THE INTERACTION BETWEEN COMPETITION LAW AND CORPORATE GOVERNANCE

Florence Thépot provides the first systematic account of the interaction between competition law and corporate governance. She challenges the 'black box' conception of the firm – or 'undertaking' – in competition law, as applied to increasingly complex corporate relations. The book opens the 'black box' of the firm to understand the internal drivers of collusive behaviour, and proposes a unified approach to cartel enforcement, based on the agency theory. It explores key issues including corporate compliance programmes, the attribution of liability in corporate groups, and structural links between competitors; and should be read by anyone interested in how the evolution of the corporate landscape impacts competition law.

Florence Thépot is a lecturer in competition law at the University of Glasgow and holds a PhD from University College London. Her research focuses on the law and economics of competition, with an emphasis on issues at the interface with corporate governance. She received the Young Writers' Award from Kluwer Law International for an article on two-sided platforms. In 2014, she was an American Bar Association International Scholar in Residence.

T0372668

GLOBAL COMPETITION LAW AND ECONOMICS POLICY

This series publishes monographs highlighting the interdisciplinary and multijurisdictional nature of competition law, economics, and policy. Global in coverage, the series should appeal to competition and antitrust specialists working as scholars, practitioners, and judges.

General Editors: Ioannis Lianos, University College London; Thomas Cheng, University of Hong Kong; Simon Roberts, University of Johannesburg; Maarten Pieter Schinkel, University of Amsterdam; Maurice Stucke, University of Tennessee

The Interaction Between Competition Law and Corporate Governance

OPENING THE 'BLACK BOX'

FLORENCE THÉPOT

University of Glasgow

CAMBRIDGE
UNIVERSITY PRESS

CAMBRIDGE
UNIVERSITY PRESS

University Printing House, Cambridge CB2 8BS, United Kingdom

One Liberty Plaza, 20th Floor, New York, NY 10006, USA

477 Williamstown Road, Port Melbourne, VIC 3207, Australia

314-321, 3rd Floor, Plot 3, Splendor Forum, Jasola District Centre, New Delhi - 110025, India

103 Penang Road, #05-06/07, Visioncrest Commercial, Singapore 238467

Cambridge University Press is part of the University of Cambridge.

It furthers the University's mission by disseminating knowledge in the pursuit of education, learning and research at the highest international levels of excellence.

www.cambridge.org
Information on this title: www.cambridge.org/9781108435420
DOI: 10.1017/9781108505185

© Florence Thépot 2019

First published 2019
First paperback edition 2022

A catalogue record for this publication is available from the British Library

Library of Congress Cataloging in Publication data
NAMES: Thépot, Florence, author.
TITLE: The interaction between competition law and corporate governance : opening the 'black box' / Florence Thépot.
DESCRIPTION: New York : Cambridge University Press, 2018. | Series: Global Competition Law and Economics Policy
IDENTIFIERS: LCCN 2018041016 | ISBN 9781108422499 (hardback)
SUBJECTS: LCSH: Competition, Unfair. | Antitrust law. | Corporate governance – Law and legislation. | BISAC: LAW / Antitrust.
CLASSIFICATION: LCC K3850 .T475 2018 | DDC 343.04/21–dc23
LC record available at https://lccn.loc.gov/2018041016

ISBN 978-1-108-42249-9 Hardback
ISBN 978-1-108-43542-0 Paperback

Contents

Figures and Tables

Figures

Tables

Preface and Acknowledgements

This book is the outcome of a long journey, which I began as a PhD candidate at University College London in September 2010, and which I now complete as a lecturer in competition law at the University of Glasgow. This monograph is a structurally and substantially revised version of my PhD thesis, defended on 18 November 2014. The experience in teaching and research accumulated since then has enabled me to strengthen the theoretical contribution and to streamline the structure of my argument. The time span between the completion of my PhD and more recent work on my monograph allowed me to incorporate discussions of some issues that have gained significance in past years. This book thus discusses the issues of the anticompetitive effects of common ownership by institutional investors, and dedicates substantial developments to the question of liability attribution in corporate groups. This book reflects the law as it stood, to the best of my knowledge, on 31 May 2018. All the URLs were also accurate as of this date.

This book would not have seen the light of day without the support and guidance of a number of people. First, I am extremely grateful to my primary PhD supervisor, Professor Ioannis Lianos, for his firm and active guidance throughout this journey. My work greatly benefited from his immense academic knowledge and his highly innovative thinking. His steering of a very dynamic and international community of competition scholars has also played a very significant role in my development as an academic researcher. I would like to thank Professor Florian Wagner-von Papp, my secondary supervisor, for our very helpful discussions on key themes of my research, during my PhD and beyond. I was honoured to have my PhD examiners, Professor Andreas Stephan and Professor William Kovacic, engage with my research. I would like to thank them for their detailed comments on my work and for a very fruitful viva discussion that has enriched my research and greatly benefited this monograph.

Specific parts of this project also benefited from the expertise of a number of people. Special thanks go to Joe Murphy for our very interesting discussions on corporate compliance programmes throughout the years. I am also very grateful to Dr Marc Moore for his insightful feedback on the corporate governance aspects of my research. To Professor Alison Diduck and Professor Valentine Korah, I give many thanks for providing very helpful comments on my research project at its very beginning. I owe special gratitude to the Section of Antitrust Law of the American Bar Association for funding a three-month research visit to Georgetown University Law Center, as part of the framework of the International Scholar-in-Residence Programme in 2014. I am particularly grateful to Professor Andy Gavil for the very warm welcome I was given, for making all the introductions and for providing me with the opportunity to present my work at the Federal Trade Commission. I would also like to express my gratitude to Clare Sandford for detailed proofreading of my thesis, and to Lisa Creevy for her excellent research assistance.

Revision of my thesis to transform it into this book took place within the very stimulating and supportive working environment of the School of Law, University of Glasgow. I often found inspiration contemplating the unique scenery of Professors' Square, and the myriad colours of the sky and of the Clyde. I will always be grateful to my colleagues and friends Professor Rosa Greaves and Professor Mark Furse for their tremendous support in every aspect of my academic career since my very first day. I thank them for their very helpful reading of some parts of this book. I wish also to thank all my colleagues who steered me, with practical and moral support, through the writing process, with special mention to my friends Maria and James. This book is a tale of different institutions and cities. I want to thank all the people and friends who have been part of this exciting adventure, in London (UCL), Washington DC (Georgetown), Strasbourg (BETA) and Munich (Max Planck Institute for Innovation and Competition).

On a more personal note, I would like to thank my godfather, Richard, for guiding me since the very beginning of my academic adventure. I profoundly thank my mother, Véronique, for her genuine support and special attention along the way, and my father, Jacques, for inspiring and advising me at all stages, as well as for reading my work with detailed interest. I also would like to thank my siblings, and my new family in Boofzheim, for their continuous support in every aspect of this adventure. Finally, I wish to dedicate this book to my husband, Thibault. I am immensely grateful for his unconditional support and love. Thanks to him, this has been a beautiful journey.

The wooden-box of the cover image is hand-crafted by Thibault, and the picture taken by us with the River Clyde in Glasgow as background.

Abbreviations

AAMS	Amministrazione Autonoma des Monopoli di Stato
ABA	American Bar Association
ASV	Axel Springer Verlag
AVG	Aschaffenburger Versorgungs GmbH
CAT	Competition Appeal Tribunal
CC	Competition Commission
CDDA	Company Directors Disqualification Act 1986 (UK)
CDO	competition disqualification order
CEO	chief executive officer
CMA	Competition and Markets Authority
D&O	director and officer insurance
DG COMP	Directorate-General for Competition
DoJ	US Department of Justice
EEA	European Economic Area
EU	European Union
FBI	Federal Bureau of Investigation
FTC	Federal Trade Commission
GmbH	Gesellschaft mit beschränkter Haftung
GWB	Gesetz gegen Wettbewerbsbeschränkungen
ICC	International Chamber of Commerce
ISO	International Organization for Standardization
NBA	National Basketball Association
NFL	National Football League
NFLP	National Football League Properties
NGO	non-governmental organisation
OECD	Organisation for Economic Cooperation and Development
OFT	Office of Fair Trading (UK)

TEU   Treaty on European Union
TFEU   Treaty on the Functioning of the European Union
UK   United Kingdom
US   United States of America
USC   United States Code

Table of Cases

Court Cases (Alphabetical Order)

US CASES

MEMBER STATES

Austria

France

Germany

Table of Legislation, Official Papers and Policy Documents

EU

Legislation

Consolidated Version of the Treaty on European Union [2010] OJ C83/01
Consolidated Version of the Treaty on the Functioning of the European Union [2010] OJ C83/01
Council Directive 86/653/EC of 18 December 1986 on the Coordination of the Laws of Member States Relating to Self-Employed Commercial Agents [1986] OJ L382/17
Council Directive 2014/104/EU of 26 November 2014 on Certain Rules Governing Actions for Damages under National Law for Infringements of the Competition Law Provisions of the Member States and of the European Union [2014] OJ L349/1
Council Framework Decision 2003/568/JHA of 22 July 2003 on Combating Corruption in the Private Sector [2003] OJ L192/54
Council Regulation (EC) No 139/2004 of 20 January 2004 on the Control of Concentrations between Undertakings [2004] OJ L24/1
EU Competition Law Rules Applicable to Antitrust Enforcement, Volume II: General Block Exemption Regulations and Guidelines (2013)
EU Competition Law Rules Applicable to Antitrust Enforcement, Volume III: Sector Specific Rules (2013)

Commission Recommendation

Recommendation complementing Recommendations 2004/913/EC and 2005/162/EC as Regards the Regime for the Remuneration of Directors of Listed Companies [2009] L120/28

Guidelines and Notices

Papers

USA

Acts

Federal Trade Commission Act 1914
Hart-Scott-Rodino Antitrust Improvements Act of 1976
Sarbanes-Oxley Act 2002
Sherman Act 1890

Guidelines, Policy Documents and Reports

Antitrust Modernization Commission, 'Report and Recommendations' (2007)
Committee on Governmental Affairs – United States Senate, 'The Role of the Board
    of Directors in Enron's Collapse', Report (8 July 2002)
Criminal Division of the US Department of Justice and the Enforcement Division
    of the US Securities and Exchange Commission, 'A Resource Guide to the
    US Foreign Corrupt Practices Act' (2012)
Department of Justice, 'Corporate Leniency Policy' (1993)
Department of Justice, 'Leniency Policy for Individuals' (1994)
Department of Justice/Federal Trade Commission, 'Antitrust Guidelines for
    Collaborations Among Competitors' (2000)
Department of Justice/Federal Trade Commission, 'Horizontal Merger Guidelines'
    (2010)
Federal Trade Commission, 'Antitrust Guidelines on Cooperation between
    Competitors' (2000)
Federal Trade Commission, 'Premerger Notification; Reporting and Waiting
    Period Requirements', 43 Fed Reg 33, 450–33, 465
SEC, 2013 Annual Report to Congress on the Dodd-Frank Whistleblower Program
    (2013)
United States Attorneys' Manual (2008)
US Senate, Committee on Governmental Affairs, 'The Role of the Board of
    Directors in Enron's Collapse' (2002)
US Sentencing Guidelines Manual (2012)

UK

Acts

Bribery Act 2010
Companies Act 2006
Competition Act 1998
Company Directors Disqualification Act 1986
Enterprise Act 2002
Enterprise and Regulatory Reform Act 2013
Insolvency Act 1986

Hansard

HL Deb 15 October 2002, vol 639, col   845

Guidelines

CMA, 'Businesses and Individuals: Competition Law Guidance' (2014)
CMA, 'Rewards for Information about Cartels' (2014)
CMA2, 'Mergers: Guidance on the CMA's Jurisdiction Procedure' (2014)
CMA73, 'CMA's Guidance as to the Appropriate Amount of a Penalty' (2018)
Ministry of Justice, 'Guidance about Procedures Which Relevant Commercial
    Organizations Can Put into Place to Prevent Persons Associated with Them from
    Bribing' (2010)
OFT423, 'OFT's Guidance as to the Appropriate Amount of a Penalty' (2012)
OFT510, 'Director Disqualification Orders in Competition Cases' (2010)
OFT1111, 'Competition Disqualification Orders: Proposed Changes to the OFT's
    Guidance' (2009)
OFT1340, 'How Your Business Can Achieve Compliance with Competition Law'
    (2011)
OFT1341, 'Company Directors and Competition Law' (2011)
OFT1495, 'Applications for Leniency and No-Action in Cartel Cases' (2013)

Reports and Policy Papers

Department of Trade and Industry, 'Productivity and Enterprise: A World Class
    Competition Regime', Cm 5233 (2001)
OFT773, 'Predicting Cartels: A Report Prepared for the Office of Fair Trading by
    P A Grout and S Sonderegger' (2005)
OFT962, 'The Deterrent Effect of Competition Enforcement by the OFT: A Report
    Prepared for the Office of Fair Trading by Deloitte' (2007)
OFT1132, 'An Assessment of Discretionary Penalties Regimes: A Report Prepared for
    the Office of Fair Trading by London Economics' (2009)
OFT1213, 'Behavioural Economics as Applied to Firms: A Primer' (2010)
OFT1218, 'Minority Interests in Competitors: A Research Report Prepared by
    DotEcon Ltd' (2010)
OFT1227, 'Drivers of Compliance and Non-Compliance with Competition Law'
    (2010)
OFT1244, 'Director Disqualification Orders in Competition Cases – Summary of
    Responses to the OFT's Consultation, and OFT's Conclusions and Decision
    Document' (2010)

OFT1391, 'The Impact of Competition Interventions on Compliance and
   Deterrence: Final Report, by London Economics' (2011)
Office of Fair Trading and Competition Commission, 'UK Competition
   Authorities' Response to DG Comp's Consultation on Reform of the EUMR':
   Annex I: 'UK Approach to Material Influence' (2013)

Financial Reporting Council

Report of the Committee on the Financial Aspects of Corporate Governance
   (Cadbury Report) (1992)
UK Corporate Governance Code (2018)

FRANCE

Code of Commerce
Competition authority, 'Antitrust compliance and compliance programmes:
   Corporate tools for competing safely in the market place' (2012)
Criminal Code Europe Economics, 'Etat des lieux et perspectives des programmes
   de conformité, Une étude réalisée pour le Conseil de la concurrence' (2008)
Ministère de l'économie, de l'industrie et de l'emploi, 'Rapport sur l'appréciation de
   la sanction en matière de pratiques anticoncurrentielles' (2010)

GERMANY

Act against Restraints of Competition (2011)
Act on Regulatory Offences (2013)Competition Authority, 'Guidelines on the setting
   of fines' (2013)
Competition Authority, 'Notice no 9/2006 on the immunity from and reduction of
   fines in cartel cases' (2006);
Criminal Code
German Stock Corporation Act

OTHER EU MEMBER STATES

Austria: Cartel Act 2005; Criminal Code
Belgium: Code de droit économique
Cyprus: Protection of Competition Law 2008
Czech Republic: Criminal Code
Denmark: Competition Act 2013
Estonia: Competition Act 2006, paragraph   148

Greece: Law 3959/2011
Hungary: Criminal Code 1978
Ireland: Competition Act 2002
Italy: Criminal Code; Art. 36 of Decree Law No 201 of 6 December 2011, converted
   into Law No 214/2011: 'Protection of Competition and Personal Cross-
   shareholdings in Credit and Financial Markets'
Latvia: Criminal Law
Malta: Competition Act
Netherlands: Competition Act 2007; Leniency Guidelines (2007)
Portugal: Competition Act, Law 19/2012
Romania: Parliament of Romania Competition Law of 1996
Slovenia: Criminal Code
Spain: Competition Act 2007

OTHER JURISDICTIONS

Australia: Trade Practices Act 1974
Brazil: Ordinance No 14 of 14 March 2004; Brazilian Secretariat of Economic Law
Indonesia: Competition Law No 5 of 1999, art 26.
Japan: Act on Prohibition of Private Monopolization and Maintenance of Fair
   Trade, Act No 54 of 1947

1

Introduction

1.1 COMPETITION LAW AND CORPORATE GOVERNANCE: TWO DISTINCT ORDERS

Antitrust is about markets; corporate [governance] is about firms. Antitrust is about competition; corporate [governance] is about cooperation. Antitrust regulates relations among firms; corporate [governance] governs relations within firms.[1]

Operating in distinct conceptual orders – that of the marketplace and that of the firm – competition law and corporate governance pursue different objectives. Competition law is oriented towards the defence of consumers' interests in the market, while corporate governance rules are designed to protect the interests of shareholders.[2] Competition law and corporate governance also constitute separate areas of academic inquiry across jurisdictions.[3] The aim of this book is to fill a gap in the scholarship, by establishing systematic connections between competition law and corporate governance, regarding both substantive and enforcement issues of contemporary relevance.

1.1.1 *Corporate Governance: the Internal Dimension of the Firm*

In this book, the term 'corporate governance' refers to any relation or mechanism that concerns the *internal dimension* of firms.[4] According to the Organisation for

---

[1] E. B. Rock, 'Corporate Law Through an Antitrust Lens', *Columbia Law Review*, 92 (1992), 497, 498. The term 'corporate law' has been replaced with 'corporate governance'. In spite of the two different meanings of 'corporate law' and 'corporate governance', I consider that the spirit of the quote is still valid, for the purpose of this introduction.
[2] For a definition of a 'firm', see Section 1.1.3. For the present purpose, the terms 'firm', 'company' and 'corporation' are used interchangeably.
[3] For a literature review, see Section 1.5.
[4] The idea is that the firm is composed of various sociological entities, or groups of participants, characterised by various aspirations and contributions to the firm. Sociological groups may be internal to the boundaries of the firm (e.g. employees, managers and shareholders) or external to the firm (e.g.

Economic Cooperation and Development's (OECD's) definition, corporate governance involves 'a set of relationships between a company's management, its board, its shareholders and other stakeholders'.[5] The definition adopted in the Cadbury Report provides that '(c) corporate governance is the system by which companies are directed and controlled'.[6] Among the different relations contributing to corporate governance, the analysis focuses mostly on that between shareholders and managers in firms where ownership is distinct from the function of control of the business. In those situations, the relationship between the owners, or shareholders, and managers – known as the *agency relation* – is characterised by a tension of interests between both parties. Due to limited information, managers may pursue their own goals, at the expense of the shareholders' interests.[7]

The *internal dimension* also refers to mechanisms and rules of corporate governance. Here, 'corporate governance' refers to mechanisms by which shareholders ensure that managers act in their best interest so as to maximise their return on investment.[8] Other conceptions of corporate governance consider that objectives that are broader than just economic aims, such as social goals, should be pursued by the firm.[9] For the sake of simplicity and conciseness, the theoretical framework for corporate governance retained for present purposes is that focusing on shareholders' interests. This approach is widely adopted in the economic literature on corporate governance, and developed along with the literature on agency costs.[10] However,

consumers, suppliers and distributors). Corporate governance is typically concerned with relations between shareholders and managers, hence the need for other areas of law to deal with other groups (e.g. competition law and consumers): S. Douma and H. Schreuder, *Economic Approaches to Organizations*, 6th edn (Pearson Education, 2017).
[5] OECD, Principles of Corporate Governance (2004), p. 11.
[6] Financial Reporting Council, Report of the Committee on the Financial Aspects of Corporate Governance (the 'Cadbury Report') (1992), p. 15.
[7] For further definition and theoretical explanations of the concept of the agency relationship, see Section 2.4.
[8] A. Shleifer and R. W. Vishny, 'A Survey of Corporate Governance', *The Journal of Finance*, 52 (1997), 737, 741.
[9] 'Corporate Governance is concerned with holding the balance between economic and social goals and between individual and communal goals. The corporate governance framework is there to encourage the efficient use of resources and equally to require accountability for the stewardship of those resources. The aim is to align as nearly as possible the interests of individuals, corporations and society' (Sir Adrian Cadbury in 'Global Corporate Governance Forum' (World Bank, 2000), p. vi).
   The stakeholder approach states that managers should take account of a much broader range of interests in making decisions: those of all of the stakeholders in a firm that impact or are affected by the firm's welfare. For discussion of the possible combination of goals, including the conception of an *enlightened* value maximisation objective, see M. C. Jensen, 'Value Maximization, Stakeholder Theory, and the Corporate Objective Function', *Journal of Applied Corporate Finance*, 14 (2010), 8, 10.
[10] E.g. S. A. Ross, 'The Economic Theory of Agency: The Principal's Problem', *American Review*, 63 (1983), 134; M. C. Jensen and W. H. Meckling, 'Theory of the Firm: Managerial Behavior, Agency Costs and Ownership Structure', *Journal of Financial Economics*, 3 (1976), 305; E. Fama and M. C. Jensen, 'Agency Problems and Residual Claims', *Journal of Law and Economics*, 26 (1983), 327; M. C. Jensen, 'Agency Costs of Free Cash Flow, Corporate Finance, and Takeovers' *The American Economic Review*, 76 (1986), 323.

a broader conception of corporate governance could arguably include the impact of managers' decisions on consumer welfare, thereby sharing concerns with competition law. In some instances, but not systematically, mechanisms of corporate *law* are part of the analysis when relevant.

1.1.2 *Competition Law: the External Dimension of the Firm*

While corporate governance is concerned with the internal dimension of the firm, competition law addresses the *external dimension* or the relations *between* firms. Competition law refers to both the substantive rules and the enforcement processes that are aimed at promoting and protecting competition in free market economies. The terms 'competition law' and 'rules on competition' are used interchangeably to refer to the European Union (EU), the United States of America (USA) and any other jurisdictions when deemed relevant. Among conduct that is regulated by competition law, this book is mostly concerned with anticompetitive agreements with a particular focus on cartel practices, which are prohibited by Article 101 of the Treaty on the Functioning of the European Union) (TFEU) in the EU and section 1 of the Sherman Act in the United States.[11] The restriction to cartel practices enables the examination of an area of competition law in which the harm to economic welfare is unambiguous and that is homogeneously prosecutable across jurisdictions.[12] The harm to economic welfare is more debated in the area of abuse of dominance or monopolisation, which is covered by Article 102 TFEU in the EU and section 2 of the Sherman Act in the United States.[13] Owing to the different enforcement approaches, abuse of dominance practices would require jurisdiction-specific analysis.[14] For the sake of conciseness, abuses of dominance will not be part of the analysis here. This study will also examine aspects of the merger control regime that demonstrate the interplay of competition law and corporate governance.[15]

1.1.3 *Concepts of the Firm*

The boundaries of the firm set the distinction between the two orders in which competition law and corporate governance operate. However, the concept of the

---

[11] Conduct prohibited by Art. 101 TFEU (EU); s. 1 of the Sherman Act 15 USC §1 (USA).

[12] Different enforcement approaches are seen in the area of vertical restraints, in which the harm to economic welfare is particularly debated. For the background of debates and contrasted approaches to resale price maintenance, see: S. Umit Kucuk and H. J. P. Timmermans, 'Resale Price Maintenance (RPM): The US and EU perspectives', *Journal of Retailing and Consumer Services*, 19 (2012), 537.

[13] Conduct prohibited by Art. 102 TFEU (EU); s. 2 of the Sherman Act 15 USC §2 (USA).

[14] For discussion of this divergence, see, e.g., W. E. Kovacic, 'Competition Policy in the European Union and the United States: Convergence or Divergence in the Future Treatment of Dominant Firms?', *Competition Law International*, 4 (2008), 8; E. M. Fox, 'Monopolization and Abuse of Dominance: Why Europe Is Different', *Antitrust Bulletin*, 59 (2014), 129.

[15] Council Regulation (EC) No 139/2004 of 20 January 2004 on the Control of Concentrations between Undertakings [2004] OJ L24/1 ('EU Merger Regulation'); s. 7 of the Clayton Act 15 USC §18 (USA).

firm is not a homogeneous one. Different conceptions and definitions of the firm are used across disciplines. In neoclassical economics, the firm is a production function. In new-institutional economics, the firm refers to the organisation of an economic activity within a hierarchy, rather than through an exchange in the marketplace.[16] The law has also long recognised the existence of firms as entities having rights and responsibilities distinguished from the individuals who compose them. The law recognises the ability of firms to govern themselves through internal processes, while also drawing their external boundaries, marking firm as entities within a larger society composed of different types of actors and institutions.[17] In corporate law, the term 'company', in all its legal variations, generally designates a legal entity that is engaged in a business activity, as distinct from the individuals who compose them.[18] A great variety of corporate forms structure the economy, including corporations, partnerships or individual proprietorship. As a feature of the modern economy, corporate groups linking legally independent entities have considerably complexified and enriched the corporate landscape.[19] Modern firms are also characterised by financial investment that is increasingly disjoined from operational control of the economic activity.[20]

Competition law has its own distinctive conception of the firm. In the EU, the concept of 'undertaking' is used to mark the external boundaries of firms that are the subject of competition law provisions. An undertaking is defined as an 'entity engaged in an economic activity, regardless of the legal status of the entity and the way in which it is financed'.[21] The conception of the firm is thus based on economic concepts and may be indifferent to the legal realities of firms.[22] In the economic literature, the expression 'black box' generally denotes the neoclassical conception that solely the amount of input and the way in which it is allocated – and not operations performed inside the boundaries of the firm – matter for economic efficiency.[23] By extension, this book uses the term 'black box' in reference to the indifference of competition law provisions and instruments to the internal dimension of what it defines as firms.

---

[16] See Chapter 2 for details of economic theories of the firm.

[17] E. W. Orts, *Business Persons: A Legal Theory of the Firm* (Oxford University Press, 2013), p. 2.

[18] The term 'company' comprises any formal business entity, including a corporation, a partnership, an association or an individual proprietorship.

[19] These include parent–subsidiary relationships, conglomerates or pyramid structures. For definitions and a taxonomy of modern business firms, see Orts, *Business Persons*, ch. 5.

[20] Separation of ownership and control is not new, but it is furthered by the financialisation of the modern economy. For discussion of the financialisation process, see, e.g., J. Crotty, *Capitalism, Macroeconomics and Reality: Understanding Globalization, Financialization, Competition and Crisis* (Edward Elgar Publishing, 2017); E. Hein, D. Detzer and N. Dodig (eds.), *Financialisation and the Financial and Economic Crises: Country Studies* (Edward Elgar Publishing, 2016).

[21] Case C–41/1990 *Klaus Höfner and Fritz Elser v. Macroton GmbH* [1991] ECR I–1979.

[22] The definition and concept of 'undertaking' or 'person' is discussed in detail in Chapter 3.

[23] 'Efficiency' is understood here as allocative or static efficiency, which refers to the optimal allocation of resources.

1.2 STATE OF PLAY OF THE INTERACTION OF COMPETITION LAW AND CORPORATE GOVERNANCE

Since its inception, competition law across jurisdictions has shown a variable interest in relations and mechanisms that are internal to the boundaries of the firm. This section takes stock of some of the notable steps in the relationship between competition law and matters of corporate governance. The evolving relationship also shows an interesting transatlantic contrast.

1.2.1 *The Emergence of Competition Law: Closing the 'Black Box'*

In the United States, which is a pioneer in the adoption of modern rules on competition, the history of competition law closely relates to the inability of corporate law to deal effectively with the social consequences of the increasing use of a form of economic organisation – trusts – in the late part of the nineteenth century. The Sherman Act, outlawing contracts, combinations, and conspiracies in restraint of trade, was introduced in 1890 as a response to concerns raised by the emergence of large trusts in the economy.[24] As corporate devices into which individual owners of businesses transferred their stocks, trusts enabled the expansion of businesses and the coordination of production, in spite of the limits set by state laws.[25] Standard Oil was the first trust created in response to the limitations to its corporate power set by state corporate law.[26] However, it was later said to qualify as 'the greatest monopoly and combination in restraint of trade in the world', reflecting a deep public aversion towards trusts.[27] Competition law in the United States (antitrust law) emerged precisely because state corporate laws could not apply to trusts, in view of their interstate dimension.[28] In addition, they were deemed inadequate to deal with the social consequences of the emergence of trusts, the most important being the concentration of economic wealth and power. Following the introduction of the Sherman Act, the United States witnessed the so-called 'great merger movement', in which thousands of business firms consolidated, at least until 1904.[29] Mergers may have been a tool for circumventing prohibitions on combinations that had been set by the newly enacted Act.[30] However, while the Sherman Act prohibited agreements to restrict price or output, it was not meant to 'limit and

---

[24] Sherman Act 15 USC§§1–7.

[25] For an account of different legal models of trusts, see H. Hovenkamp, *Enterprise and American Law, 1836–1937* (Harvard University Press, 1991), p. 249.

[26] B. Y. Orbach, 'The Antitrust Curse of Bigness', *Southern California Law Review*, 85 (2012), 605, 610–11.

[27] W. H. Taft in Orbach, 'The Antitrust Curse of Bigness', 609; W. Letwin, 'Congress and the Sherman Antitrust Law: 1887–1890', *University of Chicago Law Review*, 23 (1956), 222.

[28] Although the Sugar Trust was defeated on the basis of state corporate law: *People v. N River Sugar Ref Co* 121 NY 582, 622–3 (1890), 614.

[29] Hovenkamp, *Enterprise and American Law*, p. 242.

[30] The first targets of the Sherman Act were 'loose' combinations (or cartels); thus, mergers were a way to form 'tight' combinations and avoid prosecution ibid.

restrict the rights of corporations [. . .] in the acquisition, control, or disposition of property'.[31] Therefore a legal response was needed to address the potential negative economic consequences stemming from these consolidations.[32] For a while, state corporate laws were used as an antitrust device to solve the issue of trust combinations. However, after various developments, federal antitrust law appeared much more adequate to address concentrations of multistate companies.[33] As such, US antitrust law developed in response to the failure of corporate law to address issues of common concern to both disciplines.

In contrast to the United States, where the emergence of antitrust closely relates to corporate matters, the history of EU competition policy is linked to the goal of economic integration.[34] The development of EU competition policy occurred in a period when the European Community was working on its integration and on the realisation of the common market. At that time, in spite of the adoption of the EU treaties, the national governments of the member states still held considerable economic powers, and no single economic area existed. In such conditions the role of EU competition policy was deemed 'more extensive, more complex and even more necessary' to achieve economic integration.[35] As a result, competition law provisions were predominantly applied by the European Commission and the European Court of Justice as instruments to eliminate private restraints on trade between member states.[36] In addition, the introduction of competition rules in the European Community marked a cultural shift: in the first half of the twentieth century, cartels were commonly accepted and no member states had rules on competition.[37] EU competition law was shaped by member states who were traditionally characterised by state monopolies and had long focused on industrial policy alongside free market competition.[38] Therefore, unlike that of the United States, EU competition law has remained separate from concerns of corporate law, the latter having also largely remained a national matter.

Until a few decades ago, US antitrust law remained somehow concerned with intracorporate matters. According to the intra-conspiracy doctrine that emerged in

---

[31]　*US v. EC Knight Co* 156 US 1 (1895).

[32]　See Hovenkamp, *Enterprise and American Law*, p. 244: 'Two legal models in dealing with the Trust Problem'. This also discusses legal solutions found at state or corporate level.

[33]　Ibid., p. 267.

[34]　P. Akman and H. Kassim, 'Myths and Myth-Making in the European Union: The Institutionalization and Interpretation of EU Competition Policy', *Journal of Common Market Studies*, 48 (2010), 111, 114.

[35]　Ibid.

[36]　S. M. Ramirez Pérez and S. van de Scheur, 'The Evolution of the Law on Articles 85 and 86 EEC [Arts 101 and 102 TFEU], Ordoliberalism and Its Keynesian Challenge' in K. K. Patel and H. Schweitzer (eds.), *The Historical Foundations of EU Competition Law* (Oxford University Press, 2013).

[37]　Rules on competition such as rules that prohibit cartels and prevent abuse of dominant position: L. F. Pace and K. Seidel, 'The Drafting and the Role of Regulation 17, a Hard-Fought Compromise' in Patel and Schweitzer, *Historical Foundations*, p. 54.

[38]　M. Motta, *Competition Policy, Theory and Practice* (Cambridge University Press, 2004), 13–19.

the 1940s, companies belonging to the same corporate group could conspire within the meaning of section 1 of the Sherman Act.[39] In *United States* v. *Yellow Cab* the Supreme Court stated that being under common corporate ownership and control did not preclude the existence of a conspiracy.[40] In *United States* v. *General Motors* a parent company and its subsidiaries were considered separate entities for the purpose of antitrust analysis, even though they may have constituted a 'single corporate enterprise'.[41] In 1984, the *Copperweld* case reversed the intracorporate conspiracy doctrine, in finding that different firms forming a single economic entity were not capable of conspiring with each other and that any combination of them could not constitute an antitrust violation.[42] Through a clear adoption of the single entity doctrine, the Supreme Court thereby confirmed that antitrust law was not meant to interfere with intracorporate decisions.[43] A century after its introduction in response to corporate issues, the scope of section 1 of the Sherman Act was then rooted outside the boundaries of the corporation. In the EU, the single entity doctrine was later adopted, also marking the scope of EU competition law provisions outside the boundaries of what is defined as an undertaking.[44]

1.2.2 *Current Developments: a Renewed Interest in the Internal Dimension of the Firm?*

To date, very few competition rules are concerned with the internal dimension of firms. The only statutory provision that directly concerns corporate governance can be found in the United States, in the provision on interlocking directorates in the Clayton Act.[45] In Europe, only rarely do enforcement instruments, such as sanctions, address the internal structure of firms, or target the business participants that compose them.[46] Nonetheless, issues of corporate structure and corporate governance are very topical for competition law. The issue of corporate links among competitors has been the object of vivid debates in the United States and in the

[39]   D. V. Williamson, 'Organization, Control, and the Single Entity Defense in Antitrust', *Journal of Competition Law and Economics*, 5 (2009), 723, 731–2.
[40]   332 US 218, 228 (1947).
[41]   121 F 2d 376 (7th Cir 1941).
[42]   *Copperweld Corp* v. *Independence Tube Corp* 467 US 752 (1984).
[43]   A. I. Gavil, W. E. Kovacic and J. B. Baker, *Antitrust Law in Perspective: Cases, Concepts and Problems in Competition Policy*, 2nd edn (Thomson West, 2008), p. 239, although other provisions, such as s 2 of the Sherman Act, can still apply to single-firm conduct.
[44]   The single entity doctrine was clearly adopted in Case C–73/95P *Viho Europe BV* v. *Commission of the European Communities* [1996] ECR I–5457.
[45]   'No person shall, at the same time, serve as a director or officer in any two corporations [. . .] that are – (A) engaged in whole or in part in commerce; and (B) by virtue of their business and location of operation, competitors, so that the elimination of competition by agreement between them would constitute a violation of any of the antitrust Law' (s. 8 of the Clayton Act, 15 USC §19).
[46]   In most jurisdictions, undertakings are the primary subjects of competition rules. EU competition law does not sanction individuals. Many EU member states have individual sanctions, ranging from fines to jail sentences. The latter type of sanction is rarely used in practice (see Section 7.3.2.1).

EU. In some sectors, portfolio diversification strategies by institutional investors can result in concentration of financial ownership. Recent empirical studies suggest that such links between competitors can produce anticompetitive effects, and have triggered concerns that these may be left unchallenged.[47] In the EU, minority shareholdings not conferring control were at the heart of the project on merger control reform.[48] Although the reform has not been pursued, the issue keeps its contemporary relevance.[49] Common shareholdings links were recently discussed by the Commission in the *Dow/DuPont* merger case.[50] Commissioner Vestager also expressed the Commission's intention to examine the scope of issues raised by common institutional investors.[51]

The everlasting cartel problem also calls for greater inquiry into internal incentives and processes. The past decade has seen a significant growth in criminalisation of cartels across the world, providing jail or monetary penalties for individuals who engage their companies in collusive behaviour.[52] Recent initiatives show an increased interest by competition authorities in interactions occurring within the boundaries of the firm: guidance resources issued by the European Commission and the Competition and Markets Authority (CMA) – including 'Compliance: Why does it Matter?',[53] 'Company Directors and Competition Law' and 'How your

---

[47] For an overview of the issue, see: OECD, 'Common Ownership by Institutional Investors and Its Impact on Competition', DAF/COMP/WD (2017)10; CPI Antitrust Chronicle, 'Index Funds – A New Antitrust Frontier?' (2017) 3. For more particular legal and economic analysis, see, e.g., J. Azar, M. Schmalz and I. Tecu, 'Anti-Competitive Effects of Common Ownership', *Journal of Finance*, 73 (4), (2018), 1513; E. Elhauge, 'Essay: Horizontal Shareholding', *Harvard Law Review*, 129 (2016), 1267; J. Baker 'Overlapping Financial Investor Ownership, Market Power, and Antitrust Enforcement: My Qualified Agreement with Professor Elhauge', *Harvard Law Review Forum*, 129 (2016), 212; J. He and J. Huang, 'Product Market Competition in a World of Cross-Ownership: Evidence from Institutional Blockholdings', *The Review of Financial Studies*, 30(8) (2017), 2674–718; E. Posner, F. Scott Morton and E. G. Weyl, 'A Proposal to Limit the Anti-Competitive Power of Institutional Investors', *Antitrust Law Journal*, 81(3) (2017), 669–728; D. O'Brien and K. Waehrer, 'The Competitive Effects of Common Ownership: We Know Less than We Think', *Antitrust Law Journal*, 81(3) (2017), 729–76; M. S. Patel, 'Common Ownership, Institutional Investors, and Antitrust', *Antitrust Law Journal* (2018).
[48] European Commission, 'Towards More Effective EU Merger Control', White Paper COM (2014) 49.
[49] M. Vestager, 'Refining the EU Merger Control System', speech, *Studienvereinigung Kartellrecht*, Brussels, 10 March 2016, available at: https://ec.europa.eu/commission/commissioners /2014-2019/vestager/announcements/refining-eu-merger-control-system_en
[50] *Dow/DuPont* (Case COMP/M.7932), Commission Decision 2017/C1946 [2017] paras. 2349–52, Annex 5, p. 5.
[51] M. Vestager, 'Competition in Changing Times', FIW Symposium, Innsbruck, 16 February 2018, available at: https://ec.europa.eu/commission/commissioners/2014-2019/vestager/announcements /competition-changing-times-0_en; Commission, Management Plan 2017 of DG Competition, Ref Ares(2016)7130280. 16.
[52] A. Stephan, 'Four Key Challenges to the Successful Criminalization of Cartel Laws', *Journal of Antitrust Enforcement*, 2 (2014), 333, 335 (map of jurisdictions that criminalise cartels). For a discussion of individual sanctions in EU member states, see Section 7.3.2.1.
[53] DG Competition, 'Compliance with Competition Rules: What's in It for Business?' (2011).

Business can achieve Compliance'[54] – illustrate that corporate culture and internal compliance with competition law norms have become an important subject for competition authorities.

In addition, competition authorities, courts and practitioners face novel challenges relating to the complex corporate structures of undertakings, in which financial investments are increasingly disjoined from the economic operations of businesses.[55] In the EU, this is a very significant and highly contentious issue in cases of liability attribution for breaches of competition law by wholly owned subsidiaries.[56] National cases also suggest the critical importance of the concept of undertaking, and its internal structure, with regard to private actions in cross-border competition cases. In *Provimi*, the court noted that a wholly owned subsidiary could be held liable for the breach of its parent, thereby establishing the jurisdiction of a member state in which a subsidiary (or 'anchor defendant') is domiciled.[57] Finally, the allocation of fines among different entities forming a single undertaking was a particularly difficult question in the *Siemens* case.[58]

---

[54] OFT1341, 'How your Business can Achieve Compliance with Competition Law' (2011); and OFT1340, 'Company Directors and Competition Law' (2011). See, more generally, CMA, 'Businesses and Individuals: Competition Law Guidance', available at: www.gov.uk/government/collections/competition-and-consumer-law-compliance-guidance-for-businesses#company-directors

[55] For a description of the growing complexity of the corporate landscape, see: Orts, *Business Persons*, ch. 5; Separation of ownership and control is not new, but it is furthered by financialisation of the modern economy. For discussion of the financialisation process, see, e.g., Crotty, *Capitalism, Macroeconomics and Reality*; E. Hein, D. Detzer and N. Dodig (eds.), *Financialisation and the Financial and Economic Crises: Country Studies* (Edward Elgar Publishing, 2016).

[56] See, e.g., C. Koenig, 'An Economic Analysis of the Single Economic Entity Doctrine in the EU Competition Law', *Journal of Competition Law and Economics*, 13 (2017), 281; B. Wardhaugh, 'Punishing Parents for the Sins of their Child: Extending an EU Competition Liability in Groups and to Subcontractors', *Journal of Antitrust Enforcement*, 5 (2017), 22; S. Thomas, 'Guilty of a Fault that One has not Committed: The Limits of the Group-Based Sanction Policy Carried out by the Commission and the European Courts in EU-Antitrust Law', *Journal of European Competition Law & Practice*, 3 (2012), 11; J. Joshua, Y. Botteman and L. Atlee, '"You Can't Beat the Percentage" – The Parental Liability Presumption in EU Cartel Enforcement', *European Antitrust Review*, (2012), 3; S. Burden and J. Townsend, 'Whose Fault Is It Anyway? Undertakings and the Imputation of Liability', *Competition Law Journal*, 3 (2013), 294; B. Leupold, 'Effective Enforcement of EU Competition Law Gone Too Far? Recent Case Law on the Presumption of Parental Liability', *European Competition Law Review*, 34 (2013), 570; J. Temple Lang, 'How Can the Problem of the Liability of a Parent Company for Price Fixing by a Wholly-Owned Subsidiary Be Resolved?', *Fordham International Law Journal*, 37(5) (2014), 1481.

[57] *Provimi Ltd* v. *Aventis Animal Nutrition SA* [2003] EWHC 96; *Cooper Tyre & Rubber Co & Others* [2009] EWHC 2609 (Comm); *KME Yorkshire Ltd and others and Toshiba Carrier UK Ltd and others* [2011] EWHC 2665 (Ch); *Nokia Corp* v. *AU Optronics Corp* [2012] EWHC 731. For further discussion, see Section 4.4.

[58] In the *Siemens* case, the Commission, General Court and Court of Justice had different views with respect to the allocation of fines among companies pertaining to the same undertaking. Reversing the approach of the General Court, which noted the exclusivity of the Commission in determining the internal allocation of the fine, the Court of Justice affirmed its general indifference to the internal allocation of fines between the parent company and the infringing subsidiary, thereby leaving national courts to define such allocation: Joined Cases C–232/11P and C–233/11P *Commission* v. *Siemens AG Österreich* [2014] EU:C:2014:256.

1.3 THE SIGNIFICANCE OF OPENING THE 'BLACK BOX'

This book is the first to establish the meaningful and significant interaction between competition law and corporate governance, regarding both substantive and enforcement issues. Part I of this book will concern the *substantive* dimension;[59] and Part II the *enforcement* aspect of such interaction, with a focus on collusive behaviour.

Part I – Moving Boundaries: Substantive Issues

Competition law and corporate governance meaningfully interact when the boundaries between the firm and the market are not of clear-cut application. The substantive reach of competition law and corporate governance operates within moving boundaries. The concept of undertaking that is used in competition law to define its boundaries is based on economic concepts, applying to a wide range of evolving legal realities.[60] As such, some of the most contemporary issues for competition law are the growing complexity of corporate structures, and the increasing disconnection between financial investment and operation of the economic activity.[61] For example, the acquisition of shares in a competing undertaking renders the boundary between those unclear: two undertakings are simultaneously competitors with and shareholders of the same company.[62] Likewise, a relationship between a parent company and its subsidiary or between a company and its commercial agent constitute neither a clear market nor a clear intrafirm relation. Capturing the anticompetitive effects of such relations may require adjustment of the substantive reach of competition law vis-à-vis corporate governance. This is because relations at the border between the firm and the market may give rise to anticompetitive effects that are not adequately captured by the market/firm paradigm that underlies the theories of harm.

Examining issues of contemporary relevance, this book appraises the distinctive conception of the firm in competition law, by which it defines the boundaries of its substantive reach. Competition law submits *undertakings* (in the EU) or *persons* (in the United States) to rules relating to their conduct on the market. In EU competition law and US antitrust law, the single entity doctrine supports the idea that relationships among entities that form part of a single entity should be immune from prohibitions on anticompetitive agreements. The doctrine is thereby used to distinguish one undertaking from another, and to determine whether entities will be subject to competition law either separately or jointly. In the EU, the single entity doctrine is also critically used to attribute liability in the cases of undertakings composed of economically affiliated but legally independent companies. Showing

---

[59]   Although Part I also discusses the question of liability attribution within complex undertakings, and as such also engages with the enforcement dimension of the interaction.

[60]   Case C–41/1990 *Klaus Höfner and Fritz Elser v. Macroton GmbH* [1991] ECR I–1979.

[61]   See nn. 19 and 20.

[62]   Rock, 'Corporate Law Through an Antitrust Lens', 498.

the limits of the current approach, this book develops a new understanding of the firm that more adequately addresses the main challenges of the modern economy for competition law.

Part II – Opening the 'Black Box' for Enforcement Purposes

Competition law and corporate governance also meaningfully interact when inquiry into competition law moves within the boundaries of the firm for enforcement purposes. In that respect, this book 'opens the black box' of the firm to enable understanding of the internal dimension of compliance or non-compliance with competition law, with a focus on collusive behaviour. For example, what internal factors can explain a firm's engagement in a cartel? Mechanisms of corporate governance, such as remuneration schemes linking pay to sales figures, can produce incentives to fix and sustain prices above the competitive level.[63] In addition, poor mechanisms of corporate governance may also fail to prevent an individual from engaging in collusive behaviour. For example, participation of the company ADM in several cartels in the early 1990s occurred at a time at which the board of directors was seen as being particularly weak, owing to its passivity, large size and conflicts of interest due to personal acquaintances between the members and management.[64]

Understanding the significance of internal incentives and mechanisms as factors of collusion is of the utmost importance for enforcement purposes. Issues of imperfect information and opportunism characterising the agency relation explain some of the greatest challenges of cartel enforcement. When information is perfect, shareholders can be assumed easily to monitor, detect and punish a manager who is responsible for engaging a company in a cartel. Harsh fines imposed on an undertaking translate into adequate internal measures taken by the firm to avoid anticompetitive behaviour. As a result, responsible individuals can also expect the fine to be transferred to them. However, owing to the impossibility of fully observing their actions, shareholders may not have the incentive and ability to prevent individuals from pursuing goals that may diverge from the company's best interest. Based on corporate governance insights, this book defines the key ingredients of effective cartel enforcement. Considering that companies do not have a unity of mind and will, cartel enforcement should target individuals effectively (via sanctions and leniency) and provide greater incentives for companies to develop effective mechanisms of compliance internally.

---

[63] P. Buccirossi and G. Spagnolo, 'Corporate Governance and Collusive Behavior', in W. D. Collins (ed.), *Issues in Competition Law and Policy* 1 (American Bar Association, 2008).

[64] J. M. Connor, *Global Price Fixing (Studies in Industrial Organization)*, 2nd edn (Springer, 2008), pp. 463–4.

1.4 SCOPE AND METHODOLOGY

1.4.1 *Scope of Study*

Shedding light on the processes at work that link competition law and corporate governance, this book will offer normative suggestions for reform, essentially for EU competition law. In pioneering jurisdiction through the introduction of modern rules on competition, the United States is also leading the way to the adoption of rules targeting the internal dimension of firms. Individual sanctions have, for example, been part of antitrust sanctions since the introduction of the Sherman Act in 1890. In addition, one of the rare statutory interplays between competition law and corporate governance can be found in the Clayton Act provision on interlocking directorates.[65] It is therefore relevant to examine the US experience with regard to these questions. In addition, examples from EU member states (and sometimes from non-EU countries) may be provided when their specificity makes them relevant to the analysis. This book does not constitute a comparative law analysis, but some comparative insight will be provided when relevant.

As EU competition law targets only economic activity, only business or for-profit firms will be the object of this book. Large firms – characterised by a separation of ownership and control and typically dispersed ownership (not necessarily but also including publicly listed companies) – will be the type of company that is of interest in this study.[66] While acknowledging that the concept of 'undertaking' does not strictly coincide with that of 'company' or 'firm', most of the developments of this book will use the terms interchangeably.[67] Specific distinctions are made when relevant (e.g. regarding developments on whether a parent and a subsidiary form one or two distinct undertakings for competition law purposes).

---

[65] 15 USC §19.

[66] For the EU to have jurisdiction over an anticompetitive collusive agreement there needs to be an 'effect on trade between Member States' (Art. 101(1) TFEU). Conditions set out in the guidelines, as well as past decisions, indicate that companies subject to EU competition law prosecution are usually large. Therefore, focusing on such types of companies seems appropriate. See Commission Notice, 'Guidelines on the effect on trade concept contained in Articles 81 and 82 of the Treaty' [2004] OJ C101/81.

The widely held ownership system – centred on the ownership/control separation and associated agency problem – is quite specific to the Anglo-American environment (see Section 6.3.2). Although it may not apply to the continental Europe governance system, which is based on blockholder ownership structures, this framework is deemed relevant in the analysis of competition infringement and compliance by large multinational companies, composed of many subsidiaries in different member states: such undertakings and companies with dispersed shareholders face similar issues of internal asymmetry of information and divergent interests.

[67] The term 'company' will be used mostly in financial contexts (e.g. relationships between shareholders and managers) as well as to refer to the legal reality of a business entity. The term 'firm' will generally denote the alternative organisation to the market.

1.4.2 *Methodology and Theoretical Inspiration*

The theoretical inspiration for this book lies in the new institutional economics theory of the firm. Explaining the existence of firms as alternatives to the market for the realisation of economic transactions, the theory of the firm posits that the internal organisation matters for economic efficiency. The manner in which resources are allocated and organised within the firm is crucial to the achievement of economic performance.[68] Similarly, this book demonstrates that firms are no 'black boxes' for competition law, owing to the significance of internal processes and incentives for substantive and enforcement purposes. The theoretical framework developed here contributes also to the application of competition law. The theory of the firm, in all its variations, provides very insightful concepts for clarifying the substantive reach of competition law with respect to parent–subsidiary and commercial agency relationships as well as joint ventures. Enforcement discussions focus on the agency relationship as the object of analysis, constituting also the foundations of corporate governance mechanisms.[69] The agency theory discusses the behavioural implications[70] of limited information and tensions of interests between shareholders and managers in modern corporations.[71] Discussions on liability within corporate groups (parent–subsidiary), or within companies (shareholders or individuals) are informed by the dynamics that are characteristic of the agency relationship.

Primary sources for this book are statutes, legal instruments, policy documents and decisional practices offered in the United States, the EU and EU member states' jurisdictions. Analysis and assessment of those are made in light of the existing literature on corporate governance, competition law and economics. Chapter 8 also builds qualitatively on interviews conducted with general counsel and compliance officers of large companies in France, the United Kingdom (UK), the Netherlands, Switzerland and Germany.[72]

The general approach used throughout this book is that of the economic analysis of law: the assumption is that individuals and firms behave rationally, within the scope of limitations with regard to information, foresight and expertise.[73] Conclusions will be made only within the scope of this (rather limited) frame of bounded rationality. For example, a comprehensive study of the cartel problem would require a multidisciplinary approach encompassing, for example, beha-

---

[68] See Section 2.2.

[69] The agency relationship is also supported by well-established economic literature (see n. 10).

[70] 'Behavioural' is understood as being within the scope of 'bounded rationality'.

[71] A. A. Berle and C. C. Means, *The Modern Corporation and Private Property*, 2nd edn (Harcourt, Brace and World, 1967).

[72] More details will be found in Chapter 8, n. 131.

[73] The economic analysis of law comprises several schools of thought that link the study of law, economic institutions and organisations: A. Polinsky, A. Mitchell and S. Shavell, 'Economic Analysis of Law' in *The New Palgrave Dictionary of Economics*, 2nd edn (Harvard University, 2008).

vioural economics, sociology, psychology or criminology insights.[74] This book is enriched by some of these insights. Normative suggestions will also be made within the specific theoretical framework of the book, without consideration of all practical and legal challenges.

1.5 ORIGINALITY

This book is the first to establish the meaningful and significant interaction between competition law and corporate governance, regarding issues of contemporary relevance. The interaction of competition law and corporate governance has been subject to only a few pieces of research. Only a few articles approach the interaction in a more systematic way.[75] While taking stock of missing links in the scholarship and at policy level, this literature asserts the need for a more unified approach 'to promote the interests of both shareholders and consumers in a more systematic and meaningful way'.[76]

Some authors have touched upon the relationship between competition law and corporate governance. For example, the scholarship on corporate compliance or structural links certainly discusses relevant aspects of the interaction between the two disciplines.[77] Some authors advocate the adoption of a unified approach to

---

[74] For another approach to the firm's behaviour, which moves away from the assumption of rationality, see, e.g., behavioural economics-based studies: OFT1213, 'Behavioural Economics as Applied to Firms: A Primer' (2010). For an example of literature that enrich the study of cartels, see: B. Fisse and J. Braithwaite, *Corporations, Crime and Accountability* (Cambridge University Press, 2010); C. Parker, *The Open Corporation: Effective Self-Regulation and Democracy* (Cambridge University Press, 2002); S. S. Simpson, *Corporate Crime, Law, and Social Control* (Cambridge University Press, 2002). For a criticism of the agency relationship framework for understanding compliance, see B. Fisse, 'Reconditioning Corporate Leniency: The Possibility of Making Compliance Programmes a Condition of Immunity' in C. Beaton-Wells and C. Tran (eds.), *Anti-Cartel Enforcement in a Contemporary Age: The Leniency Religion* (Hart Publishing, 2015), ch. 10.

[75] S. Weber Waller, 'Corporate Governance and Competition Policy', *George Mason Law Review*, 18 (2011), 833; see also Buccirossi and Spagnolo, 'Corporate governance and collusive behavior', providing an overview of the relationship between competition and corporate governance, from the perspective of law enforcement against collusive behaviour). See also OECD, 'Competition and Corporate Governance' (2010) (identifying areas in which competition and corporate governance could meaningfully interact). Some economic studies explore the link between the level of competition and corporate governance. See, e.g., J. C. Cosset, H. Y. Somé and P. Valéry, 'Does Competition Matter for Corporate Governance? The Role of Country Characteristics', *Journal of Financial and Quantitative Analysis*, 51 (2016), 1231.

[76] Weber Waller, 'Corporate Governance and Competition Policy', 833.

[77] See the literature on corporate compliance, e.g.: A. Riley and D. Sokol, 'Rethinking Compliance', *Journal of Antitrust Enforcement*, 3(1) (2015), 31; D. D. Sokol, 'Policing the Firm', *Notre Dame Law Review*, 89 (2014), 785; J. E. Murphy, 'Policies in Conflict: Undermining Corporate Self-Policing', *Rutgers University Law Review*, 69 (2017), 421, 470. See also the literature on interlocking directorates and minority shareholdings, e.g.: V. Falce, 'Interlocking Directorates: An Italian Antitrust Dilemma', *Journal of Competition Law and Economics*, 9 (2013), 457–72; T. Staahl Gabrielsen, E. Hjelmeng and L. Sørgard, 'Rethinking Minority Share Ownership and Interlocking Directorships – The Scope for Competition Law Intervention', *European Law Review*, 36 (2011), 839, 840; F. Thépot, F. Hugon and

specific issues, such as in the field of competition for corporate control, or with regard to the issue of company director liability.[78] Economic research provides models or studies on managerial incentives to collude, and therefore establishes links between internal incentives and mechanisms, on one hand, and competitive outcome on the other.[79] The interaction is also subject to legal analysis, which usually focuses on particular issues and jurisdictions.[80] These studies shed light on only specific questions or concern strict legal or economic frameworks.

In an effort to bridge the gap in the scholarship, this book provides a holistic approach to the relationship between competition law and corporate governance. An analysis of the interaction, conducted at the micro level – together with an economic analysis of internal relations, feeds into the broader (or macro-level) legal discussion of EU competition law.

1.6 OUTLINE

This book is structured in two parts. Part I concerns the substantive[81] and Part II the enforcement dimensions of the interaction between competition law and corporate governance.

Chapter 2 introduces the theoretical foundations of this book. It establishes the theoretical distinction between the market and the firm, which underlies the dichotomy of conceptual orders in which corporate governance and competition law respectively operate. It explains how the economic theory, considering the firm as a 'black box', integrated the internal and organisational dimension of the firm into

M. Luinaud, 'Cumul de mandats d'administrateur et risques anticoncurrentiels: Un vide juridique en Europe?', *Concurrences*, 1 (2016), 1–11.

[78] E. B. Rock, 'Antitrust and the Market for Corporate Control', *California Law Review*, 77 (1989), 1365 (arguing that competitive processes within the market for corporate control should fall under the scrutiny of antitrust provisions); P. Hughes, 'Directors' Personal Liability for Cartel Activity under UK and EC Law – A Tangled Web', *European Competition Law Review*, 29 (2008), 632; P. Hughes, 'Competition Law Enforcement and Corporate Group Liability – Adjusting the Veil', *European Competition Law Review*, 35 (2014), 68.

[79] G. Spagnolo. 'Managerial Incentives and Collusive Behavior', *European Economic Review*, 49 (2005), 1501; G. Spagnolo, 'Debt as a (Credible) Collusive Device, or: "Everybody Happy but the Consumer"', (2000) Working paper of the Stockholm School of Economics, No 349; C. Aubert, 'Managerial Effort Incentives and Market Collusion' (2009) Toulouse School of Economics, Working Paper No 09-127; T. A. González and M. Schmid 'Corporate Governance and Antitrust Behavior' (2012) Swiss Institute of Banking and Finance, University of St Gallen, Working Paper; T. A. González, M. Schmid and D. Yermack, 'Does Price Fixing Benefit Corporate Managers?', NYU Working Paper No FIN-13-002 (2017); Azar, Schmalz and Tecu, 'Anti-Competitive Effects of Common Ownership'.

[80] UK: P. Hughes, 'Competition Law Enforcement and Corporate Group Liability – Adjusting the Veil', *European Competition Law Review*, 35 (2014), 68; Germany: J. P. Schmidt, 'Germany: Merger Control Analysis of Minority Shareholdings – A Model for the EU?', *Concurrences*, (2013), 16; Patel, 'Common Ownership'.

[81] Part I also discusses the important question of liability in parent–subsidiary and commercial agency relationships, so it includes some discussion of enforcement.

economic thinking. This echoes the necessity for competition law to 'open the black box' of the firm for various purposes, as this book advocates. The theory of the firm particularly informs developments on the substantive dimension of the interaction between competition law and corporate governance. The chapter also introduces the theory of agency – the theoretical foundation of corporate governance – that will especially feed into discussions on enforcement aspects of the interaction.

Part I – Moving Boundaries: Substantive Issues

Part I of this book discusses the distinctive conception of the firm that prevails in competition law. Chapter 3 introduces the competition law conception of the firm (the meaning of *undertaking* and of the *single entity doctrine*), and clarifies its different functions: establishing the substantive reach of competition law, and attributing liability in the EU. The theoretical claim developed throughout Part I is that these two distinct types of inquiry require a differentiated approach to the conception of the firm.[82] In the 'substantive reach' function, the boundaries of the firm are established to protect private agreements made among business participants. In its 'liability attribution' function, the firm is defined in terms of its rights and liabilities as an actor within a market or society.[83] Understanding the distinct internal or external regulation purposes clarifies the need for distinct paradigms in setting the boundaries of the firm.

Chapter 4 and Chapter 5 discuss the competition law conception of the firm in vertical and horizontal relationships that blur the market–firm boundary. These chapters offer a detailed discussion of some of the most contemporary issues of the modern economy for competition law, which are the parental liability of wholly owned subsidiaries and the competitive effects of financial and corporate links among competitors (minority shareholdings and interlocking directorates). Capturing the anticompetitive effects of such relations may require adjustment of the substantive reach of competition law vis-à-vis corporate governance. The conception of the firm, reflected in the application of the single entity doctrine, is suitable for asserting the substantive reach of competition law. However, the single entity doctrine is not adequate when used for attributing liability. It contravenes structuring legal principles without clearly enhancing deterrence. These chapters offer an alternative analytical framework, based on the agency theory, for attributing liability within complex undertakings in a manner that feeds into the objective of deterrence.

---

[82]   This is a competition law adaptation of Orts's adaptation of H. L. A. Hart's approach to the legal boundaries of the firm: 'HLA Hart's admonition ... [is] the nature and boundaries of the firm depend on the nature of the question being asked'; see H. L. A. Hart, 'Definition and Theory in Jurisprudence' in *Essays in Jurisprudence and Philosophy* (Oxford University Press, 1983); Orts, *Business Persons*, p. 108.

[83]   Orts, *Business Persons*, pp. 223–5.

Part II – Opening the 'Black Box' for Cartel Enforcement Purposes

Competition law and corporate governance also meaningfully interact when the scope of inquiry of competition law moves within the conventional boundaries of the firm. The study of cartel practice particularly demonstrates that internal relations, and the divergence of interests that characterise the separation of ownership and control in such corporations, particularly affect incentives to compete on the market.

Chapter 6 reflects on the internal drivers of non-compliance with competition law. Here, cartels are first and foremost the products of individual and organisation-specific factors. While the existing scholarship focuses mostly on external factors, the chapter suggests that, broadly speaking, elements relating to corporate governance may also explain the occurrence of collusion. An inverse relationship is also described: the degree of competition in a market may impact the quality of corporate governance mechanisms. Chapter 7 focuses on cartel enforcement and provides a normative framework for assessing the effectiveness of instrument through the lens of the agency relationship. It offers a detailed discussion of sanctions and leniency programmes as well as of the relevance of corporate tools such as derivative actions and director disqualification.

Based on the framework developed in the previous chapters, Chapter 8 discusses the significance of corporate compliance programmes as a competition enforcement tool. Taking stock of the organisational challenges of corporate compliance, as well as the relevance of issues of agency relationships that exist within firms, the chapter posits that greater incentives should be provided to companies to implement effective compliance measures. Thus, the need to move from a sanction-based to a prevention-based type of enforcement increases the need for competition law inquiry into the conventional boundaries of the firm.

Chapter 9 concludes the present inquiry and highlights the theoretical contribution and policy implications of the conclusions reached in this book.

2

Theoretical Foundations

2.1 INTRODUCTION

The purpose of this chapter is threefold. First, it provides the theoretical motivation for this book. It explains why the economic theory of considering the firm as a 'black box' integrated the internal and organisational dimensions of the firm into economic thinking. Specialisation of labour, limited information and opportunism of actors are at the heart of the existence of firms. These considerations also justify the need for competition law, metaphorically, to 'open the black box', for a variety of purposes. Secondly, this chapter describes the theoretical and analytical features of the firm and of its boundaries that are essential to determining the substantive reach of competition law vis-à-vis corporate governance. The so-called 'theory of the firm', in all its variations, explains the existence and the nature of the firm, as well as its boundary with the market.[1] Thirdly, this chapter introduces the agency theory, which focuses on the behavioural implications of bounded rationality within firms, in which ownership and control are separate functions. The agency relationship is the *raison d'être* of corporate governance mechanisms, and is designed to reduce the adverse consequences of bounded rationality. The agency relationship will be a core object of analysis in developments on enforcement of competition law. These three aspects will be discussed successively.

2.2 WHY DOES ORGANISATION MATTER?

The theory of the firm is based on the argument that the internal organisation of the firm matters for economic efficiency. It explains why a transaction is carried out either within a firm, in the market, or in the framework of a long-term contract

[1] 'An actual or nominal place where forces of demand and supply operate, and where buyers and sellers interact to trade goods, services, or contracts or instruments, for money or barter' (Businessdictionary .com).

between two firms.[2] This is also valid for understanding why two companies merge into a single firm, or why they prefer to deal via an arm's-length contract.[3]

The theory of the firm departs from the neoclassical conception of the firm as a production function.[4] In that conception, the function of production depends on the factors of production: labour, capital and land. The amount of output – what is produced – is determined by the amount of input provided inside the firm. The firm is considered to be a 'black box' as the operations performed inside its boundaries do not matter for efficiency; that depends solely on the amount of input and the way in which it is allocated.[5] The firm maximises its profit by producing a product until the cost of producing an additional unit is covered by the revenue generated by that unit.

According to neoclassical economics, the price mechanism reflects the issues inherent in dealing in the market. Specialisation and division of labour, deemed to bring productivity gains and efficiencies in free-market economies, create issues of coordination and motivation.[6] Coordination is necessary to avoid duplication of activities. It is also essential to overcoming issues of interdependency of economic agents, who do not necessarily produce what they themselves consume. Motivation issues arise in situations in which the interests of individuals are not aligned, if they do not bear the full cost of their actions or enjoy the full benefits. In the presence of interdependencies, characterising specialised economies, individuals' self-interest may, in extreme cases, lead to the failure of the economy.[7] According to both Adam Smith and Friedrich Hayek, the interdependencies and related issues of coordination and motivation may be fully internalised by a well-functioning price mechanism. The price mechanism conveys information on the knowledge available in the economy, and thus should reflect the benefits and aggregate costs of any actions.[8] Therefore, each individual, while pursuing self-interested behaviour, will be led to account for the costs incurred by society.[9]

[2] A 'transaction' refers to an economic exchange. Because of the specialised nature of the economy, agents have to undertake exchanges, as they do not produce all that they need and they do not produce for their own consumption.

[3] O. Hart, *Firms, Contracts and Financial Structure* (Clarendon Press, 1995), p. 6.

[4] O. Williamson and S. G. Winter (eds.), *The Nature of the Firm, Origins, Evolution and Development* (Oxford University Press, 1993), p. 4.

[5] 'Efficiency' is here understood as allocative or static efficiency, which refers to the optimal allocation of resources.

[6] A. Smith, *An Inquiry into the Nature and Causes of the Wealth of Nations* (University of Chicago Press, 1776), Book I, ch. I. Smith uses the example of a pin factory: The pin factory productivity of a ten-member strong team of pin-makers is about 48,000 – equivalent to 4,800 pins for each worker. The increased efficiency comes from the skills acquired by the repetition of an activity and by the gain in time from not switching between different operations. Moreover, the division and specialisation of labour enable individuals to exploit the savings realised to increase output even further.

[7] J. Roberts, *The Modern Firm, Organizational Design for Performance and Growth* (Oxford University Press, 2004), p. 75.

[8] F. Hayek, 'The Use of Knowledge in Society', *American Economic Review*, 35 (1945), 519.

[9] Smith, *An Inquiry into the Nature and Causes of the Wealth of Nations*, Book IV, ch. II, para. IX.

However, the existence of imperfect information and opportunism in the behaviour of agents raises the need to find alternative ways of organising economic exchanges, one such way being through firms. The price mechanism cannot always achieve coordination and motivation, and may produce transactional inefficiencies.[10] Asymmetry of information between parties regarding a transaction may induce opportunistic behaviour, such as adverse selection and moral hazard: adverse selection refers to a situation in which one party to an exchange has information regarding some aspect of product quality that the other does not have. An illustration of adverse selection is the tendency of people with riskier behaviour to subscribe to an insurance contract. Moral hazard, a related source of transactional inefficiencies, exists when actors do not bear the full cost of their actions, and may have an incentive to behave recklessly. When opportunism is too extreme, the transaction can simply fail to occur. The insurance company – when it cannot discriminate between people who are inclined towards risky behaviour and others who are not – may be induced to charge a higher price to everyone. This may exclude some people from purchasing insurance in the market, so that only those inclined towards riskier behaviour purchase insurance.[11]

In his pioneering article, Coase explains the existence of the firm using the notion of transaction costs, which are the costs attached to any market transaction during the different phases of the exchange.[12] Prior to entering into a transaction, the parties must search for each other, which consumes time and resources. Thereafter, the parties undertake an information exchange so as to inform each other of the opportunity of the transaction, which is also a costly process. The greater the number of parties, the more difficult and costly the decision-making will be, even before negotiating the terms of the exchange. Discussion on the terms of trade can involve costly negotiation before an agreement is reached. During the execution of the contract, the parties incur the costs of enforcement and monitoring, as each party wants to ensure that the other fulfils the obligations set out in the contract.[13] Thus, 'transaction costs' refer to the costs of participating in the market, or using the price mechanism. In the absence of transaction costs, it does not matter which form

---

[10]   Expression used in O. Williamson, 'The Vertical Integration of Production: Market Failure Considerations', *American Economic Review*, 61 (1971), 112.

[11]   To illustrate the adverse impact of asymmetry of information, see the example of the market for lemons developed in G. Akerlof, 'The Market for "Lemons": Quality Uncertainty and the Market Mechanism', *Quarterly Journal of Economics*, 84 (1970), 488.

[12]   R. H. Coase, 'The Problem of Social Cost', *Journal of Law and Economics*, 3 (1960), 1, 15.

[13]   C. J. Dahlman, 'The Problem of Externality', *Journal of Law and Economics*, 22 (1979), 141, 148. The author argues that the different types of transaction costs reduce to the single cost related to imperfect information. This view is challenged by Furubotn and Richter, who emphasise that the importance of bargaining costs, along with informational costs, should not be underestimated: E. G. Furubotn and R. Richter (eds.), *Institutions & Economic Theory, The Contribution of New Institutional Economics*, 2nd edn (University of Michigan Press, 2005), p. 52. For an account of the definitions of 'transaction' available in the economic literature, see A. Benham and L. Benham, 'The Costs of Exchange' in P. G. Klein and E. Sykuta (eds.), *The Elgar Companion to Transaction Cost Economics* (Edward Elgar, 2010), pp. 107–8.

of organisation deals with market imperfections, as the parties to a transaction can always bargain at no cost and reach an efficient outcome, thereby internalising market inefficiencies.[14] An activity will then be organised within a firm when it can organise it more cheaply than the market.[15] In other words, when there are transaction costs, the way in which an exchange is organised – whether it is in the firm or in the market – matters in terms of economic welfare.

This book is motivated by similar theoretical considerations. Imperfect information and opportunistic behaviour, together with the existence of transaction costs, requires us to 'open the black box' – that is, to understand the significance of internal dynamics within moving boundaries, for competition law purposes.

2.3 THE NATURE AND THE BOUNDARIES OF THE FIRM

The analytical and theoretical features of the firm and its boundaries aid in establishing the substantive reach of competition law vis-à-vis corporate governance. First, Coase's explanation of the firm introduced transaction cost-inspired economic theories, from which new institutional economics emerged.[16] According to these approaches based on transaction costs, the transaction is the unit of analysis that explains the distinction between the firm and the market. However, subsequent approaches challenged this distinction, claiming that the firm would simply be a nexus of contracts. Different types of organisation – e.g. the firm and the market – would then be part of a single continuum of types of contractual relationships. The approaches of property rights, although in line with transaction cost economics, focus on assets in contractual relationships in order to explain the nature of the firm.[17]

2.3.1 *The Transaction Costs Approaches*

Within the transaction costs approaches to the firm, some characterise the firm by the nature of the relationships, and others by the attributes of the transactions.

[14] Coase, 'The Problem of Social Cost'.
[15] R. H. Coase, 'The Nature of the Firm', *Economica*, 4 (1937), 386, 404. The marginal cost of a transaction also explains the size of a firm. A firm will tend to grow until the additional transaction costs in the market are less than those in the firm, due to the diminishing returns to management: ibid., 395.
[16] 'The new institutional economics is an interdisciplinary enterprise combining economics, law, organization theory, political science, sociology and anthropology to understand the institutions of social, political and commercial life. It borrows liberally from various social-science disciplines, but its primary language is economics. Its goal is to explain what institutions are, how they arise, what purposes they serve, how they change and how – if at all – they should be reformed': P. G. Klein, 'New institutional Economics' in B. Bouckaert and G. De Geest, *Encyclopedia of Law and Economics* (Edward Elgar, 2000), p. 456.
[17] O. Hart, 'An Economist's Perspective on the Theory of the Firm' in P. J. Buckley and J. Michie (eds.), *Firms, Organizations and Contracts: A Reader in Industrial Organization* (Oxford University Press, 1996), pp. 202–5.

2.3.1.1 The Firm as Characterised by the Nature of the Relation

According to Coase and Simon, the firm is characterised by the nature of the relationship between the parties to the activity.[18] The employment relationship within a firm differs from that between two parties to a transaction in the market. In the firm, the employment relationship relies on the concepts of authority and hierarchy. Coase defines the firm as a 'system of relationships which comes into existence when the direction of resources is dependent on an entrepreneur'.[19] The distinction between a firm and the market lies in the coordination of the production process. In the market, he says, the price mechanism operates as the coordinator of production. In contrast, the firm exists when an entrepreneur has the authority to coordinate production.[20] Coase's theory also analyses the existence of such an authoritative relationship in a free-market economy.[21] The existence of the entrepreneur and the specificity of the employment relationship characterise the firm as being different to the market. The role of the entrepreneur also determines the size of the firm, as developed above, with the concept of diminishing returns to the management: the difference in the sizes of firms is explained here not only by the characteristics of their activities but also by the characteristics of the entrepreneur, such as the probability of making mistakes and how this evolves with an increase in the number of transactions undertaken.[22]

Simon's model also focuses on the employment relationship that distinguishes the firm from the market.[23] His model shows the circumstances under which two individuals would rationally prefer to enter into employment contracts over sales contracts. Under certain conditions, the employment contract enables the parties to achieve better outcomes, especially given uncertainty. In the market, contracts may enable parties to overcome uncertainty to a certain extent. Parties to an exchange may have to postpone some decisions because they depend on uncertain parameters. In sales contracts, money would enable the party to be compensated for postponing the decision. The greater the uncertainty, the greater the need for flexibility. The employment contract enables the parties to postpone the choice of designing the task to be performed and may be a cheaper way of organising compensation for uncertainty between the two parties. Also, employment contracts enable the parties to save on the costs of renewing sale contracts.

---

[18]   Roberts, *The Modern Firm*, p. 103.
[19]   Coase, 'The Nature of the Firm', 393.
[20]   Ibid., 388.
[21]   Why would some economic agents want to be directed? Coase's theory provides the following answer: the cost of using the market makes it preferable for people to organise the production within a firm and to make use of an employment contract. The employment contract is 'one whereby the factor, for a certain remuneration (which may be fixed or fluctuating) agrees to obey the directions of an entrepreneur within certain limits': Coase, 'The Nature of the Firm', 404.
[22]   Ibid., 396.
[23]   H. Simon, 'A Formal Theory of the Employment Relationship', *Econometrica*, 19 (1951), 293.

2.3.1.2 The Firm Explained by the Transaction as the Unit of Analysis

Developed by Williamson, who extended Coase's analysis of the nature of the firm to all modes of organisation, transaction costs economics holds that an analysis of the dimension and characteristics of a transaction explains how an economic exchange is organised – be it within a firm, a hierarchy or any other mode of organisation.[24]

According to Williamson, transactions are characterised by the following three attributes that determine the costs of the transaction: asset specificity, uncertainty and frequency.[25]

– Asset specificity relates to the specificity of the investment realised with respect to a particular transaction. An asset is specific to a transaction if it cannot be redeployed for other types of transaction in the future.
– Uncertainty is related to non-specified aspects and non-predictable aspects of the transaction itself, as well as to external uncertainty that may affect the transaction in the course of its execution.
– The frequency of the transaction is another of its attributes. It is worth organising a transaction within a firm if that transaction is likely to occur frequently.

The more a transaction requires specific investment, and the greater the uncertainty, the more likely that the transaction will be repeated and the higher the cost of such a transaction being performed in the market. Therefore, such transactions are likely to be organised within a firm rather than in the market. Conversely, a very standard transaction with low uncertainty and low frequency is more likely to be organised in the market. The less costly solution is the most efficient way of organising that particular transaction.

Williamson identified the characteristics of three different modes of organising a transaction, called 'modes of governance'. The modes of governance under consideration are the firm (or hierarchy), the market and hybrid forms of governance.[26] These characteristics are the type of contract law supporting the transaction, the type of adaptability to change and the means used to manage the transaction. Examples of hybrid types of organisation may be given by franchising, licensing, and subcontracting agreements, repeated and long-term purchasing contracts, and joint-venture agreements.[27] The attributes of the hybrid form of governance are distinguished

---

[24] O. Williamson, *Market and Hierarchies: Analysis and Antitrust Implications* (Free Press, 1975); O. Williamson, *The Economic Institutions of Capitalism* (Free Press, 1985); O. Williamson, *The Mechanisms of Governance* (Oxford University Press, 1996); O. Williamson, 'Transaction-Cost Economics: The Governance of Contractual Relations', *Journal of Law and Economics*, 22 (1979), 233; O. Williamson, 'The Economics of Organization: The Transaction Cost Approach', *American Journal of Sociology*, 87 (1981), 548.
[25] O. Williamson, 'Comparative Economic Organization: The Analysis of Discrete Structural Alternatives', *Administrative Science Quarterly*, 36 (1991), 269.
[26] Williamson, 'Comparative Economic Organization'.
[27] C. Menard, 'The Economics of Hybrid Organizations', *Journal of Institutional and Theoretical Economics*, 160 (2004), 347–50.

among the market and the hierarchy structures of governance, following Williamson's classification in terms of transaction attributes.

2.3.2 *The 'Nexus of Contract' Approach*

Alchian and Demsetz question the assumption that authority and hierarchy are the key characteristics distinguishing the firm from the market.[28] They argue that, in effect, employment relations do not differ from relations in the market in terms of what authority may achieve in the firm. They compare the relationship between an employer and his employee to that between an independent consumer and a grocer. Both the consumer and the employer can provide incentives for the action to be performed well: the latter can fire his employee, while the former can stop purchasing from the grocer. The consumer can induce the grocer to perform a task at a negotiated price, with a similar effect as the employer assigning a task to an employee.[29] The two types of relationship involve a succession of contracts upon which the parties must agree.[30] Klein, Crawford and Alchian argue that firms are 'formed and revised in markets and the conventional sharp distinction between markets and firms may have little general analytical importance' because the firm is no different than a special class of contract: a 'nexus' of contract. The question that matters is therefore: '[W]hat kind of contracts are used for what kinds of activities, and why?'[31] The firm is characterised by the centralised position of an agent who is a common party to several contracts.

According to Alchian and Demsetz, a firm may achieve better outcomes than the market in the case of joint production, to address an inherent metering problem of assessing the marginal productivity of each factor of productivity. Jensen and Meckling recognise firms as being 'legal fictions which serve as a nexus for a set of contracting relationships among individuals'.[32] According to them, the question of personalisation of the firm – or the attempt to distinguish its boundaries – makes little sense, as the firm 'serves as a focus for a complex process in which the conflicting objectives of individuals are brought into equilibrium within a framework of contractual relations'. In other words, the firm represents the private,

---

[28] A. A. Alchian and H. Demsetz, 'Production, Information Costs, and Economic Organization', *American Economic Review*, 62 (1972), 777.

[29] 'My grocer can count on my returning day after day and purchasing his services and goods even with the prices not always marked on the goods – because I know what they are – and he adapts his activity to conform to my directions to him as to what I want each day . . . he is not my employee' (ibid.).

[30] 'To speak of managing, directing, or assigning workers to various tasks is a deceptive way of noting that the employer continually is involved in renegotiation of contracts on terms that must be acceptable to both parties' (ibid.).

[31] B. Klein, R. G. Crawford and A. A. Alchian, 'Vertical Integration, Appropriable Rents, and the Competitive Contracting Process', *Journal of Law and Economics*, 21 (1978), 297, 326.

[32] M. C. Jensen and W. H. Meckling, 'Theory of the Firm: Managerial Behavior, Agency Costs and Ownership Structure', *Journal of Financial Economics*, 3 (1976), 305, 310.

and perhaps more complex, version of market contractual transactions, and each type of organisation is no more particular than a 'standard form contract'.[33]

2.3.3 *The Property Rights Approach*

Building on the previous results, the property rights approach constitutes an alternative to the approaches presented above. The existence of transaction costs makes it impossible for contracts to be comprehensive. Contracts cannot foresee all possible future events. As a result, economic agents write incomplete contracts in which they might specify what is to be undertaken if certain events occur, while also leaving gaps in the contracts.[34] For example, utilities contracts may be pegged to the inflation rate. In those contracts, the parties choose not to fix the price of the exchange, and leave some gaps in the contract. All that can be specified in contracts may be contracted away in the market, in the 'nexus of contracts' approach of the firm.

The impossibility of writing complete contracts may give rise to disputes between parties, as well as to opportunistic behaviour, such as a hold-up on a specific investment.[35] The hold-up problem arises when each party to a contract wants to avoid granting bargaining power or 'appropriable quasi-rents'[36] to the other party – for example, when realising an investment specific to the other party's activity that may not be reused.[37] Both parties would gain from cooperating, but the hold-up problem may cause the transaction not to occur at all. The more specific the assets, the higher the cost of contracting will be, compared with that of integrating the transaction within a firm.[38]

The issue of asset specificity and the related hold-up problem can be addressed if someone can claim the *residual rights of control*: different from the specific rights of control that are foreseen in the contract, residual rights of control are used in cases of non-specified contingency.[39] Ownership amounts to holding those residual rights

---

[33] Hart, 'An Economist's Perspective on the Theory of the Firm', 204–5.

[34] O. Hart, 'Incomplete Contracts and the Theory of the Firm', *Journal of Law, Economics, and Organization*, 4 (1988), 119, 123. For an analysis and model of incomplete contracts, see O. Hart and J. Moore, 'Incomplete Contracts and Renegotiation', *Econometrica*, 56 (1988), 755.

[35] M. L. Katz, 'Vertical Contractual Relations' in R. Schmalensee and R. D. Willig (eds.), *Handbook of Industrial Organization* (North Holland, 1989), vol. 1, pp. 697–8.

[36] 'The payment that is received by a resource of production activity over the opportunity cost in the short run' (Economic Glossary).

[37] Klein, Crawford and Alchian, 'Vertical Integration', 298–302.

[38] Ibid., 298.

[39] 'Suppose that you rent my house, and that a friend of yours moves in who hates the color of the bedroom. The decision to repaint would presumably be mine, not yours. That is, you would have to persuade me to repaint the room; you could not force me to do so (so in this example, I possess the residual rights of control). On the other hand, if the paint began to peel or an effluent of a neighbouring factory reacted with it, it would probably be within your rights to insist that I repaint the room' (Hart, 'Incomplete Contracts and the Theory of the Firm', 123–4).

of control.[40] The owner of the firm controls the transaction in cases that are not specified by the contract. In the market, non-contingencies are resolved by the owners of the assets through negotiation. The negotiation of non-contingencies leads to different outcomes in terms of the division of profits, which affects the incentives of the parties.[41] As a result, there exists an optimal allocation of residual rights. The boundaries and the nature of the firm are determined by the sensitivity attached to the ownership of assets.[42] If owning those assets has a major impact on the gain expected from a party to the transaction, the transaction is more likely to be organised in a firm.

2.3.4 *Relevance of the Theory of the Firm in This Book*

The theory of the firm provides analytical features that aid in distinguishing what constitutes an internal or an external relationship for competition law purposes. Particularly in the European Union (EU), the concepts used to determine the boundaries of the firm may also be used for determining all activities that should be left outside the realm of competition law in a free market economy: non-economic activities and matters that relate to the internal organisation of companies.[43]

In addition, the theory of the firm, in all its variations, can help establish whether relations between entities are within the scope of provisions on anticompetitive agreements.[44] The single entity doctrine, used for that purpose, is particularly useful to qualify relationships among different entities that cannot merely amount to employee relations. This is the case when an undertaking is composed of legally independent but economically affiliated entities, including parent and subsidiaries, commercial agency relationships and joint ventures, all of which are discussed in this book.[45] The theory of the firm can help the application of the single entity because both are based on 'looser' concepts than the authority and hierarchy that characterise the employment relationship. For example, in the nexus of contract theory, unity of conduct and interest stem from the existence of a central actor common to different contracts, managing the coordination of all parties.[46] A similar assessment may be useful to identify the existence of a unity of will within complex undertakings. In addition, the property rights theory helps the application of the single entity doctrine when ownership and control do not coincide. An analysis of

[40] S. J. Grossman and O. D. Hart, 'The Costs and Benefits of Ownership: A Theory of Vertical and Lateral Integration', *Journal of Political Economy*, 98 (1986), 691, 692.

[41] B. Holmstrom and J. Tirole, 'The Theory of the Firm' in R. Schmalensee and R. D. Willig (eds.), *Handbook of Industrial Organization*, p. 69.

[42] Hart, 'An Economist's Perspective on the Theory of the Firm', 148–50.

[43] See Section 3.2.1.2.

[44] See Section 3.3.

[45] Parent–subsidiaries (Section 4.2.1); Commercial agents (Section 4.3); joint ventures (Section 5.2.1).

[46] H. Demsetz, 'The Theory of the Firm Revisited', *Journal of Law, Economics, & Organization*, 4 (1988), 141, 156.

residual rights of control may, for example, help to distinguish whether competitors have fully delegated control to their joint venture, operating thereby as an autonomous entity for the conduct of that activity. If competitors were to retain residual rights, this would preclude the finding of a single entity shielding their agreements with the joint venture from the scope of competition law.[47] The hybrid conception of the firm, developed by Williamson, also helps us to understand the existence of commercial agency agreements as an efficient alternative to both the firm and the market, thereby requiring a distinct legal framework.[48] Finally, the theory of the firm can also clarify whether acquisition of ownership amounts to a 'lasting change in control' that conditions the application of EU merger control.[49]

2.4 THE AGENCY THEORY

The agency theory has relevance in the modern economy, in which large companies are characterised by a separation of the functions of control and ownership. As described by Berle and Means, in such firms, financiers delegate the conduct of business to managers who control the operations of the firm, while bearing the risk of the investment.[50] Particularly in cases of dispersed and numerous shareholders, managers hold wide residual rights of control over the business.[51] The agency theory analyses the behavioural implications of rights of control allocation in relationships within such firms.

The fact that the financiers (the principal) do not themselves control the business that they own, but delegate this function to a specialised manager (the agent) creates a situation of moral hazard: the manager does not bear the full cost of their action, and their level of effort cannot be fully observed due to the informational and expertise advantage that they hold. Therefore, the agent can pursue goals of their own, such as enhanced career opportunities and improved social status, which do not necessarily coincide with the principal's best interests.

---

[47] See Section 5.2.
[48] See Section 4.3.
[49] Parent–subsidiaries (Section 4.2.1) and joint ventures (Section 5.2.1); the concept of control in EU merger control (Section 5.3.2.1.1).
[50] A. A Berle and C. C. Means, .*The Modern Corporation and Private Property*, 2nd edn (Harcourt, Brace and World, 1967). Risk aversion provides another explanation for the separation of risk and control: financiers have a better possibility of absorbing the risk of the business than managers. Managers are more likely to be risk averse, and making them bear the risk of the business could lead them to take suboptimal decisions. Risk aversion refers to how an economic agent makes a decision in the presence of uncertainty. If a person is risk averse, he will be more likely to select a project with a predictable outcome and a low pay-off, rather than an uncertain solution coupled with a higher return: Roberts, *The Modern Firm*, p. 129.
[51] The risk bearers could control those residual rights, as owning the stock of the company. This solution, however, may not be efficient if, for example, the financiers are numerous and not specialised in the conduct of a business. This may be the very reason why the financiers decide not to conduct the business but to delegate to a qualified manager: A. Shleifer and R. W. Vishny, 'A Survey of Corporate Governance', *The Journal of Finance*, 52 (1997), 741.

Jensen and Meckling's theory of agency costs is a model of the cost of the separation of ownership and control. Agency costs are inherent to the agency relationships that arise between shareholders and managers, due to asymmetry of information and divergent interests. In their analysis, they compare the value of a firm in two situations: when the manager owns all the stock of the firm (entrepreneurial firm) and when the manager sells part of the shares to outsider investors, implying some degree of separation of ownership and control. Jensen and Meckling identify three types of agency costs. The costs of *monitoring* and *bonding* respectively are costs incurred by the principal in monitoring the agent, and costs incurred by the agent in an effort to commit to acting in the best interests of the principal. Costs associated with *residual loss* are costs incurred from divergent principal and agent interests despite the use of monitoring and bonding. The monitoring and bonding schemes are examples of mechanisms of *corporate governance*, which are aimed at addressing the agency costs inherent to corporations in which ownership and control are separated.[52] Agency relationships exist whenever a relationship between two persons – a principal and an agent – involves the agent's making decisions on behalf of the principal. Agency relationships are likely to arise whenever gains can be made from the specialisation of activities.[53]

2.4.1 Relevance of the Agency Theory in This Book

Constituting the theoretical foundation of corporate governance, the agency relationship structures the developments regarding enforcement throughout this book. Issues of limited information and opportunistic behaviour are of paramount importance to the design of instruments aimed at impacting actors' behaviour. This book discusses the liability in agency relationships: (1) within a firm; (2) within a corporate group; and (3) within a commercial agency agreement in which actors do not have a unity of mind and will.[54] Depending on the liability regime, the principals of each of these relationships may bear liability for the wrongdoing of their agents. Across jurisdictions, companies are typically liable for the conduct of their employee; in the EU, a parent company usually jointly bears responsibility for the breach by a wholly owned subsidiary, and a principal may be liable for the conduct of its commercial agent. As will be explained, a 'black box' approach to liability features enforcement regimes based strictly on the liability of the principal. Such an approach may be inadequate because it is based on the premise that the incentives and ability of the principal and the agent coincide. Instead, liability should be imposed upon joint

---

[52]   Jensen and Meckling, 'Theory of the Firm'.
[53]   O. Hart and B. Holmström, 'The Theory of Contracts' in T. Bewley (ed.), *Advances in Economic Theory: Fifth World Congress* (Cambridge University Press, 1987), p. 75.
[54]   Enforcement for breach by individuals is extensively discussed throughout Part II. On liability in parent–subsidiary relationships, see Section 4.2.2.3.3 and on liability within commercial agency agreements, see Section 4.3.4.

consideration of incentives and ability within the agency relationship. Incentives may refer to the pay-offs – costs and benefits – that the principal or agent may expect from an activity (e.g. greater profits, expected cost of penalty, determined by the perceived probability of detection). The concept of ability, in turn, refers to the manner in which incentives may translate into behaviour. For example, to what extent does a principal that has the incentive to comply also have the ability to direct its agent to do so? An effective liability regime is one that incentivises the principal to internalise the social cost of non-compliance, without their incurring excessive and wasteful expenses. A fundamental message is that the existence of imperfect information and opportunism may limit the ability and incentive of the principal to internalise such costs. Therefore, whenever the incentive gap is too wide, targeting the principal exclusively may significantly limit the deterrence of sanctions. The agency relationship therefore provides a very powerful framework for the design of enforcement.

The Conception of the Firm

Moving Boundaries

Part I of this book discusses the conception of the firm that prevails in competition law. It appraises its adequacy when the boundary between the firm and the market is not clear cut. The definition of a 'firm' has very important implications for the application of competition law. It determines the substantive reach of competition law provisions. Competition law submits firms to rules relating to their conduct on the market. Defining what a 'firm' is for competition law – through the concept of 'undertaking' in the European Union (EU), or 'person' in the United States of America (USA), establishes the scope of competition law provisions. In addition, the definition of the firm serves the purpose of establishing the boundaries between different entities that are subject to competition law.[1] In EU competition law and US antitrust law, the *single entity doctrine* further reflects the competition law conception of the firm. The doctrine supports the idea that relationships among entities forming part of a single entity should be immune from prohibitions on anticompetitive agreements. The single entity doctrine is thereby used to distinguish an undertaking from the other, and to ascertain whether entities will be subject to competition law either separately or jointly. In the EU, the single entity doctrine is also used to attribute liability in cases of undertakings composed by economically affiliated but legally independent companies.

The main theoretical claim is that different types of inquiries require a differentiated approach to the boundaries of the firm.[2] In the substantive reach function, the boundaries of the firm are established to protect private agreements made among business participants. In its liability attribution function, the firm is

---

[1] The concept of undertaking is also relevant in Art 102 of the Treaty on the Functioning of the European Union (TFEU) or section II of the Sherman Act. However, this analysis will focus more on the application of Art 101 TFEU and section I of the Sherman Act.

[2] This is a competition law adaptation of Orts's adaptation of H. L. A. Hart's approach to the legal boundaries of the firm: 'HLA Hart's admonition . . . [is] the nature and boundaries of the firm depend on the nature of the question being asked' (H. L. A. Hart, 'Definition and Theory in Jurisprudence' in *Essays in Jurisprudence and Philosophy* (Oxford University Press, 1983) in E. W. Orts, *Business Persons: A Legal Theory of the Firm* (Oxford University Press, 2013), p. 108).

defined in terms of its rights and liabilities as an actor within a market or society.[3] Understanding the distinct internal or external regulation purposes clarifies the need for distinct paradigms in setting the boundaries of the firm. The economic concepts underlying the theory of the firm may inform courts and authorities in situations in which the boundaries between the market and the firm are unclear. Logically, however, the theory of the firm may be of limited use in cases of liability attribution within complex relationships.[4]

Chapter 3 introduces the competition law conception of the firm, reflected in the concept of *undertaking*, and in the *single entity doctrine*. Chapter 4 and Chapter 5 discuss the adequacy of the competition law conception of the firm in vertical and horizontal relationships that blur the market–firm boundary. As such, Part I engages with some of the most delicate issues of the modern economy for competition law, which are a growing complexity of corporate structures, and the increasing disconnection between financial investment and operation of the economic activity.[5] Chapter 4 will critically assess the application of the single economic doctrine to establish the substantive reach and to attribute liability in parent–subsidiary relationships as well as in commercial agency agreements. The chapter will offer an alternative analytical framework for attributing liability, based on the agency theory that feeds within the objective of deterrence pursued by competition law.[6] Chapter 5 will discuss the substantive reach of competition law when firms are linked via financial ownership and interlocking directorates. Capturing the anticompetitive effects of such relations may require adjustment of the substantive reach of competition law vis-à-vis, and greater insights into, corporate governance.

---

[3] Ibid, pp. 223–5.

[4] The term 'firm' will be used in the sense of the theory of the firm, merely referring to economic organisations (as opposed to the market).

[5] For a description of the growing complexity of the corporate landscape, see: Orts, *Business Persons*, ch. 5 (separation of ownership and control is not new, but it is furthered by financialisation of the modern economy). For discussion of the financialisation process, see, e.g., J. Crotty, *Capitalism, Macroeconomics and Reality: Understanding Globalization, Financialization, Competition and Crisis* (Edward Elgar, 2017); E. Hein, D. Detzer and N. Dodig (eds.), *Financialisation and the Financial and Economic Crises: Country Studies* (Edward Elgar Publishing, 2016).

[6] A framework close to that proposed by N. I. Pauer in *The Single Economic Unit Doctrine and Corporate Group Responsibility in European Antitrust Law* (Kluwer Law International, 2014) and by B. Wardhaugh in 'Punishing Parents for the Sins of Their Child: Extending EU Competition Liability in Groups and to Subcontractors', *Journal of Antitrust Enforcement*, 5(1) (2017), 22.

3

The Firm in Competition Law

3.1 INTRODUCTION

Within the European Union (EU), an entity defined as an undertaking must apply and comply with competition law, while other entities not defined as such are outside the scope of competition law.[1] In the United States of America (USA), section 1 of the Sherman Act prohibits '[e]very contract, combination in the form of trust or otherwise, or conspiracy, in restraint of trade [...]. Every person who shall make any contract or engage in any combination or conspiracy hereby declared to be illegal shall be deemed guilty of a felony'.[2] Therefore, it is the concept of *undertaking* or *persons* that determines the personal scope of competition law in the EU and the United States respectively. Although the concepts of 'undertaking' in competition law and firm in economic theories may not coincide perfectly, the theory of the firm may be useful in competition law analysis. Particularly in the EU, the concepts used to determine the boundaries of the firm may also be used for determining all activities that should be left outside the realm of competition law in a free market economy: non-economic activities and matters that relate to the internal organisation of companies.

In EU competition law and US antitrust law, the *single entity doctrine* is used to determine whether entities will be subject to provisions on anticompetitive agreements either separately or jointly. In the EU, the single entity doctrine is also used to attribute liability to complex undertakings. After explaining the foundations of the single entity doctrine in the EU and in the United States, this chapter will discuss the implications of the two functions of the doctrine. Application of the doctrine to

[1] Article 101(1) of the Treaty on the Functioning of the European Union (TFEU): Prohibition of anticompetitive agreements 'between undertakings, decisions by associations of undertakings'.

Article 102 TFEU: 'Any abuse by one or more undertakings of a dominant position within the internal market or in a substantial part of it shall be prohibited as incompatible with the internal market in so far as it may affect trade between Member States. [...]'.

[2] 15 USC §1.

33

vertical and horizontal relationships will be discussed in detail in Chapter 4 and Chapter 5 respectively.

3.2 THE MEANING OF 'UNDERTAKING' IN COMPETITION LAW

The concept of 'undertaking' is not defined in the Treaty on the Functioning of the European Union (TFEU). A functional definition emerged in the case law in *Höfner* v. *Macroton* as 'every entity engaged in an economic activity, regardless of the legal status of the entity and the way in which it is financed'.[3] The Sherman Act refers to antitrust defendants as 'persons'.[4] As such, the term 'person' is an organic concept used to attribute a conduct to its alleged originator.

3.2.1 *Undertaking and EU Competition Law*

3.2.1.1 A Functional Definition

Although defined in Article 1 of Protocol 22 to the European Economic Area (EEA) Agreement as 'any entity carrying out activities of a commercial or economic nature', the concept of undertaking is not defined in the EU Treaty. The concept of undertaking in competition law emerged through the case law, and was first mentioned in *Hydrotherm*: 'In competition law, the term "undertaking" must be understood as designating an economic unit for the purpose of the subject-matter of the agreement in question even if in law that economic unit consists of several persons, natural or legal.'[5] According to *Höfner*, it is the activity, not the type of body or entity, that determines which entity is subject to competition law.[6] In that case the Court held that a public authority, the German federal public employment agency, was an undertaking for the conduct of employment procurement, which was classified as an economic activity. Therefore, the concept of undertaking is indifferent to the legal status of the entity, which created the need for the Court to adopt a functional approach focused on the 'type of activity performed rather than on the characteristics of the actors which perform it'.[7] This approach has indeed been

---

[3] Case C–41/1990 *Klaus Höfner and Fritz Elser* v. *Macroton GmbH* [1991] ECR I–1979, para. 21; O. Odudu, 'The Meaning of Undertaking within 81 EC'. *Cambridge Yearbook of European Legal Studies*, 7 (2005), 211.

[4] P. E. Areeda and H. Hovenkamp, *Antitrust Law, An Analysis of Antitrust Principles and Their Application*, 3rd edn (Aspen, 2006), vol. IB, para. 252a.

[5] Case 170/83 *Hydrotherm Gercitebau* [1984] ECR 2999, para. 11.

[6] *Höfner* v. *Macroton* [1991] ECR I–1979.

[7] Joined Cases C–264/01, C–306/01, C–354/01 and C–355/01I *AOK Bundesverband; Bundesverband der Betriebskrankenkassen; Bundesverband der Innungskrankenkassen; Bundesverband der Landwir schaftlichen Krankenkassen; Verband der Angestelltenkrankenkassen eV; Verband der Arbeiter-Ersatzkassen; Bnndesknappschaft; See-Krankenkasse* v. *Ichthyol-Gesellschat Cordes; Mundipharma GmbH; Gödeke Aktiengesellschat; Intersan* [2003] ECR I–2493, Opinion of AG Jacobs, para. 25.

adopted by the Court in subsequent cases.[8] Therefore, the concept of undertaking may encompass several legal entities, such as a corporate group, or a natural person and companies controlled by him or her.[9]

Alternatively, the Court could have adopted an organic definition of an undertaking. In that case, the Court would have paid attention to the legal status of the entities under consideration. It could have imposed upon an entity the requirement to have a legal personality,[10] or considered the way in which the entity was financed. By not doing so, the Court clearly excluded organic considerations from the analysis, and focused on the economic concepts. By not relying entirely on the usual legal categories and concepts (i.e. those of corporate law) for the definition of 'undertaking', the Court expressed the need for economic thinking in competition law. The economic conception of an undertaking clearly shows that there is room for the theory of the firm to inform the concept of undertaking in competition law.

3.2.1.2 The Notion of Economic Activity

The notion of undertaking establishes a distinction between economic and non-economic activities. The theory of the firm also advances a distinction between an activity that is organised within a hierarchy and one that is organised in the market. Competition law avoids addressing both what is non-economic[11] and what is within a firm.[12] This section shows that what separates economic and non-economic activities corresponds to what separates the market from the hierarchy.

---

[8] E.g. Case C–218/00 *Cisal di Battistello Venanzio & C Sas v. Istituto Nazionale per l'Assicurazione contro gli In/ortuni sul Lavoro (Inail)* [2002] ECR I–691, Opinion of AG Jacobs, paras. 48–9; Case C–475/99 *Ambulanz Glöckner v. Landkreis Sidwestpfalz* [2001] ECR I–8089, AG's Opinion, paras. 71–81; Case C–343/95 *Diego Cali & Figli Sri v. Servizi Ecologici Porto di Genova SpA (SEPG)* [1997] ECR I–1547, paras. 16–17, Opinion of AG Jacobs, para. 40; Case C–67/96 *Albany International* [1999] ECR I–05751, Opinion of AG Cosmas, para. 207, citing *Hydrotherm Gercitebau* [1984] ECR 2999, para. 11; Case T–319/99 *Federacion National de Empresas De Instrumentation Cientifica, Medica, Tecnica v. Dental (FENIN) v. Commission* [2003] ECR II–357, paras. 14–19.

[9] W. P. J. Wils, 'The Undertaking as Subject of EC Competition Law and the Imputation of Infringements to Natural or Legal Persons', *European Law Review*, (2000), 99, 108.

[10] Joined Cases C–189/02P, C–202/02P, C–205/02P to C–208/02P and C–213/02P *Dansk Rørindustri and Others v. Commission* [2005] ECR I–5425, para. 113.

[11] The concept of the undertaking tries to grasp what activity needs to fall under the rules of a market economy, and what should be left outside the scope of it, which is left to the power of public authorities, such as the provision of public goods: 'It is inherent in the principle of an open market economy with free competition [...] that competition rules only apply to behaviour which is, in the widest sense, of an economic nature' (A. Winterstein, 'Nailing the Jellyfish: Social Security and Competition Law', *European Competition Law Review*, 20 (1999), 324, 325).

[12] Case 30/87 *Corinne Bodson v. SA Pompes funèbres des régions libérées* [1988] ECR 2479: 'Article [101] of the Treaty is not concerned with agreements or concerted practices between undertakings belonging to the same concern and having the status of parent company and subsidiary, if the undertakings form an economic unit within which the subsidiary has no real freedom to determine its course of action on the market, and if the agreements or practices are concerned merely with the internal allocation of tasks as between the undertakings.'

The Court has identified different factors that characterise an economic activity. Even though no clear concept of economic activity has emerged from the case law, I will examine two factors that have been used by the Court to define such an activity.[13]

3.2.1.2.1 ACTIVITY THAT OFFERS GOODS OR SERVICES TO THE MARKET. In *Commission v. Italy* the Court confirmed that the focus of the analysis must be the type of activity carried out by the entity.[14] The Court stated that an economic activity consisted of offering goods and services, irrespective of the institutional relationships that it may have with the State. It considered that a body part of the Italian State, the Amministrazione Autonoma des Monopoli di Stato (AAMS), was an undertaking, and therefore that it had to comply with a directive addressed to (public) undertakings.[15]

The theory of the firm, as developed by Coase and Williamson, focuses on the transaction as the unit of analysis. The transaction is no different from an exchange of goods or services between two parties. For a firm to exist, there needs to be a set of transactions whose characteristics determine whether it is organised within a hierarchy or within a firm.[16] In other words, both the concept of the undertaking and the theory of the firm focus on the notion of exchange: in the latter case the exchange has a conceptual status as a 'transaction' and in the former it is viewed as merely a condition ensuring the existence of the economic activity.

Financial Risk

Financial risk is another factor inherent to the notion of economic activity that has been identified by the Court. In *Wouters*, the Court argued that a bar association was engaged in an economic activity because, on top of offering goods or services in the market, 'they bear the financial risks attaching to the performance of those activities since, if there should be an imbalance between expenditure and receipts, they must bear the deficit themselves'.[17] Conversely, the absence of risk bearing justified its non-qualification as an undertaking. In *Poucet and Pistre*, the Court considered the structure of the risk in the sector of social insurance and concluded that the entities under consideration were

---

[13] The third factor upon which courts have relied is whether the activity could be carried out for profit: E. Bernard, 'L'"activité économique", un critère d'applicabilité du droit de la concurrence rebelle à la conceptualisation', *Revue Internationale de Droit économique* [2009] 353.

[14] 'The State may act either by exercising public powers or by carrying on economic activities of an industrial or commercial nature by offering goods and services on the market. [...] it is therefore necessary [...] to determine the category to which those activities belong' (Case 118/85 *Commission v. Italian Republic* [1987] ECR 2599, para. 7).

[15] Ibid.

[16] Especially in the transaction costs economics theories.

[17] Case C-309/99 *J. C. Wouters, J. W. Savelbergh, Price Waterhouse Belastingadviseurs BV v. Algemene Raad van de Nederlandse Orde van Advocaten Intervening: Raad van de Balies van de Europese Gemeenschap)* [2002] ECR I-1577, para. 48.

not engaged in an economic activity, and therefore they did not qualify as undertakings.[18] The principle of solidarity, characterising the social security system in the case, implies that people contribute according to their income, while benefiting equally from the scheme. Therefore, the risk is borne differently by the contributors. Moreover, the risk is spread across different social security schemes, as those experiencing financial difficulties benefit from the contribution of those realising surpluses.

Similarly, an employee does not constitute an undertaking, as they do not bear the financial and commercial risk of the activity.[19]

> Dependent labour is by its very nature the opposite of the independent exercise of an economic or commercial activity. Employees normally do not bear the direct commercial risk of a given transaction. They are subject to the orders of their employer. They do not offer services to different clients, but work for a single employer. For those reasons there is a significant functional difference between an employee and an undertaking providing services.[20]

The notion of risk is also relevant in the theory of the firm. It is embedded in the concepts justifying the existence of alternative arrangements to the market. The risk comes from the cost and the uncertainty of occurrence of moral hazard and adverse selection in a transaction. An analysis of risk sharing among the parties determines whether it is less costly to arrange an economic exchange within a firm or in the market.[21]

In *Poucet and Pistre*, the risk structure was prone to issues of moral hazard due to the solidarity principles across the different contributors and schemes.[22] Therefore organising such an activity differently – i.e. not as a market transaction – may have been justified in terms of risk and moral hazard issues. The cost of imposing an obligation to subscribe to insurance may have been smaller than the cost of the moral hazard attached to the activity being organised in the market.

As developed by the property rights theory of the firm, when the existence of uncertainty makes it impossible for parties to a contract to plan for every contingency; it will be more efficient to organise the activity via a firm, the owner bearing the residual risk of the activity (as well as the residual income). An employer may decide to hire an employee, rather than contracting away an activity, because

---

[18]   'There is solidarity between the various social security schemes, in that those in surplus contribute to the financing of those with structural financial difficulties' (Joined Cases C–159/91 and C–160/91 *Christian Poucet v. Assurances Generales de France (AGF) and Caisse Mutuelle Régionale du Languedoc-Roussillon (Camulrac) and Daniel Pistre v. Caisse Autonome Nationale de Compensation de l'Assurance vieillesse des Artisans (Cancava)* [1993] ECR I–637, para. 12).

[19]   L. Driguez, *Droit Social et Droit de la Concurrence* (Bruylant, 2006).

[20]   Case C–67/96 *Albany International BV v. Stichting Bedrijfspensionenfonds Textielindustrie* [1999] ECR I–5751, Opinion of AG Cosmas, para. 214.

[21]   See Section 2.2.

[22]   *Christian Poucet v. Assurances Generales de France (AGF) and Caisse Mutuelle Régionale du Languedoc-Roussillon* [1993] ECR I–637.

retaining the risk will be the most convenient approach to uncertainty.[23] Therefore, the Court is right to analyse how the risk of an activity is spread, which indicates whether the relationship or activity at stake is inside or outside an undertaking.

According to Coase, there would be no transactional inefficiencies in the absence of asymmetry of information. The manner in which a transaction is organised would not matter, as the parties could always interact and bargain so as to reach the most efficient outcome.[24] Similarly if no uncertainty is attached to an activity, the decision to hire someone or contract away may be irrelevant to the employer/owner of a company; if an entrepreneur can predict both the revenue and the outcome of an activity, there is no need to bear the administrative cost of organising an economic activity within a hierarchy, as the market already internalises the information from which the outcome can be derived. In the insurance sector, if the risk were to be predictable, insurance schemes would not need to bear additional costs to tackle the issues of opportunistic behaviour coming from the limited observability of subscribers' actions. In both cases the existence of asymmetry of information is crucial to the desirability of an alternative to the market. Therefore, the concepts of transactional efficiency underpinning the theory of the firm feed well into the concept of undertaking used in competition law.

The concept of undertaking tries to identify which activity needs to fall under the rules of a market economy, and which should be kept outside its scope and left to public authorities' power, such as the provision of 'public goods'.[25] 'Economic activity' in competition law could mean all the activities that can potentially be organised in a market, as conceived in the theory of the firm. Conversely, a non-economic activity could mean all activities that fail to be coordinated through the price mechanism in the market.[26] An employee does not offer goods and services to the market and does not bear the risk of its activity. Their activity therefore qualifies as 'non-economic' activity. This also means that this relationship is better organised inside an undertaking, which is a private form of hierarchy. In addition, the regulation of the provision of public goods lies in the hands of a public authority, which is another form of hierarchy; similarly to within the firm, the relations of authority and hierarchy – and not the price mechanism – ensure the coordination and motivation to reach the output (be it quantity, price, regulation and so on).

In sum, an economic activity may mean all that is better organised within a hierarchy, be it private (within an undertaking) or public (falling outside the logic of the free-market economy). In other words, all activities not achieved via the price mechanism may be deemed to fall outside the scope of EU competition law.

---

[23] See Section 2.3.3.
[24] Coase 'The Nature of the Firm', 390.
[25] Odudu, 'The Meaning of Undertaking within 81 EC', 228–9.
[26] See Section 2.2.

The notion of economic activity in EU competition law does not benefit from a clear-cut definition in the case law.[27] The Court has based the notion of economic activity on various factors, but none has been particularly determining. Neither the manner in which an entity is financed, the goal pursued nor the existence of a non-profit motive precludes the existence of an economic activity.[28] The difficulty of conceptualising the notion of economic activity may illustrate the discretion that the Commission and the Court retain. The absence of a systematic approach reflects the will of the EU to frame free-market competition along with its other objectives.

3.2.2 *The Concept of 'Person' in US Antitrust Law*

In the United States, 'persons' are the subject of antitrust provisions. The term 'person' is defined in section 7 of the Sherman Act:

> The word 'person', or 'persons', wherever used in [the Sherman Act] shall be deemed to include corporations and associations existing under or authorized by the laws of either the United States, the laws of any of the Territories, the laws of any State, or the laws of any foreign country.[29]

The concept of 'person' thus refers to all who are subject to US and foreign laws.[30] Agencies and instrumentalities of the federal government, which are not regarded as 'persons',[31] are therefore immune from antitrust law, even when such entities are engaged in commercial activities in competition with private firms.[32] The criteria for not finding a person stems from the institutional and organic links that the entity has with the federal government. As it relies on a rather narrow organic definition, the concept of 'person' does not determine the specific scope of antitrust law. All 'persons' are subject to the Sherman Act, unless they benefit from an exemption.

---

[27] Nor does it in the United States in the context of delimiting federal from State competences: see R. D. Cooter and N. S. Siegel, 'Collective Action Federalism: A General Theory of Article I, Section 8', *Stanford Law Review*, 63 (2010), 115.

[28] Bernard, 'L'"activité économique"', 357.

[29] 15 USC §7.

[30] Ibid.

[31] *US* v. *Cooper Corp*, 312 US 600 (1941). The United States does not qualify as a 'person' for the purpose of antitrust law: *Thomas* v. *Network Solutions, Inc* 176 F 3d 500 (DC Cir 1999), 528 US 1115 (2000). The National Science Foundation is a subsection of the federal government, and as such cannot be liable under antitrust law. *Howe* v. *Bank for Intl Settlements* 194 F Supp 2d 6 (2002): 'Greenspan, McDonough and the Secretary of the Treasury in their official capacities are not "persons" within the meaning of the antitrust laws.'

[32] *Sea-Land Service, Inc* v. *Alaska Railroad* 659 F 2d 243 (DC Cir 1981), cert. denied, 455 US 919 (1982); *IT & E Overseas, Inc* v. *RCA Global Communications, Inc* 747 F Supp 6, 11–12 (DDC 1990). 'It is well-established that the antitrust laws do not extend to actions of agencies or instrumentalities of the federal government, even when those agencies operate in competition with and to the detriment of private enterprise. Moreover, private parties acting in compliance with clearly articulated government policies and programs are immunized from antitrust liability to the same extent as the government entity.' Areeda and Hovenkamp, *Antitrust Law*, p. 63.

The exemptions are either statutory, as laid down in section 6 of the Clayton Act,[33] or judicially created, and concern specific industries or activities such as labour and labour unions, collective bargaining, some agriculture cooperatives, some newspaper joint ventures, the business of insurance and certain proceedings in the medical sector.[34] The rationale for granting the exemptions relies on the fact that free-market competition might prevent such activities from reaching their societal objectives, which outweigh the loss of consumer welfare relating to the absence of competition in such situations.[35]

Both US antitrust and EU competition law use the concepts of 'undertaking' or 'person' to delineate the boundary between a firm and the market. However, only the EU is concerned with defining the subject of competition law, while, in the United States, the scope of application of antitrust law relies on an exemption regime[36] and not on the concept of economic activity.[37] The greater reach of competition law in the

---

[33] 15 USC §17: 'The labor of a human being is not a commodity or article of commerce. Nothing contained in the antitrust laws shall be construed to forbid the existence and operation of labor, agricultural, or horticultural organizations, instituted for the purposes of mutual help, and not having capital stock or conducted for profit, or to forbid or restrain individual members of such organizations from lawfully carrying out the legitimate objects thereof; nor shall such organizations, or the members thereof, be held or construed to be illegal combinations or conspiracies in restraint of trade, under the antitrust laws.'

[34] A. I. Gavil, W. E. Kovacic and J. B. Baker, *Antitrust Law in Perspective: Cases, Concepts and Problems in Competition Policy*, 2nd edn (Thomson West, 2008), p. 1009.

[35] The thirty immunities from antitrust law identified by the Antitrust Modernization Commission have given rise to criticism. 'Many are vestiges of earlier antitrust enforcement policies that were deemed to be insufficiently sensitive to the benefits of certain types of conduct [. . .]. Immunities should rarely (if ever) be granted and then only on the basis of compelling evidence that either (1) competition cannot achieve important societal goals that trump consumer welfare, or (2) a market failure clearly requires government regulation in place of competition' (Antitrust Modernization Commission, 'Report and Recommendations' (2007) viii, available at: http://govinfo.library.unt.edu/amc/report_recommenda tion/amc_final_report.pdf).

[36] Exemptions regimes are also relevant in the application of EU competition law. In the EU, the legal exception set out in Art 101(3) TFEU may automatically apply to certain categories of agreements. Block exemption regulations include: Commission Regulation 330/2010/EU of 20 April 2010 on the application of Article 101(3) of the Treaty on the Functioning of the European Union to categories of vertical agreements and concerted practices [2010] OJ L102/1; Commission Regulation 1218/2010/EU of 14 December 2010 on the application of Article 101(3) of the Treaty on the Functioning of the European Union to certain categories of specialisation agreements [2010] OJ L335/43. For exemptions in specific sectors (agriculture, insurances etc.), see Council Regulation 1184/2006/EC of 24 July 2006 applying certain rules of competition to the production of and trade in certain agricultural products [2006] OJ L214/4; Commission Regulation 461/2010/EU of 27 May 2010 on the application of Article 101(3) of the Treaty on the Functioning of the European Union to categories of vertical agreements and concerted practices in the motor vehicle sector [2010] OJ L129/52; Notice from the Commission on the application of the competition rules to the postal sector and on the assessment of certain State measures relating to postal services [1998] OJ C39/2; Council Regulation 487/2009/EU of 25 May 2009 on the application of Article 81(3) of the Treaty to certain categories of agreements and concerted practices in the air transport sector [2009] OJ L148/1.

[37] However, the distinction between economic and non-economic activity is relevant in the delimitation of the federal and state competences: *US* v. *Morrison* 529 US 598, 617–18 (2000). For a critical analysis of this distinction, see Cooter and Siegel, 'Collective Action Federalism'.

United States may illustrate how restrictions have been approached historically. US antitrust law has been part of the legal landscape for much longer than in the EU, where, since its inception, competition policy has been part of a wider regulatory framework requiring the boundaries of its personal scope to be framed accordingly.[38]

3.3 THE SINGLE ENTITY DOCTRINE

The *single entity doctrine* supports the idea that relationships among entities forming part of a single entity should be immune from the prohibitions on anticompetitive agreements. The single entity doctrine is thereby used to distinguish one undertaking from another, and to determine whether entities will be subject to competition law either separately or jointly. In the EU, the single entity doctrine is also used to attribute liability in the cases of undertakings composed by economically affiliated but legally independent companies. After introducing the single entity doctrine, this chapter outlines the implications of the competition law conception of the firm, in its two functions.

3.3.1 *From the Intracorporate Conspiracy to the Single Entity Doctrine*

Section 1 of the Sherman Act provides that 'every contract, combination in the form of trust or otherwise, or conspiracy, in restraint of trade or commerce among the several States, or with foreign nations, is declared to be illegal'.[39] The terms used in the Act imply that a plurality of actors is needed in order to find an infringement of section 1.[40]

In the case law, the concept of 'intracorporate conspiracy' emerged between 1941 and 1951, before being subsumed by the single entity doctrine. An intracorporate conspiracy is an agreement to conspire, not between independent companies, but between companies belonging to the same corporate group.[41] According to the US courts, commonly owned or controlled entities could conspire within the meaning of section 1 of the Sherman Act.[42] Later, the *Copperweld* case and succeeding cases

---

[38] M. Motta, *Competition Policy, Theory and Practice* (Cambridge University Press, 2004), pp. 13–19. For the role of competition in regulated sectors, see A. Jones and B. Sufrin, *EU Competition Law: Text, Cases, and Materials*, 6th edn (Oxford University Press, 2016), p. 51.

[39] 15 USC §1.

[40] See *Perma Life Mufflers Inc* v. *International Parts Corp* 392 US 134, 142 (1968); J. A. Rahl, 'Conspiracy and the Antitrust Laws', *Illinois Law Review*, 44 (1950), 743, 744, n. 5; Comment, 'Combinations in Restraint of Trade: A New Approach to Section 1 of the Sherman Act', *Utah Law Review*, (1966), 75, 76–7; S. K. Wright, 'All in the Family: When Will Internal Discussion be Labelled Intra-Enterprise Conspiracy?', *Duquesne Law Review*, 14 (1975), 63; B. Kishoiyian, 'The Intra-Enterprise Conspiracy Doctrine in International Business: The Case for the Extraterritorial application of Antitrust Law', *Touro International Law Review*, 6 (1995), 191, 205.

[41] Kishoiyian, 'The Intra-Enterprise Conspiracy Doctrine', 206.

[42] E.g. *United States* v. *Yellow Cab* 332 US 218, 228 (1947) and *United States* v. *General Motors* 121 F 2d 376 (7th Cir 1941). See also Section 1.2.1.

reversed the intracorporate conspiracy doctrine, with the single entity doctrine.[43] This case concerned an agreement between a parent company and its wholly owned subsidiary. In 1972, Copperweld acquired Regal Tube Corporation, which it fully owned. Copperweld and Regal Tube Corporation undertook actions to impede the entry of a potential competitor to Regal, Independence Tube Corporation, as this entry was deemed to breach a non-compete clause included in the sale contract of Regal to Copperweld. While the first judgments held Copperweld liable for conspiracy, the Supreme Court later rejected their findings, stating that:

> The coordinated activity of a parent and its wholly owned subsidiary must be viewed as that of a single enterprise for purposes of § 1 of the Sherman Act. A parent and its wholly owned subsidiary have a complete unity of interest. Their objectives are common, not disparate; their general corporate actions are guided or determined not by two separate corporate consciousnesses, but one.[44]

The unity of interest comes from the fact that 'the parent may assert full control at any moment if the subsidiary fails to act in the parent's best interests'. In other words, 'the ultimate interests of the subsidiary and the parent are identical, so the parent and the subsidiary must be viewed as a single economic unit'.[45] In this case, the Court made it clear that the notion of common interest relies on the notion of control, rather than on the question of whether the parent and the subsidiary share financial interests and incentives.[46] 'Control' in this respect must be understood as the ability of the parent to 'assert full control at any moment' over the subsidiary.[47] Such control can be exerted by controlling voting rights enabling the parent to elect a majority of directors, and in voting on matters of fundamental importance, such as mergers, sales of substantial parts of the assets and liquidation.[48]

In the United States, this and subsequent cases found that different firms forming a single economic entity are not capable of conspiring with each other and that any combination of them cannot constitute an antitrust violation.[49] Rather than infringing the section 1 prohibition, the agreement at stake is then regarded as internal to

---

[43] *Copperweld Corp* v. *Independence Tube Corp* 467 US 752 (1984).

[44] Ibid. 770–1.

[45] Ibid. 771–2.

[46] B. Klein and A. V. Lerner, 'The Firm in Economics and Antitrust Law' in W. D. Collins (ed.), *Issues in Competition Law and Policy 1* (American Bar Association, 2008), p. 20.

[47] *Copperweld Corp* v. *Independence Tube Corp* 467 US 752 (1984), 772.

[48] R. P. Meyers, 'Ownership of Subsidiaries, Unity of Purpose, and Antitrust Liability', *The University of Chicago Law Review*, 68 (2001), 1401, 1415 (fn. 96).

[49] *Zachair* v. *Driggs* 141 F 3d 1162 (4th Circ 1998); *Advanced Health-Care Services* v. *Radford Community Hospital* 920 F 2d 139 (4th Cir 1990); *Century Oil Tool* v. *Production Specialties* 737 F 2d 1316 (5th Cir 1984); *Gudowski* v. *Hartman* 969 F 2d 211 (6th Cir 1992), cert. denied, 506 US 1053 (1993); and *Fisherman* v. *Estate of Wirtz* 807 F 2d 520 542 and n. 19 (7th Cir 1986); *Williams I. B. Fischer Nevada* 999 F 2d 445 (9th Cir 1993) in H. Hovenkamp, *Federal Antitrust Policy, The Law of Competition and its Practice*, 5th edn (West Academic Publishing, 2016), p. 246.

the organisation of a corporate group.[50] As a result, the Supreme Court confirmed that antitrust law is not meant to interfere with intracorporate decisions.[51]

3.3.2 *The Adoption of the Single Entity Doctrine in EU Competition Law*

EU competition law has long adopted the single entity doctrine, as the General Court recognised that the economic unity doctrine is an underpinning concept of the case law.[52] As for the Court, it applied the single entity doctrine in *Dyestuffs*, stressing the importance of the 'unity of [. . .] conduct on the market for the purposes of applying the rules on competition'.[53] From this perspective, what matters is not the fact that two companies might have distinct legal personalities but 'whether or not there is unity in their conduct on the market'.[54] The *Viho* judgment confirmed the adoption of this approach: Viho contested a decision by the Commission in which it held that a distribution agreement between a parent company, Parker Pen, and its subsidiaries, aimed at partitioning different national markets, were outside the scope of Article 101(1) of the Treaty on the Functioning of the European Union (TFEU). The Court upheld the Commission's decision and the General Court's judgment, stating that:

> Parker and its subsidiaries thus form a single economic unit within which the subsidiaries do not enjoy real autonomy in determining their course of action in the market, but carry out the instructions issued to them by the parent company controlling them.[55]

3.3.3 *Implications of the Single Entity Doctrine for Competition Law*

This section introduces the main implications of the single entity, which will be discussed in detail in Chapter 4 and Chapter 5.

3.3.3.1 The 'Substantive Reach' Function

The single entity doctrine is used to shield relations internal to an undertaking from prohibitions of anticompetitive agreements.[56] In doing so, definition of the outer boundaries of the firm serves the purpose of protecting the rights recognised to firms

---

[50] Hovenkamp, *Federal Antitrust Policy*, p. 246.
[51] Gavil, Kovacic and Baker, *Antitrust Law in Perspective*, p. 239.
[52] Case T–145/94 *Unimétal-Société Française des Aciers Longs SA v. Commission* [1999] ECR II–585, para. 17.
[53] *ICI v. Commission* (48/69) [1972] ECR 619.
[54] Case T–325/01 *Daimler-Chrysler AG v. Commission* [2005] ECR II–3319, para. 85.
[55] Case C–73/95P *Viho Europe BV v. Commission* [1996] ECR I–5457.
[56] This does not necessarily mean that the single entity is shielded from competition law, as provisions other than s 1 may still apply.

to self-govern regarding their private ordering.[57] Reliance on economic concepts via the single entity doctrine reflects the idea that agreements between entities impact competition only if they deprive the market of an autonomous actor. Therefore, identifying whether, from an economic point of view, there is unity of mind and will on the market enables us to reach this conclusion. As will be discussed in Chapter 4 and Chapter 5, applying the single entity doctrine may be challenging, particularly when it involves relationships that blur the boundary between the firm and the market. The application of the single entity to such complex relations is critical because of the binary outcome: arrangements will either be immune or be submitted to provisions on agreements, with possible drastic implications in the event of breach. In that respect, applying the 'single entity defence' has been important in complex corporate groups composed of parent and subsidiaries, as well as in relationships between a commercial agent and the company that it represents. Applying the single entity with care in horizontal relations is particularly important to distinguish instances in which competitors construct corporate arrangements to operate behind the shield of a single entity.[58] Too broad an application of the single entity defence could have important anticompetitive effects.

The single entity doctrine can have limitations, when the dichotomy market/firm underlying its application fails to capture relationships that are neither clearly intra- nor external relations. This is the case when companies are connected via corporate or financial links. For example, the acquisition of shares in a competing undertaking renders the boundary between those unclear: two undertakings are simultaneously competitors with and shareholders of the same company.[59] As is discussed in Chapter 5, in the EU, such links may escape antitrust scrutiny because they exist as alternatives to a market relationship, on the one hand, and to an intra-undertaking relationship, on the other hand.[60] Unlike the position in the United States, merger control in the EU seems unable to address anticompetitive effects stemming from these hybrid relations either. Addressing these effects may therefore require moving away from the paradigm underlying the single entity doctrine.

3.3.3.2 The 'Liability Attribution' Function

In the EU, unlike the United States, the single entity doctrine has been critical for attributing liability in infringement decisions. Liability is imputed to a parent company when the subsidiary has no independent conduct on the market 'but carries out, in all material respects, the instructions given to it by the parent

---

[57] Orts, *Business Persons*, p. 2.
[58] Detailed discussion at Section 5.2.
[59] E. B. Rock, 'Corporate Law Through an Antitrust Lens', *Columbia Law Review*, 92 (1992), 497, 498.
[60] See the detailed discussion at Section 5.3.

company'.[61] In applying the single entity doctrine, liability can also be attributed to a company for breach by its commercial agent.[62] Finally, the single entity doctrine may be used to establish jurisdiction in cross-border private actions. English courts have noted that a subsidiary could be an 'anchor defendant' and face private action for infringement committed by its parent domiciled in another member state, in application of the doctrine.[63] Attribution of liability within complex undertakings has been one of the most contentious issues in EU competition law.[64] Application of the doctrine has here a very different role than in the substantive function. It no longer involves granting legal privilege to the private ordering of an activity. Although it is not clearly stated, the application of the doctrine in such cases may pursue an objective of deterrence, following the logic of corporate liability regimes.[65] A company is typically responsible for the wrongdoing of employees acting within the scope of employment, so that companies have the incentive to ensure compliance by all individuals acting on their behalf.[66] Chapter 4 will demonstrate that the single entity is not suitable for such an objective. In the application of the doctrine, parent companies have been almost systematically held jointly and severally liable for infringements by wholly owned subsidiaries. Such an approach to liability, however, ignores the fundamental issues of imperfect information and opportunism at play in the agency relationships between such entities.[67] Deterrence may be undermined if the parent company does not have the ability to prevent the breach internally. In addition, such application of the single entity doctrine is shown to contravene structuring principles of the law, which

---

[61] Case C–625/13 *Villeroy & Boch v. Commission* [2017] EU:C:2017:52, para. 146; Case C–155/14P *Evonik Degussa and AlzChem v. Commission* [2016] EU:C:2016:446, para. 27; Joined Cases C–93/13 P and C–123/13P *Commission and Others v. Versalis and Others* [2015] EU:C:2015:150, para. 40; Case 48/69 *Imperial Chemical Industry v. Commission* [1972] ECR 619, para. 133.

[62] Case T–418/10 *Voestalpin v. European Commission* [2015] EU:T:2015:516, para. 138.

[63] *Provimi Ltd v. Aventis Animal Nutrition SA* [2003] EWHC 96; *Cooper Tyre & Rubber Co & Others* [2009] EWHC 2609 (Comm); *KME Yorkshire Ltd and others and Toshiba Carrier UK Ltd and others* [2011] EWHC 2665 (Ch); *Nokia Corp and AU Optronics Corp* [2012] EWHC 731. For further discussion, see Section 4.4.

[64] C. Koenig, 'An Economic Analysis of the Single Economic Entity Doctrine in the EU Competition Law', *Journal of Competition Law & Economics*, 13 (2017), 281; Wardhaugh, 'Punishing Parents', 22; S. Thomas, 'Guilty of a Fault that One has not Committed: The Limits of the Group-Based Sanction Policy Carried out by the Commission and the European Courts in EU-Antitrust Law', *Journal of European Competition Law & Practice*, 3 (2012), 11; J. Joshua, Y. Botteman and L. Atlee, '"You Can't Beat the Percentage" – The Parental Liability Presumption in EU Cartel Enforcement', *European Antitrust Review* (2012), 3; S. Burden and J. Townsend, 'Whose Fault Is It Anyway? Undertakings and the Imputation of Liability', *Competition Law Journal*, 3 (2013), 294; B. Leupold, 'Effective Enforcement of EU Competition Law Gone Too Far?: Recent Case Law on the Presumption of Parental Liability', *European Competition Law Review*, 34 (2013), 570; J. Temple Lang, 'How Can the Problem of the Liability of a Parent Company for Price Fixing by a Wholly-Owned Subsidiary Be Resolved?', *Fordham International Law Journal*, 37(5) (2014), 1481

[65] Temple Lang, 'How Can the Problem?', *Fordham International Law Journal*, 37(5) (2014), 1486–7.

[66] For a typical situation in which the regime of 'enterprise liability' involved the systematic liability of the company for the actions of its employees, see Orts, *Business Persons*, p. 138.

[67] See the theoretical framework for liability introduced at Section 2.4.1.

are limited liability and legal personality.[68] Based on an agency-relationship framework, there will be presented an alternative to the existing approach to liability that is better aligned with the objective of deterrence and with legal principles.[69]

3.4 CONCLUSION

Competition law has a distinctive conception of the firm, with important implications. In the EU, the concept of *undertaking* serves to establish the substantive reach of competition law, based on the concept of economic activity. In the United States, the concept of 'person' reflects an organic and extensive approach to the personal scope of antitrust. In the EU and in the United States, the *single entity doctrine* determines whether entities that are economically affiliated need to comply jointly or separately with provisions on anticompetitive agreements, as such agreements within what is deemed to constitute a single unit are immune from section 1 of the Sherman Act or Article 101 TFEU. Analytical features of the theory of the firm can aid the application of the single entity in the substantive reach functions. In the EU, the single entity doctrine has another far-reaching application: it has developed as a liability-attribution tool within complex undertakings.

Therefore, the claim developed throughout Part I is that different types of inquiry require a differentiated approach to the boundaries of the firm in competition law.[70] The first function is about protecting non-economic activities and the private ordering from competition law, while the second function relates to the external consequences of the action of the firm and its participants. The conception of the firm in competition law, via the application of the single entity doctrine, therefore seems inadequate in liability attribution cases in the EU. A different framework, based on the agency theory, feeds better into the goal of deterrence that is presumably pursued here.

---

[68] Argument advanced by Pauer in *The Single Economic Unit Doctrine*. See Section 4.3.4 for a full discussion.

[69] A framework close to that proposed ibid. and by Wardhaugh in 'Punishing Parents'.

[70] This is a competition law adaptation of Orts's adaptation of H. L. A. Hart's approach to the legal boundaries of the firm: 'HLA Hart's admonition . . . [is] the nature and boundaries of the firm depend on the nature of the question being asked' (H. L. A. Hart, 'Definition and Theory in Jurisprudence' in *Essays in Jurisprudence and Philosophy* (Oxford University Press, 1983)); Orts, *Business Persons*, p. 108.

4

The Single Entity Doctrine in Vertical Relationships

4.1 INTRODUCTION

This chapter appraises the application of the single entity doctrine to vertical relationships. The analysis focuses on parent–subsidiary relationships within corporate groups, and on commercial agency agreements; characterised by a combination of legally independent but economically affiliated entities. The competition law treatment of parent–subsidiaries is one of the most delicate issues in competition law. Commercial agency agreements, featuring a hybrid form of organisation between integration and a market transaction, attracted renewed scholarly attention in the context of the recent e-book and online travel agent cases.[1]

The single entity doctrine is applied to establish the substantive reach of rules on agreements to such relations; to ascertain whether entities will be subject to competition law either separately or jointly. In the European Union (EU), it is also critical for attributing liability in the event of infringement.[2] Liability is imputed to a parent company when the subsidiary has no independent conduct on the market 'but carries out, in all material respects, the instructions given to it by the parent company'.[3] In the application of the single entity doctrine, liability can also be

---

[1] A. Zhang, 'Toward an Economic Approach to Agency Agreements', *Journal of Competition Law & Economics*, 9 (2013), 553; M. Bennett, 'Online Platforms: Retailers, Genuine Agents or None of the Above?', *Competition Policy International* (2013); P. Goffinet and F. Puel, 'Vertical Relationships: The Impact of the Internet on the Qualification of Agency Agreements', *Journal of European Competition Law & Practice*, 6(4) (2015), 242; P. Akman, 'A Competitive Assessment of Platform Most-Favoured-Customer Clauses', *Journal of Competition Law & Economics*, 12(4) (2016), 781. For an account of the different investigations and outcomes, see Akman, 'A Competitive Assessment', 781 and 783 and accompanying footnotes.
[2] The two functions of the single entity doctrine are introduced and explained at Section 3.3.3.
[3] Case C–625/13 *Villeroy & Bosch* v. *Commission* [2017] EU:C: 2017:52, para. 146; Case C–155/14P *Evonik Degussa and AlzChem* v. *Commission* [2016] EU:C:2016:446, para. 27; Joined Cases C–93/13P and C–123/13P *Commission and Others* v. *Versalis and Others* [2015] EU:C:2015:150, para. 40; Case 48/69 *Imperial Chemical Industry* v. *Commission* [1972] ECR 619, para. 133.

attributed to a company for breach by its commercial agent.[4] Attribution of liability within complex undertakings has been one of the most contentious issues in EU competition law.[5] Finally, the single entity doctrine may have implications for establishing jurisdictions in cross-border private actions.

The application of the single entity doctrine may be challenged when an arrangement exists as an alternative to the firm, on the one hand, and to a market relationship, on the other hand. Persistent reliance on the single entity doctrine becomes problematic when the economic reality demands a different framework than one based on the firm/market dichotomy. This is particularly the case in commercial agency agreements. The theory of the firm may provide useful analytical tools for establishing the substantive reach of competition law, including to hybrid types of relationships.

The single entity doctrine does not provide an adequate framework for attributing liability in the event of a breach of competition law by an agent or a subsidiary. Such an approach to liability is problematic because it contradicts essential principles of corporate law and does not ensure optimal deterrence of fines. This chapter offers a framework, based on the agency theory, for attributing liability, which fits broader policy objectives of enhanced deterrence of fines in cartel cases.

4.2 PARENT–SUBSIDIARY RELATIONSHIPS

4.2.1 *The Substantive Reach of Article 101 of the TFEU and Section 1 of the Sherman Act*

4.2.1.1 The Single Entity Defence in the United States

In application of the single entity doctrine, agreements between a parent and its wholly owned subsidiary are immune from Section 1 scrutiny.[6] Following *Copperweld*, lower courts have taken two approaches with respect to relationships between parents and

---

[4] Case T–418/10 *Voestalpin v. European Commission* [2015] EU:T:2015:516, para. 138.

[5] C. Koenig, 'An Economic Analysis of the Single Economic Entity Doctrine in the EU Competition Law', *Journal of Competition Law & Economics*, 13 (2017), 281; B. Wardhaugh, 'Punishing Parents for the Sins of their Child: Extending an EU Competition Liability in Groups and to Subcontractors', *Journal of Antitrust Enforcement*, 5 (2017), 22; S. Thomas, 'Guilty of a Fault that One Has Not Committed: The Limits of the Group-Based Sanction Policy Carried Out by the Commission and the European Courts in EU-Antitrust Law', *Journal of European Competition Law & Practice*, 3 (2012), 11; J. Joshua, Y. Botteman and L. Atlee, '"You Can't Beat the Percentage" – The Parental Liability Presumption in EU Cartel Enforcement', *European Antitrust Review* (2012), 3; S. Burden and J. Townsend, 'Whose Fault Is It Anyway? Undertakings and the Imputation of Liability', *Competition Law Journal*, 3 (2013), 294; B. Leupold, 'Effective Enforcement of EU Competition Law Gone Too Far?: Recent Case Law on the Presumption of Parental Liability', *European Competition Law Review*, 34 (2013), 570; J. Temple Lang, 'How Can the Problem of the Liability of a Parent Company for Price Fixing by a Wholly-Owned Subsidiary Be Resolved?', *Fordham International Law Journal*, 37(5) (2014), 1481.

[6] *Copperweld Corp v. Independence Tube Corp* 467 US 752 (1984).

partially owned subsidiaries. Some courts have considered that ownership interest very close to 100 per cent can lead to antitrust immunity; this suggests that holding less than 75 per cent of the shares is insufficient to avoid antitrust scrutiny.[7] Other courts have adopted a 'control approach', focusing on the legal control that a parent has over its subsidiary, which determines whether the parent and subsidiary act with a unity of interest.[8]

Following the standard of legal control, courts have granted immunity to parents owning as little as 51 per cent of interest in a subsidiary,[9] and have relied on factors such as management control, contractual obligations and economic incentives.[10] Looking at the *ultimate* legal control of a parent over its subsidiary is consistent with the property rights theories of the firm, in which ownership is determined by possession of residual rights of controls.[11] Also, if a subsidiary is able to divert from acting in the best interests of its parent, this means that there is room for deviation from a collusive agreement, which indicates the existence of potential collusive relations because the companies are already not acting as a single-profit maximising firm.[12] An approach demanding both substantial voting rights and ownership interest to grant antitrust immunity would be the optimal approach for a partially owned subsidiary, in line with the idea that residual rights of control attach to ownership, and determine the boundaries of a single entity.[13]

4.2.1.2 The Single Entity Defence in the European Union

The single entity doctrine, as set out in *Viho*, also relies on the notion of control and on the implications of control with respect to the autonomy of the subsidiary. In *Viho* the parent company controlled 100 per cent of the shares of its subsidiaries, and controlled its sales and marketing operations, as well as targets, cash flows, gross margins and stocks.[14] Since *Viho*, decisive influence and absence of autonomy of those entities set the basis for establishing the existence of a single economic entity, which is part of one undertaking.[15] Decisive influence is now presumed in cases of wholly owned

---

7   *Aspen Title & Escrow, Inc v. Jeld-Wen* 667 F Supp 1477, 1482-83 (D Or 1987): immunity is granted to a parent that owns 97.5 per cent of its subsidiary, while rejecting this possibility for subsidiaries of which it owns 60 and 75 per cent.
8   *Bell Atlantic v. Hitachi Data Systems* 849 F Supp 702, 706 (ND Cal 1994).
9   *Novatel Communications, Inc v. Cellular Telephone Supply* US Dist Lexis 16017 (ND Ga 1986) in R. P. Meyers, 'Ownership of Subsidiaries, Unity of Purpose, and Antitrust Liability', *University of Chicago Law Review*, 68 (2001), 1401, 1413.
10 *Rohlfing v. Manor Care* 172 FRD 330 (ND Ill 1997) in Meyers, 'Ownership of Subsidiaries'.
11 The property rights theory of the firm is introduced at Section 2.3.3.
12 H. Hovenkamp, *Federal Antitrust Policy, The Law of Competition and Its Practice*, 5th edn (West Academic Publishing, 2016), p. 247.
13 Meyers, 'Ownership of Subsidiaries'.
14 Case C–73/95P *Viho Europe BV v. Commission* [1996] ECR I–5457.
15 Communication from the Commission – Guidelines on the applicability of Article 101 of the Treaty on the Functioning of the European Union to horizontal co-operation agreements Text with EEA relevance [2011] OJ C 11/1 ('Horizontal guidelines').

subsidiaries, and hence more straightforward to establish in such conditions.[16] When the parent company only partially or jointly owns the subsidiary, it is more difficult to establish whether the subsidiary has autonomy. In such situations, the Commission analyses other criteria in addition to the shareholding of the parent in the subsidiary: the composition of the board of directors, and the degree of influence of the parent company towards the subsidiary in terms of policy or any other related subject.[17]

As an example, in *Gosmé/Martell-DMP*, the Commission stated that a parent company and its subsidiary, of which it owned equal shares with another company, did not form a single entity. As well as holding only 50 per cent of the voting rights and half of the supervisory board members, the subsidiary had its own sales force, and was not distributing its parent company brands. Therefore, the agreement between them preventing parallel trade was found to infringe Article 101(1) of the Treaty on the Functioning of the European Union (TFEU).[18] The Commission looked at operational proof of (absence of) control of the parent over the subsidiary, which led to it finding independent conduct in the market.

The position taken by the Commission in gathering all the available evidence that supports its conclusion is reasonable. However, according to the economic principles of the firm, 'operational' criteria (e.g. sales force, or independent legal personalities) should never be analysed in isolation from residual rights of control of the parent towards the company. A corporate group can encompass different divisions that have their own brand, and sales force, and which still form a single entity, provided that the parent company holds the ultimate control rights over the divisions and the employees.[19]

4.2.2 *Attributing Liability Within Corporate Groups in the EU*

In the EU, the most important and contentious application of the single entity doctrine to parent–subsidiaries lies in the attribution of liability.[20] Parent companies of wholly owned subsidiaries are almost invariably held liable for the breach of their subsidiaries, irrespective of their participation in wrongdoing. In the United States, in contrast, courts almost never hold a parent company liable for the wrongdoing of their subsidiaries. A parent can be held responsible in rare 'veil-piercing' cases, in which a subsidiary can be proven to exist as part of a fraudulent process, or when the parent itself infringes antitrust law, bearing responsibility for its own actions only.[21]

---

[16]   Case C–107/82 AEG v. *Commission* [1983] ECR 3151, para. 50; Case C–286/98P *Stora* [2000] ECR I–9925, para. 29; or Case C–97/08P *Akzo Nobel NV v. Commission* [2009] ECR I–8237, para. 60 *et seq.*

[17]   Case C–107/82 AEG v. *Commission* [1983] ECR 3151, paras. 47–53.

[18]   *Gosmé/Martell-DMP* (Case IV/32186) Commission Decision 91/335/EEC [1991] OJ L185/23, para. 30.

[19]   B. Klein and A. V. Lerner, 'The Firm in Economics and Antitrust Law' in W. D. Collins (ed.), *Issues in Competition Law and Policy* 1 (American Bar Association, 2008), p. 21.

[20]   See n. 5.

[21]   The principles of parent liability are established in *US v. Bestfoods* 524 US 51 (1998); C. Kass, 'Holding Parents Liable for Antitrust Violations – Differences in US and EU Corporate Governance', *The Metropolitan Corporate Counsel* (2010), 38.

This section explains how the single entity doctrine has developed into a liability-attribution tool, by which a parent is, in practice, almost always liable for the act of its wholly owned subsidiary. In such cases, the parent and its subsidiary are liable jointly and severally. Such an approach to parental liability is very distinctive. Although the practice of 'veil piercing' exists in other areas of business law, it remains the exception because it interferes with the structuring principles of limited liability and legal separation. Competition law has, instead, made systematic use of this exceptional liability regime. This chapter argues that the existing approach is suboptimal in terms of the deterrence objective pursued by a liability regime, particularly in the context of a complex corporate landscape. To remedy some of the identified shortcomings, this chapter provides an alternative framework to liability, based on the agency theory, that better suits the purpose of deterrence.[22] This chapter thus substantiates the theoretical claim that different inquiries demand a distinct approach to competition law in the firm.[23] The conception of the firm whose foundation is to establish the substantive reach of competition law is inadequate for attributing liability. Liability is about protecting a third party from anticompetitive behaviour, which demands an approach consistent with that purpose.

4.2.2.1 Parental Liability and Complete Ownership

Based on the concept of economic activity, the concept of undertaking is indifferent to the legal reality of what may form the undertaking, when it is used to determine whether there is a separate undertaking, or an agreement between undertakings. However, the legal personality matters when it comes to imputing infringements of competition law:

> Although, an 'undertaking' within the meaning of Article [101](1) of the Treaty is not necessarily the same as a company having legal personality, it is necessary for the purposes of applying and enforcing decisions to identify an entity possessing legal personality to be the addressee of the measure.[24]

---

[22] For the theoretical foundations of this framework, see Section 2.4.1.

[23] This is a competition law adaptation of Ort's adaptation of H. L. A. Hart's approach to the legal boundaries of the firm: 'HLA Hart's admonition . . . [is] the nature and boundaries of the firm depend on the nature of the question being asked' (H. L. A. Hart, 'Definition and Theory in Jurisprudence' in *Essays in Jurisprudence and Philosophy* (Oxford University Press 1983)); E. W. Orts, *Business Persons: A Legal Theory of the Firm* (Oxford University Press, 2013), p. 108.

[24] See Case T–305/94 *PVC* [1999] ECR II–0931, para. 978. See also: W. P. J. Wils, 'The Undertaking as Subject of EC Competition Law and the Imputation of Infringements to Natural or Legal Persons', *European Law Review* (2000), 99, 108. 'For it to ensure that the provisions of the Treaty are applied, the Commission should be able to address decisions to undertakings or associations of undertakings for the purpose of bringing to an end infringements of Articles [101] and [102] of the Treaty' (Regulation 1/2003, para. 11). However, Art. 299 TFEU provides that 'Acts of the Council, the Commission or the European Central Bank which impose a pecuniary obligation on persons other than States, shall be enforceable. Enforcement shall be governed by the rules of civil procedure in force in the State in

When an undertaking encompasses several legal persons or companies, the question is to whom to impute the infringement.[25] For that purpose, the single entity doctrine has been used to determine the addressee to infringement decisions committed by subsidiaries forming part of a wider undertaking within the meaning of EU competition law. In various instances, the Commission has held a parent company liable for the wrongdoing of its subsidiary, even though the parent was not involved in it.[26] To do so it has been sufficient that the 'parent company and its subsidiary form a single economic unit and therefore a single undertaking [. . .] without having to establish the personal involvement of the latter.'[27]

The application of the single entity doctrine has therefore been critical for attributing fines in infringement decisions. Liability is then imputed to a parent company when the subsidiary has no independent conduct on the market 'but carries out, in all material respects, the instructions given to it by the parent company'.[28] The Commission's approach is based on a twofold test: first, liability is attributed to the parent company if it had the opportunity to exercise decisive influence. In addition, the Commission must show that this decisive influence was actually exerted on the subsidiary.[29]

When the subsidiary is wholly owned by the parent, the actual decisive influence will be presumed.[30] Some cases, such as *Bolloré* v. *Commission*, have suggested that full ownership does not mean that a parent company can be presumed to be liable, and 'something more than the extent of the shareholding must be shown, but this may be in the form of indicia'.[31] The *Akzo* case reversed those findings, affirming that a complete ownership yields a 'rebuttable presumption that a parent company does

---

the territory of which it is carried out.' Article 299 mentions 'persons' and not 'undertakings'. In national laws, this refers to entities having natural or legal personalities.

[25] Joined Cases C–231/11P to C–233/11P *Commission* v. *Siemens Österreich and Others et Siemens Transmission & Distribution and Others* [2014] EU:C: 2014:256.

[26] See, inter alia, ibid., para. 46; Case C–440/11P *Commission* v. *Stichting Administratiekantoor Portielje* [2013] EU:C:2013:514, para. 38; Cases C–628/10 and C–14/11 *Alliance One International and Standard Commercial Tobacco* v. *Commission* [2012] EU:C:2012:479, para. 43; Case T–65/89 *BPB Industries plc* v. *Commission* [1993] ECR II–389, paras. 148–55; Case T–77/92 *Parker Pen Ltd* v. *Commission* [1994] ECR II–549, para. 57; Case T–354/94 *Stora* v. *Commission* [1998] ECR II–2111, para. 79.

[27] Case C–97/08P *Akzo Nobel NV* v. *Commission* [2009] ECR I–8237, para. 59.

[28] Case C–625/13, *Villeroy & Boch* v. *Commission* [2017] EU:C:2017:52, para. 146; Case C–155/14P *Evonik Degussa and AlzChem* v. *Commission* [2016] EU:C:2016:446, para. 27; Joined Cases C–93/13P and C–123/13P *Commission and Others* v. *Versalis and Others* [2015] EU:C:2015:150, para. 40; Case 48/69 *Imperial Chemical Industry* v. *Commission* [1972] ECR 619, para. 133.

[29] Case T–314/01 *Coöperatieve Verkoop- en Productievereniging van Aardappelmeel en Derivaten Avebe BA* v. *Commission* [2006] ECR II–3085, para. 136; *Dansk Rørindustri and Others* v. *Commission* [2005] ECR I–5425, paras. 118–22; Case C–196/99P *Aristrain* v. *Commission* [2003] ECR I–11005, paras. 95–9; Case T–9/99 *HFB and Others* v. *Commission* [2002] ECR II–1487, para. 527.

[30] *Monochloroacetic Acid (MCAA)* (Case COMP/C.37.773) Commission Decision 2006/897/EC [2006] OJ C303/10, para. 219, which quotes Case C–107/82 *AEG* v. *Commission* [1983] ECR 3151, para. 50: 'as a wholly-owned subsidiary of AEG, necessarily follows a policy laid down by the same bodies as, under its statutes, determine AEG's policy'.

[31] Case T–109/02 *Bollore* v. *Commission* [2007] ECR II–94, para. 13.

in fact exercise a decisive influence over the conduct of its subsidiary'.[32] As such, joint and several liability of the parent stems from full ownership, unless the parent company provides sufficient evidence that the subsidiary acted independently.

Has this presumption been rebutted, and if so, under what circumstances? Subsequent cases led some observers to note that there is, de facto, a strict parental liability for conduct of wholly owned subsidiaries.[33] In practice, most of the time, such a presumption has led the Commission to hold a parent company jointly and severally liable for its wholly owned subsidiary. The rare exceptions to this can be explained on specific and procedural grounds, rather than providing explanation as to the type of criteria that could be considered in future attempt to rebut the presumption.

In *Alliance One*, although a complete ownership of the subsidiaries shares existed, the Commission had decided to show the two elements of the test, including that influence had actually been exerted. The General Court partially annulled the decision to attribute liability to parent companies because of lack of evidence, supporting the finding of actual decisive influence.[34] While it held that the Commission was not bound to rely exclusively on the presumption of decisive influence, the Court of Justice reaffirmed that the chosen route entailed a more onerous standard of proof that may be required in case of full ownership.[35] In that case, exempting a parent company from liability did not constitute an example of a successful rebuttal of the presumption, since it was not the chosen method for application of the single entity doctrine. However, the case was notable to the extent that a parent company operating as a pure financial investor was not held liable owing to the absence of decisive influence over the conduct of its wholly owned subsidiary.[36]

Recent cases raised the question of whether financial holdings, owning 100 per cent of the capital of a company, but having no operational take on the subsidiary should bear responsibility for the subsidiary's conduct. In *Eni* the Court held that rebutting the presumption would require evidence that the subsidiary 'could act with complete autonomy not only at the operational level but also at the

---

[32] Case C–97/08P *Akzo Nobel NV v. Commission* [2009] ECR I–8237, para. 60.

[33] See, e.g., M. Stanevicius, 'Portielje: Bar Remains High for Rebutting Parental Liability Presumption', *Journal of European Competition Law & Practice*, 5 (2014), 24. *Portielje* is the only case in which the presumption was rebutted – a finding, however, that was reversed by the Court of Justice. This case is characterised by a quite unique situation: the parent company (a foundation) was not defined as an undertaking, thereby impeding the qualification of 'undertaking' (see below).

[34] At the time, case law on the presumption was uncertain – hence the chosen approach: Case C–628/10P *Alliance One International and Others v. Commission* [2012] EU:C: 2012:479, para. 51.

[35] Ibid., paras. 47–67.

[36] 'Apart from the corporate link between the parents and their subsidiaries, there is no indication in the file of any material involvement of Universal Corporation and Universal Leaf [. . .]. It would therefore not be appropriate to address them a decision in this case. The same conclusion would apply, *a fortiori*, to Intabex insofar as its 100% shareholding in Agroexpansión was purely financial' (*Raw Tobacco-Spain* (Case COMP/C38.238/B.2) Commission Decision 2007/36/EC [2007] OJ L102/14), para. 376.

financial level'.[37] In an attempt to rebut the presumption of decisive influence, Eni held that it had no management overlap, no information on strategic and commercial plans, and no role on the definition of strategic and commercial plans of its subsidiaries that included sales volumes and prices.[38] The Court found that, although this showed a certain degree of autonomy of the subsidiaries, Eni and its subsidiaries still formed a single economic entity owing to the role of technical and financial coordinator and control over investment and budget.[39] Neither the absence of operation of Eni in the product market of its subsidiary nor the absence of direct participation in operational management played any role in rebutting the presumption. In short, although so close to a holding, the participation of Eni in any dimension of its economic activity seemed to have provided a basis for holding the finding of a single economic unit.[40] The Court's conclusions limit the availability of the presumption being rebutted in situations of financial holding having no control over operations and management of their subsidiaries.

In *Portelje*, the General Court found that the presumption had been successfully rebutted because the parent did not adopt management decisions, in compliance with the requirements of company law. The Court reversed that finding in stating that it was 'necessary for account to be taken of all the relevant factors relating to the economic, organisational and legal links which tie that author to its holding entity and, therefore, of economic reality', and that mere consideration of company law requirements could not be decisive.[41] This case is notable because it was the first in which a party had successfully rebutted the presumption, on substantive grounds, having shown that the subsidiary had an autonomous conduct on the market, until the Court reached the opposite conclusion. However, the fact that *Portielje* was a foundation, not an undertaking, made this case specific and played a role in the General Court's conclusion. On that point, the Advocate General reasserted that no consideration should be given to the legal status or form of the parent company – foundation, holding, industrial parent company etc. – in the assessment of an undertaking, and attribution of liability.[42]

In *Air Liquide*, the General Court overturned the Commission's decision of holding Air Liquide liable for its wholly owned subsidiary. Air Liquide had intended to demonstrate the autonomy of the subsidiary's autonomy in terms of strategic and commercial development of the firm's conduct.[43] The General Court only found improper examination of the evidence by the Commission, while not clarifying any

---

[37]　C–508/11P *Eni* v. *European Commission* [2013] EU:C:2013:289, para. 85.

[38]　Ibid., para. 53

[39]　Ibid., para. 64.

[40]　Kieron Beal, QC, 'The Sins of the Son or Daughter', Competition Bulletin (19 May 2013), available at: https://competitionbulletin.com/2013/05/19/the-sins-of-the-son-or-daughter/

[41]　Case C–440/11P *Commission* v. *Stichting Administratiekantoor Portielje* [2013] EU:C:2013:514, para. 66.

[42]　Ibid. (AG Opinion), para 54.

[43]　Case T–185/06 *L'Air liquide SA* v. *Commission* [2011] ECR II–02809.

aspect relating to the substantive assessment of the evidence brought by the party to rebut the presumption. In *Grolsch*, the Commission's decision to impute liability was annulled on similar procedural grounds, for it did not substantiate this finding with reference to full ownership and control of the parent company on its subsidiary.[44] Similarly, in *Edison*, the Court of Justice, upholding the General Court's judgment to quash the Commission's decision, was based on insufficient consideration of Edison's argument to rebut the presumption in the case of a holding with non-operational control over its indirectly wholly owned subsidiary Ausimont.[45]

In her opinion to *Akzo*, Advocate General Kokott clarifies that the presumption could be rebutted in case of an investment company operating like a pure financial investor.[46] In 1.*Garantanova* the General Court defines this as an 'investor who holds shares in a company in order to make a profit, but who refrains from any involvement in its management and in its control'.[47] The pure investor defence was rejected in *Gigaset*, in which an investment company specialising in restructuring was deemed to exercise decisive influence owing to its ability to make strategic decision with regard to the subsidiary.[48] In *Power Cables*, Goldman Sachs was held jointly liable with its subsidiary for the participation of its subsidiary, Prysmian, in a cartel. The investment bank was deemed to have acquired decisive influence, owing to its involvement in strategic decision-making (e.g. with the appointment of top management and the approval of business and management plans) in spite of its attempt to demonstrate its absence of operational engagement in its subsidiary's conduct on the market.[49] The definition of a pure financial investor in 1.*Garantanova* seems to be at odds with a situation of full ownership, because it corresponds to situations of minority rather than majority shareholdings. In addition, the broad interpretation of factors indicative of involvement in management and control narrows down the possibility that investors can rebut the presumption.

As the examination of these cases suggests, courts have relied on a wide range of factors to ascertain the existence of a single entity to attribute liability. This very broad interpretation of exercise of a decisive influence makes, in practice, the rebuttal of the presumption very difficult. Demonstrating full operational autonomy has never been sufficient to rebut a presumption. Parties thus need to demonstrate an absence of decisive influence, together with the absence of elements that stem from the organic relationship of ownership.

---

[44] Case T–234/07 *Koninklijke Grolsch v. Commission* [2011] ECR II–6169.
[45] Case C–446/11P *Commission v. Edison SpA* [2013] EU:C:2013:798. For comment on the case, see P. Merlino, 'Edison: A Glimpse of Hope for Parent Companies Seeking to Rebut the Parental Liability Presumption?', *Journal of European Competition Law & Practice*, 5(7) (2014), 463.
[46] Advocate General Kokott in her Opinion in Case C–97/08P *Akzo v. Commission*.
[47] T–392/09 1. *garantovaná a.s v. Commission* [2012] EU:T:2012:674, para. 52.
[48] Case T–395/09 *Gigaset AG v. Commission* [2014] EU:T:2014:23.
[49] *Power Cables*, (Case COMP/39610) Commission Decision [2014] non-official, para. 779.

The approach to parental liability raises a number of issues. The de facto liability is criticised on the ground of procedural fairness. A rule of absolute liability exists when a presumption cannot be rebutted in practice.[50] Without a legislative basis, an absolute liability contravenes fundamental rights of defence.[51] Despite confirming that the presumption is rebuttable, in line with fundamental rights, the Court has not demonstrated it in practice.[52] Another issue is that the current approach is at odd with important corporate law principles of the member states. Finally, this approach to liability is not entirely in line with the objective of deterrence that may be pursued. The subsequent sections will discuss the two latter points in detail.

4.2.2.2 A Distinctive Approach to Liability

De facto attribution of liability to the parent of wholly owned subsidiaries is an exception to *entity liability*, the default approach around most of the legal relationships of business corporations across jurisdictions. *Entity liability* is grounded on the principles of separate legal personality and limited liability. Only in particular circumstances can liability be attributed to another legal person, referring to lifting or piercing the 'entity veil'.[53] Within the *enterprise liability* approach, in contrast, a legal person may bear responsibility for the conduct of another legal person, similar to a company bearing responsibility for employees acting on its behalf.[54] EU competition law seems aligned with the enterprise approach to parental liability, which may be explained by an objective of deterrence. The following section will demonstrate that such strict approach to parental liability is not optimal for deterrence purposes.

4.2.2.2.1 ENTITY LAW. The concepts of separate legal personality and limited liability have structured the development of modern corporations. As established in the landmark English case *Salomon v. Salomon*,[55] business firms recognised as legal 'persons' bear enforceable rights and responsibilities distinct from those of the individual participants in these entities.[56] The concept of limited liability confines the responsibility of shareholders to the amount of their investment. It was introduced in the early nineteenth century in western Europe, in the form of *sociétés anonymes* in France, *Aktiengesellschaften* in Germany and *limited companies* in the United Kingdom (UK). A general rule for equity owners of many business firms since then, limited liability, and separate legal personality are drivers of economic

---

[50]   See, e.g., Case C–521/09P *Elf Aquitaine v. Commission* [2011] ECR I–8947, paras. 59–62.
[51]   M. Bronckers and A. Vallery, 'No Longer Presumed Guilty? The Impact of Fundamental Rights on Certain Dogmas of EU Competition Law', *World Competition*, 34 (2011), 535–70.
[52]   See commentators' view (n. 5).
[53]   Orts, *Business Persons*, p. 156.
[54]   Ibid., p. 137.
[55]   *Salomon v. A Salomon & Co Ltd* [1896] UKHL 1, [1897] AC 22.
[56]   Orts, *Business Persons*, p. 9.

growth promoting the value of risk-taking investments.[57] Limited liability of equity owners has also been extended to protect business enterprises themselves in complex multi-entity corporate groups, involving, for example, parents and subsidiaries.[58]

There are exceptions to the shield brought by the limited liability and legal personality principles. Courts have 'pierced' or 'lifted' the corporate veil when required in matters of justice.[59] Attributing liability to one separate legal person for the conduct of another legal person is an example of such an exception. This may intervene in situations of abuses of the protection afforded by limited liability, when, for example, a legal person is considered as merely an instrument or an agency of the company controlling it.[60] Scholars found little clarity in the circumstances around which courts lift the veil. The unifying conclusion is that courts seldom pierce the corporate veil in the United States[61] while doing so in Europe only rarely.[62] Reasons for corporate veil lifting typically include notable involvement of a parent company in the subsidiary's business activity, bankruptcy caused by a parent's conduct, or lack of good faith.[63] Thus, even if there are multiple approaches across and even within jurisdictions, the corporate veil is lifted only in particular circumstances.

4.2.2.2.2 FROM ENTITY TO ENTERPRISE LAW. The traditional approach of limited liability of an incorporated business, with exceptional veil piercing, emerged at times where a business was typically conducted by a single corporation. At that time, companies were prohibited from owning shares in other corporations in the United States.[64] Since then, the corporate landscape has evolved drastically.[65] The multiplication of corporate groups, in which business activities are conducted by legally independent but economically affiliated entities, has questioned the suitability of such an approach. Accordingly, the 'enterprise law' approach was introduced as an alternative to entity law to overcome barriers to effective regulation or policy objectives in some areas, and to respond better to the reality of modern corporate structures. Relying on the enterprise, rather than entity law, enabled the

---

[57] Ibid., pp. 135, 151.

[58] Ibid., p. 136.

[59] The term 'pierce' is mostly employed in the United States and 'lift' mostly in UK law concepts, but they will be used here interchangeably.

[60] N. I. Pauer, *The Single Economic Unit Doctrine and Corporate Group Responsibility in European Antitrust Law* (Kluwer Law International, 2014), p. 86.

[61] J. H. Matheson, 'The Modern Law of Corporate Groups: An Empirical Study of Piercing the Corporate Veil in the Parent-Subsidiary Context', *North Carolina Law Review*, 87 (2009), 1091.

[62] T. K. Cheng, 'The Corporate Veil Doctrine Revisited: A Comparative Study of the English and the US Corporate Veil Doctrines', *Boston College International and Comparative Law Review*, 34 (2011), 329; K. Vandekerckhove, *Piercing the Corporate Veil* (Kluwer Law International, 2007).

[63] Bronckers and Vallery, 'No Longer Presumed Guilty?', 551.

[64] P. Blumberg, 'The Transformation of Modern Corporation Law: The Law of Corporate Groups', *Connecticut Law Review*, 37 (2005), 605, 607.

[65] Ibid.; Orts, *Business Persons*, ch. 5.

attribution of rights or liabilities of one entity to another within a corporate group without having recourse to the exceptional frame of 'veil-piercing' practices.[66]

The enterprise approach entails an assessment of the economic rather than legal relationships, grounded on the concept of 'control' of a parent company over its subsidiary.[67] The aim of this is to ascertain whether a subsidiary is deprived of decision-making power on markets owing to its economic relationships with the parent company. In most jurisdictions and areas of the law, economic integration of the business activity within a corporate group is another important factor that supplements control for reliance on enterprise rather than entity law for attributing liability. Blumberg identifies a set of characteristics that should be decisive in attributing enterprise liability to corporate groups: a common public persona, including a common trade name, logo and marketing plan, financial as well as administrative interdependence and group identification of employees.[68] Although many other statutes across jurisdictions adopt variations of the test of control and integration to apply enterprise law, the entity law approach remains the norm in many respects.[69]

In EU competition law, attributing liability of the misconduct of a subsidiary to a parent company shows clear endorsement of the enterprise law approach to corporate groups. However, it goes beyond the enterprise approach as described above. In competition law, decisive influence may be established based on a wide range of structural elements inherent to the parent–subsidiary relationship; thus, involving a different inquiry than that of whether the subsidiary is deprived of decision-making power on the market.[70] In addition, in the case of full ownership, the burden of proof lies on the parties to rebut the presumption of decisive influence, which contrasts with the enterprise approach. Finally, while enterprise law shifts liability from one entity to the other, EU competition law expands it. Parents are indeed jointly and severally liable with the subsidiary. As a result, the turnovers of both parent and subsidiary are taken into account in the final calculation.[71]

As Blumberg states it 'whether entity or enterprise law prevails depends on which doctrine best implements the underlying objectives and policies of the law in the particular area'.[72] One set of policy justifications for disregarding the corporate form is to bring a corporate actors' behaviour into compliance with a statutory requirement.[73]

[66] For a description of some of the regulatory issues that motivated the adoption of the enterprise law approach in the United States, see Blumberg, 'The Transformation of Modern Corporation Law', 608.

[67] A. Berle, 'The Theory of Enterprise Entity', *Columbia Law Review*, 47(3) (1947), 343.

[68] Blumberg, 'The Transformation of Modern Corporation Law', 610.

[69] Orts, *Business Persons*, p. 146.

[70] See previous section for details.

[71] Cheng, 'The Corporate Veil Doctrine Revisited', 397.

[72] Blumberg, 'The Transformation of Modern Corporation Law', 611.

[73] J. Macey and J. Mitts, 'Finding Order in the Morass: The Three Real Justifications for Piercing the Corporate Veil', *Cornell Law Review*, 100 (2014), 99.

4.2.2.2.3 DETERRENCE AS POLICY OBJECTIVE. What are the policy objectives that are pursued in liability attribution cases? Do these adequately support the endorsement of an 'enterprise liability' approach that even goes beyond the framework of that doctrine? Policy considerations have not been clearly stated by the European Commission. An analysis of cases may lead to assumptions that the attributing liability approach is guided by the objective of deterrence, based on the following rationale. The turnover of a group of companies, on which a fine is based, will be significantly larger than that of the subsidiary involved in the infringement. Secondly, the aim is to provide strong incentives for parent companies that can control the subsidiaries' conduct towards compliance with competition law. Sharing responsibility for the infringement aligns the incentives of the parent companies and the subsidiary on which it exerts decisive influence.[74] This deterrence-related objective, justifying an exceptional regime, is confirmed by the Court in *Eni*, in which it recalls that the presumption of decisive influence in the case of a wholly owned subsidiary 'seeks precisely to find a balance between the importance [...] of the objective of penalising conduct contrary to the competition rules, in particular Article 101 TFEU, and to prevent its repetition and [...]the requirements of certain general principles of European Union law, such as, in particular, the principles of the presumption of innocence, that penalties should be applied only to the offender, legal certainty and the rights of the defence, including the principle of equality of arms'.[75]

4.2.2.3 Framework for Attributing Liability Based on Deterrence

This section provides a framework for assessing the existing approach to liability as a tool for deterrence. Based on the agency relationship, this framework also provides an alternative approach to liability attribution that furthers the objective of deterrence, while addressing some of the legal issues discussed above. Embracing the legal standard of negligence, parent companies of wholly owned subsidiaries should be able to demonstrate that they have taken adequate steps to prevent the occurrence of the infringement, to escape liability. The existence of effective compliance programmes could constitute such evidence. This framework builds on arguments by Pauer and Wardhaugh.[76]

4.2.2.3.1 INCENTIVE AND ABILITY: THE THEORY. From a law and economics perspective, an efficient liability regime is one that incentivises the parent company to

---

[74] J. Temple Lang, 'How Can the Problem of the Liability of a Parent Company for Price Fixing by a Wholly-Owned Subsidiary Be Resolved?', *Fordham International Law Journal*, 37(5) (2014), 1486–7.

[75] C–508/11P *Eni* v. *European Commission* [2013] EU:C:2013:289, para. 50.

[76] B. Wardhaugh, 'Punishing Parents for the Sins of Their Child: Extending EU Competition Liability in Groups and to Subcontractors', *Journal of Antitrust Enforcement*, 5(1) (2017), 22; Pauer, *The Single Economic Unit Doctrine*.

internalise the social cost of non-compliance, without its incurring excessive and wasteful expenses.[77] A parent may not be encouraged to detect misconduct internally if this increases the likelihood of liability, or if the expected cost outweighs the expected benefit.[78] When the *incentive* exists, internalisation of the non-compliance cost is effective if the parent has the *ability* to direct the subsidiary's conduct on the market.[79]

When the parent can easily monitor its subsidiary's conduct, parental liability helps to align incentives towards greater compliance. Owing to a relationship of power and to an informational advantage, the parent may ensure compliance at a lower cost than the authority.[80] These arguments are those typically advanced to support corporate liability of a company over its employees' behaviour.[81] Similarly, parental liability may effectively restrain opportunistic behaviour caused by the shield of limited liability. In the absence of parental liability, parent companies may externalise the legal risk of entering into illegal agreements from which they benefit, without bearing the full consequences, especially if subsidiaries are undercapitalised.[82] In addition, the limited liability of shareholders may reduce the need for them to monitor the business activity as well as the conduct of other shareholders.[83] These are examples of inevitable tensions between the protection and promotion of investment in business activity, and the protection of third parties from misconduct associated with that activity.

How does the decisional practice embrace the importance of internal dynamics in its approach to liability? The focus on exercise of decisive influence in the case of non-complete ownership may seem to fit the proposed framework in which a parent should be responsible only if there is evidence of both incentive and ability to direct the subsidiary's conduct on the market. The approach to liability in cases of complete ownership is the focus of the subsequent developments.

4.2.2.3.2 INCENTIVE AND ABILITY IN THE DECISIONAL PRACTICE. The decisional practice shows that the Commission and the Court will usually rely on a very broad set of indicia to assert lack of autonomy: 'the parent company's influence over its subsidiaries as regards corporate strategy, operational policy, business plans, investment, capacity, provision of finance, human resources and legal matters may have indirect effects on the market conduct of the subsidiaries and of the whole group.'[84] This

---

[77] Wardhaugh, 'Punishing Parents for the Sins of Their Child', 26.
[78] J. Arlen and R. Kraakman, 'Controlling Corporate Misconduct: An Analysis of Corporate Liability Regimes', *New York University Law Review*, 72 (1997), 687.
[79] In line with the theoretical framework introduced at Section 2.4.1.
[80] Arlen and Kraakman, 'Controlling Corporate Misconduct'.
[81] For further development on this issue see Section 7.3.1.1.
[82] Koenig, 'An Economic Analysis of the Single Economic Entity Doctrine', 319.
[83] F. H. Easterbrook and D. R. Fischel, 'Limited Liability and the Corporation', University of Chicago Law Review, 52 (1985), 89.
[84] Case T–104/13 *Toshiba Corp* v. *European Commission* [2015] EU:T:2015:610, para. 121.

reflects confusion between what characterises the *incentive* (that is, organic elements associated to ownership) and *ability* (that is, the actual ability to control the subsidiary's commercial conduct). A relation of financial ownership necessarily aligns the *incentives* of companies towards the benefits of successful price-fixing conduct. However, the *ability* of financial ownership to confer control over the pricing conduct is much less evident, even in the case of full ownership.

Irrespective of whether ownership and control coincide, both incentive and ability to control ultimate pricing behaviour are presumed. Such presumption, as shown, seems in practice impossible to rebut. As such, it ignores the agency nature of the relationship between a parent and its subsidiary, and the fundamental dynamics that impact deterrence.[85] The financialisation of modern capitalism, characterised by the investment function increasingly disjoined from business operations, further the need of an agency-based approach for greater deterrence. As in every agency relationship, imperfect information and opportunistic behaviour are likely to feature the relationship between a parent and a subsidiary, even in the case of full ownership.

The following examples further illustrate the confusion between *incentives* from *ability*.[86] In *Eni*, the Court stated that rebutting the presumption requires to show that the subsidiary 'could act with complete autonomy not only at the operational level but also at the financial level'.[87] Financial supervision, however, is an organic consequence of the financial relationship between a parent and its subsidiary. A degree of supervision, in all the forms it can take, may not be incompatible with financial autonomy, because it does not confer an ability to control conduct on the market. *Akzo* also suggests that the existence of limited reporting between a parent and its subsidiary is insufficient to rebut the presumption.[88]

In *Groupe Gascogne*, the Court relied on the approval by the parent of investment decisions and budgets to attribute liability, as well as of monthly reports. Operating in different relevant markets was regarded as irrelevant to the finding of a single economic entity.[89] While indicating a certain level of influence, approval of large investments may not create a unity of conduct with respect to pricing decisions. Requirement of such approval may be an organic consequence of the financial link, since these may affect the parent's market valuation. Financial safeguards and economic conduct thus need to be distinguished.

It is also important to distinguish legal obligations stemming from the financial relationship, from the existence of a relationship of control. As a shareholder,

---

[85] Parents and subsidiaries have the features of an agency relationship: see Section 7.3.1.1.

[86] The following developments are based on Temple Lang, 'How Can the Problem?', 1514–21.

[87] C–508/11P *Eni v. European Commission* [2013] EU:C:2013:289, para. 68.

[88] Case C–97/08P *Akzo Nobel NV v. Commission of the European Communities* [2009] ECR I–8237. 'It is not clear whether these were findings of fact in the cases before the General Court or general statements about the legal effects of financial reporting' (Temple Lang, 'How Can the Problem?', 1514).

[89] Case T–72/06 *Groupe Gascogne v. Commission* [2011] :EU:T:2011:671, para. 81.

a parent may be required to comply with obligations including participation in annual shareholders' meetings, approval of accounts, and appointment of directors and auditors. While appointment of a director could be an element of influence, auditors may not be deemed to be the expression of the exercise of influence. Consolidation of the subsidiary's account into that of the parent company may also be a requirement of company law; and does not imply control of the parent over pricing conduct. Anti-bribery and anti-money laundering legislation may also impose certain obligations that a parent company cannot avoid. Finally, in the case of publicly listed companies, parents may be required to comply with certain stock exchange obligations. As Temple Lang explains, all these elements may not, on their own, establish the existence of a decisive influence.[90]

Another very relevant question for deterrence is the extent to which an internal policy of compliance within a corporate group may or should trigger parental liability. In *General Quimica*, the Court seems to imply that general instructions to comply with the law could not be regarded as decisive influence.[91] However, in *Schindler* the Court found that: 'the implementation of [a] code of conduct suggests [. . .] that the parent company did in fact supervise the commercial policy of its subsidiaries'.[92] In addition, in *United States* v. *EI du Pont de Nemours*,[93] the existence of a common compliance programme was an indication of decisive influence of parent companies over their jointly-owned subsidiary. This approach is ill suited because a parent company should be free to ensure compliance within a corporate group, without it being evidence of unity of conduct on the market. In addition, the adoption of internal measures should, from a deterrence point of view, not be expanding liability, owing to the residual risk that cannot be removed. However, in light of *Schindler*, the existence of compliance programmes within corporate groups extends rather than narrows down liability. A structural element of the organic relationship is here confounded with a positive behavioural response to the competition rules. This approach to liability is therefore inadequate for the policy objective of enhanced deterrence.[94]

All the above confirms that EU competition law has a far-reaching understanding of the exercise of decisive influence in the case of complete ownership. The persistent reliance on structural elements makes the presumption impossible to rebut: many of these factors are inherent to the organic relationship between a parent and a subsidiary in the case of full-ownership. When financial ownership co-exists with economic autonomy of the subsidiary on the market, this creates agency costs that may have adverse effects for deterrence. Internalisation of such costs may cause wasteful expenditures, which is not desirable from a social welfare

---

[90] Temple Lang, 'How Can the Problem?', 1511–12.
[91] Case C–90/09P *General Química SA* v. *Commission* [2011] ECR I–0001, para. 101.
[92] Case C–501/11P *Schindler Holding and Others* v. *Commission* [2013] ECR I–0, para. 114.
[93] *United States* v. *EI du Pont de Nemours & Co* 353 US 586 (1957).
[94] Temple Lang, 'How Can the Problem?', 1510–13.

point of view. In addition, the current regime may disincentive any internal mechanisms of detection, since this could enhance the liability risk for the parent company.[95] This is not just a theoretical risk since, in *Schindler*, an internal code of conduct was used to evidence a relationship of decisive influence between a parent and its subsidiaries.[96]

4.2.2.3.3 OPERATIONAL FRAMEWORK FOR ATTRIBUTING LIABILITY. The proposed framework, structured on the concepts of incentive and ability, addresses some of the problems of the existing approach to liability. First, it better integrates the factor that, even in the case of full ownership, financial incentives may exist without the ability to control conduct. This typically refers to financial holdings or passive investments, but not strictly. A parent company operating in a different sector, and/or only having oversight of the subsidiary as required by legal obligations, could be deemed to lack the ability. Secondly, this framework reconciles the idea that liability should be attributed based on some level of parental fault, in line with the requirement set by Regulation 1/2003 for imposing fines. What has indeed triggered concerns of non-respect of fundamental principles of procedural fairness is that, under the current approach, a parent may be held liable irrespective of its behaviour.[97] An approach to liability that integrates actors' behaviour is also one that incentivises greater control and oversight within the corporate group.

Assessment of Incentive and Ability: Case-by-Case Analysis or Rebutting the Presumption

To identify whether the parent may have an *incentive* to influence its subsidiary's conduct, it is reasonable primarily to assess the structural relationship between a parent and its subsidiary. The *ability* to conduct the subsidiary's conduct should be assessed based on operational factors of decisive influence. A distinction should be made between organic and operational elements of such decisive influence, as explained previously.[98] Quite logically, the higher the financial incentive, the higher the likelihood that a parent will be able to direct its subsidiary's conduct.[99] In the case of complete ownership, if the case-by-case approach to liability is too expansive, and requires instead using a presumptive approach, companies should be able to rebut the presumption on the basis that they lack the ability to direct the subsidiary's conduct on the market. Such assessment should be made upon careful analysis of operational rather than organic factors.

---

[95]   J. Arlen, 'The Potentially Perverse Effects of Corporate Criminal Liability', *The Journal of Legal Studies*, 23 (1994), 833–67.
[96]   Case C–501/11P *Schindler Holding and Others* v. *Commission* [2013] ECR I–0, para. 114.
[97]   Temple Lang, 'How Can the Problem?', 1510.
[98]   For a discussion of the practical details, see, e.g., ibid.
[99]   Wardhaugh, 'Punishing Parents for the Sins of Their Child', 47.

A Negligence-Based Defence

When the presumption may not be rebutted, a defence should be available to the parent, as a means of incentivising corporate groups to organise compliance internally. Even when companies have influence over their subsidiary, collusion still exists as a residual risk. This risk is inherent in every relation characterised with imperfect information and opportunism. Regulation 1/2003 requires that fines can be imposed to an undertaking if it has 'intentionally or negligently' infringed Article 101 or 102 TFEU.[100] Any direct or indirect involvement on the part of the parent should obviously trigger liability, being a manifestation of an intentional restriction of competition through a subsidiary.[101] The contentious and relevant question is whether a parent should be held liable when it did not participate to the wrongdoing. Based on the developed framework, a parent should be able to prove that the wrongdoing did not occur as part of negligence.[102]

The legal content of negligence is not defined in the case law. In his opinion in *General Motors*, Advocate General Mayras asserts that 'the concept of negligence must be applied where the author of the infringement, although acting without any intention to perform an unlawful act, has not foreseen the consequences of his action in circumstances where a person who is normally informed and sufficiently attentive could not have failed to foresee them'.[103] In *Rubber Chemicals*, the Commission refers to the obligation of a parent to ensure compliance of their wholly owned subsidiaries. It can be derived that failure to prevent the infringement by the subsidiary may result in parental liability.[104]

Negligence is commonly used to ground criminal and civil liability in domestic laws of the EU member states. Therefore, attributing parental liability on a negligence-based standard would be based on a common principle.[105] In the context of corporate groups, negligent conduct could refer to the failure of the organisation to take action to ensure compliance with competition law. The degree of fault should therefore be assessed with respect to the internal incentives and mechanisms put in place within the corporate group.[106] Corporate compliance programmes, broadly referring to all the management tools used to prevent and detect misconduct, would therefore be a cornerstone of such

---

[100] Council Regulation (EC) No 1/2003 of 16 December 2002 on the implementation of the rules on competition laid down in Articles 81 and 82 of the Treaty [2003] OJ L 1/1 ('Regulation 1/2003'), art. 23(2).

[101] This chapter will not further discuss the technicalities of intentional breach of competition law provisions, since this issue would be less specific to the case of parent–subsidiaries relationships.

[102] Wardhaugh, 'Punishing Parents for the Sins of Their Child'.

[103] Opinion of Advocate General Mayras in Case 26/75 *General Motors* v. *Commission* [1975] ECR 1389.

[104] *Rubber Chemicals* (Case COMP/F/38.443) Commission Decision 2006/902/EC [2006] OJ L353/50 in Wardhaugh, 'Punishing Parents for the Sins of Their Child', 32.

[105] Ibid., 33.

[106] Pauer, *The Single Economic Unit Doctrine*, pp. 232–3.

assessment.[107] If a programme provides effective internal measures, a parent company should be able to be exempt from liability for the wrongdoing of its subsidiary.[108] The burden of proof for showing that adequate internal measures have been put in place must lie on the company.

As Chapter 8 discusses in detail, providing positive incentives for the implementation of internal mechanisms further enhances the effectiveness of competition law enforcement. This would contrast with the current approach, in which compliance measures implemented within the corporate groups are rather used to incriminate the parent. From a law and economics perspective, a negligence-based approach to liability would mitigate some of the perverse effects of what is currently a strict parental liability that is, encouraging rather than deterring parent companies from detecting internally a wrongdoing.[109]

4.2.3 *Conclusion on Parental Liability*

The single entity doctrine has far-reaching implications, especially when used to attribute liability within corporate groups in the EU. This section showed that the impossibility to rebut the presumption of decisive influence in case of full ownership is not in line with the policy objective of deterrence. It also contradicts structuring legal principles. An agency-based framework provides that a parent company should be held liable only if it has the ability and incentive to direct the subsidiary's conduct on the market. Distinguishing between the incentive, on the one hand, and the ability, on the other, is of utmost importance in the design of an optimal approach to liability. In addition, a defence based on the standard of negligence should be available to parent companies, if they prove they have implemented adequate internal measures for compliance. This would provide incentives for corporate groups to implement mechanisms that help overcome issues of imperfect information and opportunistic behaviour that is inherent to every agency relation.

4.3 COMMERCIAL AGENCY AGREEMENTS

The single entity doctrine also applies to establish the substantive reach of competition law to the commercial agency agreement.[110] The relationship between

---

[107] Defined in Chapter 8 as schemes designed to educate employees about illegal activities, monitor their behaviour, and discipline them in cases of illegal conduct. C. Angelucci and M. A. Han, 'Monitoring Managers Through Corporate Compliance Programs', Amsterdam Center for Law & Economics Working Paper No 2010-14, 2.

[108] The key elements of effective compliance programmes, and how to verify such effectiveness, are discussed in length in Chapter 8.

[109] Wardhaugh, 'Punishing Parents for the Sins of Their Child', 35.

[110] Agency agreements are a relevant subject of study in this chapter; they are understood here in the legal sense. Economic issues that arise due to such types of relationships, and legal implications, will be major themes of the subsequent chapters.

a company and its commercial agent may exist as an alternative to a market relation-ship, on the one hand, and to an employment relationship on the other hand. In light of the decisional practice, this section discusses the adequacy of the single entity for the legal qualification of hybrid types of relationships. It is argued that the competition law conception of the firm may need refinement to accommodate relationships that do not fit within the market/firm paradigm underlying the single entity doctrine. In the EU, as in the case of corporate groups, the use of the single entity is inadequate to attribute liability within such relationships characterised with dynamics of the agency relationship.

4.3.1 *Substantive Reach of Article 101 TFEU*

In the EU, agreements between the principal and the agent in what qualifies as a genuine agency relationship are immune from Article 101 TFEU. According to the Vertical Guidelines, 'an agent is a legal or physical person vested with the power to negotiate and/or conclude contracts on behalf of another person (the principal), either in the agent's own name or in the name of the principal', for the purchase, or sales of goods or services (supplied) by the principal.[111] The determining factor for the non-applicability of Article 101(1) TFEU to 'genuine' agency agreements is the 'financial or commercial risk borne by the agent in relation to the activities for which he has been appointed as an agent by the principal'.[112] Therefore, the agent's role, limited to purchasing or negotiating sales on behalf of the principal, bears limited risk or responsibility for the products or services of the principal. A lack of autonomy on the market and interrelated interests make them part of a single economic unit for the purpose of Article 101 TFEU.[113] A principal may therefore impose territorial or price restrictions on the agent for the sale of its goods or services which would be prohibited in other vertical relationships.

From a theoretical perspective, distributing via an agent is an alternative to vertical integration, on the one hand, and to selling through an independent retailer, on the other hand.[114] The agency relationship is therefore a hybrid between a relationship within a *hierarchy*, and a *market* relationship. An analysis of transac-tion costs can help to determine which distribution method is the most efficient.[115]

The practical application of the exemption of agency relationships from Article 101 TFEU is a binary analysis, based on the single economic doctrine. The criteria used in the decisional practice suggests that an agency relationship will be genuine only if it is akin to a relationship internal to one undertaking – that is, pertaining to

---

[111]   Guidelines on Vertical Restraints [2010] OJ C130/1, para. 12.
[112]   Ibid.
[113]   A. Jones and B. Sufrin, *EU Competition Law: Text, Cases, and Materials*, 6th edn (Oxford University Press, 2016), p. 756.
[114]   Zhang, 'Toward an Economic Approach to Agency Agreements', 571.
[115]   See Section 2.3.1.2.

a hierarchy rather than a market type of economic relationship. This conception of the agency relation raises practical problems. It is argued that agency relationships are best analysed and explained as hybrid types of organisations. Theoretical insights of the property rights theory of the firm can support the legal assessment of genuine agency relationships.

4.3.1.1 An Assessment Based on the Single Economic Doctrine

Earlier case law focused on the notion of integration and economic dependence between the agent and the principal. In *Pittsburgh Corning*, a case of alleged concerted practice, the Commission concluded that Article 101(1) TFEU was applicable to the relationship between Pittsburgh Corning and Formica Belgium because of the absence of integration and the economic dependence of the latter with respect to the former.[116] Even though it was acting as an agent for Pittsburgh Corning during the relevant period, the Commission found that Formica was an economic actor independent of its principal, operating independently on other markets and being integrated with a group other than Pittsburgh Corning. In *Sugar*, the Commission considered the 'real economic function' of the agents who 'do not work exclusively for one employer, but act on their own to a considerable extent, as independent dealers'.[117] The Commission concluded that the agents were not part of the undertaking of the principal, and hence could not benefit from the exemption. In these cases, the relationships between the principal and its agent were analysed through the lens of authority and hierarchy, which characterise employment relationships according to Coase and Simon's theories of the firm.[118]

Subsequent cases adopted the criterion of the allocation of risks in order to determine the scope of the specific regime. In *Volkswagen*, the Court justified the absence of an exemption because the agent was not bearing all the risk related to the transaction: 'Representatives can lose their character as independent traders only if they do not bear any of the risks resulting from the contracts negotiated on behalf of the principal.'[119] It did not mention the economic independence of integration of the agent towards its principal. The Court still related its decision to the fact that the agent is not 'an auxiliary organ forming an integral part of the principal's undertaking'. While relying on a looser concept (that is, the allocation of risk), the single entity doctrine was still the standard focus in asking whether the agency agreement could be assimilated to an employment relationship.

---

[116] *Pittsburgh Corning Europe* (Case COMP IV/26894) – *Formica Belgium* (Case COMP IV/26.892) – *Hertel* (Case COMP IV/26876) Commission Decision 72/403/EC [1972] L272/35.

[117] *European Sugar Industry* (Case COMP IV/26918) Commission Decision 73/109/EC [1973] OJ L140/17, para. 4.

[118] See Section 2.3.1.1.

[119] Case C–266/93 *Bundeskartellamt v. Volkswagen AG and VAG Leasing GmBH* [1995] ECR I–3477, para. 19.

The *Daimler Chrysler* case illustrates a refinement of the risk allocation criteria.[120] The General Court annulled the Commission's decision in *Mercedes-Benz*,[121] rejecting the application of Article 101(1) TFEU to the relationships between Daimler Chrysler and its dealers for the sale of Mercedes-Benz vehicles. In doing so, the General Court moved away from the criterion of integration to focus on the relationship of control and authority between the agent and the principal.[122] The Court focused on the fact that the agent's conduct was determined by its principal, with regard to carrying out the instructions given. In particular, the principal determined the conditions attached to all car sales, and the agent was prevented by contractual obligations from purchasing and holding stocks of cars for sales.[123] Yet the Court concluded that, as a result, they should be treated in the same way as employees and considered as forming an economic unit with it.[124] Here, the Court adopted a less restrictive approach towards the risk allocation criterion, and stated that there was no need for the principal to bear all the costs in order to benefit from an exemption. However, the Court still purported to determine whether or not the agent and the principal could be considered as a single economic unit. The concept of undertaking preserves its importance as a unifying concept in delineating the scope of the specific regime.

4.3.1.2 Vertical Guidelines: a Strict and Uncertain Framework

The Vertical Guidelines specify the factors that are material in the definition of an agency relationship. An agent will qualify as genuine if it does not incur any (or a very negligible part) of the contract-specific risk or market-specific investment of the activities for which it is appointed. Costs that would be related to the agent's provision of services are not incompatible with qualification as genuine agency. The Guidelines provides a non-exhaustive list of the type of cost borne by the agent that would preclude the qualification of genuine agency. This includes transport cost, stock-related, advertising, customers cost of default etc. In essence, the level of risk that ought to be borne by a genuine agent, restricted to its cost of labour, requires a level of economic integration akin to that of an employee.[125]

---

[120] I. Lianos, 'Commercial Agency Agreements, Vertical Restraints, and the Limits of Article 81(1) EC: Between Hierarchies and Networks', *Journal of Competition Law & Economics*, 3 [2007], 625, 642.

[121] *Mercedes-Benz* (Case COMP/36.264) Commission Decision 2002/758/EC [2001] OJ L 257/1.

[122] Lianos, 'Commercial agency agreements', 644

[123] 'Where an agent, although having separate legal personality, does not independently determine his own conduct on the market, but carries out the instructions given to him by his principal, the prohibitions laid down under Article 81(1) EC do not apply to the relationship between the agent and the principal with which he forms an economic unit. In those circumstances, it must be held that the relationship between the agents and the applicant is such that the former sell Mercedes-Benz vehicles in all material respects under the direction of the applicant' (emphasis added) (Case T-325/01, *Daimler-Chrysler AG v. Commission* [2005] ECR II-3319, para. 2).

[124] Ibid., para. 102.

[125] Zhang, 'Toward an Economic Approach to Agency Agreements', 571.

The framework of the Guidelines does not, however, unequivocally adopt the single entity approach to qualifying agreements as genuine ones. It is stated that where the risk-based criteria for finding a genuine relation do not apply, 'the agent will be treated as an independent undertaking and the agreement between agent and principal will be subject to Article 101(1) as any other vertical agreement'.[126] But for agency relationships that qualify as genuine, Article 101(1) TFEU can still apply to provisions concerning the relationship 'since the agent is a separate undertaking from the principal'.[127] This may concern some categories of single-branding and non-compete agreements. Thus, based on the wording of the Guidelines, it is not clear whether qualification as genuine agency relationship defines one or two distinct undertakings. In addition, the Commission still considers the possibility of collusion between the agent and the principal of a genuine agency relationship, as an agreement that would facilitate collusion is excluded from the Article 101(1) TFEU exemption.[128] This seems to contradict the idea that internal arrangements are deemed to stem from the internal organisation of the undertaking, as is suggested by the approach focused on the single entity doctrine taken in the decisional practice.[129] A clearer framework based on hybrid types of relationships may help to solve the apparent contradiction.

4.3.1.3 Recent Developments

Recent cases involving online platforms have attracted a renewed attention among competition law scholars as to what constitutes a genuine agency agreement.[130] The *e-book* and *online travel agent* cases involved vertical agreements, and most-favoured-nation clauses that restrained the retail price levels of e-books and hotel rooms.[131] One question that these cases raised was whether publishers or hotels and the online platforms could be principals and agents in genuine agency relationships. If so, the vertical price-fixing clauses could fall outside Article 101 TFEU.[132] However, this particular question was not systematically addressed and in none of the cases did an authority adopt the view that vertical restraints were falling within

---

[126] Guidelines on Vertical Restraints [2010] OJ C130/1, para. 21.
[127] Ibid., para. 19.
[128] Ibid., para. 20.
[129] Lianos, 'Commercial agency agreements', 641.
[130] Zhang, 'Toward an Economic Approach to Agency Agreements; M. Bennett, 'Online Platforms: Retailers, Genuine Agents or None of the Above?', *Competition Policy International* (2013); P. Goffinet and F. Puel, 'Vertical Relationships: The Impact of the Internet on the Qualification of Agency Agreements', *Journal of European Competition Law & Practice*, 6(4) (2015), 242. P. Akman, 'A Competitive Assessment of Platform Most-Favoured-Customer Clauses', *Journal of Competition Law & Economics*, 12(4) (2016), 781.
[131] For an account of the different investigations and outcomes, see Akman, 'A Competitive Assessment', 781 and 783 and accompanying footnotes.
[132] Most of the cases were national cases but, owing to Regulation 1/2003, national competition authorities cannot prohibit an agreement that would be permitted under EU Competition law: Regulation 1/2003, art. 33(2).

the agency exemption.[133] In the German case *HRS*, the competition authority stated that the platform was no genuine agent, because the restraints at stake originated from the agent themselves, and not from the principal.[134] In addition, it is noted that such platforms sell on behalf of not a single hotel but a multitude of them, which, in line with the *VVR* case, requires this agent to be regarded as operating on an independent basis.[135] However, it contrasts with the Vertical Guidelines approach, which states that it is not 'material for the assessment whether the agent acts for one or several principals'.[136] Although these justifications may not be fully supported by economic or legal reasoning, a contrary conclusion may not have prevented the finding of anticompetitive concerns, owing to the exclusion from the exemption of agreements that facilitate collusion.[137]

To sum up, the decisional practice illustrates the difficult application of the single entity doctrine in cases in which a relationship is at the interface between the firm and the market. Although the Guidelines seem to embrace a looser approach to the agency relationship, its framework seems to assimilate an agent with an employee. It is not without contradiction. In addition, recent cases that touched upon the legal qualification of agency in digital markets did not provide further clarity. This confirms that authorities find it uneasy to apply competition law to agreements that are clearly neither external nor internal relationships. The conception of the firm, based on the single entity doctrine, here needs some refinement.

4.3.2 *Alternative Approach to Agency Agreements*

The existing framework in the EU adopts a conception of agency aligned with that of a situation of hierarchy, with the relationship being akin to the internal organisation of a firm. In such a perspective, a genuine agent should bear little or no risk, at a level similar to that of an employee, in carrying out business activities on behalf of the principal.[138] However, this conception ignores the business and economic justification for delegating the commercial function to an agent in the first place. The commercial agency relationship is a hybrid between a hierarchy and a market relationship. It means that the principal retains most control over the activity in

[133] E.g. in the UK case Booking.com/Expedia/IHG, the Office of Fair Trading (the precursor to the Competition and Markets Authority) noted that the platforms do not take title or hold inventory to hotel accommodation, possibly suggesting the agency nature of the relationship. Office of Fair Trading, Hotel Online Booking: Decision to Accept Commitments to Remove Certain Discounting Restrictions for Online Travel Agents, OFT1514dec in Akman, 'A Competitive Assessment', 807.
[134] Bundeskartellamt [Federal Cartel Office], *HRS-Hotel Reservation Service* (20 December 2013) B 9 – 66/10 [hereinafter 'HRS Decision'] in Akman, 'A Competitive Assessment', 783.
[135] Case C–311/85, *VZW Vereniging van Vlaamse Reisbureaus v. VZW Sociale Dienst van de Plaatselijke en Gewestelijke Overheidsdiensten* [1987] ECR 3801, para. 20.
[136] Guidelines on Vertical Restraints [2010] OJ C130/1, para. 13.
[137] Ibid., para. 20.
[138] Zhang, 'Toward an Economic Approach to Agency Agreements', 589.

a way that may be compatible with some discretion and risk for the agent. An estate agent can indeed have discretion in setting the price of a property, because of the market-intelligence held, and bear some of the activity cost, if such costs help the alignment of incentives between both parties.

An adequate conception of the firm is one that enables the efficient organisation of transactions and suitable pricing decision-making. Otherwise parties may be adopting alternative but less efficient contractual arrangements, which is not socially desirable.[139] The difficulty lies, however, in identifying tangible criteria for assessing whether an agreement should be exempted. To do so, it is fundamental to identify whether an agency, rather than a distribution agreement, is the most efficient way of organising a vertical relationship between parties.[140] An analysis of the agency costs in the relationship (including, for example, the costs of monitoring) indicates whether the relationship is likely to be one of agency or one between independent dealers. In the case of high agency costs, the principal will need to provide high-powered incentives for a proper performance of the task.[141] The principal could, for example, transfer some of the risk with revenue-based incentive for the marketing, distribution or selling of the products.[142] If the agent were to hold a significant part of such residual income rights, they would likely be holding residual control rights, which, based on the property rights theory of the firm, determines ownership of the agent over the activity.[143] In such a case, the transaction characterises a market transaction; and a commercial agency agreement may be unnatural possibly indicating the existence of sham, used to circumvent prohibitions applying to vertical agreements.[144] Therefore, an analysis of risk allocation between the principal and the agent can indicate whether it makes business sense to have an agency as opposed to an agreement with an independent distributor.

4.3.3 *The US Case Law on Agency Agreements*

The US approach to agency seems to be more in line with the economic and business reality of agency. It provides insightful examples of how a principled-approach to agency can come into practice. Since *General Electric*, if agency or consignments agreements qualify as genuine, they are immune from the prohibition

---

[139] Ibid.

[140] Ibid., 583.

[141] An analysis of attributes of the transaction (uncertainty, frequency and asset-specific investment), in line with the transaction approach to the firm may also inform on the scope of the agency costs: Lianos, 'Commercial agency agreements', 663.

[142] Residual income rights may be defined as 'the difference between stochastic inflow of resources and the promised pay-outs involved in marketing, distributing and selling the goods': Zhang, 'Toward an Economic Approach to Agency Agreements', 583.

[143] See Section 2.3.3.

[144] Zhang, 'Toward an Economic Approach to Agency Agreements', 584.

of vertical price-fixing in restraint of trade.[145] Until *Leegin*, this was a very important defence to the illegality per se of resale price maintenance.[146] Still illegal per se in some US states, the treatment of resale price maintenance remains unclear; therefore, cases on consignment agreements maintain contemporary relevance.

In practice, courts examine whether consignment agreements are used to circumvent the possible unlawfulness of imposing retail prices.[147] To do so, courts assess the business rationale of adopting an agency rather than a distribution agreement, by 'objectively viewing whether the arrangement serves one of the economic functions of agencies in general, such as apportioning risk to the firm best able to bear risk, or loading pricing decisions in the firm best able to gauge market conditions'.[148] An inquiry into economic risk allocation has been the focus of the courts' assessment. In *Simpson*[149] the property title was retained by Union Oil, which paid property taxes on the goods, while the agent Simpson bore the storage cost and was liable for any loss or damage. The consignee, through commission revenue calculation, also bore most of the market risk. Upon examination of which of those costs and revenues were deterministic, it could be said that the agent was bearing most of the residual risk and was entitled to most of the residual income. It was therefore unnatural for residual income rights not to be accompanied by residual rights of control, with Union Oil, the principal, still holding the property titles. An analysis through the lens of property rights indicates that the agency relationships may have been a sham. Circumstantial evidence supported this finding in the present case.[150] Similar analysis of *General Electric*, an earlier but similar case, suggests that the Supreme Court was incorrect to find genuine agency agreement.[151] More recently, in *Valuepest.com v. Bayer Corporation*, the Fourth Circuit examined the risk allocation between Bayer and its agent, as well as the business rationale for Bayer adopting such distribution systems. In that case, the Court understood the business justification for retaining more control over the distribution, and the request by distributors to switch to such a distribution model.[152]

Application of the single entity doctrine to commercial agency agreements requires a legal understanding of the existence of commercial agreements as a hybrid form, alternative to the firm and to the market. An approach based on business justifications, informed by the property rights theory of the firm, provides an adequate framework to that end.

---

[145]   *US v. General Electric Co.*, 272 US 476 (1926).
[146]   Resale price maintenance was a violation per se according to *Dr Miles Medical Co. v. John D Park & Sons Co* 220 US 373, until *Leegin Leather Products, Inc. v. PSKS, Inc.*, 127 S Ct 2705 reversed the per se violation.
[147]   *Morrison v. Murray Biscuit Co.*, 797 F 2d 1430, 1436 (7th Cir 1986).
[148]   Easterbrook in *Illinois Corporate Travel v. American Airlines* 806 F 2d at 725–6.
[149]   *Simpson v. Union Oil Co.*, 377 US 13 (1964).
[150]   Zhang, 'Toward an Economic Approach to Agency Agreements', 586–7.
[151]   Ibid., 588.
[152]   *Valuepest.com of Charlotte, Inc. v. Bayer Corp.*, 561 F 3d 282, 288 (4th Cir 2009).

4.3.4 *Attribution of Liability*

An important implication of the single entity doctrine is its use to impute fines when an agent breaches competition law.[153] As in parent–subsidiary relationships, a principal will bear responsibility for the conduct of its agent, on the ground that they form part of one single economic entity.[154] In *Voestalpin* v. *European Commission*, the General Court confirmed the fine imposed on a principal for involvement of its agent in the pre-stressing steel cartel, in the absence of direct evidence of the principal's involvement. The General Court states here that 'if an agent [. . .] works for the benefit of his principal he may in principle be treated as an auxiliary organ forming an integral part of the latter's undertaking, who must carry out his principal's instructions and thus, like a commercial employee, forms an economic unit with that undertaking'.[155] The rationale for imputing liability to the principal is, in the Court's view, similar to that of holding an employer responsible for breach of an employee, irrespective of whether the principal was aware of the agent's conduct:

> 'where the agent acts on behalf of and on account of the principal without assuming the economic risk of the activities entrusted to him, the anti-competitive conduct of that agent in the context of those activities can be imputed to the principal, just as the offending acts committed by an employee can be imputed to the employer, even without proof that the principal was aware of the agent's anti-competitive conduct'.[156]

In its assessment the Court recalls two conditions that will be critical to attributing liability: whether the agent takes on any economic risk, and whether there is exclusivity in the provision of service by the agent. Economic risk is assessed in light of financial risk – echoing the position of the Vertical Guidelines on the scope of the exemption granted to agreements in a genuine agency relationship. The exclusivity requirement precludes the principal from bearing liability if the agent also undertakes a significant part of business for its own account on the same market.[157] Whether the agent acted for two competing undertakings was, however, considered immaterial to the finding of a single entity. The delegation by

---

[153] Case T–66/99 *Minoan Lines* v. *Commission* [2003] ECR II-5515, para. 125; *Candle wax* (Case COMP/39181) Commission Decision of 01.10.2008 [2008] OJ C295/17, paras. 338 and 397–409; *Butadiene Rubber and ESBR* (Case COMP/38.638) Commission Decision 2008/C 7/07 [2006] OJ C7/11, paras. 414–22.

[154] 'It is clear from [. . .] the case-law relating to the imputation of subsidiaries' conduct to their parent companies that the imputation of ETA's conduct to the applicant rests on the principles which govern the relationship between agent and principal and on the principal's liability for its agent's actions, interpreted with reference to the notion of a single economic entity, which is generally used where the conduct of undertakings is analysed from the point of view of competition law' (T–66/99 *Minoan Lines* v. *Commission* [2003] ECR II–5515, para. 119).

[155] Case T–418/10 *Voestalpin* v. *European Commission* [2015] EU:T:2015:516, para. 138.

[156] Ibid., para. 175.

[157] Ibid., paras. 139–41.

competitors of some commercial activity to a single agent can indeed serve as a facilitator to collusion. What mattered instead was whether the agent is commercially independent from its principal.[158]

Although consistent with the overall approach to liability in corporate groups, such application of the single entity doctrine is problematic. First, extending liability for the conduct to a separate legal entity contravenes important corporate law principles, and no defence seems to be available to the principal. The liability scheme is therefore exceptional. Is this regime justified by strong policy objectives, such as deterrence?

In the *pre-stressing steel* case, the Commission justified the imposition of fines on the ground of compliance: 'if an undertaking decides to delegate its commercial activity in a particular country or market to a genuine agent, it is under an obligation to put in place the necessary mechanisms to ensure its control'.[159] On appeal, however, the General Court did not build on this argument, and the incentives for internal mechanisms that are supposed to be triggered do not appear clearly. Instead, the approach to liability rests strictly on structural elements of the relationship, which are essentially related to financial risk. A principal will therefore be held liable irrespective of its behaviour.

A similar argument to that employed in the case of parent and subsidiaries can be advanced.[160] A strict approach to liability is not optimal from a deterrence perspective, because it ignores the specificity of an agency relationship, as opposed to a relationship with an employee. It particularly ignores the existence of agency costs – associated with imperfect information and opportunism – that may be very difficult for the principal to internalise. Depending on the scope of such agency costs, the principal may incur excessive costs to ensure liability, in a way that may be detrimental from a social welfare point of view. In addition, strict liability for the principal may have perverse effects, such as that of deterring internal detection if this increases likelihood of liability.[161]

From an economic point of view, if the agent represents the principal on the market, the principal should bear some responsibility for wrongdoing associated with its market conduct. The closer the economic incentives of both parties, the more likely it is that the principal should be liable. It is here posited that the principal in a genuine agency relationship should be held liable if it has the incentive *and* the ability to direct the commercial conduct of its agent on the market. The reasons for delegating commercial tasks to an agent are the very same that explain that a principal may not be able to direct its conduct or prevent the occurrence of a breach. For example, a manufacturer may hire an agent for its knowledge of a given geographic market, otherwise it would not have entered into such a contractual relationship. This also means that a commercial agency is

---

[158]   Ibid., paras. 149–63.
[159]   *Prestressing steel* (Case COMP/38.344) Commission Decision 2010/4387 [2010] OJ C339/7, para. 777.
[160]   See Section 4.2.2.3.3.
[161]   Arlen, 'Potentially Perverse Effects', 833.

characterised by a degree of asymmetry of information, which also complicates the monitoring of the agent's conduct. In practice, a principled approach to liability should also include a defence to the principal's liability. A defence based on the standard of negligence would provide the additional behavioural incentive for the principal to take adequate organisational steps to prevent a breach of competition law. A principal in a genuine agency relationship would therefore be able to avoid liability if it proves that it has taken adequate internal measures for compliance.[162]

An undifferentiated approach to both substantive reach and liability in agency relationships is not adequate. A very strict approach to the first function makes it less likely that a company will, in any case, be at risk of bearing responsibility for the conduct of its commercial intermediary. But it also means that efficient methods of organising an economic transaction may not be chosen, if they may not be exempt from the scope of Article 101 TFEU, on the one hand; or if there is extended liability risk, on the other. Therefore, this substantiates the need for having distinct approaches. An approach based on the property rights theory enables the protection of efficient forms of economic organisations, including hybrid relationships. An agency-based framework ensures that anticompetitive behaviour is not left unchallenged; while providing adequate incentives for internal compliance schemes.

4.4 THE SINGLE ENTITY DOCTRINE AND PRIVATE ENFORCEMENT

The single entity doctrine may also have far-reaching implication regarding private enforcement. Recent cases suggest the importance of the concept of undertaking with regard to private actions in competition cases. In *Siemens*, the General Court referred to a principle of private law, that of joint debtors, from which competition law could seek guidance in respect to the allocation of fines among different entities jointly and severally liable. Based on such principles, the General Court further relied on private claims that these legal entities could bring against each other, to determine that allocation of shares of fine should reflect each entity's relative liability.[163]

UK cases also demonstrate the significance of the single entity doctrine, when entities that form undertakings are multi-defendants in cross-border private actions. According to the private European law provision, Article 8(1) of the Brussels I Regulation Recast, a defendant can be sued in a member state in which a co-defendant is domiciled. This is very relevant in private actions brought by a cartel's victim seeking to recover damages from an undertaking formed by entities domiciled in various member states. Several cases raised the question of whether

---

[162] See Section 4.2.2.3.3 for references and further justification of such an approach.

[163] Joined Cases T–122/07 to T–124/07 *Siemens Österreich* [2011] ECR 2011 II–793, paras. 155–9. On appeal, the Court reversed the General Court's approach affirming its general indifference to the internal allocation of fines between the parent company and the infringing subsidiary, thereby leaving national courts to define such allocation. Joined Cases C–231/11P and C–233/11P Commission v. Siemens AG Österreich [2014] EU:C:2014:256.

a subsidiary domiciled in the UK, could face private action for the conduct of its parent company, while it had no knowledge of it.[164]

In *Provimi* the court established that a subsidiary can be sued on the basis of the single entity doctrine:

> [T]he legal entities that are a part of the one undertaking [. . .] have no indepen-
> dence of mind or action or will. They are to be regarded as all one. Therefore [. . .]
> the mind and will of one legal entity is, for the purposes of art [101], to be treated as
> the mind and will of the other entity. There is no question of having to 'impute' the
> knowledge or will of one entity to another, because they are one and the same.[165]

In *Cooper*, the Court of Appeal discussed whether some sort of knowledge of the wrongdoing by the subsidiary was required for its liability. Although it did not decide on that matter, it seemed to be sufficient for the subsidiaries to be anchor defendants if there was the possibility that the subsidiaries were either parties or aware of the anticompetitive conduct.[166] In *KME Yorkshire* v. *Toshiba*, the Court states that knowledge of illegality would need to be established unless a parent exerts decisive influence over a subsidiary.[167] In *Nokia*, the High Court confirmed that a claim could be made against a subsidiary that does not have knowledge of the cartel, provided that significant influence or control of the parent participating results in the implementation of the subsidiary of the cartel arrangement.[168]

These cases suggest that wholly owned subsidiaries are presumed to be liable for a breach of competition law by their parent company – thereby establishing the jurisdiction of a member state in which a subsidiary (or 'anchor defendant') is domiciled.[169]

This is a very far-reaching application of the single entity doctrine. A finding of decisive influence can occur at quite a low level of shareholding, and will be presumed in the case of complete ownership. As in situations of parental liability, such cases go beyond the principles of legal separation and limited liability and even consist in 'reverse' corporate veil piercing. As in other liability attribution cases, only

---

[164]   *Provimi Ltd* v. *Aventis Animal Nutrition SA* [2003] EWHC 96; *Cooper Tyre & Rubber Co & Others*
     v. *Shell Chemicals UK Ltd* [2009] EWHC 2609 (Comm); *KME YorkshireLtd and others* v. *Toshiba
     Carrier UK Ltd and others* [2011] EWHC 2665 (Ch); *Nokia Corp* v. *AU Optronics Corp* [2012] EWHC
     731 (Ch). For further discussion, see: I. Lianos, P. Davis and P. Nebbia, 'Cross-Border Damages
     Actions in the EU: Managing Inter-Jurisdictional Competition in the EU Mixed Enforcement
     System' in *Damages Claims for the Infringement of EU Competition Law* (Oxford University Press,
     2015). For discussion of international aspects of public and private enforcement of the application of
     the single entity doctrine to international corporate groups see: E. Bouton (2016), 'The Single
     Economic Unit Doctrine under EU Competition Law: Application and Consequences for the
     Scope and Enforcement of the Substantive Rules of Competition Law', Unpublished LLM disserta-
     tion, University of Glasgow.
[165]   *Provimi*, para. 31.
[166]   *Cooper Tyre* .
[167]   *KME Yorkshire*, paras. 37–8.
[168]   *Nokia Corporation and AU Optronics Corporation*, para. 82.
[169]   P. Hughes, 'Competition Law Enforcement and Corporate Group Liability – Adjusting the Veil',
     European Competition Law Review, 35 (2014), 68, 81–2.

a clearly stated policy objective may justify an exceptional regime. While holding a parent liable for the conduct of a subsidiary that it controls may be consistent with deterrence, holding liable the entity controlled by the infringer is not. Incentives towards greater compliance are impacted only if a company has control over its market conduct. Here, subsidiaries may be held liable for the whole cartel activity, irrespective of their behaviour. A subsidiary should bear responsibility only in the case of a negligent or intentional infringement of competition law, in line with Regulation 1/2003 for the imposition of a fine.[170] Thus, applying the doctrine for holding a subsidiary liable would create issues of foreseeability and procedural rights. In the United States, there is no such instance of suing a subsidiary company for reselling products of a cartel, where the subsidiary had no knowledge of the cartel.[171] Jurisdiction in cross-border cases depends on whether injury was caused by a conduct that has an effect on US commerce.[172] Interestingly, such application of the single entity doctrine has not been confirmed at EU level, either by the Commission or by the Court, since no reference for preliminary ruling was made to the Court in spite of the uncertainty that it triggered.[173] This confirms the inadequacy of such application of the single entity doctrine.

4.5 CONCLUSION

The application of the single entity doctrine to parent–subsidiary relationships and commercial agency agreements demonstrates that the competition law conception of the firm is very much based on a market/firm paradigm that may be challenged when complex relationships blur the boundaries of the firm. The application of the doctrine to establish the substantive reach is more critical regarding commercial agency agreements. The theory of the firm, in all its variations, provides useful analytical tools that can aid the legal qualification of such agreements. The application of the single entity doctrine to attribute liability has far-reaching implications, contradicting important legal principles, and not adequate to the objective of deterrence that it presumably follows. This chapter thus offers a principled framework for liability attribution that furthers deterrence, valid across the types of relations discussed, and that features the availability of a defence based on the standard of negligence. The principal, or parent company, would have the burden of proving that effective internal measures have been implemented in order to benefit from such a defence.

---

[170] Regulation 1/2003, art. 23(2).

[171] B. Kennelly, 'Antitrust Forum-Shopping in England: Is Provimi Ltd v Aventis correct?', *CPI Antitrust Journal*, 2 (2010), 1, 5–6.

[172] Foreign Trade Antitrust Improvements Act, 15 U.S.C.A. §6a.

[173] Hughes, 'Competition Law Enforcement', 6 and B. Rodger, 'EU Competition Law and Private International Law: A Developing Relationship' in I. Lianos and D. Geradin (eds.), *Handbook on European Competition Law: Enforcement and Procedure* (Edward Elgar Publishing, 2013), pp. 456, 474.

5

The Single Entity Doctrine in Horizontal Relationships

5.1 INTRODUCTION

As discussed in Chapter 3, the *single entity doctrine* supports the idea that relationships among entities forming part of a single entity should be immune from prohibitions on anticompetitive agreements.[1] A very significant implication of the doctrine is that entities within it are not capable of conspiring,[2] and that competition among them is impossible.[3] May an undertaking or a single entity encompass potentially competing entities? Such a situation can exist when two competitors are wholly owned by the same parent, or when two competitors form a joint venture to which they delegate part of their economic activity. Competitors can also belong to umbrellas associations that impact companies' conduct on the market. The setting of such corporate arrangements will be submitted to antitrust scrutiny, either via merger control if the business integration falls within its scope, or *ex post*, under provisions on anticompetitive agreements. In application of the single entity doctrine, the critical question will be whether agreements between entities of *lawful* cooperation may be exempted from further scrutiny. In such cases, the single entity doctrine, if applied consistently with the principles of the theory of the firm, will adequately capture all possible anticompetitive effects of corporate arrangements.[4]

The competitive effects of some other corporate arrangements, however, may fall short of antitrust scrutiny. As is currently highly debated, competitors are commonly tied via structural links, such as financial or corporate board links, which can create

---

[1] The single entity was adopted in *Copperweld Corp* v. *Independence Tube Corp* 467 US 752 (1984) in the EU and in Case C–73/95P *Viho Europe BV* v. *Commission of the European Communities* [1996] ECR I–5457. For discussion of the implications of the single entity doctrine for establishing the substantive reach of competition law, see Section 3.3.

[2] *Copperweld Corp* v. *Independence Tube Corp* 467 US 752 (1984).

[3] Case 170/83 *Hydrotherm Gercitebau* [1984] ECR 2999, para. 11.

[4] For a discussion of how the theory of the firm, in all its variations, can aid in the application of the single entity doctrine, see Section 2.3.4.

anticompetitive effects.[5] These links may escape antitrust scrutiny, because they exist as alternatives to a market relationship, on the one hand, and to an intra-undertaking relationship, on the other hand. For example, the acquisition of shares in a competing undertaking renders the boundary between those unclear: two undertakings are simultaneously competitors with and shareholders of the same company.[6] The market/firm dichotomy on which the single entity doctrine is based explains here the limited substantive reach of competition law. The second part of this chapter will be dedicated to the contemporary debate on financial ownership and interlocking directorates in the European Union (EU) and in the United States. As such, this chapter engages with some of the most delicate issues of the modern economy for competition law, which are a growing complexity of corporate struc-tures, and the increasing disconnection between financial investment and operation of the economic activity.[7]

5.2 JOINT VENTURES AMONG COMPETITORS

In the EU and in the United States, the assessment of joint ventures between competitors involves two distinct inquiries. Is the cooperation between competitors, by way of creation of a joint venture, lawful? If so, do the companies and their joint venture form a single entity?

In the United States, the formation of the joint venture is subject to scrutiny of section 1 of the Sherman Act, assessed under the rule of reason. It can also be subject to *ex ante* control if the acquisition falls within the scope of merger control, under section 7 of the Clayton Act.[8] The Department of Justice (DoJ) and the Federal Trade Commission (FTC) *Antitrust Guidelines for Collaborations Among Competitors* clarify the approach of the agencies on such forms of cooperation.[9] In the EU, corporate arrangements between competitors fall either under the scrutiny of the Merger Control Regulation or within the scope of Article 101 of the Treaty on the Formation of the European Union (TFEU).[10] It is relevant to apply

---

[5] For an account of the debate, see Section 5.3.

[6] E. B. Rock, 'Corporate Law Through an Antitrust Lens', *Columbia Law Review*, 92 (1992), 497, 498.

[7] For a description of the growing complexity of the corporate landscape, see: E. W. Orts, *Business Persons: A Legal Theory of the Firm* (Oxford University Press, 2013), ch 5. Separation of ownership and control is not new, but it is furthered by financialisation of the modern economy. For discussion of the financialisation process, see, e.g., J. Crotty, *Capitalism, Macroeconomics and Reality: Understanding Globalization, Financialization, Competition and Crisis* (Edward Elgar Publishing, 2017); E. Hein, D. Detzer and N. Dodig (eds.), *Financialisation and the Financial and Economic Crises: Country Studies* (Edward Elgar Publishing, 2016).

[8] 15 USC §18.

[9] Department of Justice and Federal Trade Commission, 'Antitrust Guidelines for Collaborations Among Competitor' (2000).

[10] Council Regulation (EC) No 139/2004 of 20 January 2004 on the Control of Concentrations between Undertakings [2004] OJ L24/1 ('EU Merger Regulation'), Article 101 TFEU.

Article 101 only when there is no concentration or merger in the meaning of the Merger Regulation. A joint venture will be considered as *concentrative* if it is full function, involving the formation of an autonomous entity, in an operational sense.[11] The *Horizontal Cooperation Guidelines* also provide guidance for the assessment of non-concentrative, but cooperative, joint ventures among competitors.[12]

Secondly, should the companies and their joint venture be considered a single economic entity, and therefore not capable of conspiring with each other?[13] If so these agreements will fall short of section 1 of the Sherman Act and Article 101 of the TFEU. This section will focus on this second inquiry. It will be shown that the property rights theory of the firm provides a suitable analytical framework for applying the single entity doctrine to joint ventures.

5.2.1 *A Property Rights Framework*

In the United States, following *Copperweld*, the single entity doctrine was applied to a series of more complex corporate arrangements, including less than complete ownership or joint ventures.[14] One contentious issue was the conditions under

---

[11] 'The creation of a joint venture performing on a lasting basis all the functions of an autonomous economic entity shall constitute a concentration within the meaning of paragraph 1(b)' (EU Merger Regulation, Article 3(2)). It needs to have enough resources to operate independently in the market and it needs to have an activity that does not coincide with a function of the parent companies. In the process, commercial relationships with parents are assessed, as well as the length of the operation of the joint venture. Those practical criteria can be deemed to reflect the degree of control that the parents have over the joint venture, and consequently, the control that they have over each other.

[12] Communication from the Commission – Guidelines on the applicability of Article 101 of the Treaty on the Functioning of the European Union to horizontal co-operation agreements Text with EEA relevance OJ C11/1 ('Horizontal guidelines').

[13] B. Klein, 'Single Entity Analysis of Joint Ventures After American Needle: An Economic Perspective', *Antitrust Law Journal*, 78 (2013), 669, 675.

[14] *Dagher v. SRI*, 369 F 3d 1108, 1112 (9th Cir 2004): 'In Equilon, Shell has a 56% interest while Texaco owns 44%. In Motiva, Shell owns 35%, while SRI and Texaco each own 32.5%. Despite the collective assumption of risk and resource pooling in its joint ventures, Shell and Texaco continued to operate as distinct corporations. Each retained its own trademarks and kept control over its own brands pursuant to separate Brand Management Protocols, each of which prohibited the joint ventures from giving preferential treatment to either brand'; *HealthAmerica Penn Inc v. Susquehanna Health Sys* 278 F Supp 2d 423, 428 (MD Pa 2003): 'The Alliance Agreement further provides that the Boards of Directors of the respective PHS and NCPHS Affiliates retain authority and responsibility for mission and values, governance, credentialing, medical staff issues and quality assurance of the Affiliates. [. . .] the parties will share equally in the financial risks and rewards of the joiner[..] Each party to the Alliance Agreement retains 'its respective separate legal identity and the ownership of all of its assets, real and personal, tangible and intangible, and shall continue to be governed by its respective Board of Directors subject to Section III. An Affiliate must seek approval of Susquehanna Alliance before it acquires, purchases, sells, leases or otherwise transfers any property. No Affiliate may incur any capital indebtedness unless expressly authorized by the Alliance'; *Mt Pleasant v. Assoc Elec Cooperative Inc* 838 F 2d 268, 276 (8th Cir 1988): 'Thus, an analysis solely in terms of legal ownership and control would probably lead to the conclusion that, as in Topco, 405 US at [. . .], the subsidiary cooperatives here could conspire with their owners'; *Thomsen v. Western Electric Co* 512 F Supp 128, 133 (ND Cal 1981): 'Activities inherently connected with common ownership or control by their very definition fall

which the single entity doctrine could apply to agreements between competitors and their joint venture.

In their application of the single entity doctrine, courts have relied on various factors to ascertain the existence of a single entity. In *Copperweld*, the Court justified the impossibility of conspiring because of the 'unity of interests' afforded by full ownership by the parent company.[15] The role of a unity of interest in applying the single entity doctrine has been debated by commentators. In the context of a joint venture, a unity of interest should not merely be interpreted as common economic incentives, since competitors may have a common, but not socially desirable, interest, in delegating pricing decision to a third party. In addition, disparate interests can coexist within the most tightly controlled entity.[16] The key question is whether the joint venture corresponds to a true integration of a business activity to the extent that companies no longer compete on the function assigned to the joint venture. The joint venture should then have full control over the conduct of the function to which it is assigned.

An assessment of the type of control rights held by the joint venture helps that inquiry. Such assessment needs to be specific to the function assigned to the joint venture. Companies can retain their rights of control for other business activities, which does not preclude the finding of a single entity.[17] According to the property rights theory of the firm, an analysis of residual rights of control can inform the extent to which control over the activity at stake is concentrated and integrated within the joint venture. Residual rights of control are used in cases on non-specified contingency and determine ownership.[18] A distinction needs to be made between contractual (or reserved) and residual rights of control. Control can frequently be delegated, or reserved, to non-owners via contractual arrangements, not implying that ownership is transferred.[19] Residual rights of control indicated by ownership of the underlying assets necessary for the conduct of the activity is the important factor.[20] If such rights are concentrated within the joint venture, and not retained by the companies, it means that the joint venture constitutes a single entity doctrine. If ownership of assets is fragmented and retained by the parties, control is therefore fragmented and a single entity is not deemed to exist.[21]

outside the single instance where the conspiracy of affiliated companies would be actionable under §1 arising out of or inherently connected with common ownership or control.'

[15] *Copperweld Corp*, paras. 770–1.
[16] Klein, 'Single Entity Analysis'; D. V. Williamson, 'Organization, Control, and the Single Entity Defense in Antitrust', *Journal of Competition Law and Economics*, 5 (2009), 723; N. G. Menell, 'The Copperweld Question: Drawing the Line Between Corporate Family and Cartel', *Cornell Law Review*, 101 (2016), 467.
[17] Klein, 'Single Entity Analysis', 687.
[18] See Section 2.3.3.
[19] Williamson, 'Organization, Control', 735.
[20] Ibid., 736.
[21] Ibid.

The property-rights approach to joint ventures may be illustrated with the following scenario: two competitors create a joint venture of which they share the governance. The joint venture is assigned some veto rights concerning decisions on production capacity taken by the two companies. Investment decisions are then assumed by the joint venture. The two competitors may want to argue that all three companies constitute one single economic entity, because the joint venture assumes control over investment decisions. However, in this scenario the joint venture does not own any asset of the companies. The competitors retain the residual rights of control over their underlying assets, meaning that they keep control of the right to reallocate or redeploy such assets in the event of unforeseen or uncontracted events. Residual rights of control over these, determining ownership, are therefore not concentrated within the joint venture. This would preclude the finding of a single entity. It means that decisions taken with the joint venture should not be insulated from competition law screening.[22]

In summary, evidence that residual control rights are concentrated might allow a court or authority to accept a single entity defence. In contrast, evidence that control rights are fragmented and are distributed across the parties may preclude the finding of a single entity.[23]

5.2.2 A Property Rights Framework Applied to US Cases

Such an approach offers clarity to cases that have dealt with the single entity doctrine. In *HealthAmerica Pennsylvania Inc v. Susquehanna Health System*[24] the Court judged that the hospitals affiliated to Susquehanna Alliance formed a single economic entity, on the ground that 'an affiliate must seek approval of Susquehanna Alliance before it acquires, purchases, sells, leases or otherwise transfers any property'.[25] The Court considered here the possession of the rights to redeploy assets as one criterion for finding that control is concentrated. In *Chicago Professional Sports*, the judge considered wholesale redeployment rights, which amounts to a residual control right, as indicating fragmentation of control. 'All of this makes the [NBA] league look like a single firm. Yet the 29 clubs [in the National Basketball Association (NBA)], unlike GM's plants, have the right to secede (wouldn't a plant manager relish that!), and rearrange into two or three leagues.'[26] Single entity status was, however, granted by the Court to the NBA league on grounds other than control.[27]

---

[22]   Ibid.
[23]   Ibid., 744.
[24]   278 F Supp 2d 423 (MD Pa 2003).
[25]   Ibid. 428.
[26]   95 F 3d 593, 598–9 (7th Cir 1996).
[27]   Ibid.: 'It produces a single product; cooperation is essential (a league with one team would be like one hand clapping); and a league need not deprive the market of independent centers of decision making. The NBA has no existence independent of sports. It makes professional basketball; *only* it can make

In *American Needle*, it was explained that National Football League Properties (NFLP) had been created to support National Football League (NFL) teams in operation of their intellectual property rights.[28] The Supreme Court, while reversing the findings of the district court and the court of appeal, found that the NFL was not a single entity. This case was understood to restrict the possible application of the single entity to cases of complete control and ownership, because of its focus on economic incentives and profits. The Court stated that the NFL and the thirty-two 'teams are acting as "separate economic actors pursuing separate economic interests" and that each team is a potential "independent center of decision making"'. However, this case can be also interpreted in light of the property rights theory.[29] The reasoning in *American Needle* seems to be grounded on the distinction between contractual (or reserved) and residual control. Although NFLP and the teams were contractually bound, the teams retained ownership on the key asset here – their intellectual property – which they 'are able to and have at times sought to withdraw from this arrangement'.[30] The fact that the teams still owned their own trademarks was a key element in rejection of the single entity doctrine. This may mean that a long-term contractual arrangement on intellectual property could not amount to integrated ownership. Overall, this judgment was criticised because it supposedly lacked clarity. For the first time in over two decades, the Supreme Court addressed the issue of the scope of section 1 of the Sherman Act, and the delineation of the unilateral action and concerted practice.[31] The Court failed to provide guidance on the meaning of 'independent decision making' and 'separate economic interest' while relying on those concepts to conclude that there was no single entity. The Court would have benefited from adopting an approach to the single entity that was more consistent with the theory of the firm, in particular with regard to the ownership of residual rights of control.

"NBA Basketball" games; and unlike the NCAA the NBA also "makes" teams. After this case was last here the NBA created new teams in Toronto and Vancouver, stocked with players from the 27 existing teams plus an extra helping of draft choices. All of this makes the league look like a single firm. [. . .] [F]rom the perspective of college basketball players who seek to sell their skills, the teams are distinct, and because the human capital of players is not readily transferable to other sports (as even Michael Jordan learned) the league looks more like a group of firms acting as a monopsony. That is why the Supreme Court found it hard to characterize the National Football League in *Brown* v. *Pro Football* 116 S Ct 2116, 2126 (1996): "the clubs that make up a professional sports league are not completely independent economic competitors, as they depend upon a degree of cooperation for economic survival . . . In the present context, however, that circumstance makes the league more like a single bargaining employer, which analogy seems irrelevant to the legal issue before us." [. . .][W]e conclude that when acting in the broadcast market the NBA is closer to a single firm than to a group of independent firms.'

28 H. Hovenkamp, '*American Needle*: The Sherman Act, Conspiracy and Exclusion', *The CPI Antitrust Journal* [2010] 1, 2.
29 Klein, 'Single Entity Analysis', 678.
30 *American Needle, Inc.* v. *National Football League*, 560 U.S. 183.
31 N. Grow, '*American Needle* and the Future of the Single Entity Defense Under Section One of the Sherman Act', *American Business Law Journal*, 48 (2011), 449, 455.

5.2.3 *Joint Ventures in the EU*

In the EU, the application of the single entity doctrine for establishing the sub-stantive reach did not give rise to as many cases. The highly debated issue is rather the use of the doctrine to attribute liability within corporate groups. As in vertical relationships, inquiries in substantive reach and liability attribution cases demand different paradigms.[32]

In *Ijsselcentrale*, four electricity companies controlling a joint venture claimed that the agreement between them was outside of the scope of Article 101(1) of the TFEU because they formed a single economic entity.[33] The Commission found that the four companies were able to behave independently in the market, as they were not separate legal persons and they were not controlled by a single organisation. As such, agreements between them could not be exempt from Article 101(1) scrutiny. Although the legal separation should have been immaterial, this conclusion seems consistent with the concepts of the firm and the single entity doctrine focusing on control. A property rights approach, examining concentration of asset ownership within the joint venture, could have provided further argument. In the case, the agreement seemed beyond the scope of the internal organisation of the integrated activity anyway.

There has been a broad application of the single entity doctrine to hold parents liable for the misconduct of a joint venture. In *Shell Petroleum NV v. Commission*, the General Court went as far to apply the presumption of decisive influence because the two parents were deemed to be in an analogous situation as a single parent with full control.[34] Does this mean that the two parents and their common subsidiary form part of a single undertaking, and that all the agreements between them fall outside the scope of Article 101(1)? Endorsing a single approach to both functions would potentially exclude a wide range of behaviour from its scope. In this context, however, it can be expected that only the agreements relating to the internal workings of the joint venture could fall outside Article 101, while all the others could be submitted to its review.[35]

Although all points to a single interpretation of the concept of undertaking in the general application of competition law, *Dow* seems to support the need of having a context-based approach:

> Where two parent companies each have a 50% shareholding in the joint venture which committed an infringement of the rules of competition law, *it is only for the purposes of establishing liability for participation in the infringement of that law and only in so far as the Commission has demonstrated, on the basis of factual evidence,*

---

[32] For discussion of a single versus a context-specific approach to the concept of undertaking, see A. Jones and B. Sufrin, *EU Competition Law: Text, Cases, and Materials*, 6th edn (Oxford University Press, 2016), p. 133.

[33] *Ijsselcentrale* (Case IV/32.732) Commission Decision 91/50/EEC [1991] OJ L28/32, paras. 22–4.

[34] Case T–343/06 *Shell Petroleum NV v. Commission* [2012] EU:T:2012:478.

[35] Jones and Sufrin, *EU Competition Law*, p. 133.

that both parent companies did in fact exercise decisive influence over the joint venture, that those three entities can be considered to form a single economic unit and therefore form a single undertaking for the purposes of Article [101 of the TFEU].[36] [emphasis added]

This judgment confirmed that all the three companies constituted a single undertaking, extending liability to the parent companies of the subsidiary for its involvement in the Chloroprene Rubber cartel. In such cases, however, the Commission must produce evidence of the actual exercise of decisive influence to attribute liability. The Court rejected the argument that the joint venture was a separate undertaking because of its being a full-function joint venture for the purposes of the EU Merger Regulation. It confirms that, in the assessment of joint ventures, the EU adopts a differentiated approach depending on the inquiry.

The competition law treatment of joint ventures substantiates the theoretical claims that different inquiries demand a distinct approach to the boundaries of the firm.[37] The substantive reach of Article 101 of the TFEU to joint ventures is based on a different paradigm than liability attribution cases. Recourse to the property rights theory of the firm could clarify the substantive reach of Article 101 of the TFEU to agreements between competitors and the joint ventures. As in vertical relationships, an approach more in line with deterrence and corporate law principles should be adopted when attributing liability.[38]

5.3 STRUCTURAL LINKS BETWEEN COMPETITORS

This section discusses the issue of structural links between competitors, created via corporate arrangements such as financial ownership links and interlocking directorates.[39] Structural links between competitors connect undertakings through both corporate and market relationships, and involve relationships at the very border of the firm and the market.

The issue of financial links among competitors is currently highly debated in the United States and in the EU. Portfolio diversification strategies by institutional investors can result, in some sectors, in concentration of financial ownership. In the United States, the debate focuses on anticompetitive effects of common

---

[36] Case C–179/12P *The Dow Chemical Company* v. *Commission* [2013] EU:C:2013:605, para. 58

[37] This is a competition law adaptation of Orts's adaptation of H. L. A. Hart's approach to the legal boundaries of the firm. 'HLA Hart's admonition . . . [is] the nature and boundaries of the firm depend on the nature of the question being asked' (H. L. A. Hart, 'Definition and Theory in Jurisprudence' in *Essays in Jurisprudence and Philosophy* (Oxford University Press, 1983); E. W. Orts, *Business Persons: A Legal Theory of the Firm* (Oxford University Press, 2013), p. 10) 8.

[38] Liability framework is established in Section 3.3.3.2 and Section 4.2.2.

[39] It is necessary to point out that the concept of 'structural link' has also been used in the context of collective dominance cases (to refer to cross-ownership, long-term contracts etc. between competitors) see, for example: Case T–102/96 *Gencor Ltd* v. *Commission of the European Communities* [1999] ECR II–753.

ownership,[40] which may be unchallenged.[41] Recent empirical studies have demonstrated the impact on prices of structural ownership links in oligopolistic markets.[42] In the EU, minority shareholdings not conferring control were at the heart of the project of merger control reform. In the *Ryanair/Aer Lingus* case, the European Commission could not review the acquisition of an anticompetitive minority shareholding because it fell short of the EU Merger Regulation.[43] Although the reform has not been pursued, the issue keeps its contemporary relevance.[44] Common shareholdings links were recently discussed by the Commission in the *Dow/DuPont* merger case.[45] Commissioner Vestager also expressed the Commission's intention to examine the scope of issues raised by common institutional investors.[46]

Interlocking directorates, created by directors sitting on the board of several companies, can also create coordinated and unilateral anticompetitive risks that may fall short of antitrust scrutiny.[47] The practice of interlocking directorates is

---

[40]   For an overview of the debate, see, e.g., OECD, 'Common Ownership by Institutional Investors and Its Impact on Competition', DAF/COMP/WD(2017)10; CPI Antitrust Chronicle, 'Index Funds – a New Antitrust Frontier?' (2017) 3. For more particular legal and economic analysis, see, e.g., J. Azar, M. Schmalz and I. Tecu, 'Anti-Competitive Effects of Common Ownership', *Journal of Finance*, 73 (4) (2018), 1513–65; E. Elhauge, 'Essay: Horizontal Shareholding', *Harvard Law Review*, 129 (2016), 1267; J. Baker 'Overlapping Financial Investor Ownership, Market Power, and Antitrust Enforcement: My Qualified Agreement with Professor Elhauge', *Harvard Law Review Forum*, 129 (2016), 212; J. He and J. Huang, 'Product Market Competition in a World of Cross-Ownership: Evidence from Institutional Blockholdings', *The Review of Financial Studies*, 30(8) (2017), 2674–718; E. Posner, F. Scott Morton and E. G. Weyl, 'A Proposal to Limit the Anti-Competitive Power of Institutional Investors', *Antitrust Law Journal*, 81(3) (2017), 669–728; D. O'Brien and K. Waehrer, 'The Competitive Effects of Common Ownership: We Know Less than We Think', *Antitrust Law Journal*, 81(3) (2017), 729–76, M. S. Patel, 'Common Ownership, Institutional Investors, and Antitrust', *Antitrust Law Journal* (2018).

[41]   Although the FTC recently obtained divesture of assets on the ground of competitive concerns of common ownership links in competing companies: FTC, Holdco and Bankrate, N°1710196 (2018), available at: www.ftc.gov/enforcement/cases-proceedings/file-no-1710196/red-ventures-holdco-bankrate

[42]   The most cited study is Azar, Schmalz and Tecu, 'Anti-Competitive Effects of Common Ownership'.

[43]   European Commission, 'Towards More Effective EU Merger Control', White Paper COM (2014) 449; Commission, DG Competition, Annex I to the Staff Working Document, Towards More Effective EU Merger Control: 'Economic Literature on Non-Controlling Minority Shareholdings ("Structural links")' (2013).

[44]   M. Vestager, 'Refining the EU Merger Control System', speech, *Studienvereinigung Kartellrecht*, Brussels, 10 March 2016, available at: https://ec.europa.eu/commission/commissioners/2014-2019/ves tager/announcements/refining-eu-merger-control-system_en

[45]   *Dow/DuPont* (Case COMP/M.7932) Commission decision 2017/C1946 [2017] paras. 2349–52, Annex 5, 5.

[46]   M. Vestager, 'Competition in changing times', FIW Symposium, Innsbruck, 16 February 2018, available at: https://ec.europa.eu/commission/commissioners/2014-2019/vestager/announcements /competition-changing-times-o_en; Commission, Management Plan 2017 of DG Competition, Ref. Ares(2016)7130280. 16.

[47]   F. Thépot, F. Hugon and M. Luinaud (2016), 'Cumul de mandats d'administrateur et risques antic-oncurrentiels: Un vide juridique en Europe?', *Concurrences*, 1 (2016), 1–11; J. Buhart and L. Lesur, 'Minority Shareholders and Competition: Is a European Reform Necessary?', *Concurrences*, 4 (2013), 57.

widespread in Europe, particularly in France and Germany.[48] While interlocking directorates among competitors are prohibited in the United States, there is no such prohibition in Europe with the exception of Italy, where such links are prohibited in the banking and insurance industry.[49]

After providing a brief overview of the anticompetitive effects of structural links, this chapter will compare the manner in which the EU and the United States deal with structural links. An enforcement gap may exist because structural links – being at the very border of market and corporate relationships – may not fit into the firm/market paradigm underlying the application of EU provisions. In moving away from that distinction, the US provisions seem more adequate for the review of structural links that blur the boundary between the market and the undertaking.

The competition law conception of the firm thus needs to adjust, when the boundary between the firm and the market blurs. Such adjustment involves greater insight into corporate governance and finance matters. Protection of minority shareholdings may be a key feature of the quality of corporate governance.[50] The board of directors is a central component of the corporate governance system of a company. Its composition, with members being elected according to their expertise or experience, is an important aspect of the quality of corporate governance.[51] Although corporate structural links seem to cause anticompetitive concerns, this chapter will show that corporate governance (and corporate law) and competition law may have convergent objectives with regard to issues raised by structural links.

To the extent that interlocking directorates are attached to a partial acquisition, or constitute a means of corporate influence, the analysis for minority shareholdings may apply to interlocking directorates. They will be examined as a separate issue, when the developments on minority shareholdings do not apply to them. This chapter will provide normative justification for the need for regulatory change in

---

[48]   K. van Veen and J. Kratzer, 'National and international interlocking directorates within Europe: corporate networks within and among fifteen European countries', *Economy and Society*, 40(1) (2011), 1–25. 'France (83.7 per cent) and Germany (85.2 per cent) have the lowest number of individuals with only one board seat. Only in the Netherlands was the percentage Approved lower (82.5 per cent) (. . .) The biggest European linkers are mostly from Germany and France.'

[49]   United States: s. 8 of the Clayton Act, 15 USC §19; Italy: Art. 36 of Decree Law No 201 of 6 December 2011, converted into Law No 214/2011: 'Protection of competition and personal cross-shareholdings in credit and financial markets'.

[50]   See, for example: R. La Porta, F. Lopez-de-Silanes, A. Shleifer and R. W. Vishny, 'Law and Finance', Journal of Political Economy, 106 (1998), 1113. Note that a conflict of interests between minority and majority shareholders may also be a relevant issue both for competition and corporate governance in the following scenario: a minority shareholder may have a reduced incentive to control the management in a manner that benefits the long-term interest of the company. A company having a minority acquisition will benefit indirectly from the target being in a cartel if the cartel causes prices to be at the cartel level throughout the industry (umbrella price), while not fearing the risk of fines in the event of detection.

[51]   B. M. Gerber, 'Enabling Interlock Benefits While Preventing Anticompetitive Harm: Toward an Optimal Definition of Competitors Under Section 8 of the Clayton Act', *Yale Journal on Regulation*, 24 (2007), 107, 109.

the EU with regard to structural links, through the lens of the need for a change of paradigm. The practical challenges of addressing such an enforcement gap will not be addressed in a comprehensive manner.

5.3.1 *Anticompetitive Effects of Structural Links*

A minority shareholding refers to a share of less than 50 per cent of the voting rights or equity rights in a company that can confer financial and corporate rights.[52] It is not uncommon that companies own minority interests in their competitors. The process of financialisation of the global economy has also led many sovereign funds, banks and hedge funds to acquire controlling and non-controlling shareholdings in various corporations operating in the same markets.[53] Structural links between competitors can thus be direct, in cases of direct ownership links, but can also be indirect. This is the case when competitors have common ownership links by such institutional investors. Structural links may also create relationships between companies that are vertically related, which have effects that are relevant for competition law analysis.[54] Structural links between competitors can impact their incentives to compete, through unilateral and coordinated effects. Another important question is the corporate channels through which such anticompetitive effects may materialise. In other words, a joint analysis of *incentives* and *ability* is required for understanding possible anticompetitive effects of structural links.

5.3.1.1 Financial Links

5.3.1.1.1 THEORIES OF HARM. The acquisition of a minority interest in a competitor may induce a company to reduce its competitive effort, as the value of the investment is affected by the performance of the other company. Fierce competition affects the profit of the competitor and, as such, affects the return on the minority shareholding. Because of the financial interest held by firm A in firm B, firm A has a unilateral incentive to raise its price. An increase in price by A normally results in some of the sales being diverted to its competitor B. Owing to the stake held, part of the loss is recaptured in the form of dividends or a rise in share price related to the greater revenues earned by B. The magnitude of the incentive depends on the

---

[52] 'Financial rights' refers to the entitlement to a share of the profits of the acquired firm. 'Corporate rights' can take the form of voting rights, or rights to appoint a board member that may provide the acquirer with a degree of influence over the target company: S. C. Salop and D. P. O'Brien, 'Competitive Effects of Partial Ownership: Financial Interest and Corporate Control', *Antitrust Law Journal*, 67 (2000), 568.

[53] J.E. Fichtner, J. Heemskerk and J. Garcia-Bernardo, 'Hidden power of the Big Three? Passive Index Funds, Re-Concentration of Corporate Ownership, and New Financial Risk', *Business and Politics*, 19 (2) (2017), 298.

[54] A. Perrot, 'Minority Shareholdings: Is there a Need for Reform?' Law & Economics Workshop, Institute of Competition Law (15 October 2013). This chapter focuses on the effects of horizontal links.

portion of shares held.[55] Thus, a minority shareholding, although not conferring control, is shown to produce a unilateral incentive for company A to raise its price.[56] The same unilateral effect is deemed to arise from common ownership by institutional investors. For an institutional investor owning stakes in competitors, the expected loss of sales following a price increase by one competitor could be recouped via gains realised by competitors. In that context, common ownership could also affect negatively the intensity of innovation in sectors in which innovation competition is an important factor. Such an assessment was made in the *Dow/ DuPont* merger case.[57]

Financial ownership in a competitor may also enable the holder to sustain a collusive agreement because it increases the cost of deviation, if competitors can expect a price war that will impact negatively on the holders of those shares. In addition to the impact on incentives, such ownership arrangements increase the transparency in a market, which can help to sustain a collusive agreement, in particular if relevant information regarding companies is not publicly available, because they are not listed.[58]

Due to the unilateral effects of partial ownership on competition, however, the potential gain from collusion is not maximal. The gap between the collusive and non-collusive outcomes is smaller in a market in which competition is softer due to partial ownerships. As a result, companies gain relatively less from collusion, and fear less from the abandonment of collusion if one of them deviates.[59] The scope of the anticompetitive effects associated with minority shares in a competitor depends on a number of factors relating to the market structure but that may also be specific to the company.[60] Common ownership by institutional investors could also facilitate coordination of the collusive practice, as an investor common to multiple firms may

---

[55] This also depends on the ability of the acquirer actually to capture the benefits of a price increase through the financial entitlements provided by the acquisition: J. B. Dubrow, 'Challenging the Economic Incentives Analysis of Competitive Effects in Acquisitions of Passive Minority Equity Interests', *Antitrust Law Journal*, 69 (2001), 131.

[56] D. Gilo, 'The Anticompetitive Effect of Passive Investment', *Michigan Law Review*, 99 (2000), 1.

[57] *Dow/DuPont* (Case COMP/M.7932) Commission Decision 2017/C1946 [2017] para. 2350. The decision taken by one firm, today, to increase innovation competition has a downward impact on its current profits and is also likely to have a downward impact on the (expected future) profits of its competitors. This, in turn, will negatively affect the value of the portfolio of shareholders who hold positions in this firm and in its competitors. Therefore, as for current price competition, the presence of significant common shareholding is likely negatively to affect the benefits of innovation competition for firms subject to this common shareholding.

[58] K. U. Kühn and X. Vives, *Information Exchanges Among Firms and Their Impact on Competition* (Office for Official Publications of the European Communities, 1995).

[59] OFT1218, 'Minority Interests in Competitors: A Research Report prepared by DotEcon Ltd' (2010), 10. For an analysis of the conditions in which cross-ownership induces collusive behaviour, see: D. D. Gilo, Y. Moshe and Y. Spiegel, 'Partial Cross Ownership and Tacit Collusion', *The RAND Journal of Economics*, 37 (2006), 81. For a contrasting view, see D. Malueg, 'Collusive Behavior and Partial Ownership of Rivals', *International Journal of Industrial Organization*, 10 (1992), 27. Malueg shows that, in a repeated game, cross-ownership decreases the likelihood of collusion

[60] OFT1218, 9.

act as a 'cartel ringmaster'.[61] Financial links, unless used to complement joint ventures agreements to align incentives, are unlikely to generate efficiencies.[62] In addition, although common ownership may enable successful diversification strategies, the benefits are likely to accrue to the funds customers while affecting negatively consumers. Similar diversification benefits could be reached by less restrictive measures with investments across sectors rather than within sectors.[63]

5.3.1.1.2 IMPACT OF STRUCTURAL LINKS ON COMPANY'S BEHAVIOUR. How may incentives to reduce competition be implemented in practice? Corporate channels of influence are at the heart of the debate on common ownership in the United States.[64] Corporate rights, such as voting rights, or the right to appoint a board member, may be attached to financial interests.[65] This may confer shareholders' influence on strategic decisions eventually impacting the competitive stance.[66] Shareholders may even be able to block strategic decisions, or appoint a board member who will be sympathetic to a less aggressive commercial policy.[67] Even in the absence of a majority, a minority share of voting could confer influence, especially in the event of dispersed shareholdings, or a low rate of attendance at meetings.[68]

Regarding institutional investors, the influence may also materialise more informally through active participation in private engagement meetings. Such interactions, deemed to be much more frequent, may provide greater influence than formal contacts via voting rights at shareholders' meetings.[69] Some institutional investors publicly request, for example, long-term strategic plans regarding growth and profitability; and express that their evaluation strategy of management depends on the implementation of such plans.[70] In addition, institutional investors may also exert influence via a threat of selling shares.[71] As an anecdotal example of the impact on product market competition, mutual funds representatives admitted having

---

[61] E. B. Rock and D. Rubinfeld, 'Antitrust for Institutional Investors', NYU Law and Economics Research Paper No 17-23 (2017), 2.

[62] OFT1218, 5.23–5.26.

[63] Elhauge, 'Essay: Horizontal Shareholding', 1303.

[64] Rock and Rubinfeld, 'Antitrust for Institutional Investors'; O'Brien and Waehrer, 'The Competitive Effects of Common Ownership'; Azar et al. 'Anti-Competitive Effects of Common Ownership'.

[65] Salop and O'Brien, 'Competitive Effects of Partial Ownership', 568.

[66] Azar et al., 'Anti-Competitive Effects of Common Ownership'.

[67] See Section 5.3.3 on corporate rights typically attached to different levels of shareholdings.

[68] OECD, 'Common Ownership by Institutional Investors and its Impact on Competition', para. 54.

[69] J. McCahery, Z. Sautner and L. Starks, 'Behind the Scenes: The Corporate Governance Preferences of Institutional Investors', *Journal of Finance*, 71(6) (2016), 2905, 2906. 'Our survey's 143 respondents, mostly very large institutional investors with a long-term focus, indicate that voice, especially when conducted behind the scenes, is important. For example, 63% of respondents state that in the past five years they have engaged in direct discussions with management, and 45% state that they have had private discussions with a company's board *outside* of management's presence.'

[70] Azar, 'Anti-Competitive Effects of Common Ownership'.

[71] McCahery, Sautner and Starks, 'Behind the Scenes'.

encouraged pharmaceutical firms to maintain pricing levels and to be united towards consumers and policymakers.[72] However, one may also question the scope of such possible influence with respect to that of majority shareholders.[73] As such, Patel shows that the ability of common ownership to translate into actual competitive harm depends on several factors, including the structure of shareholder incentives. Some shareholders may have interests in other firms outside the relevant market, which may mitigate the anticompetitive effect produced by common ownership. Thus, the scope of anticompetitive effects critically depends on how managers set their competitive strategy. Managerial decision-making is determined by a range of factors including compensation schemes, and their approach to maximising shareholders' interests.[74] Indeed, setting a competitive strategy in response to common ownership requires managers to put the interests of certain shareholders above others.[75]

Recent empirical studies evidence the potential effects of common ownership. The most commonly cited, a study by Azar et al. (2018) identified a possible 3–7 per cent price increase in the US airline industry due to concentration of financial ownership in the hands of a few institutional investors.[76] Azar et al. (2016) studied the relationship between financial ownership links and fees for banking deposit services in the United States. They concluded that cross-ownership between bank and common ownership by institutional investors is strongly correlated with an increase in fees observed over the period of study.[77] Research on the impact on institutional investors is still in its infancy, and evidence on actual impact on competition is likely to build in the coming years.

5.3.1.2 Interlocking Directorates

5.3.1.2.1 THEORIES OF HARM. Interlocking-directorates, when held among competing companies, may give rise to unilateral and coordinated effects.[78] The practice of interlocking directorates is widespread, particularly in Europe. In France, large

---

[72] C. Chen, 'Mutual Fund Industry to Drug Makers: Stand Up and Defend Yourself' (2016) *Bloomberg News* in OECD, 'Common Ownership by Institutional Investors and its Impact on Competition', para. 58.

[73] OECD, 'Common Ownership by Institutional Investors and Its Impact on Competition', para. 55.

[74] Patel, 'Common Ownership, Institutional Investors, and Antitrust'.

[75] N. J. Phillips, 'Taking Stock: Assessing Common Ownership', remarks to the Global Antitrust Economics Conference (1 June 2018).

[76] Azar, 'Anti-Competitive Effects of Common Ownership'.

[77] J. Azar, S. Raina and M. Schmalz, 'Ultimate Ownership and Bank Competition' (2016), available at: https://papers.ssrn.com/sol3/papers.cfm?abstract_id=2710252

[78] E. M. Fich and L. J. White, 'Why Do CEOs Reciprocally Sit on Each Other's Boards?', *Journal of Corporate Finance*, 11 (2005), 175; M. S. Mizruchi, 'What Do Interlocks Do? An Analysis, Critique, and Assessment of Research on Interlocking Directorates', *Annual Review of Sociology*, 22 (1996), 273; e.g. H. Buch-Hansen, 'Interlocking Directorates and Collusion: An Empirical Analysis', *International Sociology*, 29 (2014), 253; V. Petersen, 'Interlocking Directorates in the European Union: An Argument for Their Restriction', *European Business Law Review*, 27(6) (2016), 821–64; F. Thépot, F. Hugon and M. Luinaud, 'Cumul de mandats d'administrateur et risques anticoncurrentiels: Un vide juridique en Europe?', *Concurrences*, 1 (2016), 1–11.

companies are connected through their boards with a high number of CEOs sitting as independent board members of competitors.[79] Similarly, Germany has long been characterised by dense networks of companies in which banks play a central role, leading to 'cooperative capitalism' being regarded as a feature of the German economy.[80]

In contrast to financial links, the competing companies are related not via their financial performance but by individual directors sitting on the boards of the different companies. The first impact on the competitive outcome stems from the information and communication flows facilitated by interlocking-directorates. Board members have access to strategic, accounting and commercial information as well as information regarding the appointment and compensation of executives.[81] Information and communication between competitors has been shown to facilitate collusion, even when not specifically related to prices and quantities. Information flows may help in reaching a collusive agreement and also provide monitoring tools for competitors to prevent deviation from the collusive agreement.[82] As an example, a network of interlocking directorates has helped to stabilise a number of cartels, including the international uranium and diamond cartels.[83] Accordingly, the purpose of the US prohibition of interlocking directorates is expressly to 'avoid the opportunity for the coordination of business decisions by competitors and to prevent the exchange of commercially sensitive information by competitors'.[84] Anticompetitive agreements can also be facilitated by indirect interlocks in which competitors sit on the board of a third party. Information exchanges can be more discrete, with indirect rather than direct interlocks.[85]

Interlocks may also affect unilateral incentives to compete. Social ties created by the attendance of common board meetings may discourage aggressive commercial strategies towards rivals. If interlocks are widespread within industries this may reduce the overall intensity of competition.[86] When attached to financial interests,

[79]   H. J. Yeo, C. Pochet and A. Alcouffe, 'CEO Reciprocal Interlocks in French Corporations', *Journal of Management and Governance*, 7 (2003), 87–108.
[80]   F. Ferraro, G. Schnyder, E. M. Heemskerk et al., 'Structural Breaks and Governance Networks in Western Europe' in B. Kogut (ed.), *The Small Worlds of Corporate Governance* (MIT Press, 2012), pp. 151–82; P. Windolf and J. Beyer, 'Co-operative Capitalism: Corporate Networks in Germany and Britain', *British Journal of Sociology*, 47(2) (1996), 205–31
[81]   OFT, 11. J. P. Schmidt, 'Germany: Merger Control Analysis of Minority Shareholdings – A Model for the EU?', 16(2)*Concurrences*,2-2013.
[82]   K. U. Kühn, 'Fighting Collusion by Regulating Communication Between Firms', *Economic Policy*, 16 (2001), 167; X. Vives, *Oligopoly Pricing: Old Ideas and New Tools* (MIT Press, 1999); P. Buccirossi and G. Spagnolo, 'Corporate Governance and Collusive Behavior' in W. D. Collins (ed.), *Issues in Competition Law and Policy 1* (American Bar Association, 2008), p. 10.
[83]   V. Petersen, 'Interlocking Directorates in the European Union: An Argument for Their Restriction', *European Business Law Review*, 27(6) (2016), 821, 842.
[84]   *Square D Co v. Schneider SA* 760 F Supp 362 (SDNY 1991).
[85]   H. Buch-Hansen, 'Interlocking Directorates and Collusion: An Empirical Analysis', *International Sociology*, 29 (2014), 53.
[86]   L. Flochel, 'The Competitive Effects of Acquiring Minority Shareholdings', *Concurrences*, 1 (2012), 16–17; D. Spector, 'Some Economics of Minority Shareholdings', *Concurrences*, 3 (2011), 14.

interlocking directorates may provide the ability to influence a competitor's conduct. The remuneration schemes in place may also affect the incentive to compete, especially if closely tied to the firm's performance.[87]

Economic efficiencies are nevertheless more likely to exist in the area of interlocking directorates than in the situation of minority shareholdings.[88] Information exchange, enabled by such links, may reduce strategic uncertainty, which may under certain circumstances be pro-competitive if it improves business decision-making. The presence of the board member of a competitor offers the benefit of his expertise and experience, which may improve decision-making. Moreover, the exchange of information can create synergies in the control and management of companies facing similar technical and economic issues. A business can also benefit from the reputation of an independent board member and use it in situations in which the asymmetry of information may be an obstacle in negotiations to obtain financing from banks or investors. Similarly, the expertise and reputation of the board member of a competitor can facilitate contractual negotiations with suppliers and customers – especially in small businesses.[89]

The anticompetitive effects of interlocking directorates are exacerbated if the corporate governance of the competing companies is weak. A director sitting on several boards may influence the decision process in one company, as a way of favouring another company of which he is a board member. Directors may also be tempted to disclose confidential information of a company at another company's board meeting. These issues may be mitigated by the quality of the fiduciary duty. A strong fiduciary duty, which indicates good corporate governance, may prevent the director from engaging in such practices. A director's fiduciary duty to one company, however, may naturally conflict with his fiduciary duty to another.[90] Overall, bad-quality corporate governance is more likely to induce directors with shared directorship to compete less aggressively.[91]

5.3.1.2.2 EMPIRICAL STUDIES. The few existing empirical studies draw contrasting conclusions regarding the actual effectiveness of interlocks as a collusive device. Based on data from a sample composed of 225 firms convicted of participating in cartels between 1986 and 2010, González and Schmidt found that there is a greater

---

[87] OFT 1218, 'Minority Interests in Competitors: A Research Report prepared by DotEcon Ltd' (2010), pp. 60–3.

[88] Ibid., para. 6.11.

[89] The welfare effect of a reduction in uncertainty depends on the type of decision variable (price or quantity), the type of uncertainty (common demand versus idiosyncratic costs) and the characteristics of the goods (substitutes or complements, homogeneous or heterogeneous products): Kühn and Vives, *Information Exchanges Among firms*. For a comprehensive analysis of impact of board interlocks on firms' performance, see, e.g., E. Prinz, *Les effets des liens personnels interconseils sur la performance de l'entreprise: une analyse comparée entre France et Allemagne* (Peter Lang, 2011).

[90] OECD, 'Common Ownership by Institutional Investors and Its Impact on Competition', DAF/COMP/WD (2017), 34.

[91] OFT, para. 6.5.

likelihood of collusion when companies have a higher fraction of 'busy' board members, referring to members sitting on the boards of other companies, owing to the impact of board connections on collusion.[92] Based on data from EU cartel cases between 1969 and 2012 and corporate links between the companies, a study by Hubert Buch-Hansen concluded that only twelve of the 3,318 corporate ties among the 890 companies involved in the cartel cases seem to have been conducive to collusion. Three of them were direct and nine were indirect interlocks. Interestingly, however, earlier cases of cartels seem to have been more correlated to interlocking directorates than those of today.[93] A possible interpretation is that, since the 1990s, there has been stricter enforcement against cartel practices. Consequently, companies would refrain from using interlocking directorates to sustain collusion, possibly to avoid attracting the authority attention. Although inherent to the study of typically hidden illegal practices, the correlation is limited to cases of detected explicit collusion. This prevents any conclusion from being made on corporate links and undetected collusion between competitors. Based on estimation of the probability of detection (of cartels that were eventually detected), we can imagine that the population of undetected collusion largely outweighs that of detected cases.[94] A few older studies by Pennings and Burt based on US firms establish a positive correlation between an industry concentration and interlocks.[95] The latter study, however, found a negative relationship between interlocks and concentration, as being of intermediate level of concentration. This may be explained by the fact that firms in highly concentrated industries have little need for interlocks to achieve collusive outcomes.[96]

5.3.2 *The Reach of EU and US Competition Laws over Structural Links*

In the EU, a structural link is scrutinised under the Merger Regulation if it is part of an acquisition that confers a 'lasting change in the control of the undertaking'.[97] Minority shareholdings or interlocking directorates not conferring control can be captured by Article 101 of the TFEU only to the extent that there is an agreement or concerted practice between undertakings, or by Article 102 of the TFEU if there is dominance. In application of the competition law conception of the firm, a relationship between

---

[92]   T. A. González and M. Schmid, 'Corporate Governance and Antitrust Behavior', Swiss Institute of Banking and Finance, University of St. Gallen, Working Paper (2012).

[93]   Buch-Hansen, 'Interlocking Directorates and Collusion', 253.

[94]   E. Combe, C. Monnier and R. Legal, 'Cartels: The Probability of Getting Caught in the European Union', Bruges European Economic Research Papers (2008), 2.

[95]   J. M. Pennings, *Interlocking Directorates: Origins and Consequences of Connections Among Organizations' Board of Directors* (Jossey-Bass Inc Pub, 1980); R. S. Burt, *Corporate Profits and Cooptation* (Academic, 1983); Mizruchi, 'What Do Interlocks Do?', 273–4.

[96]   Mizruchi, 'What Do Interlocks Do?', 273.

[97]   EU Merger Control Regulation, Recital 20.

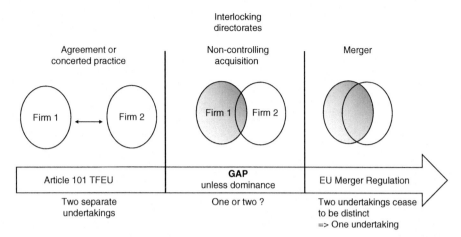

FIGURE 1 – The EU approach to structural links. *Enforcement gap: a matter of boundaries between undertakings When a relationship is neither clearly a market nor an intra-undertaking relationship, it is unclear whether Article 101 of the TFEU or merger control can apply to the anticompetitive links between competitors.*

two distinct undertakings – a sign of the existence of a market relationship – falls within Article 101 of the TFEU, while an intra-undertaking relationship is immune from its scrutiny.[98] A similar paradigm can be extrapolated to the application of merger provision. A relevant merger situation is created if, via the proposed acquisition, two undertakings cease to be distinct. In practice, the acquisition of control – or decisive influence – determines the creation of a merger situation.[99] Therefore, the concept of undertaking for Article 101 of the TFEU and the concept of control for merger review are used to determine whether a relationship is either a market or an intrafirm relationship.[100] It will be shown that an enforcement gap exists because of the difficulty of applying the paradigm of inter/intra-undertaking – underlying the different provisions- to structural links.

In the United States, merger control applies to anticompetitive minority shareholdings, irrespective of whether they confer control over the target company.[101] In addition, section 8 of the Clayton Act specifically prohibits interlocking directorships between competitors. The scrutiny of structural links does not depend on the question of control or, of whether the relationship between, two economic entities ceases to be a market relationship. Therefore, the United States seems to be adopting a different paradigm: one that is based on anticompetitive effects rather than one that is built on the

---

[98] An intra-undertaking can fall within the scope of Article 102 of the TFEU only if there is dominance.
[99] EU Merger Control Regulation, Recital 20.
[100] I acknowledge here that this paradigm does not work for distinguishing the application of merger control and Article 101 of the TFEU, as the former applies *ex ante* and the latter *ex post*.
[101] Under the conditions established in the Hart-Scott-Rodino Act: Hart-Scott-Rodino Antitrust Improvements Act 15 USC §18a.

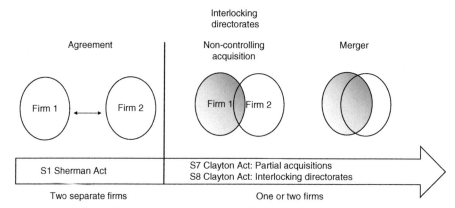

FIGURE 2 – The US approach to structural links: *non-controlling acquisitions can be scrutinised in spite of being neither a clear market nor an intra-entity relationship.*

dichotomy of market/firm relationships.[102] Although the United States does not display a similar enforcement gap to that of the EU, ongoing debates concerning common ownership by institutional investors also question the suitability of the substantive reach of provisions, when confronted with new types of relationships. In addition, one critical question is whether existing tools used in the competitive assessment adequately capture effects that may not have been accounted for before.

5.3.2.1 The Substantive Reach of EU Competition Law

5.3.2.1.1 STRUCTURAL LINKS UNDER EU MERGER CONTROL.

A Focus on Control

In the paradigm of inter/intra-undertaking relationships, the concept of control enables the identification of the elimination of a market relationship and the creation of an intra-undertaking relationship. The shortcomings of the EU Merger Regulation relate to the difficulty of applying the framework of control – or the creation of an undertaking in the paradigm – to relationships that are at the frontier of the firm and the market. The *Ryanair/Aer Lingus* case is an illustration of such difficulty.

In 2007, the Commission prohibited the proposed acquisition of Aer Lingus by its competitor Ryanair. Following the prohibition decision, Ryanair still held a 29.4 per cent non-controlling stake in its competitor. Aer Lingus requested that the Commission order the divestment of this shareholding, arguing that the minority stake was being held to interfere with Aer Lingus's strategic and financial decisions and was

---

[102]   In the actual application of those provisions, however, the concept of boundaries between undertakings is essential, in the application of either s. 1 of the Sherman Act (15 USC §1) or s. 8 of the Clayton Act (15 USC §19).

weakening competition.[103] The Commission declared that it could not scrutinise such minority interests on a stand-alone basis as it only has jurisdiction to examine *ex ante* acquisitions conferring control.[104] This was later confirmed by the General Court, which recalled that 'the concept of concentration cannot be extended to cases in which control has not been obtained'.[105] In 2010, proceedings were also opened in the United Kingdom (UK). In 2012, the Office of Fair Trading (OFT) (later the Competition and Markets Authority (CMA)) referred the case to the Competition Commission.[106] The UK authorities found that Ryanair's stake conferred the possibility of exerting 'material influence', with regard to its ability to block special resolutions and to the sales of Heathrow's slots under the transaction agreement terms. This merger situation was found to lessen competition in the supply of air passenger services due to the interference of Ryanair in Aer Lingus's strategic commercial decisions.[107] Subsequently, the Competition Commission required Ryanair to divest the shareholding down to 5 per cent.[108] The Competition Appeal Tribunal dismissed Ryanair's appeal against the Competition Commission's decision.[109] The different approach to control adopted in the Ryanair case by the EU and UK authorities highlighted a lack of consistency between the approaches of member states and that of the EU with regard to minority interests.

Structural links that have a community dimension fall under the scope of the EU Merger Regulation if the acquisition brings about a 'lasting change in the control of the undertakings concerned and therefore in the structure of the market'.[110] According to the EU Merger Regulation, 'control shall be constituted by rights, contracts or any other means which, either separately or in combination and having regard to the considerations of fact or law involved, confer the possibility of exercising decisive influence on an undertaking, in particular by: (a) ownership or the right to use all or part of the assets of an undertaking; (b) rights or contracts which confer decisive influence on the composition, voting or decisions of the organs of an undertaking'.[111] Therefore, the existence of 'decisive influence' is central to the existence of control triggering the application of merger review. Interlocking directorates that confer influence are therefore theoretically part of merger control scrutiny.

In practice, the Commission considers that control may be established through different means: in addition to the acquisition of property rights, such as shares or

---

[103] Case T–411/07 *Aer Lingus Group Plc v. Commission* [2008] ECR II–41, paras. 62 and 64.
[104] *Ryanair /Aer Lingus* (Case COMP/M.4439) Commission Decision 2008/C 047/04 [2007] OJ C47/7.
[105] *Aer Lingus Group* v. *Commission*, para. 65.
[106] OFT, Press release, OFT refers Ryanair's minority stake in Aer Lingus to Competition Commission (15 June 2012), available at: https://webarchive.nationalarchives.gov.uk/20140402144835/; www.oft.gov.uk/news-and-updates/press/2012/47-12
[107] CC Report, Ryanair Holdings plc/Aer Lingus Group plc, 28 August 2013, para. 6.
[108] Ibid.
[109] *Ryanair Holdings plc* v. *Competition and Markets Authority* [2014] CAT 3.
[110] EU Merger Control Regulation, Recital 20.
[111] Ibid., Art. 2.

assets, control can be acquired on a factual basis by economic relationships.[112] Such an approach seems to echo the property rights theory of the firm, in which residual rights of control confer decision rights for their owner, when a situation not foreseen in the contract occurs. Ownership amounts to holding those residual rights of control.[113] As exemplified throughout this book, an approach based on the property rights theory is particularly insightful in cases in which the coincidence of ownership and control is not obvious.[114]

In the context of merger control, the acquisition of residual rights of control is an obvious way to confer on the owner 'decisive influence' in unforeseen situations. Voting rights can be used not only for decisions regarding the general policy orientation of a company, but also with respect to unforeseen situations, such as a decision to change a board member. In considering de facto situations leading to control, the EU Merger Regulation also seems to identify factual elements in which a company may hold some 'last resort' decisional power. For example, lease contracts that provide control over management or resources are considered as conferring control within the meaning of the EU Merger Regulation.[115] This means that consideration is given to which actors can ultimately make decisions regarding business operations and workers' assets. Control can also be established in relation to veto rights over strategic business decisions that are held in conjunction with management contracts.[116] It can be assumed that holding veto rights confers some sort of residual rights of control over the company, which, together with some power of oversight over the operations of the company, confer decisive influence in the sense of the EU Merger Regulation.

The question of ownership and control is crucial in minority shareholdings. The Commission notice specifically foresees the possibility of minority stakes conferring control 'in situations where specific rights are attached to this shareholding'.[117] The rights considered will typically enable the shareholder to determine the strategic commercial behaviour of the target, or grant the power to appoint more than half of the board members. For example, in *Accor/Wagon-Lits*, the Commission considered that the long-term management agreements entered into by the minority stakeholder conferred decisive influence over the target, because of the day-to-day oversight over the hotel's operation that included budgetary matters.[118] In *CCIE/GTE*, in which CCIE acquired 19 per cent of the voting

---

[112] Commission Consolidated Jurisdictional Notice under Council Regulation (EC) No 139/2004 on the control of concentrations between undertakings [2008] OJ C95/1, paras. 16–23.

[113] The theory of property rights is introduced at Section 2.3.3.

[114] The theoretical framework based on the property rights is introduced at Section 2.3.4 and is applied to parent–subsidiaries at Section 4.2.1 and to joint ventures at Section 5.2.1.

[115] Commission Notice [2008] OJ C95/1, para. 18.

[116] *Lehman Brothers/SCG/Starwood/Le Meridien* (Case COMP/M.3858) Commission Decision [2005] OJ L24/1, para. 9.

[117] Commission Notice [2008] OJ C95/1, para. 57.

[118] *Accor/Wagons-Lits* (Case COMP IV/M.12) Commission Decision 92/385/EEC [1992] OJ L204/1.

rights in GTE, the equity was held in conjunction with a permanent seat on the board, a right to appoint the CEO and the chairman, as well as veto rights on all essential decisions (the appointment and dismissal of board members and senior employees, material capital expenditure, the disposal of significant assets and approval of the annual budget).[119] By granting a substantial degree of decision-making power to the shareholder, those rights seem to echo the concept of residual rights of control. The Commission found that this acquisition constituted a concentration.

The previous developments illustrate that the EU Merger Regulation conditions its inquiry of minority shareholdings to the creation of a new 'firm', metaphorically, as echoed by the property rights theory of the firm. The underlying approach to minority shareholdings is that only partial acquisitions that lead to a change in market structure, via acquisition of either de jure or de facto control, will be scrutinised by the EU Merger Regulation. As a result, the acquisition of a minority interest that does not confer control is left unchallenged.

Pre-Existing Non-Controlling Participations

Pre-existing or acquired non-controlling stakes can be assessed as part of the overall anticompetitive effects of a merger.[120] Referring to previous case law, the Commission considered in *Newscorp/Telepiù* 'that any decision under the Merger Regulation must cover a transaction bringing about a concentration in its entirety, including minority shareholdings', which involves analysing their possible adverse effects in all relevant markets.[121] In a number of merger cases, pre-existing structural links were therefore found to raise anticompetitive concerns.[122] In *Dow/DuPont*, the Commission specifically discussed the impact of common shareholdings. Significant ownership links characterising the agrochemical industry were deemed to affect negatively the intensity of innovation competition. In addition, passive investors admitted that they exerted influence on individual companies, through active discussions with boards and management, with an industry-wide strategy. Such influence was exacerbated due to the dispersed structure of shareholdings.[123]

In addition, the Commission notice on remedies specifically addresses structural links: 'The divestiture of a minority shareholding in a joint venture may be necessary

---

[119]   *CCIE / GTE* (Case COMP IV/M.258) Commission Decision 92/C 258/15 [1992] OJ C258, para. 8.
[120]   This issue was critical in the Ryanair case: *Ryanair Holdings plc v. Competition and Markets Authority* [2014] CAT 3.
[121]   *Newscorp/Telepiù* (Case COMP/M.2876) Commission Decision 2004/311/EC [2003] OJ L110/73, paras. 278–9.
[122]   See, for example, *AXA/GRE* (Case COMP/M.1453) Commission Decision 2000/C30/05[1999] OJ C30/6; *Allianz/AGF* (Case IV/M.1082) Commission Decision 98/C246/04 [1998] C246/4; *Toshiba/Westinghouse* (Case COMP/M.4153) Commission Decision 2007/C010/01 [2006] OJ L24/1; *Glencore/Xstrata* (Case COMP/M.6541) Commission Decision 2014/C109/01 [2012] OJ C109/1; *Siemens/VA Tech* (Case COMP/M.3653) Commission Decision 2006/899/EC [2005] OJ L353/19.
[123]   *Dow/DuPont* (Case COMP/M.7932), pp. 5–10.

in order to sever a structural link with a major competitor or, similarly, the divestiture of a minority shareholding in a competitor."[124] The divestment of minority interests and the termination of interlocking directorships are examples of remedies imposed in the context of a merger raising competitive issues.[125]

While the Commission and courts grasp the potential anticompetitive effects of minority shareholdings that do not confer control, such effects are unchallenged on a stand-alone basis.[126] The existence of an enforcement gap results from the reliance of EU merger review on the concept of control – which excludes acquisitions that do not eliminate a market relationship.

5.3.2.1.2 STRUCTURAL LINKS UNDER ARTICLE 101 OF THE TFEU. Following the doctrine established in the *Philip Morris* case, share acquisitions that do not confer control can be captured by Article 101 of the TFEU, which prohibits anticompetitive agreements and concerted practices.[127] After presenting the Court's judgment in that case and the subsequent application of that ruling, this section will identify possible shortcomings of Article 101 of the TFEU with regard to capturing anticompetitive effects emanating from structural links. First, the reach of Article 101 of the TFEU is limited because coordinated effects seem to be persistently analysed through the lens of control. Other shortcomings relate to the difficulty of identifying the existence of an agreement between undertakings – or a clear market relationship between undertakings – in the context of structural links. The application of Article 101 of the TFEU to information exchange stemming from interlocking directorates will also be examined.

The *Philip Morris* Doctrine

The *Philip Morris* case concerned the acquisition (from Rembrandt) by Philip Morris of a 30.8 per cent share, corresponding to 24.9 per cent of the voting rights, in Rothmans International, another company operating in the market for cigarettes. The Commission cleared this agreement, subject to the following commitments: Philip Morris would not be represented in the management of Rothmans, and Philip Morris would not access sensitive information about Rothmans that might influence Philip Morris's strategic behaviour.[128] A complaint lodged by British-American Tobacco and Reynolds triggered a review of the case by the Court of

---

[124]   Commission Notice on remedies acceptable under Council Regulation (EC) No 139/2004 and under Commission Regulation (EC) No 802/2004 [2008] OJ C267/1, para. 58.

[125]   See, for example, *Glencore/Xstrata* (Case COMP/M.6541), para. 1, in which Glencore committed to divest its minority interest in Nyrstar as one of the remedies. In *AXA/GRE* (Case COMP/M.1453), one of the undertakings to address the competitive issues raised by the merger was that members of the board of directors nominated by GRE would resign upon their replacement by an individual, approved by the Commission, and not employed by AXA (para. 34).

[126]   G. D. Pini, 'Passive–Aggressive Investments: Minority Shareholdings and Competition Law', *European Business Law Review*, 23 (2012), 575, 653.

[127]   Cases 142 and 156/84 *British-American Tobacco/Reynolds* [1987] ECR 4487.

[128]   Ibid., para. 9.

Justice. The Court thereby admitted the possible scrutiny of anticompetitive effects of share agreements between competitors:

> Although the acquisition by one company of an equity interest in a competitor does not in itself constitute conduct restricting competition, such an acquisition may nevertheless serve as an instrument for influencing the commercial conduct of the companies in question so as to restrict or distort competition on the market on which they carry on business.[129]

At the time of this case, there was no merger control in EU competition law. In recognising the potential application of competition law provisions to acquisitions leading to control, the *Philip Morris* case constituted a stepping stone towards the creation of merger control as acquisitions potentially producing anticompetitive effects could be submitted to Articles 101 and 102 scrutiny.[130] In addition, in the *Philip Morris* case, the Court ruled that minority shareholdings may restrict competition if they enable commercial cooperation or require that companies take each other's interest into account in defining their commercial policy.[131] This means that as well as explicit commercial cooperation corporate arrangements that enable the exchange of sensitive information would restrict competition.[132] This part of the Court ruling remains of contemporary relevance in relation to non-controlling acquisitions, as it constitutes the only case in which share agreements were ruled to potentially fall within Article 101 (and Article 102) of the TFEU.[133]

In the specific circumstances of the case, the Court concluded that the share agreements did not confer control to Philip Morris over Rothmans, nor did the agreements require the parties to take each other's interest into account in defining their commercial strategy.[134] In its reasoning regarding the incentives produced by an investment in a competitor, the Court recognised the relevance of the unilateral effects arising from non-controlling investments.[135] However, no further analysis of the unilateral effects of the investment was conducted. In *Philip Morris*, the Court had a narrow interpretation of the scope of Article 101 of the TFEU: anticompetitive effects of minority interests seemed to arise strictly in relation to coordination or control. In that case, the Court focused on anticompetitive effects arising from de

---

[129] Ibid., para. 37.
[130] A. J. Burnside, 'Minority Shareholdings: An Overview of EU and National Case Law'. e-Competitions N° 566761 (2013), 1.
[131] *Philip Morris*, para. 39.
[132] T. Staahl Gabrielsen, E. Hjelmeng, and L. Sorgard, 'Rethinking Minority Share Ownership and Interlocking Directorships – The Scope for Competition Law Intervention', European Law Review, 36 (2011), 839, 849.
[133] Ibid., 847.
[134] *Philip Morris*, paras. 49–54.
[135] Ibid., para. 50: 'Philip Morris, because of its share in the profits of Rothmans International, has an interest in the success of that company.'

facto control, cooperation and a long-term plan to collude or to take-over a competitor.[136]

Application to Minority Share Acquisitions

In subsequent cases, the Commission applied the *Philip Morris* doctrine to minority share acquisitions. In such cases the Commission assessed whether the acquisition of minority shares had the effect of coordinating and influencing the companies' competitive behaviour. A shortcoming of the doctrine in its later application is the reliance (direct or indirect) on the concept of control. The *BT/MCI* case concerned the acquisition by British Telecom of a 20 per cent equity stake, with proportional board representation, in its competitor MCI. The Commission confirmed the relevance of the *Philip Morris* case by stating that Article 101(1) of the TFEU may apply to agreements on the sale or purchase of shares 'given the specific contractual and market contexts of each case, if the competitive behaviour of the parties is to be coordinated or influenced'.[137] The Commission subsequently assessed the question of coordination, as well as that of influence and control, and concluded that there was no restriction of competition.[138] In that case, the concept of influence seems to have been understood as a synonym of de facto control. The question was whether the acquisition could confer influence over the target company's activities,[139] but each company's influence over the other's unilateral behaviour was left out of the scope of the doctrine. In *Olivetti/Digital*, the Commission cleared a cooperation agreement together with an acquisition of an 8 per cent share by Digital in Olivetti – two companies active in the field of computer systems.[140] Here again, the Commission examined whether the agreement would lead to a change in control, and whether the share acquisition would enable the coordination of competitive behaviour or the exchange of information through the nomination by Digital of a board representative.[141] Digital's representative was found not to have any control over commercial management, as they would be involved in board meetings that were strictly responsible for financial review only four times per year.[142] The impact on companies' competitive behaviour is therefore still analysed through the lens of control.

Unilateral effects, such as an incentive to compete less fiercely on prices, stemming from an acquisition of a competitor, or from common institutional ownership, remain unchallenged. In *Philip Morris*, the Court referred to possible anticompetitive effects of partial acquisitions when they 'serve as an instrument for influencing

[136] A. Ezrachi and D. Gilo, 'EC Competition Law and the Regulation of Passive Investments Among Competitors', *Oxford Journal of Legal Studies*, 26 (2006), 327.
[137] *BT/MCI* (Case COMP IV/34.857) Commission Decision 94/579/EC [1994] OJ L223/36, para. 44.
[138] Ibid., para. 44.
[139] Ezrachi and Gilo, 'EC Competition Law and the Regulation of Passive Investments', 241.
[140] *Olivetti/Digital* (Case COMP IV/34.410) Commission Decision 94/771/EC [1994] OJ L309/24.
[141] Ibid., para. 27.
[142] Ibid., para. 26.

the commercial conduct of companies'. In that and subsequent cases, the term 'influence' is understood as a proxy for de facto control. Such influence over commercial conduct could also be interpreted as an influence over pricing behaviour: an acquisition of a competing company is indeed capable of influencing the acquirer's pricing behaviour. Therefore, the influence over a company's competitive behaviour does not just amount to the impact on operations and management. A share acquisition can also influence the independence of a company's pricing behaviour, irrespective of whether it confers control over internal affairs. As has been discussed, institutional investors can also use various channels of influence over competitors, including active participation in management meetings, which go beyond the scope of traditional corporate control.

In the interpretation of *Philip Morris*, the unilateral effects remain unchallenged. Such a shortcoming relates to the insistence on looking at minority shareholdings exclusively through the lens of control and coordination. A wider interpretation of the concept of influence beyond the realm of traditional corporate control could enable Article 101 to capture anticompetitive unilateral effects of minority shareholdings.[143]

The Condition of the Existence of an Agreement/Concerted Practice Between Undertakings

In the cases that have been discussed previously, minority interests were analysed as part of a bigger transaction that clearly involved an agreement between undertakings. However, if a minority interest is to be examined in isolation, the application of Article 101 of the TFEU still requires the existence of a concerted practice or agreement between two separate undertakings. This may be complex to assess in the context of minority share acquisitions. Share agreements are not necessarily contracted between undertakings, in the sense of Article 101 of the TFEU. In addition, the 'meeting of the minds' requirement for finding an agreement or a concerted practice may not be easily established.[144]

The Existence of an Undertaking

Holding or purchasing shares does not, in itself, constitute an economic activity for the purpose of Article 101 of the TFEU.[145] In *Reuter/BASF*, however, Dr Reuter, controlling his company Reuter-Holding GmbH, was considered 'as an undertaking since he engages in economic activity through those firms of the Elastomer group which remain under his control'.[146] In *Vaessen/Moris*, the principal shareholder and managing director, Mr Moris, held a patent relating to a process that he licensed to his own

---

[143]   Such unilateral effects would still be the outcome of a share agreement between two competitors, which differs from unilateral conduct that could not fall within the scope of Article 101 anyway.

[144]   A. Tzanaki, 'The Legal Treatment of Minority Shareholdings Under EU Competition Law: Present and Future' in *Essays in Honour of Professor Panayiotis I. Kanellopoulos* (Sakkoulas Publications, 2015), pp. 861–86; Staahl Gabrielsen, Hjelmeng, and Sorgard, 'Rethinking Minority Share Ownership', 851.

[145]   Case C–22/04 *Cassa di Risparmio di Firenze and Others* [2006] ECR I–289, para. 111.

[146]   *Reuter/BASF* (Case COMP IV/28.996) Commission Decision 76/743/EEC [1976] OJ L254, para. II.1.

company. As such, he 'exploit[ed] his invention commercially via his company and in this way he carr[ied] on the business of an undertaking'.[147] Both Mr Moris and his company ALMO qualified as undertakings. In both cases the controlling shareholder and the company entered into agreements. But the Commission seemed to imply that, in exceptional cases, the controlling shareholder could constitute an undertaking for the purpose of Article 101(1) of the TFEU. In those cases, controlling shareholdings were thought of as performing an economic activity, consisting of the 'commercial exploitation of the results of the shareholder's activity'.[148] Most recently, the discussion about whether a controlling shareholder can constitute an undertaking separately from its company has been raised in the case *HFB Holding* v. *Commission*. The Commission found that four companies had formed a de facto undertaking as they were all controlled, directly or indirectly, by the same individual, Mr Henss. The applicants asserted that Mr Henss could not be considered as an undertaking, in his capacity as the majority shareholder in two companies. The General Court confirmed the Commission's position that the four companies could be considered as an undertaking, as they were run by the same individual pursuing a single economic activity. However, the Court did not consider it relevant to discuss further whether Mr Henss could himself qualify as an undertaking for the purpose of Article 101(1) of the TFEU.[149]

Only under very specific circumstances, and only in the case of majority shareholdings, have the courts and the Commission considered the possibility that a controlling shareholder constitutes an undertaking on their own. Authorities are reluctant to 'pierce the corporate veil' in defining a shareholder as an undertaking separately from their company. The first difficulty may therefore be being in the presence of two or more undertakings within the meaning of Article 101 of the TFEU.

The Existence of an Agreement or Collusive Practice

The main obstacle to the application of Article 101 of the TFEU is distinguishing unilateral from joint conduct, through the finding of an agreement or a concerted practice.[150] Purchasing minority shares in a company on the stock exchange does not necessarily involve a 'mental consensus' or a 'concurrence of wills' between the two undertakings. The sale of shares to a competitor may occur due to the decision by a shareholder to sell their shares, independently from the company as a whole.[151]

---

[147]   *Vaessen/Moris* (Case COMP IV/C-29.290) Commission Decision 79/86/EEC [1979] OJ L019/32, para. 12.

[148]   F. Caronna, 'Article 81 as a Tool for Controlling Minority Cross Shareholdings Between Competitors', *European Law Review*, 29 (2004), 485, 497.

[149]   Case T-9/99 *HFB* v. *Commission* [2002] ECR II-1487, paras. 54–67.

[150]   'The concept of concerted practice does in fact imply the existence of reciprocal contacts [. . .]. That condition is met where one competitor discloses its future intentions or conduct on the market to another when the latter requests it or, at the very least, accepts it' (Joined Cases T-25/95 and others *Cimenteries CBR* [2000] ECR II-491, para. 1849).

[151]   Caronna, 'Article 81 as a Tool for Controlling Minority Cross Shareholdings Between Competitors', 494; Elhauge, 'Essay: Horizontal Shareholding', however, takes the view that the requirement of agreement or concerted practice is no obstacle to the application of Article 101 of the TFEU.

Regarding interlocking directorates, if the nomination of a board member emanates from an appointment by the general assembly of shareholders, this will not constitute an agreement between undertakings. If the right to nominate a board member is part of a shareholding agreement, the board nomination may constitute an agreement between undertakings and may therefore fall within the prohibition under Article 101(1) of the TFEU.

A relevant question is whether flows of information stemming from structural links could fall within the scope of Article 101 of the TFEU. The mere exchange of information between competitors can constitute a restriction of competition by 'object', if the information relates to individualised and future price information.[152] In practice, though, to what extent could strategic information received at a board meeting or as part of a share agreement be in breach of Article 101 of the TFEU? In *Suiker Unie*, the Court established that Article 101 of the TFEU 'preclude[d] any direct or indirect contact between [competitors], the object or effect whereof is either to influence the conduct on the market [. . .] or to disclose to such competitor the course of conduct which they themselves have decided to adopt or contemplate adopting on the market'.[153] In addition, *Hüls* provides that the presumption that competitors take into account the information in determining their conduct is even greater 'where the undertakings concert together on a regular basis over a long period'.[154] Therefore the nature of the contact is irrelevant as long as such contact produces an anticompetitive effect. A concerted practice may exist even in the event of a passive reception of information, provided that there is reciprocity of acceptance.[155] Financial ownership and interlocking directorships may amount to direct and close contact between undertakings. Depending on the nature of the information disclosed on the occasion of board meetings, or of general assembly of shareholders, and the manner in which it is circulated within the companies, such conduct can, in principle, meet the requirements of a concerted practice.

Having a common board member, as part of or separate from a minority shareholding, does not bring the two companies within the same economic entity. Therefore, information exchange between those two companies cannot be considered as an intracorporate relationship precluding the application of Article 101 of the TFEU.[156] It is, however, difficult to consider that the mere exchange of information during a board or shareholders' meeting, which is internal to the company, can be sufficient to establish a concerted practice. To our knowledge, there is no case in which a concerted practice has been identified in such a context, reflecting the

---

[152] Communication from the Commission – Guidelines on the applicability of Article 101 of the Treaty on the Functioning of the European Union to horizontal co-operation agreements: Text with EEA relevance OJ C11/1 ('Horizontal Guidelines'), General Principles on the competitive assessment of information exchange.

[153] Case 40/73 *Suiker Unie* v. *Commission* [1975] ECR 1663, para. 174.

[154] Case C–199/92P *Hüls* [1999] ECR I–4287, para. 162.

[155] See n. 150.

[156] Staahl Gabrielsen, Hjelmeng and Sorgard, 'Rethinking Minority Share Ownership', 857.

practical difficulty for competition authorities in producing tangible evidence of a concerted practice based on the mere existence of structural links.[157] In summary, Article 101 of the TFEU theoretically applies to an information exchange relating to structural links, but the establishment of an agreement or concerted practice between undertakings may prove difficult.[158]

5.3.2.1.3 ARTICLE 102 OF THE TFEU. Pursuant to the *Philip Morris* doctrine, Article 102 of the TFEU, which prohibits abuses of a dominant position, may also apply to minority interests, if the acquisition confers the possibility of reinforcing a dominant position.[159] In that case, there is a close interaction between concerns of collusion and the abuse of a dominant position raised by the acquisition. In *Warner Lambert/ Gillette* the Commission found that Gillette had abused its dominant position in the context of a transaction involving a series of agreements between Gillette and its competitor Eemland. The agreements also involved the acquisition by Gillette of a 22 per cent stake in Eemland. The Commission held that the 'structure of the wet-shaving market in the Community has been changed by the creation of a link between Gillette and its leading competitor'.[160] The equity, together with Gillette being Eemland's main creditor, conferred on Gillette 'at least some influence on Eemland's commercial policy', which was found to be problematic.[161] Although the partial acquisition did not confer voting rights, the influence was established based on financial reasoning. In contrast with previous cases applying the *Philip Morris* doctrine, 'some influence' was sufficient for the partial acquisition to raise competitive concerns. Some argued that this illustrated a lower standard of control, enabling the extension of scrutiny over minority acquisitions.[162] This would imply that Article 102 of the TFEU would better capture the anticompetitive effects raised by non-controlling shareholdings. An important limitation, however, lies in the prerequisite of dominance for the application of Article 102 of the TFEU.

In addition, anticompetitive effects could be reviewed in the context of collective dominance, the abuse of which may also be in breach of Article 102.[163] Collective

---

[157]   Thépot et al., 'Cumul de mandats d'administrateur et risques anticoncurrentiels'.

[158]   Elhauge clearly states that the requirement of concerted practice or agreement is no obstacle in the case of structural links. Although he is right in theory, in practice the obstacles presented complicate the reach of Article 101 of the TFEU to structural links: E. Elhauge, 'Tackling Horizontal Shareholding: An Update and Extension to the Sherman Act and EU Competition Law', Background Paper for 128th meeting of the OECD Competition Committee (2017).

[159]   *Philip Morris*, para. 39.

[160]   *Warner-Lambert/Gillette and Bic/Gillette and others* (Case COMP IV/33.440 and IV/33.486) Commission Decision 93/252/EEC [1993] OJ L116/21, para. 23.

[161]   Ibid., para. 24.

[162]   Ezrachi and Gilo, 'EC Competition Law and the Regulation of Passive Investments', 342 and B. E. Hawk et al., '"Controlling" the Shifting Sands: Minority Shareholdings Under EEC Competition Law', *Fordham International Law Journal*, 17 (1993), 321.

[163]   'Any abuse by one *or more undertakings* of a dominant position within the internal market or in a substantial part of it shall be prohibited' [emphasis added] (Article 102 of the TFEU).

dominance can exist when economic links between undertakings make them together hold a dominant position vis-à-vis other competitors in the same market.[164] In *Irish Sugar*, a situation of collective dominance was established based on a combination of economic and corporate ties between two companies, including interlocking directorates.[165] Therefore, structural links falling short of Article 101 of the TFEU could be theoretically be challenged under Article 102, even if undertakings are individually not dominant. However, the main difficulty would be to establish an abuse of that position of collective dominance. To date, there are only very few cases of collective dominance. One of the reasons is that anticompetitive issues raised in such cases may not fit the analytical framework and legal standards developed in cases of single undertaking abuses, more focused on exclusionary conduct. Cases of collective dominance based on structural links would, instead, be exploitative types of abuses, typically involving higher prices, which are far more difficult to establish.[166]

Elhauge, however, argues that a case of excessive pricing could have better substantial grounds where high prices result from structural links rather than from monopoly power or tacit collusion. High prices set by a single company may well be the outcome of a successful innovative process, which authorities do not want to deter. High prices resulting from tacit collusion in oligopolistic markets are deemed to be the natural adaptation of companies to specific market conditions. Effects of structural links do not result from prima facie efficient and desirable conduct, nor are they the outcome of natural and inevitable market processes.[167] However, the usual difficulties relating to administrability, and the willingness of authorities to bring exploitative abuse cases, remain. In addition, the limited decisional practice on collective dominance provides little guidance on how to handle the anticompetitive effects of structural links.

5.3.2.1.4 CONCLUSION ON THE REACH OF ARTICLES 101 AND 102. To sum up, the limits in application of Article 101 of the TFEU relate to the difficulty in finding an agreement between undertakings, as the transaction or relationship may not be reciprocal and may only involve some shareholders acting independently of their company. Coordinated effects stemming from information flows may be caught, but there is no case of violation based on the type of information usually communicated within the private remit of a board, or of shareholders' meetings. Additionally, applications of the doctrine laid down in *Philip Morris* remain focused on the concept of control of one undertaking over the other. As a result, problematic unilateral effects of partial acquisitions may be left unchallenged. Article 102 of the TFEU, potentially enabling an extension of the concept of influence to capture

---

[164] O. Okeoghene, 'Collective Dominance Clarified?', *Cambridge Law Journal*, 63(1) (2004), 44.
[165] *Irish Sugar* (Case COMP 97/624) Commission Decision 7/624/EC [1997] OJ L258/1, para. 112.
[166] Jones and Sufrin, *EU Competition Law*, p. 707.
[167] Elhauge, 'Tackling Horizontal Shareholding', 22.

non-cooperative effects, applies only in the context of dominance. Collective dominance may provide a better avenue for controlling structural links in concentrated markets; this would, however, require willingness from the Commission to re-open the excessive prices line of cases. The current enforcement shortcomings stem from the paradigm underlying the provisions, which require either the existence of an agreement between two undertakings or the creation of a new undertaking. A comparison with the United States will show whether abstracting from the strict undertaking or control framework enables the anticompetitive effects of structural links to be captured better.

5.3.2.2 The Substantive Reach of US Antitrust Law

5.3.2.2.1 PARTIAL ACQUISITIONS. In the United States, minority shareholdings are submitted to the scrutiny of both section 1 of the Sherman Act and section 7 of the Clayton Act, along with the Hart-Scott-Rodino Act, which establishes the federal premerger notification programme.[168] Section 1 of the Sherman Act applies to anticompetitive links between competitors, including structural links:

> Where, as here, merging companies are major competitive factors in a relevant market, the elimination of significant competition between them, by merger or consolidation, itself constitutes a violation of §1 of the Sherman Act.[169]

Section 7 of the Clayton Act prohibits acquisitions of 'the whole or any part' of shares of assets the effect of which may be to substantially lessen competition.[170] No threshold of control or minimum share of stock is required for the application of section 7.[171] Partial acquisitions not conferring control are thus within the scope of this prohibition, which has been confirmed by the Supreme Court.[172] On a number of occasions, the US state and federal courts have therefore rejected equity acquisitions of less than 25 per cent in a competitor.[173] More recently, the Department of Justice and the Federal Trade Commission have reviewed and entered into consent orders limiting partial acquisitions below 25 per cent.[174] Even though courts have

---

[168]   15 USC §18a.

[169]   15 USC §1; *US v. First National Bank & Trust* 376 US 665, 671–2 (1964).

[170]   15 USC §18.

[171]   However, the Hart-Scott-Rodino Act sets some turnover thresholds: 15 USC §18a.

[172]   *US v. El. du Pont de Nemours & Co* 353 US 586, 592 (1957).

[173]   Ibid. 602–11 (1957) (23 per cent stock acquisition breaches s. 7 of the Clayton Act); *Denver & Rio Grande* 387 US 485, 501–4 (1967). (20 per cent stock acquisition warrants ICC assessment of anticompetitive effects under s. 7); *American Crystal Co v. Cuban-American Sugar Co* 259 F 2d 524 (1958) (23 per cent stock acquisition infringes s. 7 of the Clayton Act).

[174]   See, for example: *US v. Gillette Co* Proposed Final Judgment, Stipulation and Competitive Impact Statement, 55 Fed Reg 12,567, 12,569 (1990) (imposing restrictions to sterilise acquisition of 23 per cent non-voting shares); *US v. MCI Communications Corp* Proposed Final Judgment, Stipulation and Competitive Impact Statement, 59 Fed Reg 33,009 (1994) (restrictions imposed on 20 per cent stock holding); *Time Warner Inc* Proposed Consent Agreement with Analysis to Aid Public Comment, 62 Fed Reg 67,868, 67,871 (1996) (requiring divestiture of 7.5 per cent equity

addressed this issue since the 1950s, the agencies have only recently introduced an explicit reference to possible anticompetitive effects in their guidelines. In its Antitrust Guidelines on Cooperation between Competitors, the FTC draws attention to direct equities in competitors that 'reduce the incentives of the participants [to a joint venture] to compete with each other'.[175] Furthermore, the updated version of the Horizontal Merger Guidelines of 2010 introduced a specific section on partial acquisitions:

> Partial acquisitions that do not result in effective control may nevertheless present significant competitive concerns and may require a somewhat distinct analysis from that applied to full mergers or to acquisitions involving effective control.[176]

The *Dairy Farmers* case provides a good example of the manner in which the US courts consider anticompetitive effects of non-controlling minority interests in a competitor.[177] In 2003, the Department of Justice filed a complaint against Dairy Farmers of America (DFA), alleging that DFA's partial acquisition in Southern Belle breached section 7 of the Clayton Act. DFA is a milk marketing organisation, and the largest dairy farmer cooperative in the United States. Its primary activity is to secure a steady sale of raw milk for its farmer members at the highest price. To do so, DFA began vertically integrating and investing in dairy businesses. Instead of wholly acquiring downstream dairies, DFA decided to take 50 per cent ownership and leave the daily operations to experienced business partners.[178] In that context, in 2001, DFA acquired 50 per cent of ownership of the dairy Flav-O-Rich, and other business partners were put in charge of daily operations. In 2002, DFA acquired, through its subsidiaries, a 50 per cent controlling interest in Southern Belle. For many school districts in Kentucky and Tennessee, Southern Belle and Flav-O-Rich were the only two school milk competitors. According to the Department of Justice, the partial interests of DFA in the two rival dairies eliminated competition in the supply of school milk.[179] In addition, it was argued that DFA would have the incentive and ability unilaterally to raise prices, as it would be indifferent to the school district purchasing from either dairy.

Prior to the district court trial, DFA changed the governance of its partial interest from voting to non-voting interests in Southern Belle. Therefore, DFA could no longer vote on any matter or sit on Southern Belle's board. On the basis of the revised

position or acceptance of capped non-voting shares); *US* v. *AT&T Corp* Proposed Final Judgment, Stipulation and Competitive Impact Statement, 64 Fed Reg 2506 (1999) (full divestiture of 23.5 per cent stock holding). *US* v. *TC Group, LLC*, Decision and Order, 72 Fed Reg 4508 (2007) (challenged the acquisition of a 22.6 per cent equity interest in KMI by private equity funds managed by the Carlyle Group and Riverstone Holdings LLC because of KMI's ability to appoint board members in two competitors and exchange competitively sensitive non-public information).
[175] FTC, Antitrust Guidelines on Cooperation between Competitors (2000), 3.34(c) 'Financial Interests in the Collaboration or in Other Participants'.
[176] Department of Justice, FTC, Horizontal Merger Guidelines (2010), s. 13.
[177] *US* v. *Dairy Farmers of America, Inc* 426 F 3d 850, 852–5 (6th Circuit 2005).
[178] OECD Policy Roundtable, 'Minority Shareholdings' (2008), 177.
[179] Department of Justice complaint, *US* v. *Dairy Farmers*, No 03-206-KSF, paras. 2 and 3.

terms of the acquisition, the District Court concluded that the acquisition did not 'increase the percentage of the market that DFA "controls" or even enhance DFA's ability to influence the market because DFA's non-voting interest in Southern Belle does not give it any control over the business decisions made by Southern Belle'.[180] Consequently, the District Court rejected the Department of Justice's complaint, concluding that the transaction did not raise any competitive issues. The case was appealed by the US government, and the Court of Appeal reversed the judgment, considering that the lower court should have examined the original instead of the revised terms of the partial acquisition. While it accepted that 'control or influence may be the mechanism through which an acquirer causes competitive harm, the Sixth Circuit [did] not agree with the district court's conclusion that a lack of control or influence precludes a Section 7 violation'.[181] Referring to the Supreme Court in the *du Pont* judgment,[182] the Court of Appeal stated that 'even without control or influence, an acquisition may still lessen competition'.[183] Indeed, the Court considered that the voluntary abandonment of voting rights by DFA did not remedy the competitive concerns: DFA and its partner in Southern Belle, which would retain all voting rights under the revised terms of the transaction, had 'closely aligned interests to maximise profits via anticompetitive behaviour'. In addition, DFA could 'leverage its position as Southern Belle's financier to control or influence Southern Belle's decision'. Therefore, the Court considered that this might be a 'mechanism that causes anticompetitive behaviour other than control'.[184] DFA was subsequently required to divest its 50 per cent interest in Southern Belle.

The importance of that case lies in the assessment of anticompetitive effects independently of the mere concept of control. The subsequent assessment first of the controlling and then of the non-controlling partial interest by the Sixth Circuit provides an interesting point of comparison. In analysing the effect of the revised agreement – or non-controlling interest, the Court had to move away from the concept of control and analyse the change in incentives resulting from the acquisition.[185] This case confirms that any partial acquisition can potentially reduce competition, either by way of control, or by way of another 'mechanism'.[186] While scrutiny by the EU Merger Regulation depends explicitly upon the creation of control, US antitrust law adopts the opposite view: that acquisition of control is not necessary for a violation of section 7.[187] Therefore US merger control clearly distances itself from the paradigm of

---

[180] *United States v Dairy Farmers of America* 2004 WL 2186215 (ED Ky 2004) 3.
[181] US v. Dairy Farmers of America, Inc 426 F 3d 850, (6th Circuit 2005) 859.
[182] US v. El du Pont de Nemours & Co.
[183] US v. Dairy Farmers of America, Inc 426 F 3d 850, (6th Circuit 2005) 860.
[184] Ibid., 862.
[185] J. G. Krauss and C. T. Cronheim, 'Partial Acquisitions After Dairy Farmers: Got Answers?', *Antitrust* magazine, ABA Section of Antitrust Law [2006], 49, 52.
[186] US v. Dairy Farmers of America, Inc 426 F 3d 850, (6th Circuit 2005) 862.
[187] US v. El du Pont de Nemours; Dairy Farmers. However, this does not mean that the concept of control or influence is not important in the substantial competitive assessment: 'Control or influence may be the mechanism through which an acquirer causes competitive harm' (*Dairy Farmers* case).

intra-inter undertaking relationships on which EU merger control is based, and adopts a different paradigm focusing on anticompetitive effects.[188]

'Solely for Investment Purposes' Acquisition

Acquisition solely for investment purposes may benefit from a substantive and filing notification exemption. What are the implications for acquisitions by competitors or institutional investors?

Substantive Exemption

Section 7 stipulates that acquisitions 'solely for investment' purposes are exempted from the prohibition, provided that persons are 'not using the same *by voting or otherwise* to bring about, or in attempting to bring about, the substantial lessening of competition'.[189] It has been clarified that the 'solely for investment' element is narrowly construed, requiring a complete lack of influence over management. Therefore, investors without control but having a direct or indirect ability to reduce competition would not benefit from this exemption. In addition, acquisitions solely for investment purposes will also be challenged if they actually restrict competition. This exception is therefore rather understood as a different liability standard, requiring *actual* rather than *potential* lessening of competition, rather than a true exemption.[190]

Filing Exemption

In addition, solely for investment purposes acquisitions of 10 per cent and less are exempt from the filing notification requirement set out in the Hart-Scott-Rodino Act. A filing exemption, however, does not preclude the violation of section 7 if the acquisition does have anticompetitive effects, as set out above. According to further rules adopted by the Federal Trade Commission and the Department of Justice, a financial ownership is acquired 'solely for the purpose of investment' if the person holding or acquiring such voting securities has no intention of participating in the formulation, determination, or direction of the basic business decisions of the issue.[191] If the acquirer is an institutional investor, the exemption is raised to 15 per cent on condition that they do not participate in business decisions. While mere voting stock will not amount to participation in business decisions, representatives of investors on the board, or right to nominations, will preclude the application of the exemption.[192] However, this means that investors holding up to 10–15 per cent with an equivalent share of voting rights may not need to file a notification. In view of the recent empirical studies on possible negative impacts of financial ownership, the exemption should be narrowed down, so that the notification requirement comes into line with associated anticompetitive effects.[193] In 2015, the

---

[188]   For discussion of the possible explanations behind such different approaches, see Section 5.3.2.4.
[189]   15 USC §18.
[190]   Elhauge, 'Essay: Horizontal Shareholding', 1305.
[191]   16 CFR §801.1(i)(1) (2015).
[192]   Premerger Notification; Reporting and Waiting Period Requirements, 43 Fed. Reg. 33,450,33,465.
[193]   Elhauge, 'Essay: Horizontal Shareholding', 1308.

Federal Trade Commission found that a 0.2 per cent acquisition by a hedge fund had failed to be notified; the fund had gauged interest for candidates to CEO or board positions, amounting to interference with business decisions.[194]

In summary, US antitrust law has jurisdiction to address anticompetitive effects stemming from financial acquisitions not conferring control. Even the existence of a passive investment, although exempted from the notification requirement under certain conditions, does not preclude the challenge of its actual anticompetitive effects. Indeed, the Federal Trade Commission recently ordered the divestment of assets over anticompetitive concerns arising from common ownership links held by the parties in two close competitors in the market for a third-party paid referral service for senior living facilities.[195] However, the analysis of such effects may be challenging in practice. Some advocate the need to use a modified Herfindahl-Hirschman Index to incorporate ownership links into the measure of concentration; and to adjust thresholds accordingly.[196] The ongoing debate on the question of common ownership link also reflects the difficulty, in practice, of intervening on links that are so closely related to corporate finance matters.

5.3.2.3 Interlocking Directorates

Interlocking directorates are subject to a specific provision. Section 8 of the Clayton Act prohibits any 'person' from simultaneously serving as a director or officer of two competing corporations.[197] The degree of competition required for the application of section 8 is such that its elimination 'by agreement between [the companies] would constitute a violation of any antitrust laws'.[198] The section 8 prohibition applies only to companies of a certain size.[199] In addition, the section does not apply when the overlap between the competing companies is *de minimis*.[200]

The United States has a particular approach to interlocking directorates, a specific provision on which exists in only very few jurisdictions.[201] In addition, those

[194] FTC, Third Point Funds Agree to Settle FTC Charges that They Violated U.S. Pre-merger Notification Requirements (2015), available at: https://perma.cc/F9HZ-S8YP
[195] FTC, Red Ventures Holdco and Bankrate.
[196] Salop and O'Brien, 'Competitive Effects of Partial Ownership'; Elhauge, 'Essay: Horizontal Shareholding'; OECD, 'Common Ownership by Institutional Investors and Its Impact on Competition', 31.
[197] 15 USC §19(a)(1)(A).
[198] Ibid. §19(a)(1)(B).
[199] The Act applies if each of the corporations has capital, surplus and undivided profits of more than $10 million, adjusted for inflation.
[200] '(A) the competitive sales of either corporation are less than $1,000,000, adjusted for inflation; (B) the competitive sales of either corporation are less than 2 per centum of that corporation's total sales; or (C) the competitive sales of each corporation are less than 4 per centum of that corporation's total sales.'
[201] Japan: Act on Prohibition of Private Monopolization and Maintenance of Fair Trade, Act No 54 of 1947, ch. IV, Art. 13; Indonesia: Indonesia Competition Law No 5 of 1999, Art. 26; Italy (financial sector): Art. 36 of Decree Law No 201 of 6 December 2011, converted into Law No 214/2011: 'Protection of competition and personal cross-shareholdings in credit and financial markets.'

jurisdictions enable the interlock to be justified based on a lack of competitive injury, which contrasts with the 'per se' prohibition in section 8.[202] A brief historical background will shed some light on the US antitrust peculiarity. The introduction of section 8 in 1914 is closely related to concerns about monopolies in a period of broad public mistrust in business.[203] Following a law proposal by the Democratic Party in 1908, all three political parties called for legislation on interlocking directorates in 1912. In that context, several reports were issued to publicise the scope of interlocking directorates in sectors such as the railroad and steel markets, as well as in financial institutions.[204]

Section 8 is the outcome of a political and legislative process, largely influenced by the work of Louis Brandeis, adviser to President Wilson. His position with regard to the harm created by interlocking directorates was as follows:

> The practice of interlocking directorates is the root of many evils. It offends laws human and divine. Applied to rival corporations, it tends to the suppression of competition and to violation of the Sherman law. Applied to corporations which deal with each other, it tends to disloyalty and to violation of the fundamental law that no man can serve two masters. In either event it tends to inefficiency; for it removes incentives and destroys soundness of judgment. It is undemocratic; for it rejects the platform: 'A fair field – and no favors' – substituting the pull of privilege for the push of manhood.[205]

In an address to Congress, President Wilson defended the necessity for stricter antitrust laws with the necessity to 'open the field to scores of men who have been obliged to serve when their abilities entitled them to direct'. Interlocking directorates were then perceived as an obstacle to the opportunities that the American economy was supposed to provide.[206] Therefore, much broader concerns than unilateral and coordinated effects, also including the issue of conflicts of interests between shareholders and directors, drove the introduction of section 8. The Act that was finally adopted in 1914 reflected a narrower approach taken by Congress, to limit the scope of the prohibition to certain types of interlocks.[207] The last amendment of the Act, in 1990, was aimed at providing greater exceptions to the 'per se' prohibitions (raising the jurisdictional threshold and exempting interlock from having *de minimis* overlap) while extending the prohibition to officers in addition to directors.[208]

---

[202] American Bar Association Section of Antitrust Law, *Interlocking Directorates: Handbook on Section 8 of the Clayton Act* (ABA Publishing, 2011), pp. 94–6: except for Italy, which has a 'per se' prohibition of interlocks in the financial sector.
[203] Ibid., p. 1.
[204] See, for example, the Stanley Committee and Pujo Committee reports; ibid., p. 3.
[205] L. D. Brandeis, *Other People's Money and How Bankers Use It* (Seven Treasures Publications, 1914), p. 51.
[206] A. H. Travers, 'Interlocks in Corporate Management and the Antitrust Laws', *Texas Law Review*, 46 (1968), 819, 830.
[207] ABA Section of Antitrust Law, p. 4.
[208] Ibid., pp. 8–9.

Section 8 of the Clayton Act is enforced by counsel to corporations, and there has been very little litigation.[209] Private litigation cases show that section 8 is closely related to issues of corporate governance. Claims have typically been lodged by corporations in order to prevent an acquisition or a proxy fight, or to remove an interlocked director; they have also been brought by shareholders of an alleged interlocked company to reject a merger or in support of a derivative action.[210] For example, recent investigations by the Federal Trade Commission led to the resignation from the board of Google of Arthur Levinson, a member of Apple's board. Google's CEO Eric Schmidt, who was director of both companies, stepped down from Apple's board.[211] In 2016, the Department of Justice obtained the restructuring of a transaction that would have given a company the right to appoint a member on its competitor's board.[212] In addition, anticompetitive effects of interlocking directorates that may not be reached by section 8 can be reviewed under section 1 of the Sherman Act as well as under section 5 of the Federal Trade Commission Act.[213] A specific historical and economic context in which the US provision emerged explains the far-reaching prohibition of interlocking directorates between competitors, irrespective of whether they actually harm competition.

US scrutiny of anticompetitive interlocks is therefore independent of the paradigm of market or intracorporate relationship. In the EU, interlocking directorates may be challenged only if they raise competitive concerns, either as part of a merger transaction, or *ex post* if leading to information exchange. Thus, the review of interlocking directorates in the EU once again depends on the existence of a change in control, or on the establishment of an agreement or concerted practice between undertakings. Should further regulation be needed, discussions need to take into account the specific features of the corporate landscape, as well as the possible legal constraints exerted by national corporate laws.[214]

[209]   Ibid., p. 2. Cases include *US v. W T Grant Co* 345 US 629 (1953); *SCM Corp v. FTC* 565 F 2d 807 (1977); *TRW, Inc v. FTC* 647 F 2d 942 (9th Circ 1981); *Borg-Warner Corp v. FTC* 746 F 2d 108 (2nd Circ 1984).
[210]   ABA Section of Antitrust Law, pp. 22–3; e.g. *Charming Shoppes v. Crescendo Partners* II 557 T Supp 2d 621 (ED Pa 200) (attempt to prevent an acquisition or proxy fight); *Protectoseal Co v. Barancik* 484 F 2d 585 (7th Circ 1973) (or to remove an interlocked director).
[211]   FTC, 'Statement of FTC Chairman Jon Leibowitz Regarding the Announcement that Arthur D. Levinson Has Resigned from Google's Board' (2009).
[212]   Department of Justice, 'Tullett Prebon and ICAP Restructure Transaction after Justice Department Expresses Concerns about Interlocking Directorates' (2016), available at: www.justice.gov/opa/pr/tullett-prebon-and-icap-restructure-transaction-after-justice-department-expresses-concerns
[213]   'Terra Incognita: Vertical and Conglomerate Merger and Interlocking Directorate Law Enforcement in the United States', Remarks of J Thomas Rosch, Commissioner, FTC, before the University of Hong Kong (2009); s. 5 of the FTC Act prohibits 'unfair methods of competition' (15 USC §45).
[214]   Interlocking directorates indeed have distinctive national features. France and Germany have typically been characterised by denser networks, while in the UK fewer companies share directors. Such a trend is confirmed by a recent study of the evolution of the structure of networks over the period 2006–15: I. Allemand, B. Brullebaut, E. Prinz and F. Thépot, 'Structure et évolution des réseaux d'administrateurs', Conférence internationale de gouvernance, 15–16 May 2017, Lausanne,

5.3.2.4 Conclusion on EU Versus US Approaches to Structural Links

In the United States, the question whether structural links are captured does not revolve around the issue of the boundary between the market and the firm. As a result, the United States has far-reaching jurisdiction over problematic structural links. The ongoing debate on common ownership raises the question of how to integrate the anticompetitive effects of structural links into the competitive assessment. In the EU, the enforcement gap is due to too strict boundaries between the firm and the market, underlying the application of the provisions. Therefore, the transatlantic discrepancy in the ability to challenge structural links relates to the different paradigms underlying the application of competition law provisions.

In the case of minority shareholdings, a contrasted approach may reflect the different enforcement strategies pursued in the EU and the United States. EU enforcement is based on clear rules establishing the legality or illegality of practices. Relying on the concepts of undertaking and control contributes to the legal clarity of competition law jurisdiction. In the United States, most practices are subject to case-by-case scrutiny, with an emphasis on effect analysis.[215] The US merger review may allow for a more open-ended approach: unlike the position in the EU, where the Commission has to justify either way whether a merger is anticompetitive, a decision not to prosecute is left to the discretion of US agencies. Such a decision cannot be subject to appeal in court.[216] As a result, a decision to extend merger control to non-controlling acquisitions has different implications in terms of the enforcement burden in the EU. A stricter framework in the EU, that establishes a sort of 'per se' legality of practices outside its scope, may also explain its more cautious approach towards minority shareholdings. A contrasted approach around structural links may reflect the different choices regarding enforcement trade-offs faced by enforcers, such as legal clarity, the administrative burden, and over- and under-deterrence (type I or type II antitrust errors).[217] In addition, notification processes in the EU are

Switzerland. Another study compares the nature of interlocking directorates in five countries. In France, Italy and Germany, a high number of companies are linked to each other through a small number of shared directors who serve on several company boards at the time, while in the UK fewer companies are linked to each other by directors sitting on a maximum of two boards. The US model seems to be halfway between the French/Italian/German model and the UK model: P. Santella, C. Drago, A. Polo, and E. Gagliardi, 'A Comparison of the Director Networks of the Main Listed Companies in France, Germany, Italy, the United Kingdom, and the United States', Working Paper [2008].

[215] 'Rule of reason'. For a detailed account of antitrust evolutions from 'per se' to 'rule of reason' approaches to anticompetitive practices, see A. I. Gavil, W. E. Kovacic and J. B. Baker, *Antitrust Law in Perspective: Cases, Concepts and Problems in Competition Policy*, 2nd edn (Thomson West, 2008).

[216] W. E. Kovacic, P. C. Mavroidis and D. J. Neven, 'Merger Control Procedures and Institutions: A Comparison of the EU and US Practice', *Antitrust Bulletin*, 59 (2014), 55, 57.

[217] Given the difficulty of identifying an anticompetitive conduct by a firm with market power, enforcers are likely to commit errors. The important issue is whether enforcers favour erring on the side of overenforcement (type I errors) or underenforcement (type II errors) in light of consumer welfare. See, for example: F. H. Easterbrook, 'The Limits of Antitrust', *Texas Law Review*, 63 (1984), 1.

much more expansive than those in the United States; therefore, a broader jurisdiction in the United States does not mean that companies face a significant administrative burden regarding filing requirements.[218]

The enforcement choice of a 'per se' prohibition on interlocking directorates in the United States may be explained by the perception of clear anticompetitive effects of interlocks at the time of the introduction of the Clayton Act. The prohibition, which is restricted to some conditions, such as roles within the company, has not expanded much since the introduction of the Clayton Act. Although there are some points of discussion, the relative clarity brought by the 'per se' prohibition may help to explain why there has been very little litigation.[219] Should the EU decide to introduce a similar provision, the enforcement approach would need to discuss parameters such as object- or effect-based restriction.

The United States and EU antitrust regimes are very different, and this section does not advocate a mere transplantation of the US system to the EU one.[220] The procedural implications of a change in regime are critical to the issue of competition regime changes. As stated above, such questions are outside the scope of this chapter. The US perspective suggests that the EU should adopt a more relaxed approach to the concept of control and undertakings in an area in which the boundaries between the market and the firm are not clear cut.

5.3.3 *Need for a Shift in Paradigm in EU Competition Law?*

This section will present and discuss possible regulatory approaches to structural links in the EU. In its 2001 Green Paper on Merger Review, the Commission recognised the possible anticompetitive effects of structural links. Yet no regulation was deemed necessary at that time.[221] While there was deemed to be insufficient evidence to prove the existence of a gap, Articles 101 and 102 of the TFEU were considered capable of addressing *ex post* potential anticompetitive effects. Since then, the *Ryanair/Aer Lingus* case, as well as various member states' regulatory approaches, have triggered discussions about regulating an enforcement gap at EU level.[222] In 2014, the Commission issued a White Paper proposing a reform of the

---

[218]   Spark Legal Network and Queen Mary University of London, 'Support Study for Impact Assessment Concerning the Review of Merger Regulation Regarding Minority Shareholdings' (2016), 35.

[219]   American Bar Association Section of Antitrust Law, *Interlocking Directorates*.

[220]   For a comparison of, for example, EU and US merger control, see: S. R. Miller, M. E. Raven and D. Went, 'Ownership Interest Acquisitions : New Developments in the European Union and United States', *Competition Policy International Antitrust Chronicle* [2012] 1; J. B. Baker, 'My Summer Vacation at the Commission', *The Antitrust Source* [2005]; I. Platis, 'Competition Law Implications of Minority Shareholdings: The EU and US Perspectives', *Hellenic Review of European Law* [2013] 181; Kovacic, Mavroidis and Neven, 'Merger Control Procedures and Institutions'.

[221]   Green Paper on the Review of Council Regulation (EEC) No 4064/89 COM (2001) 745.

[222]   DG Competition, Commission Staff Working Document, 'Towards More Effective EU Merger Control' (2013), 4.

Merger Regulation to cover non-controlling structural links.[223] In its White Paper, the Commission sought input on the proposal to extend EU merger control to non-controlling structural links. Among the different options considered, partial acquisitions could be scrutinised at the discretion of the Commission, via a 'targeted transparency' system. Only acquisitions conferring a 'competitively significant link' would be notified (information notice), based on which the Commission would decide whether further investigation was required.[224] Following the consultation process, in which many parties expressed concern over significant burdens of the extension of merger control, relative to the identified issue, the Commission decided not pursue the proposed reform.[225] More recently, however, the EU has started paying attention to the possible anticompetitive effects of common ownership by institutional investors.[226] Depending on its scope in Europe, this phenomenon could revive discussions of the shortcomings of EU competition law around structural links.

The following national approaches show that the enforcement gap can be regulated by extending merger control, implying a greater scrutiny within the conventional boundaries of the firm. In both the jurisdiction and competitive assessment, minority interests require a detailed scrutiny of corporate rights. A corporate law perspective provides useful insights into possible constraints exerted by corporate governance mechanisms on structural links.[227] Based on these developments, this chapter posits a necessary examination of the potential synergies between competition law and corporate law. An attempt by the EU to cover structural links may step in to bridge a gap that national corporate governance systems have so far failed to address.

5.3.3.1 UK

As highlighted by the *Ryanair/Aer Lingus* case, the UK addresses the issue of minority acquisitions by stretching the concept of control. According to the Enterprise Act 2002, acquisitions that confer 'material influence' on the policy of the target fall under the scrutiny of the merger provisions. Thus, a lower threshold than 'decisive influence', which is used in the EU, enables non-controlling acquisitions to be challenged in the UK.[228] A case-by-case analysis of the overall relationships between the acquirer and the target seeks to identify whether the acquiring

---

[223] European Commission, 'Towards More Effective EU Merger Control'.

[224] 'There needs to be a competitive relationship between acquirer and target); and the competitive link would be considered significant if the acquired shareholding is (1) around 20% or (2) between 5% and around 20%, but accompanied by additional factors such as rights which give the acquirer a "de-facto" blocking minority, a seat on the Board of Directors, or access to commercially sensitive information of the target' (European Commission, 'Towards More Effective EU Merger Control', para. 47).

[225] '[T]here appears to be no need, at this stage, to carry out any further evaluation in this field' (European Commission, Management Plan 2017 of DG Competition).

[226] Vestager, 'Competition in changing times'.

[227] Concepts and mechanisms of corporate governance are introduced at Section 6.3.1.

[228] UK merger control is characterised by a voluntary notification system. As such, having a lower-level threshold for control has different implications, as in the case of a mandatory regime. Similarly, a less

company has the ability to influence the target's management of its business in relation to its competitive conduct. This includes the strategic direction of the competitor and its ability to define and achieve its commercial objectives. The assessment of material influence involves, for example, an examination of the dispersion of the remaining shares, the existence of special veto rights, patterns of attendance and voting at shareholders' meetings.[229]

The CMA considers that a shareholding of more than 25 per cent may confer the ability materially to influence the target. In addition, material influence unusually arises for acquisitions below 15 per cent, unless a combination of other factors indicates influence.[230]

The *ITV/BSkyB* and *Ryanair/Aer Lingus* cases (developed above) exemplify the competitive assessment of non-controlling interests carried out by the UK competition authorities. The *ITV/BSkyB* case concerned the acquisition of a 17.9 per cent interest in ITV by BskyB. The UK authorities found that such a partial acquisition would confer on BSkyB the ability materially to influence its competitor. While BSkyB was unlikely to be represented on ITV's board, veto rights would enable the blocking of strategic decisions, which in turn was likely to lessen competition in that market. Other elements, such as BSkyB being the largest shareholder, voting weights based on the history of voting patterns, and shareholders' attendance, confirmed that influence.[231] To remedy the likely negative effects on quality, innovation and prices, BSkyB was required to divest its stake down to 7.5 per cent to eliminate its key veto rights.[232]

Theories of harm developed in the assessment of minority interests seem to move away from traditional unilateral and coordinated effects analysis. In the UK *Ryanair/ Aer Lingus* case, the Competition Commission (CC) found that the minority interest was not likely to produce unilateral or coordinated effects,[233] due to the ongoing rivalry between the two competitors. Rather, it required divestment because of the possibility that Ryanair could interfere with its competitor's strategic decisions concerning possible mergers and the management of Heathrow slots.[234] Similarly, in *BskyB*, the CC concluded that unilateral effects and coordinated effects would be unlikely.[235] A loss in rivalry was found to arise from the possibility of Sky influencing

---

well-defined concept of influence seems to be less problematic than in a mandatory notification regime: OECD, Competition Committee, 'The concept of merger transaction' (2013), 5.

[229]   CMA2, 'Mergers: Guidance on the CMA's jurisdiction procedure' (2014), paras. 4.14–4.17.

[230]   Ibid., para. 4.20.

[231]   Competition Commission, *Acquisition by British Sky Broadcasting Group plc of 17.9 per cent of the shares in ITV plc* (2007), Appendix D: Material influence: ability to block resolutions.

[232]   Ibid.

[233]   Competition Commission Report and Appendices, *Ryanair/Aer Lingus*, para. 18: 'We found that the minority shareholding was unlikely to cause Aer Lingus's management to compete less fiercely with Ryanair in order to avoid antagonizing its largest shareholder; to cause Ryanair to compete less fiercely with Aer Lingus in order to protect the value of its investment; or to lead to coordinated effects.'

[234]   Ibid., paras. 7.178 and 7.180.

[235]   *BskyB/ITV*, paras. 4.185 and 4.192.

ITV's strategic financial decisions, affecting the effectiveness of ITV as a competitor in the market for all TV.[236] Additionally, in their response to the Commission's consultation, the OFT and the Competition Commission (CC) (now both combined within the Competition and Markets Authority) expressly identified the corporate influence on non-pricing business decisions afforded to the acquirer as a potential source of competitive harm. Such harm may arise if the acquirer uses its rights as a shareholder to prevent its competitor from raising capital or engaging in mergers.[237] As such, the OFT and the CC considered that a loss in rivalry also possibly emanates from an ability to interfere with non-price strategic decisions.[238] The effects laid down in those decisions seem to stem from the organisation of corporate governance and the presence of 'unwelcome shareholders'.[239] One may wonder whether such issues should remain outside the realm of competitive law, as they mostly constitute an issue of corporate governance.[240] Alternatively, issues of dissident shareholders could be considered to be common issues of corporate and competition law.

5.3.3.1.1 CORPORATE LAW INSIGHTS. The extension of the concept of control to 'material influence' affords the UK competition authorities greater insight into corporate matters. Corporate rights, either granted by law, or held in practice by shareholders, may help us to understand their potential influence on the target company. The Companies Act 2006 provides that a shareholder of more than 25 per cent may block special resolutions at shareholders' meetings.[241] Special resolution is required for amending the articles of association, changing the company's name, reducing the share capital of the company, and changing the nature of the company, as well as for voluntary dissolution of the company.[242] On top of such legal requirements, 25 per cent shareholdings typically grant, in practice, right to block decisions relating to nuclear issues (e.g. change in tax structure), and constitutional as well as operational issues (e.g. concerning memorandum of association, capital expenditure, or salaries threshold decisions).[243] Shareholders owning shares

---

[236]   Ibid., paras. 4.197–4.198.
[237]   Office of Fair Trading and Competition Commission, 'UK Competition Authorities' Response to DG Comp's Consultation on Reform of the EUMR', Annex I: UK Approach to Material influence.
[238]   The UK authorities' approach would then be more in line with the theory of harm laid down in the US Horizontal Merger Guidelines, which mention the influence on 'competitive conduct', which broadly include pricing and non-pricing decisions. 'First, a partial acquisition can lessen competition by giving the acquiring firm the ability to influence the competitive conduct of the target firm' (US Horizontal Merger Guidelines, Section 13. Partial acquisitions).
[239]   Burnside, 'Minority Shareholdings', 9.
[240]   B. Ignjatovic and D. Ridyard, 'Minority Shareholdings, Material Effects?', *CPI Antitrust Chronicle* (2012), 7.
[241]   Companies Act 2006, s. 283.
[242]   Ibid., s 21(1), ss. 77(1) and 641(1); Insolvency Act 1986, s. 84.
[243]   Spark Legal Network and Queen Mary University of London, 'Support Study for Impact Assessment', 43.

in the area of 20 per cent may typically expect board representation, and veto rights in relation to material issues such as a change in direction of the company, a decision to embark on material litigation and disposal or acquisition of certain assets. Going down the scale, shareholders holding around 10 per cent may expect to have a seat on the board, or an observer right – implying the possibility of information on internal matters. Shareholders in that range may also negotiate veto rights on certain nuclear issues. Therefore, it seems reasonable that, even with low shareholdings, an investor may be able to achieve a reduction of competition, via material influence conferred by corporate rights. It is, however, important to stress that shareholders' rights greatly differ, depending on a variety of factors such as the valuation of the company, the existence of other investors.[244]

Both the analysis of the threshold of material influence and the competitive assessment require a greater understanding of corporate governance structure, and corporate law. This different level of inquiry into the boundaries of companies may be reflected in decisional practice. In *Ryanair/Aer Lingus*, the assessment of control by the Commission and the UK Competition Commission displays such a contrast. In its decision to reject Aer Lingus's request to challenge Ryanair's minority interest, the Commission made the following assessment regarding control: 'Ryanair's rights as a minority shareholder (in particular the right to block so-called "special resolutions" pursuant to Irish Company Acts) are associated exclusively to rights related to the protection of minority shareholders. Such rights do not confer control in the sense of Article 3(2)'. In contrast, the assessment by the UK Competition Commission of the creation of a situation of merger involved a more extensive analysis of elements of corporate governance, such as the level of shareholding, patterns of attendance and voting at shareholder meetings, Ryanair's ability to pass or reject ordinary resolutions, the board representation and the distribution and holders of the remaining shares. The analysis of these elements of corporate governance was the focus of six pages of the report. The details of the extensive analysis are available in the Appendices.[245] Such a contrast is logical and stems from the different thresholds of control used in the EU and the UK.[246] This reflects that a lower threshold would impose a more intensive competition law scrutiny within the boundaries of the firm.

5.3.3.2 Germany

Under the German merger regime included in the Act against Restraints of Competition (Gesetz gegen Wettbewerbsbeschränkungen (GWB)), the German

---

[244]   Ibid., 44.

[245]   Competition Commission Report and Appendices, *Ryanair/Aer Lingus*.

[246]   However, the General Court judgment provides a greater analysis of corporate governance elements, in response to Aer Lingus's request to consider those as harming its effectiveness as a competitor (*Aer Lingus v. Commission*).

Competition Authority can scrutinise the acquisition both of controlling and non-controlling minority interests that qualify as a 'concentration' within the meaning of §37 GWB. Acquisitions of 25 per cent or more of shares (capital or voting rights) meet the threshold to qualify as a 'concentration'.[247] In addition, a situation of concentration arises when a transaction enables the acquiring company to exercise a 'competitively significant influence' on the acquired undertaking.[248] Therefore even acquisitions of less than 25 per cent that do not confer control may be challenged by the Bundeskartellamt. The provisions extending merger control to acquisitions conferring significant influence were introduced in 1990. The extension addressed issues of companies attempting to circumvent merger scrutiny in combining acquisitions of less than 25 per cent with special corporate rights.[249]

Any type of link between undertakings that allows the acquirer to influence the competitive behaviour of the target company will be considered. The influence must be established by means of corporate law, and mere economic dependency by way of supply or financing agreements is not sufficient for granting influence.[250] In addition, the acquisition must confer on the acquirer the status of a minority shareholder with a blocking minority, which a 25 per cent interest is presumed to provide. This is established in the light of 'plus factors' such as information rights, rights to appoint supervisory board members, aligned business interests of minority and majority shareholders, veto rights that do not confer control, specific industry expertise and management interlocks. To establish a competitive significant influence, the contractual and factual relationship must suggest that the majority shareholder will take into account the minority's interest.[251] Pursuant to the relevant provisions on merger control, a concentration will be found anticompetitive if it creates or strengthens a dominant position.[252] Accordingly, the competitive assessments conducted in several cases have rested largely on an analysis of dominant position.

In the *Axel Springer Verlag (ASV)/Stilke* case, the proposed acquisition of a 24 per cent interest by Axel Springer Verlag (ASV), a major media publisher, was found to confer significant competitive influence over Stilke, a chain of train station bookshops. The transaction would have conferred on ASV information rights that would have strengthened its dominant position in the promotion of its own products. Therefore, the proposed acquisition was prohibited by the Bundeskartellamt, and this decision was later confirmed by the Federal Court of Justice.[253] In 2004, the Bundeskartellamt prohibited the acquisition of a 17.5 per cent interest in

---

[247] Act against Restraints of Competition, § 37(1) No 3.
[248] Ibid §37(1) No 4.
[249] OECD Policy Roundtable, 'Minority Shareholdings', 111.
[250] Bundesgerichtshof, II ZR 171/83, BGHZ 90, 381, *BuM/WestLB*, 26.3.1984 in Schmidt, 'Germany: Merger Control Analysis'.
[251] Schmidt, 'Germany: Merger Control Analysis', 208.
[252] Act against Restraints of Competition, §36(1).
[253] Federal Court of Justice, Decision of 21 November 2000, WuW/E DE-R 607 *et seq.*, *Minderheitsbeteiligung im Zeitschriftenhandel* in OECD, 114.

Aschaffenburger Versorgungs GmbH (AVG) by Mainova AG, two companies active in the energy sector. It was deemed that this would give rise to corporate influence of Mainova over AVG through corporate rights such as supervisory board mandates and pre-emption rights. As a source of further factual influence, this acquisition would reinforce Mainova's position as gas supplier to AVG, a local gas distributor. With regard to the competitive assessment, vertical foreclosure upstream would be permitted by AVG's incentive to give Mainova a privileged supplier position, due to its existing energy sector expertise. This is because other shareholders in AVG were expected to respect Mainova's interest with respect to concluding supply contracts. In addition, Mainova's participation would entail the possibility of its recouping losses due to lower prices through participation in AVG. Difficulties regarding entry into regional and local gas supply markets would also be a likely consequence of the interest acquisition, since Mainova would have reduced incentives to enter the market for gas distribution. The existing dominant position of AVG in that market would then be strengthened.[254] Statistics on decisional merger practice show that non-controlling minority interests have been a relevant antitrust issue. Between 1990 and 2010, approximately 10 per cent of all notifications concerned minority acquisitions.[255] More specifically, while non-controlling acquisitions conferring 'competitive significant influence' amount to 0.7 per cent of notified cases, they represent 11 per cent of all prohibition decisions.[256]

5.3.3.2.1 CORPORATE LAW INSIGHTS. In Germany, all acquisitions above the threshold of 25 per cent are reviewed without any inquiry into corporate rights being attributed to that acquisition. Acquisitions that induce a degree of influence usually provided by an acquisition meeting the threshold also fall within merger review scrutiny. This threshold of 25 per cent stems from corporate law principles. Such acquisitions confer corporate rights enabling the acquiring company to significantly influence the target company. German corporate law also provides some legal constraints to this possible influence.

Holding a minority shareholding of 25 per cent in a listed company typically provides the right to attend shareholders' meetings, which in general are held on an annual basis. Depending on the type of corporation, different levels of matters may be discussed at such meetings. In listed companies, Aktiengesellschaft (AG) minority shareholders can vote on all the matters discussed, which usually do not relate to business matters. Owing to the simple majority system, such voting rights cannot influence the outcome. However, corporate matters that require a special resolution

---

[254]   Annex II to the Staff Working Document, 'Towards More Effective EU Merger Control': 'Non-Controlling Minority Shareholdings and EU Merger Control' (2013), paras. 56–7.
[255]   Although the 12.5 per cent refer to minority shareholdings as a whole, not only non-controlling acquisitions: Schmidt, 'Germany: Merger Control Analysis', 208.
[256]   A. Bardong, 'The German Experience' in 'Merger Control and Minority Shareholdings: Time for a Change?', *Revue Concurrences*, 3-2011 (2011), 14, 34.

can be blocked by 25 per cent (plus one) of the voting rights. Such owners can veto amendment to the articles of associations, a capital increase or decrease, and a recall of the supervisory board. In addition, the management of listed companies typically operates independently from shareholders, which prevents minority shareholders from directly influencing companies' substantial business matters. In the case of limited liability companies, Gesellschaft mit beschränkter Haftung (GmbH) corporate governance law is more flexible.[257] Meetings are usually held more frequently and shareholders have a greater ability to interfere in the management's actions. Nevertheless, minority shareholders holding 25 per cent or less cannot usually influence the outcome of shareholders' meetings. As with listed companies, major decisions may be blocked by a minority of 25 per cent as decisions normally require a majority of 75 per cent of the votes.

German corporate law also provides insights into the level of information that a shareholder can have over its target, and the limits set to the acquisition of such information. Any shareholder of a listed company has a right to be informed about the company's matters, to the extent that this information is used to evaluate a question on the agenda of the shareholders' meeting.[258] However, this information is to be disclosed orally only at the shareholders' meeting. In addition, based on statutory restrictions, the board has a right to refuse an information request if, among other grounds, the disclosure is likely to cause material damage to the company.[259] In the case of GmbH companies, shareholders have a more extensive right to information. Shareholders may request, at any time, access to information relating to any of the company's matters, and can access documents such as correspondence and invoices.[260] No statutory restriction on this information right exists. However, based on a shareholder's decision, the managing director may refuse an information request if there are concerns that the minority shareholder may use the information in a way that causes material damage to the company.[261]

Consequently, German statutory corporate law provisions regulate matters relating to the right of shareholders to influence business matters and access information. This means that corporate law sets some constraints on the possible damaging interference of a minority shareholder. Influence and information rights, especially in listed companies, may be legally constrained, so that a minority shareholder holding 25 per cent of the voting rights cannot interfere with business matters.[262] However, much weaker legal constraints exist for limited liability companies. In addition, the *Ryanair/Aer Lingus* decision suggests that even the ability to block decisions on raising capital may be problematic from a competition law perspective.[263] Control over

---

[257]   Ibid.
[258]   AktG (German Stock Corporation Act), s. 131(1).
[259]   Ibid., s. 131(3).
[260]   GmbHG, s. 51a(1).
[261]   Ibid., s 51a(2).
[262]   Schmidt, 'Germany: Merger Control Analysis', 211.
[263]   Competition Commission Report and Appendices, *Ryanair/Aer Lingus*.

raising capital decisions was also a source of competitive harm in the US *Univision* decision.[264] The power to block such a decision, via the voting system, is even referred to by Salop and O'Brien as a situation of 'total control' over the target.[265] Such rights may not be constrained by statutory provisions in Germany.

German corporate law seems to be quite unique in the manner in which a company can be protected from the possible negative influence of shareholders.[266] Yet, corporate statutory provisions do not sufficiently address competitive concerns that are broader than just the possible influence of a competitor over its target. This has justified the necessity of expanding the ambit of merger control over partial acquisitions in Germany.

5.3.3.3 Austria

In Austria, all transactions above 25 per cent must be notified to the competition authority, irrespective of whether the acquisition confers control.[267] Unlike in Germany and the UK, no provision entails the possibility of challenging acquisitions that confer corporate influence. However, decisional practice has developed to challenge acquisitions that circumvent the legal threshold. The Austrian courts have challenged acquisitions below 25 per cent when they have conferred rights normally attributed to acquisitions meeting the threshold.[268] In 2011, minority interests represented approximately 15 per cent of a total of 236 mergers notified in Austria, irrespective of whether control was acquired.[269] Over the period 2006–16, minority acquisitions represented 12.2 per cent of all notifications, with a steady number of thirty-three to forty notifications per year.[270] The Austrian competition authority has intervened in two cases involving acquisitions of just above 25 per cent. In *Saubermarcher*, remedies were required to address concerns of possible discriminatory access to the waste plant of the target company.[271] In *Funke Mediengruppe*, the concern was potential negative impact on media diversity.[272] In both cases

---

[264]   'Univison's rights to veto Entravision's issuance of equity or debt, or acquisitions over $25 million give it a significant degree of control or influence and will likely impair Entravision's ability and incentive to compete with Univision/HBC' (Complaint for Injunctive Relief, US v. *Univision Communication, Inc* (No CV03-00758). 2003 WL 23781621 (DDC 2003) 26).

[265]   Salop and O'Brien, 'Competitive Effects of Partial Ownership', 579.

[266]   In Austria, and in the UK, no statutory provision limits shareholders' right in a way that could limit the competitive concern.

[267]   Austrian Cartel Act 2005, s. 7(1).

[268]   Annex II to the Staff Working Document, 'Towards More Effective EU Merger Control', paras. 67–8.

[269]   Ibid.

[270]   Spark Legal Network and Queen Mary University of London, 'Support Study for Impact Assessment', 27.

[271]   BWB/Z-2121 *Saubermacher Dienstleistungs-AG/KärntnerRestmüllverwertungs GmbH*.

[272]   BWB/Z-2660 *Funke Mediengruppe GmbH & Co KGaA/Axel Springer Media Impact GmbH & Co KG*.

neither corporate rights attached to the shareholdings nor the issue of control were discussed.[273]

5.3.3.4 Regulatory Approaches to Interlocking Directorates

The problem of interlocking directorates is, first and foremost, a matter of corporate law in the member states. In France, the French Commercial Code governs different aspects of the composition and functioning of the board of directors of limited companies.[274] The law limits to five the number of seat appointments held as top executives or board members. In addition, the recent 'Macron law'[275] has reduced that number to three appointments for publicly listed companies of more than 5,000 employees in France, or at least 10, 000 worldwide.[276]

In the Netherlands, the (binding) code of corporate governance prohibits conflicts of interest and limits the number of appointments held.[277] Moreover, approval from the board of directors is required for any transaction that may give rise to a conflict of interests between the members of the board and the company.

Italy is the only country to have adopted a specific regulation entitled 'Protection of competition and cross corporate ties in the banking and finance industry' to deal with the anticompetitive effects of interlocks among competitors.[278] In 2011, following a report of the competition authority on problems of corporate governance and competition in the financial industry, Italy adopted a series of specific economic measures.[279] These measures aim to increase competition and ethical governance in industries in which low economic performance seemed to stem from the multitude of personal ties linking corporate governance bodies.[280] This regulation prohibits any person appointed as a manager, supervisor or auditor of a company operating in the financial and insurance industry from holding a similar appointment with a competitor. Persons holding more than one such appointment must comply within ninety days and decide which one to keep. Failure to comply leads to the termination of all appointments, either by the company or by the national regulator.[281]

---

[273]   Spark Legal Network and Queen Mary University of London, 'Support Study for Impact Assessment', 27.

[274]   Article L. 225-17 of the French Commercial Code.

[275]   Law N° 2015-990 of 6 August 2015.

[276]   This gives binding force to the provision set by the non-binding AFEP/MEDEF code of conduct that provides that 'the board member of a public company may not hold more than two other appointments in public companies outside of his own group, including foreign companies' (Article 19).

[277]   Dutch Corporate Governance Code, article III.3.5.

[278]   V. Falce, 'Interlocking Directorates: An Italian Antitrust Dilemma', Journal of Competition Law and Economics, 9 (2013), 457–72.

[279]   Article 36 Protection of Competition and Personal Cross Shareholdings in the Credit and Financial Markets of the Law Decree N° 201/2011, converted by Law N° 214/2011.

[280]   Falce, Interlocking Directorates', 460.

[281]   F. Ghezzi, 'Interlocking Directorates in the Financial Sector: The Italian Job (art. 36 law 214/2011) – An Antitrust Perspective', Università Bocconi, 2012.

With the exception of Italy in the banking and financial industry, limitations of interlocking directorates do not specifically target competitors. These tools, which exist at national level in a few EU member states, offer a variety of solutions and have, in practice, a limited impact on cross-border operations.

5.3.3.5 Principles of Corporate Governance

Structural links are at the heart of corporate governance systems. This section discusses whether principles of corporate governance can set constraints over the anticompetitive effects of minority shareholdings and interlocking directorates. Competition law may adjust its boundaries to address common issues that corporate laws and corporate governance fail to address. Overall, this shows that the discussion at the EU level requires a multidisciplinary approach to the issue of structural links.

5.3.3.5.1 LIMITED REACH OF CORPORATE GOVERNANCE. While protection of minority shareholders and the freedom to appoint board members are essential to corporate governance, these corporate arrangements can also hinder rivalry between companies. In addition, policies regarding corporate governance encourage an active role by institutional investors in the corporate governance, which seems to conflict with the competitive concerns raised by common ownership.[282]

Yet, corporate governance and competition law seem to converge on other issues. A core principle of corporate governance is the fiduciary duty of management to shareholders.[283] Fiduciary obligation may mitigate the anticompetitive effects of structural links. In the context of interlocking directorates, a strong fiduciary duty may prevent a common board member from disclosing information from one company to the other. However, a director's fiduciary duty to one company may naturally conflict with their fiduciary duty to another.[284] As for minority shareholdings, a fiduciary obligation imposes on the management of a company that it should act in the company's best interest as opposed to the interest of a specific shareholder. Minority shareholders may have reduced incentives to ensure the long-term interest of a company, including a weaker interest in seeking to avoid participation into illegal anticompetitive agreements.[285]

[282] OECD, 'Common Ownership by Institutional Investors', 36.
[283] As an example, the French Court of Cassation reaffirms the legal requirement of fiduciary duty for top management: Cass. com., 27 February 1996, JCP G 1996, II, 22665, note J. Ghestin.
[284] OECD Policy Roundtable, 'Minority Shareholdings', 34.
[285] Such an effect may be particularly strengthened if the existence of a cartel in which the target participates indirectly benefits the competing companies due to prices being inflated across the market. However, the *Kone* case implies that, under certain conditions, damage actions may be brought even in relation to prices offered by non-cartelised companies: Case C–557/12 *Kone AG and Others* v. *ÖBB Infrastruktur AG* [2014] EU:C:2014:1317.

Independence of decision-making is another important principle of corporate governance.[286] Accordingly, decisions should be made in the company's best interest, without consideration of other companies.[287] The French Asset Management Association warns against the risk of interlocking directorates as undermining transparency and independence of decision-making, when not attached to a common strategic economic cooperation project.[288] In practice, however, an increase in price taken in the interest of some shareholders may be difficult to identify. Collecting evidence and taking action, such as voting to remove a director in breach of fiduciary obligation, could be difficult and risky for the shareholders. In addition, a fiduciary duty may be ineffective in counteracting the ability of 'unwelcome shareholders' to reduce the effectiveness of a competitor. The influence of a competitor over its target, and the related anticompetitive effects, do not necessarily involve a decision by the board. In the *Ryanair* and *Sky* cases, the competitive harm originated from the ability of the acquirer unilaterally to block resolutions. Further exploration of corporate governance mechanisms is therefore critical to understanding the practical ability of a board to raise prices unfavourably for the company, for the financial benefits of a competitor.[289]

As an example, the French Court of Cassation has reaffirmed the legal requirement of fiduciary duty for top executives, which then applies to those sitting on the board of a competing company. In addition, the court has clarified that this duty forbids the chief executive from commercial negotiation in his capacity as manager of another company within the same industry.[290] However, such a requirement, which is rather limited to apprehending the whole spectrum of anticompetitive effects, only applies to executives (and not to directors) of French companies. In addition, the code of corporate governance recommends that, as an ethical rule, a board member should be bound to report to the board any actual or potential conflict of interest, and refrain from voting on the related resolution.[291] However, no mention is made of conflicts of interests arising from individuals sitting in multiple board meetings.

Interlocking directorates may pose additional problems both for corporate governance and for competition law, if top managers select or exclude directors according

---

[286] See, e.g., AFEP-MEDEF Code of Corporate Governance of Listed Corporations (2016), ss. 8 and 19.

[287] See the scenario of fiduciary duty limiting the anticompetitive effects of partial acquisitions in Salop and Brien, 'Competitive Effects of Partial Ownership', 580.

[288] AFG, 'Recommandations sur le gouvernement d'entreprise' (2018), 19, available at: www.afg.asso.fr /wpcontent/uploads/2017/01/Recommandations_sur_le_gouvernement_d_entreprise_2018.pdf

[289] 'Real-world' corporate governance factors that affect the financial incentives to competition – incomplete information, management's incentives and ability to capture benefits (J. B. Dubrow, 'Challenging the Economic Incentives Analysis of Competitive Effects in Acquisitions of Passive Minority Equity Interests', *Antitrust Law Journal*, 69 (2001), 131).

[290] *Affaire Clos du Baty*, Chambre commerciale de la Cour de cassation, 15 novembre 2011, n 10-15049. The scope of this duty seems to be expanding, as is illustrated by recent decisions. See Thépot et al., 'Cumul de mandats d'administrateur et risques anticoncurrentiels'.

[291] AFEP-MEDEF, Code of Corporate Governance of Listed Corporations (2016), s. 19.

to their experience on other boards, in an effort to retain control over the board.[292] In addition, mutual interlocks can reflect and contribute to CEO entrenchment, resulting in higher compensation and lower turnover.[293]

5.3.3.5.2 COMPETITION LAW 'STEPPING IN'? Legal constraints provided by corporate laws do not bridge the regulatory gap that exists at the EU level. General principles of corporate governance, such as independence of decision-making, have a limited ability to address competitive concerns, even when they closely relate to common issues. In Italy, for example, a competition approach may have stepped in to address issues that corporate governance modernisation has so far insufficiently addressed.[294] In *Ryanair* and *Sky*, competition law seemed possibly to tackle issues relating to 'unwelcome shareholders' that are both detrimental to competition law and the value of the company.

One strong argument for an EU-wide solution structural links is that corporate systems differ across member states. Corporate law may give minority shareholders different levels of influence over the target that directly impact the scope for competitive concerns.[295] Those means of influence include the right to influence the agenda of the general meeting, the right to see the company's documents, and the right to appoint non-executive directors.[296] EU law may then be able to ensure that enforcement over structural links is addressed beyond the framework of very different national corporate or competition law regimes. As proposed by the Commission in 2014, the extension of the concept of control with an effect-based approach to acquisitions of non-controlling minority shareholdings seems to be a valuable option in that respect.[297]

Regarding interlocking directorates, some have argued that these should remain beyond the realm of competition law.[298] Corporate laws of member states may provide effective *ex ante* solutions to the problem, especially if the practice of interlocks primarily has national features. The need of an EU-wide solution depends on whether there is a growing tendency for cross-border interlocking directorates.

---

[292]   E. J. Zajac and J. D. Westphal, 'Director Reputation, Power, and CEO-Board the Dynamics of Board Interlocks', *Administrative Science Quarterly*, 41 (1996), 507.

[293]   E. M. Fich and L. J. White, 'CEO Compensation and Turnover: The Effects of Mutually Interlocked Boards', *Wake Forest Law Review*, 38 (2003), 935.

[294]   L. Enriques and P. Volpin, 'Corporate Governance Reforms in Continental Europe', *Journal of Economic Perspectives*, 21 (2007), 117.

[295]   For a comparative insight into the different rights associated with different levels of shareholdings, see Spark Legal Network and Queen Mary University of London, 'Support Study for Impact Assessment'.

[296]   P. Kalbfleisch, 'Minority Shareholdings in Competing Companies', 'Merger Control and Minority Shareholdings: Time for a Change?', *Revue Concurrences* (2011), 39.

[297]   Although this proposition was not implemented following concerns of disproportionate burden compared with the potential risks: European Commission, 'Towards More Effective EU Merger Control'.

[298]   Gerber, 'Enabling Interlock Benefits', 112.

If an EU-wide regulation prohibiting interlocks among competitors may seem too ambitious, significant limitations of interlocking directorates could be introduced nationally to remedy issues that are of concern for both corporate governance and competition law. In any case, a comprehensive impact assessment of the extent of such issues in Europe should form part of any proposal for reform, and would supplement the identification of theoretical concerns provided here.[299] Overall, a close scrutiny of corporate law and corporate governance is essential to the debate.

5.4 CONCLUSION

The existence of an enforcement gap around the issue of structural links calls for a rethinking of the boundaries of competition law. This chapter argues that the enforcement gap in the EU relates to the difficulty in applying the concept of undertaking to relationships at the interface of the firm and the market. Regulating that gap by extending merger control, as exemplified by an examination of the US's and some member states' regimes, requires either abstracting from or extending the concept of control and as such implies a greater scrutiny of the internal boundaries of companies. In both the jurisdiction and competitive assessments, minority interests require a detailed scrutiny of corporate rights. The corporate law perspective has provided useful insights as to the possible legal constraints exerted by corporate governance. In addition, the existing provisions on interlocking directorates show that a debate over competitive concerns closely relates to special features of corporate landscapes. Based on these developments, this chapter posits a necessary examination of the potential synergies of competition and corporate law. An EU-wide response to cover structural links may step in to bridge a gap that national corporate systems have so far failed to address.

---

[299] For an example of such studies, see Allemand et al., 'Structure et évolution des réseaux d'administrateurs'.

Conclusion of Part I

Part I has developed an understanding of the competition law conception of the firm, highlighting its implications for very contemporary issues. Clearly endorsing an economic vision, competition law recognises the efficiency of alternatives to the market, and does not purport to interfere with such alternative forms of transactions. As such, agreements within what forms a single entity are outside its scope. Public services functions that may fail to be provided in markets are equally protected from the reach of competition law. The property rights theory of the firm, in particular, helps to distinguish what ought to be treated as a firm or a market transaction, in relationships such as joint ventures, or parent and subsidiary, as well as in commercial agency agreements. In doing so it helps to minimise type I and type II errors. Efficient forms of economic transactions, including hybrid forms such as commercial agency relationships, are not deterred if their specific features are recognised and protected by competition law. Arrangements that may produce anticompetitive effects, such as joint ventures, may also be adequately captured if they are correctly qualified in terms of the theory of property rights. Competition law may, however, need to stretch its boundaries to capture effects of relationships that blur the market/firm boundaries. This is the case when competitors are connected via both a market and a corporate relationship, owing to common ownership or board links. In the United States, jurisdiction over structural links does not depend on the market/firm dichotomy. In the European Union (EU), challenging anticompetitive effects of such relationships may require a greater inquiry into corporate matters.

Part I has substantiated the claim that an inquiry different from establishing the substantive reach demands a different conception of the firm. The conception of the firm is inadequate when it is used to attribute liability in the EU. It contradicts important legal principles, and is not optimal for deterrence. Competition law needs to adopt an agency vision of relationships when it attributes liability among economically affiliated but legally independent entities. Therefore, Chapter 5 offers a unifying framework for attributing liability, that applies across relations that may qualify as 'agency relationships', including those between parents and subsidiaries, and commercial agency agreements, within joint venture. An analysis in terms of incentives and ability helps to account for the imperfect information and opportunism that characterise all the relationships. A defence based on organisational negligence would also provide adequate incentives for organising compliance internally.

PART II

Opening the 'Black Box': the Case of Cartels

Competition law and corporate governance also meaningfully interact when the inquiry of competition law moves within the boundaries of the firm for enforcement purposes. In that respect, Part II 'opens the black box' of the firm to understand the internal dimension of compliance or non-compliance with competition law, with a focus on collusive behaviour. The study of cartel practice particularly demonstrates that internal relations, and the divergence of interests that characterise the separation of ownership and control in such corporations, affect the incentives to compete on the market. Agency relationships, which are the *raison d'être* of corporate governance theories and mechanisms, are the object of the analysis. This reflects the fact that modern firms do not have a unity of mind and will. Characterising the cartel problem as one of agency has fundamental implications for effective cartel enforcement. This restriction to cartel practices also enables the examination of an area of competition law in which the harm to economic welfare is unambiguous and that is homogeneously prosecutable across jurisdictions.

Chapter 6 reflects on the internal drivers of non-compliance with competition law. Explaining collusion as a specification of the agency problem, it establishes the theoretical framework that will be used to discuss cartel enforcement in Part II. While the existing scholarship focuses mostly on external factors, Chapter 6 suggests that elements relating to corporate governance, broadly speaking, also provide a powerful explanation for the occurrence of collusion. An inverse relationship is also described: the degree of competition in a market may impact the quality of corporate governance mechanisms.

Chapter 7 assesses the effectiveness of 'traditional' enforcement tools against cartels, sanctions and leniency, through the lens of the agency-based framework. It makes the case for better targeting individual incentives, including greater recourse to individual sanctions.

Chapter 8 discusses the significance of corporate compliance programmes as a complementary enforcement tool. Taking stock of the organisational challenges of corporate compliance, as well as the relevance of agency relationship issues that exist within firms, the chapter posits that greater incentives should be provided to companies to implement effective compliance measures. Thus, the need to move from a sanction-based to a prevention-based type of enforcement increases the need for competition law inquiry into the conventional boundaries of the firm.

Part II relies mostly on a specific theoretical framework of analysis – that of the agency relationship. This allows the analysis to be limited to specific relationships within the firm, the study of which is also supported by a well-established body of theories and literature. Accordingly, and for the sake of conciseness, it will mostly be assumed that actors within the firm are somehow rational (with limitations brought by limited expertise or imperfect information being part of the foundations of the agency problem).[1] However, it is acknowledged and illustrated in several instances that the study of cartels needs to be enriched by approaches that move away from the assumption of rationality.[2] In addition, criminology studies analyse a greater range of factors that are related to the individual as well as to the organisation, the explanatory power of which complements the framework developed here.[3]

---

[1] Following the methodology of the economic analysis of law. See, e.g., A. Polinsky, A. Mitchell and S. Shavell, 'Economic Analysis of Law' in *The New Palgrave Dictionary of Economics*, 2nd edn (Harvard University, 2008).

[2] For another approach to the firm's behaviour, which moves away from the assumption of rationality, see, e.g., behavioural economics-based studies: OFT1213, 'Behavioural Economics as Applied to Firms: A Primer' (2010).

[3] See, e.g., Study focused on antitrust infringements, S. S. Simpson and C. S. Koper, 'Deterring Corporate Crime', *Criminology*, 30(3) (1992), 347–75. More generally: S. S. Simpson, 'Making Sense of White Collar Crime: Theory and Research', *Ohio State Journal of Criminal Law*, 8 (2011), 481–502.

6

Corporate Governance Insights into Cartels

6.1 INTRODUCTION

Theoretical insights afforded by corporate governance literature enable us to understand cartels as products of individual and of organisational-specific factors. Collusive behaviour by companies may be explained by their internal dynamics, in addition to factors related to the economic environment in which they operate. Engagement in cartel practice often emanates from rather senior employees or managers.[1] Such positions are often characterised by a degree of discretionary power, which the mechanisms of corporate governance, aim to control, via the board of directors. Poor supervision by the board may facilitate engagement in a cartel. Remuneration schemes, which intend to align the interests of shareholders and managers, may induce managers to enter into cartels, if such schemes are inadequately designed. The artificial inflation of short-run profits, via a price-fixing agreement, may be a response to a remuneration scheme that provides managers with incentives that are too strong. As a result, the quality of its corporate governance is a very important component of a firm's compliance. A company in which managerial activity is better monitored may be less likely to engage in illegal practices that restrict competition, as this may reduce the scope for illegal use of managerial discretionary power.

This chapter characterises collusive behaviour as a problem of agency, which justifies the importance of internal dynamics in the study of cartels. Thus, an

---

[1] A. Stephan 'See no Evil: Cartels and the Limits of Antitrust Compliance Programs', *The Company Lawyer*, 31 (2010), 231, 236; J. E. Harrington, 'How Do Cartels Operate?', *Foundations and Trends in Microeconomics*, 2 (2006), 1, 78. Stephan and Nikpay suggest that a great variety of positions are occupied by employees engaging their companies in cartels, ranging from local sales managers to senior executives, but all of them have discretion over prices: A. Stephan and A. Nikpay, 'Leniency Decision-Making from a Corporate Perspective: Complex Realities' in C. Beaton-Wells and C. Tran (eds.), *Anti-Cartel Enforcement in a Contemporary Age: The Leniency Religion* (Hart Publishing, 2015), p. 146.

examination of corporate governance mechanisms that seek to address problems in the agency relationship provides fundamental insights into internal drivers to collusion.

6.2 COLLUSIVE BEHAVIOUR AS A TYPE OF AGENCY PROBLEM

This section asks whether collusive behaviour constitutes a specification of the agency problem, both in the absence and in the presence of detection. It is argued that, in the event of detection, cartel practices tend to benefit managers at the expense of shareholders, and are detrimental to the value of the firm. As such, practices that restrict competition seem to be a *manifestation* of the agency problem. It will be shown that restriction of competition may also be a *source* of the agency problem, as it exacerbates issues related to what is called *free cash flow*.

6.2.1 *The Agency Problem and Theory of Agency Costs*

As was explained in Chapter 2,[2] agency relationships exist whenever a relationship between two persons – a principal and an agent – involves the agent making decisions on behalf of the principal. Agency relationships are likely to arise whenever gains can be made from the specialisation of activities. The agency problem emanates from the fact that, in many companies, the financiers – *the principal* – do not themselves control the business that they own, but delegate this function to a specialised manager, who is *the agent*. There is a moral hazard in the context of separation of ownership and control, for the following reason: the manager does not bear the full cost of their action, and their level of effort cannot be fully observed due to the informational and expertise advantage that they hold. Therefore, the agent can pursue goals of their own, such as enhanced career opportunities and improved social status, which do not necessarily coincide with the principal's best interests. Jensen and Meckling's theory of agency costs is a model of the cost of the separation of ownership and control. They identify three types of agency costs: the costs of *monitoring* and *bonding* (those incurred by the principal to monitor the agent, and costs incurred by the agent in an effort to commit to acting in the best interest of the principal), and costs associated with *residual loss* (those incurred from divergent principal and agent interests despite the use of monitoring and bonding). The monitoring and bonding schemes are examples of mechanisms of *corporate governance*, which are aimed at addressing the agency costs inherent in corporations in which ownership and control are separated.[3]

---

[2]   For further explanation, see Section 2.4.
[3]   M. C. Jensen and W. H. Meckling, 'Theory of the Firm: Managerial Behavior, Agency Costs and Ownership Structure', *Journal of Financial Economics*, 3 (1976), 305.

6.2.2 *Collusive Behaviour as a Manifestation of the Agency Problem*

Asking whether participation in a cartel is an illustration of the agency problem differs from considering whether such participation is profitable to an undertaking in the absence of detection, or in the short run. When undetected, collusion, rather than competition, is undoubtedly profitable. According to industrial organisation theories, cartels enable companies to maximise a joint profit rather than individual profits, which leads to inflated profits.[4] Although cartels are theoretically unstable in nature, owing to each member's incentive to deviate, they are widely observed, and some companies have repeatedly engaged in collusive behaviour.[5] Fines imposed on cartel members are becoming increasingly higher, as a way of deterring participation.[6] Intervention of authorities by way of strong sanction policies is necessary to deter such profitable practices, if undetected. Profitability from collusive behaviour has been analysed by Levenstein and Suslow, among others who have examined the scope of cartel profitability and have explained the reasons behind the success of cartels.[7]

6.2.2.1 In the Event of Detection/In the Long Run

Cartel detection has been the subject of several empirical studies. By definition, it is impossible to identify the number of undetected cartels in the economy. Bryant and Eckard's study provided the first estimation of the probability of an undertaking's being caught by the competition authorities.[8] Based on statistics for 184 detected cartels in the United States between 1961 and 1988, they found that there is a 13–17 per cent probability of an undertaking's being detected annually, conditional on the cartel being detected eventually. This estimation is not a global estimation of the cartel detection rate, but concerns cartels that are eventually detected. In other words, the annual probability of 13–17 per cent is the upper rate, and the actual probability of detection is likely to be much lower. Combe, Monnier and Legal conducted a similar investigation into cartel cases detected at European Union (EU) level and estimated that there is a 13 per cent probability of companies being caught.[9] The following developments are based on the contingency of detection, in spite of low probabilities.

---

[4] M. Motta, *Competition Policy, Theory and Practice* (Cambridge University Press, 2004), p. 138.

[5] For statistics on international cartels, see: J. M. Connor, 'Cartel Detection and Duration Worldwide', *CPI Antitrust Chronicle* (2011); J. M. Connor, 'Recidivism Revealed: Private International Cartels 1990–2009', *Competition Policy International*, 6 (2012), 101. For access to a data set of cartels over the period 1990–2012, see J. M. Connor, Private International Cartels Full Data 2012-4-13 2012-1 Edition (Purdue University Research Repository, 2017).

[6] EU Commission, cartel statistics (2017), available at: http://ec.europa.eu/competition/cartels/statistics /statistics.pdf

[7] M. C. Levenstein and V. Y. Suslow, 'What Determines Cartel Success?', *Journal of Economic Literature*, 44 (2006), 43.

[8] P. G. Bryant and E. W. Eckard 'Price Fixing: The Probability of Getting Caught', *The Review of Economics and Statistics*, 73 (1991), 531.

[9] E. Combe, C. Monnier and R. Legal, 'Cartels: The Probability of Getting Caught in the European Union', Bruges European Economic Research papers (2008), 2.

When detection occurs, participation in a cartel may be the manifestation of conflicting interests between shareholders and managers. The corporate governance literature explains such an interest gap by the fact that managers may have a different time horizon, and may not bear the full cost of their actions. A situation of moral hazard is typical of the agency problem, which negatively affects the value of the firm. Several factors may, however, limit the agency problem described by the traditional corporate governance literature.

While shareholders are more likely to benefit from the return on their investment over a long period of time, managers benefit from the company's return on only a fixed-term basis. This time difference may lead the manager to select investments that yield shorter-term returns irrespective of whether such investments are in the interests of the company. For example, the manager may have fewer incentives to invest in research and development projects, as these are likely to create losses in the short run even though they bring long-run benefits.[10] Differences in time horizons between managers and shareholders also exist with respect to the costs and benefits of cartels. Managers may have shorter time horizons than shareholders, and they may make decisions that ensure short-run profits at the expense of future losses related to the sanctions imposed due to detection of the cartel. Finally, the manager may leave before the cartel is prosecuted, which adds to the different time horizons between the shareholders and managers.

The scope of the time-span gap depends on several factors. Some economies are characterised by a tradition of lifetime employment, where time horizons between employees and shareholders are more aligned.[11] In addition, recent trends in modern capitalism nuance the view that shareholders have longer-term prospects. In particular within the Anglo-American corporate governance system, shareholders have frequently shown themselves to be just as short term as managers in many instances, and sometimes even more so.[12] Recent evidence has shown the average holding period of a share on the New York Stock Exchange to be less than a year, which seems too short for shareholders to be sensitive to cartel detection in the future.[13] Therefore, the assumption of the managers' short-term approach does not hold in a wide range of scenarios, and particularly so in the case of publicly listed companies on the main stock exchanges.

Another source of moral hazard lies in the difference in the costs of cartel participation for managers and shareholders, particularly in the absence of

---

[10] S. Douma and H. Schreuder, *Economic Approaches to Organizations*, 6th edn (Pearson Education, 2017), pp. 178–9.

[11] E.g. the Japanese economy features a particularly high rate of lifetime employment compared with other industrialised economies: H. Ono, 'Lifetime employment in Japan: Concepts and measurements', *Journal of Japanese International Economies*, 24 (2010), 1–27.

[12] For a presentation and discussion of the issue of investors' short-termism, see M. T. Moore and E. Walker-Arnott, 'A Fresh Look at Stock Market Short-termism', *Journal of Law and Society*, 41 (2014), 416.

[13] R. J. Rhee, 'Corporate Short-Termism and Intertemporal Choice', *Washington University Law Review*, 96 (2018), 2, 34, quoting several studies.

individual sanctions.[14] The benefits of cartel membership are common to share-holders and managers alike. Any increase in the revenues of a company results in an increase in its share value and therefore benefits the shareholders. Managers also gain from an increase in the company's value; the extent of this gain is determined by the remuneration scheme that is in place. Shareholders may be willing to encourage managers to participate in a cartel. Taking into account the antitrust sanctions, however, the situation becomes somewhat different. In the absence of individual sanctions, detection leads, in most jurisdictions, to administrative and/or monetary fines that are borne by the undertaking. In addition, private enforcement can cause additional financial consequences for shareholders. Consequently, shareholders bear the costs of these sanctions, while managers may completely avoid direct personal punishment for their actions. The scope of fines as compared with that of cartel profit is an important factor.[15] Fines are typically considered as being sub-optimal to achieve deterrence, implying that the cost of sanctions may not be hugely significant compared with cartel benefits.[16] In addition, the 10 per cent worldwide turnover cap for fines, as is provided for in the EU, further limits the scope of the interest gap.[17] The development of damages action, as encouraged by the 2014 Damages Directive in the EU, may, however, widen the cost of detection and thereby the interest gap towards cartel participation.[18]

Adverse reputational impacts of detection can affect both shareholders and managers. Reputational effects may be stronger for managers than for shareholders: it is more difficult to know the identity of shareholders, and dispersed shareholders are not supposed to have known about the cartel. In addition, detection may lead to the dismissal of the responsible manager, who thus personally faces a human capital risk. However, by the time that the participation of a company in a cartel is detected and sanctioned, the manager responsible for it may have left the company.[19] In this respect, Stephan points out that the average time span between the end of a cartel and the fine being imposed on an undertaking is in excess of five years.[20] Therefore, a company that wants to fire or punish its managers may not be able to do so. In this

[14] For an overview of jurisdictions imposing individual sanctions, see Section 7.3.2.1.
[15] In the EU: Guidelines on the method of setting fines imposed pursuant to Article 23(2)(a) of Regulation No 1/2003 [2006] OJ C210/02.
[16] W. P. J. Wils, *The Optimal Enforcement of EC Antitrust Law* (Kluwer Law International, 2002), p. 200.
[17] Council Regulation (EC) No 1/2003 of 16 December 2002 on the implementation of the rules on competition laid down in Articles 81 and 82 of the Treaty [2003] OJ L1/1 ('Regulation 1/2003'), Art. 23(1).
[18] Directive 2014/104/EU of the European Parliament and of the Council of 26 November 2014 on certain rules governing actions for damages under national law for infringements of the competition law provisions of the Member States and of the European Union [2014] OJ L349/1 ('Damages Directive').
[19] C. Leslie, 'Cartels, Agency Costs, and Finding Virtue in Faithless Agents', *William and Mary Law Review*, 49 (2008), 1621.
[20] A. Stephan, *Should Individual Sanctions Be Part of Deterrence Efforts?* 'Deterring EU Competition Law Infringements: Are We Using the Right Sanctions?' Conference by TILEC and the Liege Competition and Innovation, 3 December 2012.

context, the manager stands to benefit more from the participation in a cartel than the shareholders.

It is expected that any legal investigation of a publicly listed company may impact negatively the value of its shares. The market may indeed respond negatively due to the prospect of legal costs, or to the reputational loss. Markets could also react to changes in profit streams from cartel to competitive prices. A study by Motta, Langus and Aguzzoni found an estimated loss of 2.89 per cent in the value of shares on the day of the dawn raid on a company for alleged antitrust breach, and an aggregate estimated loss of 3.57 per cent due to the infringement decision. Overall, antitrust actions relate to a drop between 3.03 per cent and 4.55 per cent in market value. They find little significance in courts' decisions on this market reaction and explain most of the decrease by readjustment to a competitive level of profits.[21] A study on Dutch companies involved in cartel and dominance cases between 1998 and 2008 found that, on average, firms lose 2.3 per cent of their market value when an investigation is uncovered. The loss is explained in greater proportions by the adjustment effect and by reputational impact.[22] Finally, a study showed that the stock price of cartel companies fell by 10 per cent following a television show about the Dutch construction cartel, while information on this cartel was already publicly available. This drop may be explained by a reputational loss.[23]

On balance, shareholders may be relatively more harmed than managers by the consequences of cartel detection; even though several factors mitigate the extent of the loss. Managers rarely face the consequences of cartel detection, due to the absence of individual liability (eg. in Europe), or because companies may fail to punish responsible individuals, especially if they have left the firm. As such, a moral hazard situation may exist since managers may not bear the full cost of collusive behaviour. The next section discusses whether cartels may be characterised as a typical form of corporate misconduct.

6.2.2.2 Collusive Conduct: a Typical Form of Corporate Crime?

Participation in a cartel and thereby violating competition law has the characteristics[24] of a corporate crime, such as corruption or corporate fraud.[25]

---

[21] L. Aguzzoni, G. Langus and M. Motta 'The Effect of EU Antitrust Investigations and Fines on a Firm's Valuation', *Journal of Industrial Economics*, 61 (2013) 61, 290.

[22] S. van den Broek, R. G. M. Kemp, W. F. C. Verschoor and A. C. de Vries, 'Reputational Penalties to Firms in Antitrust Investigations', *Journal of Competition Law and Economics*, 8 (2012), 231.

[23] J. J. Graafland, 'Collusion, Reputation Damage and Interest in Code of Conduct: The Case of a Dutch Construction Company', *Business Ethics: A European Review*, 2 (2004), 127.

[24] For further discussion of whether competition law infringements are distinctive compared with other forms of corporate crimes, see Section 8.3.1.

[25] 'As an illegal activity involving many agents, cartels can be considered a form of organized crime, certainly not the most harmful. Long term corruption [. . .], collusion between agents and supervisors [. . .], large scale frauds (including financial ones), and most kinds of illegal trade (in drugs, arms and

A corporate crime is, in criminology, 'the conduct of a corporation (or of employees acting on its behalf) which is proscribed and punishable by civil, administrative, or criminal statutes'.[26] Corporate crimes are typically seen as detrimental to the value of the firm, and are analysed as emanating from the misbehaviour of the managers and working against the interest of the shareholders.[27] The critical question, however, is the extent to which cartel conduct requires a different analysis. As was explained, collusive behaviour is very profitable when undetected, while other types of corporate crime, such as embezzlement, may directly harm shareholders, irrespective of whether the wrongdoing is sanctioned.

Mullin and Snyder make the assumption that corporate crimes, and in particular antitrust infringement, benefit shareholders.[28] This may be a valid approach in the specific context of their analysis, which is the analysis of indemnification of employees by companies, in the absence of sanctions.[29] Alexander and Cohen's empirical study provides further evidence that restriction of competition, as a form of corporate crime, affects the interests of shareholders and constitutes an agency cost. Some of the corporate crimes highlighted in this study are cases of antitrust infringement.[30] The study examines the ownership structure of infringing and non-infringing companies. The authors collected data on the proportion of stock held by the top management of companies before the commencement of the corporate crime, and from companies that supposedly remained virtuous. In their econometric

---

people trafficking, where at least a buyer and a seller repeatedly interact) are similar to cartels in terms of the incentive structure they generate for the involved agents, and the social costs of these activities to society are enormous' (G. Spagnolo, 'Divide et Impera: Optimal Leniency Programs' (2004) CEPR Working Paper No 4840, 5).

[26] S. Simpson, N. Leeper Piquero and R. Paternoster, 'Rationality and Corporate Offending Decisions' in A. Piquero and S. G. Tibbetts (eds.), *Rational Choice and Criminal Behavior: Recent Research and Future Challenges* (Routledge, 2002), p. 26.

[27] H. A. Newman and D. W. Wright, 'Strict Liability in a Principal-Agent Model', *International Review of Law and Economics*, 10 (1990), 219; J. R. Macey, 'Agency Theory and the Criminal Liability of Organizations', *Boston University Law Review*, 71 (1991), 315; J. Arlen, 'The Potentially Perverse Effects of Corporate Criminal Liability', *Journal of Legal Studies*, 23 (1994), 833; C. Y. Chu and Q. Yingyi, 'Vicarious Liability under a Negligence Rule', *International Review of Law and Economics*, 15 (1995), 305; M. L. Davis, 'The Impact of Rules Allocating Legal Responsibilities Between Principals and Agents', *Managerial and Decision Economics*, 17 (1996), 413; J. Arlen and R. Kraakman, 'Controlling Corporate Misconduct: An Analysis of Corporate Liability Regimes', *New York University Law Review*, 72 (1997), 687; S. Shavell, 'The Judgment Proof Problem', *International Review of Law and Economics*, 6 (1986), 458.

[28] W. P. Mullin and C. M. Snyder, 'Should Firms Be Allowed to Indemnify Their Employees for Sanctions?', *Journal of Law, Economics, and Organization*, 26 (2010), 41. The model developed by Privileggi et al. also features an illegal activity that benefits the principal of the agency relationship: F. Privileggi, C. Marchese and A. Cassone, 'Agent's Liability Versus Principal's Liability When Attitudes Toward Risk Differ', *International Review of Law and Economics*, 21 (2001), 181–95.

[29] 'This is the natural framework for studying our central issue – indemnification – because a firm would presumably not choose to indemnify its agent for crimes against itself' (Mullin and Snyder, 'Should Firms Be Allowed to Indemnify Their Employees for Sanctions?', 41).

[30] C. R. Alexander and M. A. Cohen, 'Why Do Corporations Become Criminals? Ownership, Hidden Actions, and Crime as an Agency Cost', *Journal of Corporate Finance*, 5 (1999), 1.

model, the dependent variable is the occurrence of corporate crime and the independent variable is the proportion of stock held by the top management. The study concludes that the rate of corporate crime is higher when top management owns less than 10 per cent of the shares of the company. This result validates the theory of agency cost developed by Jensen and Meckling. Fewer shares being held by the top management indicates a greater separation of ownership and control, and thus wider scope for agency cost. The cases under examination in this study do not specifically concern situations in which top management were personally involved in the illegal behaviour, but mostly relate to hidden actions of other employees. The cost related to the hidden actions of employees can be addressed with monitoring schemes, but cannot be reduced completely, as it is inherent to the separation of ownership and control. Consequently, there are more corporate crimes in situations of greater separation of ownership and control. Therefore, antitrust infringements, like other corporate crimes, affect the value of the firm and are a manifestation of the existence of agency cost in companies in which ownership and control are distinct.[31]

6.2.3 Collusion as a Source of the Agency Problem

In addition to being a particular specification of the agency problem, the restriction of competition may also constitute a source of the agency problem.[32] Some companies in mature industries may produce significant cash flow from their operations; however, as the industry reaches a level of maturity, the company may be unable to make any further investments and therefore generate a surplus. Surpluses that are generated and that cannot be invested in other projects constitute *free cash flow*, over which the manager exerts his residual control. Free cash flow may serve to distribute dividends to the shareholders. However, the manager may have an incentive not to return the free cash flow to the shareholders because investing in a new line of business, buying another company, or *empire building*, may better serve the manager's goal of increasing the size of the company. In the event, however, that such investment fails, both the value of the company and the interests of the shareholders may be in jeopardy.

Participation in a cartel may exacerbate the divergence of interests related to the existence of free cash flow. If successful, a cartel agreement increases the profits of the company because it allows companies to set prices higher than competitive levels, i.e. greater than its marginal cost. Increased profits for the company are likely to result in more free cash flow, which may leave more room for the potential misuse

[31] Only six observations out of seventy-eight relate to the specific case of antitrust infringement. Owing to the low number of observations, this study cannot constitute strong evidence for antitrust infringement being an agency cost, but it illustrates the intuition. The empirical study is based on an econometric model that takes into account several variables. Focusing on one variable in isolation from the others necessarily yields erroneous conclusions.
[32] M. C. Jensen, 'Agency Costs of Free Cash Flow, Corporate Finance, and Takeovers', *American Economic Review*, 76 (1986), 323.

of such discretionary power by managers. However, it must be stressed that this effect is likely to arise whenever a company makes profit in a mature industry, due, for example, to a successful innovation.

In general, the degree of competition in a market may impact the scope of the agency problem. A firm operating in a highly competitive market must optimise costs and internal processes, to sustain its position in the market, including agency costs.[33] Competition also improves the ability of a company to evaluate a manager, as the performance of similar competing companies may provide a basis for comparison. In addition, competition enables the design of reward schemes based on relative performance.[34] As such, competition can be considered a disciplining device in companies, which compels them to adopt efficient mechanisms of corporate governance.[35] Several economic studies have therefore analysed the impact of product market competition on the performance of firms.[36] Finally, the opportunism of top executives can be disciplined by effective competition in the market for corporate control.[37]

Restriction of competition via participation to a cartel displays a number of characteristics of the agency problem that are inherent to the relation between managers and shareholders. Managers and shareholders may have different time horizons towards the benefits of participating in a cartel: managers may not bear the full cost of their action, and participation in a cartel may be detrimental to the firm, taking the legal and market consequences of an investigation. A reduction in competition may also mean that managers face less external discipline device. As such, it is essential to analyse the interplay between corporate governance mechanisms and collusion, as a specification of the agency problem.

[33]　F. Machlup 'Theories of the Firm: Marginalist, Behavioral, Managerial', *American Economic Review*, 57 (1967), 1–33.
[34]　B. Holmström, 'Moral Hazard in Teams'. *Bell Journal of Economics*, 13 (1982), 324; B. J. Nalebuff and J. E. Stiglitz, 'Prices and Incentives: Towards a General Theory of Compensation and Competition', *Bell Journal of Economics*, 14 (1983), 21; B. J. Nalebuff and J. E. Stiglitz, 'Information, Competition, and Markets', *American Economic Review*, 73 (1983), 278.
[35]　E. Fama, 'Agency Problems and the Theory of the Firm', *Journal of Political Economy*, 88 (1980), 288.
[36]　R. D. Willig, 'Corporate Governance and Market Structure' in A. Razin and E. Sadka (eds.), *Economic Policy in Theory and Practice* (Macmillan, 1987); S. J. Nickell, 'Competition and Corporate Performance', *Journal of Political Economy*, 104 (1996), 724, 727; M. Baily and H. Gersbach, 'Efficiency in Manufacturing and the Need for Global Competition' in M. Baily (ed.), *Brookings Papers on Economic Activity: Microeconomics* (Brookings, 1995), p. 307; S. Januszewski, J. Koke and J. K. Winter, 'Product Market Competition, Corporate Governance and Firm Performance: An Empirical Analysis for Germany', *Research in Economics*, 56 (2002), 299.
[37]　B. Warner, R. L. Watts and K. H. Wruck, 'Stock Prices and Top Management Changes', *Journal of Financial Economics*, 20 (1988), 461; M. S. Weisbach, 'Outside Directors and CEO Turnover', *Journal of Financial Economics* (1988), 431; E. Fama and M. C. Jensen 'Agency Problems and Residual Claims', *Journal of Law and Economics*, 26 (1983), 327, 328; H. G. Manne, 'Mergers and the Market for Corporate Control', *Journal of Political Economy*, 73 (1965), 110; and B. Rock, 'Antitrust and the Market for Corporate Control', *California Law Review*, 77 (1989), 1365.

6.3 CORPORATE GOVERNANCE AND COLLUSION

This section discusses the impact of mechanisms of corporate governance used to master the agency problem on collusive behaviour. After a brief presentation of the relevant mechanisms of corporate governance, the impact of the monitoring function of the board of directors and the top management and of remuneration schemes will be examined. As will be seen, corporate governance mechanisms may help to explain the occurrence of collusion. Mechanisms of corporate governance that are not optimally designed produce undesirable effects most of the time, with respect to both shareholders' interests and the level of competition. Finally, this section will consider the possible links between different systems of corporate governance and statistics on cartel decisions.

6.3.1 *The Mechanisms of Corporate Governance*

The mechanisms of corporate governance are designed to reduce the agency problem between the shareholders and the managers of a company. Monitoring helps to reduce the informational gap, and can be achieved internally, by the board of directors, or externally, by auditing companies, stock analysts or debt holders. A second category of mechanisms addresses the issue of conflicting interests between the shareholders and managers. These mechanisms contend to provide the right incentives, seeking to align the interests of the parties. The incentives can be provided internally – for example, by way of a remuneration scheme for the managers – or externally, by the competitive forces operating in markets such as the market for corporate control or the product market.[38] These mechanisms of corporate governance are present across the jurisdictions under consideration.[39]

6.3.1.1 The Role of the Top Management and Internal Monitoring

The way that internal monitoring is achieved in a company provides an understanding of how the responsibilities of running the company and control are divided. This helps to identify the level at which practices that restrict competition should be internally monitored and sanctioned. This also shows the impact that such mechanisms of corporate governance have on the competitive behaviour of the company.

6.3.1.1.1 THE BOARD OF DIRECTORS. For the purposes of corporate governance, the board of directors is the main tool for performing monitoring tasks. In large companies with dispersed shareholders, it is difficult for them to monitor the managers'

---

[38]   Douma and Schreuder, *Economic Approaches to Organizations*, p. 158.

[39]   Some mechanisms of corporate governance may be imposed by the law. For present purposes, I focus on the functionalities of the mechanisms rather than the regulatory provisions of corporate or company law. As such, corporate law will not be part of this section, although some principles of corporate law will be considered.

behaviour. Shareholders holding a very small portion of shares have very little incentive to invest time and effort in monitoring managers, as this would be likely to benefit all the other shareholders, including those holding a controlling interest, rather than merely the shareholder who undertakes the exercises. The returns would therefore be small compared with the effort. Coordinating the monitoring effort is also a challenging task in companies with numerous shareholders, and therefore more easily performed by the board of directors.

In most jurisdictions, the board of directors, comprising both executive and non-executive directors, ensures internal monitoring. Executive directors are internal managers in the company. The top manager of the company is part of the board, and is called the chief executive officer (CEO) in both the United States and in the United Kingdom (UK). Non-executive directors are external to the company and, depending upon the jurisdiction, they can be top managers from other companies, or large shareholders. The board is chaired by one executive and one non-executive director. This type of board structure or 'one-tier board' governance system, which is present in the UK and in the US, contrasts with 'two-tier board' systems in which there are two distinct boards: an executive board and a supervisory board. The latter are present in continental Europe (required in Germany and in the Netherlands, found in Italy and in France).[40] While the former comprises directors internal to the company, the latter comprises exclusively external directors. The structure of the board illustrates different corporate governance approaches, which will be explained below.

The executive directors of the board, or members of the executive board in the two-tier system, are responsible for running the company and monitoring the lower-level management. In large companies, the executive members are removed from the day-to-day business decisions, which are delegated to lower-level managers. The executive members in such structures focus on the strategy of the company, or take major decisions such as those on the sales of the division, large investment decisions, or an increase in capital.[41] The non-executive part of the board, or the supervisory board, in this system, has the duty of monitoring the executive part of the board, typically appointing and selecting the top managers, monitoring their performance, replacing them and taking legal action against them if necessary, taking decisions regarding remuneration, controlling the information systems internal to the company, and setting and implementing the compliance of executive directors with their obligations and duties.[42] The board derives its authority from the shareholders, who delegate their corporate power to the board, so that it may control and run the company on their behalf. The directors of the board have a duty to act in the best interests of the company, which means that they are legally required to remain

---

[40]   B. Tricker, *Corporate Governance, Principles, Policies and Practices*, 2nd edn (Oxford University Press, 2012), pp. 102–3.

[41]   D. Kershaw, *Company Law in Context: Text and Materials* (Oxford University Press, 2009), p. 224.

[42]   Ibid., p. 227.

loyal to it. The director's duty is not restricted to his actions when acting for the company, but extends to his personal actions as well. Therefore, directors may not make personal investments or enter into contracts that conflict with the company's interests.[43]

6.3.1.1.2 INTERNAL MONITORING AND COLLUSIVE BEHAVIOUR. The board of directors is ultimately responsible for ensuring the best interests of the shareholders. The board must not be passive just because good financial results are achieved by the managers of the company. It needs to ensure that results are not achieved via illegal corporate behaviour, which includes price-fixing.[44] The decision-making process for participating in a cartel shows that corporate governance schemes may be at stake in the wrongdoing of a company. This is the case when a senior executive is either directly or indirectly involved in the wrongdoing, or when management ought to have known of or prevented employees from breaching competition rules.

As is shown by a list of individuals responsible for past cartel cases, decisions to enter into a cartel may occur at a high level of the hierarchy, which encompasses the positions responsible for corporate governance within the undertaking.[45] CEOs of companies, presidents of subsidiaries and senior managers appear a number of times among the positions listed as being involved in decisions to enter into cartels. The involvement of these persons took the form of either personal and direct engagement in the decision, or indirect involvement (i.e. being aware of the decisions and allowing collusive behaviour). Sales managers, being directly exposed to pricing decisions, are also among the most active individuals participating in cartel decision-making. The common feature between individuals involved in cartel decisions is that they have some decision-making power over pricing, output or the geographical aspects of markets.[46]

The manner in which some European cartels have been organised confirms that the decision to participate in a cartel may emanate from the highest level of management.[47] The meetings of these cartels often took place at trade association meetings at which many top executives of companies from the same industry were gathered and at which they were therefore able to combine a business meeting with a collusive discussion.[48] The manner of implementation of cartel decisions reveals

---

[43] Ibid., p. 291.
[44] J. M. Connor, *Global Price Fixing (Studies in Industrial Organization)*, 2nd edn (Springer, 2008), p. 463.
[45] Stephan, 'See no Evil', 236.
[46] See ibid., 236, although this finding was somehow nuanced in A. Stephan and A. Nikpay, 'Leniency Decision-Making', pp. 144–6.
[47] Harrington, 'How Do Cartels Operate?', 78.
[48] *Choline Chloride* (Case COMP/E-2/37.533) Commission Decision 2005/566/EC [2004] OJ L190/22, para. 98; *Citric Acid* (Case COMP/E-1/36.604) Commission Decision 2002/742/EC [2001] OJ L239/18, para. 87; *Copper Plumbing Tubes* (Case COMP/E-1/38.069) Commission Decision [2006] OJ L192/2, para. 112; *Industrial and Medical Gases* (Case COMP/E-3/36.700) Commission Decision 2003/355/

that the decisions were monitored and implemented at lower and more local levels of management.[49]

Based on the assumption that cartel practices harm a company when detected, the direct involvement of the highest layers of the hierarchy in the decision to participate in a cartel implies a degree of failure in the corporate governance of the company. The board of directors has a duty to monitor the top management closely and to ensure that it, as well as the lower levels of the hierarchy, acts in the best interests of the shareholders. Corporate crimes are typically characterised by a failure of the board of directors to fulfil its duty.[50] In that sense, a company in which the senior management is involved in cartel practices gives rise to questions regarding the quality of the monitoring function achieved by its board of directors and by the top management. Involvement in cartels by local sales managers also questions the quality of internal mechanisms of control. The key question here is whether senior management ought to have questioned and controlled the origin of, for example, unusually good results.

Failure in a board's monitoring is exemplified by the poor quality of corporate governance at ADM, when that company was involved in several price-fixing scandals in the early 1990s. In 1996, ADM's board of directors was rated by a survey of management experts as one of the worst in the United States. This was based on the poor structure of the board, and its failure to respond adequately when evidence of the company's involvement in a cartel was presented to it. The board's passivity to management control was explained by the charismatic personality of the chairman, whose legitimacy relied on the excellent financial results achieved by the company over the past decades. The board was seen as being too large. It comprised seventeen members, few of whom could be considered as outsiders as many of them were personal acquaintances of the chairman. Conflicts of interests stemming from personal and family relationships in the company explained the slow response of the board when the management appeared to be involved in price-fixing scandals. Following a series of price-fixing scandals, the company made significant changes to its corporate governance, since when no further scandals have been reported.[51] The analysis of the organisation of a cartel shows that the individuals involved in

EC [2002] OJ L123/49, para. 105; *Industrial Tubes* (Case COMP/E-1/38.240) Commission Decision [2003] OJ L125/50, para. 10.

[49] Harrington, 'How Do Cartels Operate?', 78.

[50] The corporate scandal at Enron illustrates the role of the board of directors in the collapse and bankruptcy of a company: 'The Enron Board of Directors failed to safeguard Enron's shareholders and contributed to the collapse of the seventh largest public company in the United States, by allowing Enron to engage in high risk accounting, inappropriate conflict of interest transactions, extensive undisclosed off-the-book activities, and excessive executive compensation. The Board witnessed numerous indications of questionable practices by Enron management over several years, but chose to ignore them to the detriment of Enron's shareholders, employees and business associates' (US Senate, Committee on Governmental Affairs, 'The Role of the Board of Director in Enron's Collapse' (2002)).

[51] Connor, *Global Price Fixing*, pp. 463–4.

cartels are those whose parameters of employment depend on the profitability of the company.[52] This is surely inherent to the allocation of responsibility and power across the hierarchy, but also has implications for the quality of corporate governance.

The empirical study by González and Schmid shows a link between some characteristics of the board and the likelihood of a company participating in a cartel. Companies with a high proportion of busy directors, who are members of more than one board, are more likely to engage in a cartel.[53] Multiple directorships may indicate a low rate of attention by a director to each company's board and may provide a channel of cooperation for potential collusion. In addition, an empirical study by González et al. shows that companies involved in cartels may favour passive directors, are less likely to replace directors who resign, and may change auditing companies less often than the norm. Therefore, the governance function exerted by these boards may be seen as weaker than in those of companies not involved in cartels.[54]

A study by Sonnenfeld and Lawrence identifies some characteristics of the top management of companies involved in collusive practices.[55] The corporate culture conveyed from the top management to the lower level of the hierarchy plays a key role in price-fixing behaviour. In some companies, price-fixing may have been considered an accepted practice in the past. In such companies, long-tenured executives are more likely to maintain the habit of engaging in price-fixing, while the lower layers of management merely conform to the prevalent culture of the company. To illustrate the importance of specific culture characteristics of the top management, Sonnenfeld and Lawrence take the example of the acquisition of one company by another, to show that the executives of the parent company realised how different the ethics and culture of the acquired company were, even though they were operating in a similar industry. In other words, if the specific corporate culture conveyed by the top management is in favour of collusion, this increases the likelihood of collusive behaviour. This, however, does not minimise the role of external industry-specific factors in the likelihood of collusion.

6.3.1.2 The Impact of Remuneration Schemes on the Level of Competition

6.3.1.2.1 REMUNERATION AND CORPORATE GOVERNANCE. The economic literature suggests that the remuneration of senior managers must be linked to the

---

[52] American Bar Association, *Antitrust Compliance: Perspectives and Resources for Corporate Counselors*, 2nd edn (ABA Section of Antitrust Law, 2005), p. 30 in Stephan, 'See no Evil', 235.

[53] T. A. González and M. Schmid 'Corporate Governance and Antitrust Behavior', Swiss Institute of Banking and Finance, University of St. Gallen, Working Paper 5–6 (2012).

[54] T. A. González, M. Schmid and D. Yermack, 'How Managers Behave When They Have Something to Hide', NBER Working Paper No 18886 (2013). This study also found that cartel firms engage more in evasive financial reporting strategies, including earnings smoothing, segment reclassification, and restatement

[55] J. Sonnenfeld and P. R. Lawrence, 'Why Do Companies Succumb to Price Fixing?', *Harvard Business Review* (1978), 145.

performance of the company, as a way to reduce the agency problem.[56] As such, the design of remuneration contracts determines the incentives for managers to act in the best interests of shareholders. Bonuses, shares and option plans are examples of incentives contracts linking remuneration to economic performance. These remuneration schemes differ from the base salary that managers receive independently of the performance of the company. A bonus, paid annually, is linked to the accounting results of the firm. A manager receives this bonus if the company meets specific targets, which are based on ratios such as the return on assets, or on capital employed, the evolution of the sales growth or the market share achieved by the company. Share plans consist of awarding a stock of shares to the manager so that they have a personal interest in making decisions that result in an increase in the price of a share of the company. The allocation of shares can be conditional on the shares reaching a specific price target. Stock options constitute another incentive scheme through which a manager's pay is linked to the performance of the company. A stock option is a right to purchase shares at a given moment in the future, at a price specified in advance. The value of this scheme will increase with the price of the share, since the manager receives the difference between the price fixed in the option and the price of the share at the time of purchase. The manager is then provided with a strong incentive to improve the results of the company, and therefore the price of the share.

However, remuneration schemes that link pay and performance may be either suboptimal or capable of providing wrong incentives. First, factors outside the manager's control may affect the results of a company. The price of commodities, currency rates or other economic variables can negatively affect the price of the share, in a way that cannot be controlled by the manager. Conversely, periods of general economic growth can result in a rise in share prices despite poor management. Therefore, linking pay to performance may lead to inappropriate outcomes: managers performing badly in a period of economic boom may receive a high bonus, while high-performing managers whose businesses are highly dependent on the price of a commodity may not reach the target required for a bonus. This can reduce the strength of incentives, as managers may realise that considerable effort is not necessarily going to be adequately rewarded.[57]

The remuneration of managers can help to align the interests of managers and shareholders but, if not well designed or controlled, it can exacerbate agency relationship issues. Compensation of top executives is the object of regulation and policy documents, since its design is crucial to the outcome of corporate governance

---

[56] M. J. Conyon and C. A. Mallin, Directors' Share Options, Performance Criteria and Disclosure: Compliance with the Greenbury Report (1997) ICAEW Research Monograph, London in C. A. Mallin, *Corporate Governance*, 3rd edn (Oxford University Press, 2010), p. 190.

[57] Douma and Schreuder, *Economic Approaches to Organizations*, p. 373.

mechanisms.[58] Financial scandals, as exemplified by the Enron case in 2000, show how remuneration schemes may provide the wrong incentives to managers. In order to maximise the remuneration derived from stock options and bonuses, managers had very strong incentives to attain high share prices in the short term. Remuneration schemes linking performance and pay too strongly may have been partly to blame for the artificial manipulation of companies' results. The Enron case illustrates the issues of agency relationships and how the failure of corporate governance mechanisms may cause the failure of a company.[59]

6.3.1.2.2 REMUNERATION AND COLLUSION: ECONOMIC EVIDENCE. The economic literature discusses how the design of compensation schemes may impact the collusive incentives of managers. Remuneration based on high shares of profits paid as bonuses can foster collusion, because it may provide incentives for achieving such targets based on collusion rather than on effort.[60] Price-fixing agreements may then be a way of artificially inflating the profits derived from sales in the short-term to 'get the numbers no matter what'.[61] Thus, schemes linking pay to performance can be adjusted by the company to impact collusion incentives, or to promote or prevent collusive behaviour. Remuneration schemes also help to sustain a collusive agreement, preventing individuals within cartel firms from unilateral defection from a cartel engagement. While inherent incentives to deviate make cartels unstable, the prospect of retaliation and a price war may help to sustain a cartel agreement.[62] Managers may then sustain such an agreement if they expect to suffer from a price war in the future.

Herold shows how different types of remuneration schemes (e.g. capped bonus, threshold-linear or linear contracts) can be adjusted to reduce managerial incentives to collude.[63] Paha's model analyses how managerial incentives can affect the pattern of cartel formation, through the response of managers to profit shocks. Overall, it suggests that factors including remuneration schemes should be carefully designed to account for the collusive behaviour that they may induce.[64] Thépot and Thépot also explore the impact of managerial compensation on choice of collusive outcome by managers. The model shows that firms may choose to collude on parameter of

---

[58] For example, in the UK: Financial Reporting Council, Corporate Governance Code (2018); in the EU: Recommendation Complementing Recommendations 2004/913/EC and 2005/162/EC as regards the regime for the remuneration of directors of listed companies [2009] L120/28.

[59] For failure of the corporate governance function by the board, see n. 50.

[60] C. Aubert, 'Managerial Effort Incentives and Market Collusion' (2009) Toulouse School of Economics, Working Paper No 09-127.

[61] Sonnenfeld and Lawrence, 'Why Do Companies Succumb to Price Fixing?', 75.

[62] Motta, *Competition Policy, Theory and Practice*, p. 139.

[63] See also D. Herold, 'The Impact of Incentive Pay on Corporate Crime', MAGKS Discussion Paper No. 52-2017 (2017).

[64] J. Paha, 'Antitrust Compliance: Managerial Incentives and Collusive Behavior', *Managerial and Decision Economics*, 38(7) (2017), 992–1002.

remuneration, rather than on product market prices, to obtain cartel profits.[65] Spagnolo (2005), and Buccirossi and Spagnolo examine the interplay between remuneration schemes such as stock options and bonuses, and the ability to sustain a collusive agreement.[66] They find that certain remuneration schemes can have the effect of sustaining collusive behaviour. Stock-based bonuses link the manager's present remuneration to the future profits of the company. Under the assumption of perfect information, the market anticipates the effect of deviation from a cartel agreement if detected by the competitors. The stock price therefore incorporates the information that profit losses are to be expected in the deviating company. As the manager's present compensation depends on the future profits earned by the firm, the loss suffered from a price war directly affects his compensation. Therefore, this remuneration scheme reduces the incentive for the manager to deviate from a collusive agreement.[67] In contrast, a capped bonus plan reduces the manager's valuation of higher profits in the future and increases his sensitivity to a potential loss resulting from a price war.[68]

Sonnenfeld and Lawrence examined the internal characteristics of companies within an industry particularly affected by illegal price-fixing practices in the United States. It transpires that the performance of sales managers in the convicted companies was mainly assessed according to the price levels and profits achieved. Bonuses and commissions, which were directly related to a manager's ability to increase the price of the company's goods, constituted a significant part of the compensation awarded to managers. Conversely, the most virtuous companies in the industry under consideration were compensating their sales managers via straight salary bases, and assessing their performance according to the volume of sales achieved, rather than profits and price levels.[69] To give a complementary example, at Lufthansa, the introduction of a personal performance scheme based on the results of the company over a rather long period (three years, contrasting with most performance schemes) possibly reflected a change in corporate culture, eventually leading to internal discovery of Lufthansa's involvement in the air cargo cartel.[70] Finally, data collected on the car glass cartel, the lifts and escalators cartel and the marine hose cartel suggests that the presence of a range of performance-based and

---

[65] F. Thépot and J. Thépot, 'Collusion, Managerial Incentives and Antitrust Fines', Working Papers of LaRGE Research Center 2017-06 (2017).

[66] G. Spagnolo, 'Managerial Incentives and Collusive Behavior', *European Economic Review*, 49 (2005), 150; P. Buccirossi and G. Spagnolo, 'Corporate Governance and Collusive Behavior' in W. D. Collins (ed.), *Issues in Competition Law and Policy 1* (American Bar Association, 2008).

[67] Buccirossi and Spagnolo, 'Corporate Governance and Collusive Behavior', 6.

[68] This is due to the concave form of the manager's objective function, and the related decreasing marginal utility from higher profits: Buccirossi and Spagnolo, 'Corporate Governance and Collusive Behavior'.

[69] Sonnenfeld and Lawrence, 'Why Do Companies Succumb to Price Fixing?', 79.

[70] H. Bergman, and D. D. Sokol, 'The Air Cargo Cartel: Lessons for Compliance' in Beaton-Wells and Tran, *Anti-Cartel Enforcement in a Contemporary Age*, p. 310.

stock-based compensation schemes may have created incentives for managers and other employees to sustain collusive agreements.[71]

Corporate governance produces effects on incentives to collude, either by the weaknesses of the mechanisms, or by the type of incentives induced. Mechanisms of corporate governance that are not optimally designed produce undesirable effects most of the time, with respect to both shareholders' interests and the level of competition.

6.3.2 *The Impact of the Systems of Corporate Governance on Competition*

The mechanisms of corporate governance previously described do not apply homogeneously across the jurisdictions, and can also differ within legal systems, according to the company's characteristics; its size, activity, and presence on or absence from the stock exchange can all affect the mechanisms at play. This section will introduce the main features of different corporate governance systems. The aim is to discuss possible correlation links between the systems and the occurrence of cartels. This section finds a potentially higher rate of cartel recidivism in countries displaying network-oriented rather than market-oriented governance.[72]

6.3.2.1 Market-Oriented Systems

The UK and the United States display market-oriented systems of corporate governance. Market oriented governance is characterised by widely dispersed shareholders and no shareholders owning a controlling part of the company. Minority shareholders are strongly protected by the law. In market-oriented systems, all large companies are listed on the stock exchange. The legal protection of minority shareholders reduces the potential long-running relationships between companies listed on the stock exchange and institutional actors, as these relationships could provide inside information to institutional investors, which is not available to smaller investors. Due to being widely dispersed and holding only a small portion of the stock, shareholders have less incentive to monitor managers closely. Instead of using voting rights to replace the management, widely dispersed shareholders tend to sell their share of a company if it is performing badly. The non-executive members of the board may also have a reduced incentive to monitor the management. Therefore, the market for corporate control and the fear of a hostile takeover may act as the most important monitoring devices in market-oriented systems.[73]

---

[71]   A. Petersone, 'Managerial Compensation and Cartel Behavior' (2010), available at: http://dare.uva.nl /cgi/arno/show.cgi?fid=222247

[72]   This classification of governance system follows that adopted in S. Douma and H. Schreuder, *Economic Approaches to Organizations*, 5th edn (Pearson, 2013). The term 'network' is generally used in distinction to 'market' and refers to blockholders' governance systems.

[73]   Ibid., p. 391.

6.3.2.2 Network-Oriented Systems

Some EU countries, such as continental European countries, are characterised by network-oriented systems of governance, or by the presence of a small numbers of shareholders holding large parts of the stock, otherwise known as block-holders. Some companies are owned by one investor or a few investors. Large companies are not necessarily listed on the stock exchange, and shares are not intensely traded. Large block holders are typically members of the board of directors, and can be institutional investors such as banks, as is often the case in Germany, or families, as is common in France and Italy.[74] Other stakeholders take part in the governance structure, with the example of employees in Germany being represented on the supervisory board. The investors therefore directly monitor the manager's actions by sitting on the board and using their voting rights. As such, the network-oriented system maintains a strong and long-running relationship between the shareholders and managers. Monitoring is therefore mostly done by the board, rather than by the market for corporate control.[75]

6.3.2.3 Governance System and Collusion

Connor has established a list of recidivist companies, which were convicted of engagement in several international cartels between 1990 and 2009.[76] As previously explained, companies from Germany and France are characterised by network-oriented corporate governance, while companies from the UK and the US follow the market-oriented system of corporate governance. A substantial difference in the level of cartel participation between countries with different corporate governance features is noticeable (see Table 1). Building on Connor's statistics, Table 1 establishes the rate of cartel recidivism according to country. For each country, two types of figures are presented: the proportion of recidivist companies and the proportion of cartel formations in that country. In addition, the figures are combined for the US and the UK on one side, and for France and Germany on the other side. The latter represents the network-oriented system and the former the market-oriented system of corporate governance.

– Among the fifty-two leading recidivist companies, seventeen originated in France and Germany, and those companies engaged in a total of 213 cartels. This means that French and German companies were liable for 35,3 per cent of the international cartels in that period.

---

[74] Tricker *Corporate Governance, Principles, Policies and Practices*, p. 157.
[75] Douma and Schreuder, *Economic Approaches to Organizations*, 5th edn, p. 406.
[76] Connor, 'Recidivism Revealed', Annex: Table 1: 'Fifty-Two Leading Recidivists, 1990–2009'. For methodology, see J. M. Connor and G. Helmers, 'Statistics on Modern Private International Cartels' Working Paper 07-01: American Antitrust Institute (2007), 7. For criticism of the data set and the definition of recidivism used, see: G. J. Werden, S. D. Hammond and B. A. Barnett, 'Recidivism Eliminated: Cartel Enforcement in the United States Since 1999', *Competition Policy International Antitrust Chronicle*, 10 (2011).

TABLE 1 – *Cartel recidivism per country of incorporation*[77]

	Number of companies	Proportion	Number of cartels	Proportion
Austria	1	1.9%	7	1.2%
Belgium	1	1.9%	7	1.2%
Denmark	1	1.9%	15	2.5%
Finland	3	5.8%	23	3.8%
France	10	19.2%	125	20.7%
Germany	7	13.5%	88	14.6%
Italy	2	3.8%	26	4.3%
Japan	5	9.6%	63	10.4%
Korea	3	5.8%	35	5.8%
Luxembourg	1	1.9%	9	1.5%
Mexico	1	1.9%	12	2.0%
Netherlands	3	5.8%	34	5.6%
Spain	1	1.9%	7	1.2%
Sweden	1	1.9%	13	2.2%
Switzerland	3	5.8%	51	8.5%
United Kingdom	2	3.8%	25	4.1%
United States	7	13.5%	63	10.4%
Total	52		603	
UK and US	9	17.3%	88	14.6%
France and Germany	17	32.7%	213	35.3%

– In contrast, a total of nine UK and US companies were among the top cartel recidivists, engaging in a total of eighty-eight cartels, which amounts to 14,6 per cent of the international cartels accounted for.

The structure of the French and German industries surely plays a key role in explaining the substantial difference in cartel participation. Both economies are characterised by industries that are particularly prone to cartel formation because of the type of goods produced and the high barriers to entry into the market. It has been shown that cartel formation is more likely in industries producing homogeneous goods, which are characterised by rather stable demand, or a demand affected by common shock. Moreover, cartel formation is deemed more likely in markets in which entry and exit is difficult. If barriers to entry are low, new entrants are attracted by the high profits realised in such markets. Gains from collusion are then reduced, while the costs of punishment in the event of a deviation are relatively lower.[78]

[77] Based on Connor 'Recidivism Revealed', Annex: Table 1: 'Fifty-Two Leading Recidivists, 1990–2009'.
[78] OFT, 'Predicting Cartels', A Report Prepared for the Office of Fair Trading by P. A. Grout and S. Sonderegger (2005). See also R. C. Marshall and L. M. Marx, *The Economics of Collusion* (MIT Press, 2012).

Corporate features may also explain the higher rate of cartel prosecution in some countries. As discussed in Chapter 5, continental Europe may be characterised by a dense corporate network of financial and non-financial companies in continental Europe.[79] Corporate networks are created by relationships, such as shared ownership and interlocking directorates, between investors, board members and managers.[80] In Germany, corporate governance is characterised by a dense corporate network, with banks occupying central positions in the network. Despite transformations of capitalism, some suggest that corporate networks still play a role as an 'institutional infrastructure for coordination, information exchange, and control in Germany'.[81] In France, during the 1990s and 2000s, cross-shareholdings among major companies increased, intensifying the network of corporate ownership. Some related these new ties to the wave of liberalisation in the 1990s.[82] As outlined in the previous section, corporate links created by minority shareholdings and interlocks between competitors can soften competition. In addition, when corporate networks are dense, competitors may not be directly related but may be influenced by indirect corporate relationships. Therefore, corporate ties that establish a 'small world' of corporations may have been correlated with the multiple cartel convictions in France and Germany between 1990 and 2010.

In addition, a parallel between the rate of recidivism and investor protection can be suggested. La Porta, Lopez, Shleifer and Vishny state that the legal protection of investors is a key factor in determining the size of capital markets.[83] Countries with legal systems of French and German origin are characterised by a lower level of legal investor protection and a high concentration of share ownership. In contrast, countries with Anglo-Saxon legal origins have stronger legal protection for investors, and companies are characterised by a dispersed structure of ownership.[84] In the narrow sense of corporate governance, meaning the mechanisms by which shareholders ensure a return of their investment, the legal protection of investors acts as a proxy for corporate governance features. One may wonder whether less investor protection indicated a greater likelihood that managers would enter into collusive behaviours, hence the higher recidivism rates in countries with poorer investor protection. In countries with weaker investor protection, however, companies may achieve corporate governance differently. Companies may, for example, compensate

---

[79] Section 5.3.

[80] F. Ferraro, G. Schnyder, E. M. Heemskerk et al., 'Structural Breaks and Governance Networks in Western Europe' in B. Kogut (ed.), *The Small Worlds of Corporate Governance* (MIT Press, 2012), p. 151.

[81] B. Kogut and G. Walker, 'The Small World of Germany and the Durability of National Networks', *American Sociological Review*, 66 (2001), 317.

[82] V. A. Schmidt, 'Privatization in France: The Transformation of French Capitalism', *Environment and Planning C: Government and Policy*, 17 (1999), 445. In subsequent periods, the intensity of these links seems to have reduced, with the emergence of foreign investors in French major companies.

[83] R. La Porta, F. Lopez-de-Silanez, A. Shleifer and R. W. Vishny, 'Legal Determinants of External Finance', *The Journal of Finance*, 52 (1997), 1131.

[84] Ibid.

a lower level of legal protection for investors with greater control by the board of directors. In network-oriented systems, corporate governance is indeed characterised by a more concentrated ownership structure, which enables investors to have more control over the firm's conduct.[85]

However, as is exposed in Chapter 5, dispersion of shareholders, which is rather an Anglo-American feature, may also yield different competition problems. Recent debates on common ownership by institutional investors provide examples of competitive effects that may be specific to such corporate governance systems. Activism of minority shareholders, and 'stewardship approaches', are aimed at addressing some agency problems created by different time horizons of various shareholders.[86] The stewardship approach may even expressly encourage institutional investors to act collectively.[87] In addition, while positive for better corporate governance, such approaches may also provide greater means by which institutional investors may restrict competition.[88]

Looking at past cartel statistics, network-oriented systems, which are traditionally characterised by stronger corporate links between companies, may have favoured the emergence of softer competition, including collusive practices, between companies. Systems characterised by greater legal protection for shareholders may have been associated with greater protection for shareholders against the risk of participation in a cartel. However recent debates on common ownership links show that measures that ensure shareholders' protection may produce competitive effects not traditionally accounted for in competition law. Thus, no causality can be established between the type of governance and the level of competition, as other important economic factors explain the level of collusion in a country or industry. Cartel prosecution is only the tip of the iceberg; this does not say anything about collusive practices that have not been detected. Finally, the difference in cartel cases may be explained by the much longer tradition of antitrust enforcement in the United States than in the EU. In the United States, antitrust and sanctions against cartels were in place much earlier than in the EU, where harsh fines only started to be imposed at the start of the period of observation.[89] This means that, at least in the United States, companies have surely developed an awareness of non-compliance risks at a much earlier stage than in France and Germany.

---

[85]   A. Shleifer and R. W. Vishny, 'A Survey of Corporate Governance', *The Journal of Finance*, 52 (1997), 737, 754.

[86]   M. C. Corradi and A. Tzanaki, 'Active and Passive Institutional Investors and New Antitrust Challenges: Is EU Competition Law Ready?', *CPI Antitrust Chronicle* (2017).

[87]   Financial Reporting Council, The UK Stewardship Code, 2012; K. Sergakis, 'EU Corporate Governance: the Ongoing Challenges of the "Institutional Investor Activism" Conundrum', *European Journal of Law Reform*, 4 (2014), 726–48.

[88]   For example, behind-the-scenes activism, described at Section 5.3.1.1.2.

[89]   EU Commission, cartel statistics (2017).

6.4 CONCLUSION

The issue of collusive behaviour may be characterised as a specification of the agency problem arising in a relationship in which there is imperfect information and opportunistic behaviour. Collusive practices exacerbate the agency issue and may be a type of agency cost, when they stem from hidden managerial actions that are detrimental to the shareholders' interest. The practical implication is that mechanisms of corporate governance, which seek to address the agency problem, are closely related to the internal drivers of collusion. As has been shown, wrongly designed compensation schemes, or poor internal monitoring, may explain the participation of firms in cartels. In addition, an analysis of corporate governance systems may shed some light into additional driving forces of cartels. This chapter provides the necessary inquiry into internal drivers that was for long absent from economic analysis of collusion. As such, this chapter opens the 'black box' of the firm disentangling internal dynamics that are fundamental to the study of cartels. The chapters that follow incorporate these findings into the discussion of optimal enforcement against cartels.

7

Cartel Enforcement: Sanctions and Leniency

7.1 INTRODUCTION

Based on the agency-based framework developed in Chapter 6, this chapter provides normative suggestions for enhancing the deterrence and detection effects of cartel enforcement. In the EU, sanctions for infringing competition law are typically imposed on undertakings, while actors within the firm are rarely liable for engaging their companies into anticompetitive practices.[1] Recent policy trends suggest that sanctions – instruments seeking to *deter* anticompetitive practices – should increasingly target the incentives of individuals, in addition to the companies' incentives. In the United States, prison terms have been regularly imposed for breach of the Sherman Act, and the average sentence went up from eight months in the 1990s to twenty months over the last two decades.[2] In 2015 and 2017, after a period of low success with criminal cases, the UK Competition and Markets Authority's (CMA's) criminal investigations led to the imposition of suspended prison sentences and director disqualification in relation to the galvanised steel tanks and the construction product cartels.[3] Among other EU member states, a growing number of competition regimes incorporate individual sanctions; although the enforcement level of such sanctions remains rather low.[4] Instruments seeking to *detect* ongoing anticompetitive practices, such as leniency policy or bounty programmes, aim to destabilise the relationships between cartel members by producing effects on relations that are

[1] For example, in EU competition law, undertakings are the subject-matter of competition law provisions, and decision sanctions are addressed to undertakings. See, for example, in the UK: Enterprise Act 2002, ss. 188 and 204; in the United States: Sherman Act, 15 USC §1. As will be explained below, many EU member states have sanctions against individuals, but the enforcement level is low.

[2] Department of Justice, Antitrust Division, Criminal Enforcement Trend Charts (2017), www.justice .gov/atr/criminal-enforcement-fine-and-jail-charts

[3] *R* v. *Snee*: see CMA Press Release, 'Director Sentenced to 6 months for Criminal Cartel' (14 September 2015); CMA Press Release, 'Supply of Precast Concrete Drainage Products: Criminal Investigation' (15 September 2017).

[4] K. Jones and F. Harrison, 'Criminal Sanctions: An Overview of EU and National Case Law' (2014) e-Competitions N° 64713.

internal to companies.[5] One of the most striking (but non-typical) examples is given by Mark Whitacre, who denounced his own company for participation in the lysine cartel. His cooperation with the Federal Bureau of Investigation (FBI), in return for which he hoped to gain amnesty, enabled it to bring down other related cartels in the international chemicals industry.[6]

This chapter assesses the effectiveness of cartel enforcement instruments that seek to *deter* and *detect* collusive behaviour. It provides normative justification for better targeting individual incentives, including greater recourse to individual sanctions. The effectiveness of enforcement instruments critically depends on their effects on internal dynamics, analysed through the lens of agency relationships. It explores how sanctions or leniency policy modify the incentives of the actors of the agency relationship between shareholders and managers, depending on whether the principal or the agent is targeted. Under certain circumstances, competition law instruments should help to align interests between managers and shareholders, while, in others, enforcement instruments need to aggravate the agency problem for greater effectiveness.

Forming and sustaining a cartel involves different types of actors within a company. The chapter first examines different types of agency relationships that are relevant in the context of a cartel activity. The second section will examine instruments that aim to *deter* anticompetitive practices, including sanctions that range from corporate administrative fines, to individual criminal penalties. The third section will focus on instruments that aim to *detect* existing anticompetitive practices. Normative suggestions for greater effectiveness require an understanding of the desired impact of such tools on the dynamics of the agency relation. The fourth section will analyse the *ex post* reaction by shareholders to a cartel investigation and possible tools of corporate governance that may be used.

This chapter relies on the specific theoretical framework of the agency relationship, supported by a well-established body of literature. However, the study of collusive behaviour cannot be restricted to such a framework, which largely rests on the assumption that actors within the firm are somehow rational (with limitations brought by limited expertise or imperfect information are part of the foundations of the agency problem).[7] Criminology, or behavioural economics that provide very relevant insights into the study of collusion, are, however, not part of subsequent

---

[5] These instruments, of course, also aim to increase the cost of cartel participation and to deter cartel practice.

[6] However, it seems that his actions were driven by the need to hide other criminal practices, and were probably influenced by his mental health problems. After exposing the cartel and working for three years with the FBI on the investigation, Mark Whitacre was eventually convicted and given a 10-and-a-half-year prison sentence for other criminal infringements.

[7] Following the methodology of the economic analysis of law. See, for example, A. Polinsky, A. Mitchell and S. Shavell, *Economic Analysis of Law*, 2nd edn (The New Palgrave Dictionary of Economics, 2008).

developments, for the sake of conciseness.[8] The agency relationship is here under-stood more generally as any mismatch of information and interests, and any beha-viour, driven by rational or irrational motives, that would put the company at risk of a violation of competition.

7.2 AGENCY RELATIONSHIPS IN THE CONTEXT OF FORMING AND SUSTAINING A CARTEL

7.2.1 *Example of Agency Relationships in Cartels*

Forming and sustaining a cartel may involve multi-level types of relationships within the firm.[9] As discussed in Chapter 6, in the short run, benefits of cartel participation accrue for shareholders and managers, implying that their interests in price-fixing are aligned. When there is detection, or in the longer run, cartel participation is a manifestation of the agency problem, which is the case when managers are not individually liable.[10]

In addition, the operation and implementation of the cartel within the firm may involve delegation of tasks between various actors, as described here:

> The senior executives responsible for determining the broad outline of the [citric acid] cartel agreement were nicknamed 'the masters.' The lower level executives responsible for the day-to-day workings of the cartel were 'the sherpas'. They shared monthly sales figures and took stock at the end of the year of each company's total sales.[11]

The distinction between the cartel decision-making – by the 'principals' – and its implementation by the 'agents', is particularly relevant in cases in which decisions to participate in cartels originate from the higher level of the hierarchy.[12] In such situations, the cartel may be implemented by lower-level management, whose role is to guarantee the actual return of the cartel practice for higher level management.[13]

The delegation of the operation and implementation of the cartels to lower-level employees intervenes for reasons similar to the delegation of a task in the classic agency relationship. The principal employs someone who is better positioned to

---

[8] See Introduction to Part II (n. 3).
[9] D. H. Ginsburg and J. D. Wright, 'Antitrust Sanctions', *Competition Policy International*, 6 (2010), 3, 16.
[10] See Section 6.2.2.
[11] K. Eichenwald 'US Wins a Round Against Cartel', *New York Times*, 30 January 1997 in M. C. Levenstein and V. Y. Suslow, 'What Determines Cartel Success?', *Journal of Economic Literature*, 44 (2006), 73.
[12] A. Stephan, 'See No Evil: Cartels and the Limits of Antitrust Compliance Programs', *The Company Lawyer*, 31 (2010), 231, 236. In some cases, the top level of management was personally involved, and in other cases it permitted the collusion while not being directly involved.
[13] J. E. Harrington, 'How Do Cartels Operate?', *Foundations and Trends in Microeconomics*, 2 (2006), 78; see table of allocation of authority.

perform a task, be it for his specialised expertise or the time that he can dedicate to such a task. In the context of a price-fixing cartel, it seems logical that sales divisions specialising in business decisions related to pricing are very often involved in the operation of the cartel.[14]

With the objective of pursuing personal goals, an employee may decide not to comply with the cartel implementation instructions. In the context of a cartel operation, the agent maximises the principal's value if he or she implements the cartel agreement, under strict confidentiality, which includes not keeping hard evidence of any meetings and refraining from exposing the cartel to the authorities. In some cartel cases, some agents have been 'faithless' to their principals as they failed to comply with the instructions emanating from the high-level executives, due to the pursuit of personal goals.[15] The cartel between the auction houses Sotheby's and Christie's provides an example, in which Christie's chief executive officer (CEO), who was responsible for the implementation of the cartel in practice on behalf of his chairman, generated a huge amount of evidence, in spite of a promise not to leave any written notes relating to the secret meetings he was holding with his counterpart.[16] His personal goal was to gather the maximum amount of incriminating evidence on the illegal practice, as a potential source of bargaining power against his own company, and as a way of ensuring protection through an immunity scheme should the cartel be detected and prosecuted.[17] The lysine cartel provides another example of a faithless agent in the context of a cartel operation.[18] Mark Whitacre, a corporate executive of one of the cartelist companies, ADM, kept a significant amount of evidence on its price-fixing practices, which he thought would attract the investigation's attention to the case of the cartel being detected. By doing so, he was pursuing his own interest, which was to dissimulate other illegal activities that he was undertaking at the time. He hoped that the evidence provided, and his

[14] 'Sales managers and pricing specialists possess the knowledge about prices, costs, sales history, etc., needed to reach an agreement as to who will bid for what job or what price will be set for what goods' (R. R. Faulkner, E. R. Cheney, G. A. Fisher and W. E. Baker, 'Crime by Committee: Conspirators and Company Men in the Illegal Electrical Industry Cartel, 1954–1959', *Criminology*, 41 (2003), 511).

[15] Leslie uses the expression of 'faithless agent' to refer to an employee who is a weak link in the cartel organisation, and therefore not maximising the principal's value by adequately implementing the cartel agreement: C. Leslie, 'Cartels, Agency Costs, and Finding Virtue in Faithless Agents', *William & Mary Law Review*, 49 (2008), 1621.

[16] The collusion was prosecuted both in the United States and in the EU. For the EU decision, see: *Fine Art Auction Houses* (Case COMP/E-2/37.784) Commission Decision IP/02/1585 [2006] 4 CMLR 90; for the US case (civil), see: *In Re Auction Houses Antitrust Litigation*, 135 F Supp 2d 438 (SDNY 2001); DoJ Press Release, Former Chairmen of Sotheby's and Christie's Auction Houses Indicted in International Price-Fixing Conspiracy (2 May 2001).

[17] C. Mason, *The Art of the Steal* (G. P. Putnam & Sons, 2004), p. 246.

[18] The lysine cartel occurred in the mid-1990s, when five companies fixed the price of the animal feed additive lysine. The sanctions imposed by the US authorities included a total of $105 million in fines, and jail sentences for some executives. For the final US legal decision, see: *US v. Michael D Andreas and Terrance S Wilson*, 216 F 3d 645 (2000). The EU Commission issued an infringement decision in 2000 and imposed a total of €110 million in fines: *Amino Acids* (Case COMP/36.545/F3) Commission Decision 2001/418/EC [2000] OJ L152.

cooperation in the cartel investigation, would impede the FBI from discovering his other crimes.[19] It also seems that Mark Whitacre suffered from mental illness at that time, which may also explain his behaviour against his firm.[20] The impossibility of fully controlling the behaviour of each actor, and diverging interests towards cartel participation, be they on rational or less rational grounds, may complicate the implementation of a cartel agreement.

Participation in a cartel may also involve relevant agency relationships outside the boundaries of the firm. The *AC Treuhand* case is one such (unusual) examples, in which a consultancy was commissioned to facilitate the operation of the cartel, in exchange for remuneration.[21] The judgment made it clear that even companies operating in a different market than that affected by the cartel could be liable. Therefore, *AC Treuhand* clarified that incentives in this type of agency relationship may be aligned regarding both the costs and the benefits of cartel participation.

7.2.2 *Alignment of Interests*

The company can easily align the incentives between the cartel decision-makers and those who are responsible for implementing the cartel.[22] In some companies, price-fixing may have been an accepted practice in the past. In such companies, long-tenured executives are more likely to maintain the habit of engaging in collusive conduct, while the lower layers of management merely conform to the prevalent culture of the company.[23] Employees may also find it natural to comply with price-fixing instructions, as they would comply with any other business instruction. For example, one of the companies of the lysine cartel, ADM, fired an employee who refused to cooperate with the cartel operations.[24] In the electrical equipment cartel, a vice-president at General Electric admitted to having used strong social pressure to coerce executives to fix prices.[25]

As was explained in Chapter 6, a company may provide incentives to employees so that they benefit from a sustained price-fixing outcome financially.[26] Sonnenfeld and Lawrence, who examined some characteristics of companies within an industry affected by price-fixing practices, found that compensation schemes in place may have been a powerful tool to align the interests of senior management and

[19]   Leslie, 'Cartels, Agency Costs, and Finding Virtue in Faithless Agents', 1643. After exposing the cartel and working for three years with the FBI on the investigation, Mark Whitacre was given a 10-and-a-half-year prison sentence, for embezzlement.
[20]   K. Eichenwald, *The Informant* (Random House, 2000), p. 390.
[21]   Case C-194/14 P, AC Treuhand v. Commission, ECLI:EU:C:2015:717.
[22]   Leslie, 'Cartels, Agency Costs, and Finding Virtue in Faithless Agents', 1649.
[23]   J. Sonnenfeld and P. R. Lawrence, 'Why Do Companies Succumb to Price Fixing?', *Harvard Business Review* (1978) 145.
[24]   J. Connor, *Global Price Fixing (Studies in Industrial Organization)*, 2nd edn (Springer, 2008), p. 141, n. 7.
[25]   Sonnenfeld and Lawrence 'Why Do Companies Succumb to Price Fixing?', 148.
[26]   See Section 6.3.1.2.

employees in the price-fixing activity.[27] In contrast, the most virtuous companies were compensating their sales managers via straight salary bases. The managers' performance was assessed according to volumes of sales achieved, rather than profits and price levels.[28] Therefore, in these types of compensation schemes, sales managers' gains from a price-fixing agreement were not aligned to those of the company. Data collected on the car glass cartel, lifts and escalators cartel and marine hose cartel suggests that the presence of a range of performance-based and stock-based compensation schemes may create incentives for managers and other employees to sustain collusive agreements.[29]

Competition policy instruments have the potential to affect relationships at different levels within the firm. Depending on the actors considered, the agency problem operates either against or in favour of the cartel formation and stability. Therefore, it is of the utmost importance to specify and identify the relationship under consideration. The remainder of this chapter will merely focus on the agency relationship between managers and shareholders, but will consider the relationship between top executives and lower-level employees in several instances when relevant.

7.3 ENFORCEMENT INSTRUMENTS THAT AIM TO DETER CARTELS

Both in the European Union (EU) and in the United States, sanctions for breaching competition law have two objectives: sanctioning the illegal action, for which the infringer caused harm to society; and preventing a future breach of competition law.[30] The scope of sanctions imposed does not just intend to repair the loss to society that is associated with the breach, but attempts to deter it by making such an action unprofitable. In the cases of cartels, while the infringement, if not punished, may be highly profitable to the companies, it is also highly harmful to consumer welfare. To address the necessity of making infringements unprofitable, competition authorities have been imposing increasingly higher fines on companies breaching competition law.[31] Private enforcement is also another source of sanction cost for

---

[27] Sonnenfeld and Lawrence, 'Why Do Companies Succumb to Price Fixing?', 149.

[28] Ibid., 153.

[29] A. Petersone, 'Managerial Compensation and Cartel Behavior', unpublished B.Sc. thesis, University of Amsterdam (2010).

[30] Commission guidelines on the method of setting fines imposed pursuant to Article 23(2)(a) of Regulation No 1/2003 [2006] OJ C210/2, para. 4: 'Fines should have a sufficiently deterrent effect, not only in order to sanction the undertakings concerned (specific deterrence) but also in order to deter other undertakings from engaging in, or continuing, behaviour that is contrary to Articles [101] and 82 [102] of the EC Treaty (general deterrence).' In the United States, a cartel conviction opens the possibility of civil damages, and antitrust sanctions in general seek to deter anticompetitive practices (Department of Justice, G. J. Werden, S. D. Hammond and B. A. Barne, 'Deterrence and Detection of Cartels: Using all the tools and sanctions' (2012)).

[31] Statistics on fines imposed by the Commission between 1990 and 2017, available at: http://ec.europa.eu/competition/cartels/statistics/statistics.pdf; for the United States, see: Antitrust Division Criminal Enforcement Trends, available at: www.justice.gov/atr/criminal-enforcement-fine-and-jail-charts

companies that can affect incentives; particularly so in the United States, which has a long tradition of damages actions.[32] In subsequent developments, the cost of private enforcement will be integrated to that of corporate sanctions and will not be subject to specific analysis.

This section will provide normative suggestions for greater effectiveness of sanctions, in the light of their effects on the agency relationship. Sanction instruments range from administrative monetary fines, imposed on companies, to sanctions of a criminal nature, targeting the individuals. This section will first discuss sanctions that are imposed on companies exclusively, irrespective of their criminal or administrative nature. In the context of the agency relationship, corporate fines target shareholders – or the principal – of the agency relationship. Sanctions targeting the agent refer to sanctions imposed on individuals, ranging from monetary fines and imprisonment, to professional disqualification.

7.3.1 *Corporate Sanctions: Targeting the Principal in the Agency Relationship*

Throughout jurisdictions, administrative sanctions are almost invariably imposed on companies in case of participation of their employees to cartels.[33] In the EU, corporate sanctions are of an administrative nature, and are imposed on 'undertakings' that are the subject of competition law provisions, regardless of any internal dynamics within the undertaking.[34] Some member states criminalise participation to cartels, mostly with a low level of actual enforcement.[35] This section provides a normative justification for sanctions that target the principal of the agency relationship; and an assessment of their effectiveness. Corporate sanctions are necessary and effective when they induce companies to monitor individuals internally, provided that such controlling costs are not excessive and that they do not create 'perverse' effects. An analysis of *incentives* and *ability* informs such assessment.

7.3.1.1 The Normative Justification for Corporate Liability: the Necessity

On top of general arguments on deterrence of corporate sanctions, corporate liability seems desirable if it is very costly or difficult for society to enforce the law.[36] Corporate liability, instead of or in combination with individual liability, is justified

---

[32]   See, e.g., W. P. J. Wils, 'Private Enforcement of EU Antitrust Law and Its Relationship with Public Enforcement: Past, Present and Future', *World Competition*, 40(1) (2017), 3–45; for discussion of the deterrent effect of private enforcement in the United States, see, e.g., R. H. Land and J. P. Davis, 'Comparative Deterrence from Private Enforcement and Criminal Enforcement of the U.S. Antitrust Laws', *Brigham Young University Law Review* (2011), 315.
[33]   International Competition Network, *Anti-Cartel Enforcement Manual* (2011).
[34]   Article 23(5) of Regulation 1/2003 provides that sanctions for competition law infringement shall not be of a criminal nature.
[35]   See Section 7.3.2.1.
[36]   The same argument was advanced in the discussion on liability attribution in Chapter 4, based on the framework introduced in Chapter 2.

on the ground that companies have an informational advantage on their employee's action, and can implement internal monitoring and control at a lower cost than would be incurred for society.[37] Sanctioning companies exclusively may spare society from the potential costs associated with the prosecution of individuals, especially when it involves prison sentences. Also, individuals may not be as rational as companies and may be unresponsive to individual sanctions.[38] In addition, individuals may have a limited ability to pay a monetary fine corresponding to the value of economic harm to society.[39] When individuals are personally liable, corporate sanctions are necessary so that companies do not operate behind the shield of individual liability while profiting from inflated cartel profits.[40]

Corporate liability is desirable if it induces the company to internalise the social cost of the individual's wrongdoing. If so, the company incurs costs to reduce the agency problem associated with corporate liability. Companies can implement measures aimed at preventing individuals from entering into anticompetitive agreements, including, for example, compliance training for individuals who are particularly at risk. In addition, companies may run internal investigations and set up reporting mechanisms, with internal sanction schemes designed to increase the cost for an individual to enter into an illegal practice.[41] The agency costs incurred solve the agency problem when the company can align incentives by punishing individuals internally. The company can do so in firing, demoting or disciplining responsible individuals whose actions expose the company to liability.[42]

In competition law, as in many non-criminal matters, companies cannot avoid liability for infringements undertaken by their employees. It means that companies are liable even if they do not initiate, encourage or know of the individual's act.[43] In contrast, corporate liability for criminal matters is typically attributed based on much higher standards. The different rules for attributing liability may produce a differentiated impact on the agency dynamic.[44] As an example, the *identification* approach, the common law doctrine in the UK, establishes that a company will be criminally liable only if the mental element of the offence can be attributed to the

---

[37] L. Kornhauser, 'An Economic Analysis of the Choice Between Enterprise and Personal Liability for Accidents', *California Law Review*, 70 (1982), 1345, 1351.

[38] R. J. Herrnstein and J. Q. Wilson, *Crime and Human Nature* (Simon and Schuster, 1985); J. Arlen and R. Kraakman, 'Controlling Corporate Misconduct: An Analysis of Corporate Liability Regimes', *New York University Law Review*, 72 (1997), 687, 696.

[39] G. S. Becker, 'Crime and Punishment: An Economic Approach', *Journal of Political Economy*, 76 (1968), 169.

[40] W. P. J. Wils, 'Antitrust Compliance Programmes and Optimal Antitrust Enforcement', *Journal of Antitrust Enforcement*, 1 (2013), 59.

[41] Arlen and Kraakman, 'Controlling Corporate Misconduct',693.

[42] R. Kraakman, 'Corporate Liability Strategies and the Costs of Legal Controls', (*Yale Law Journal*, 93 (1984), 857.

[43] A. Sykes, 'The Economics of Vicarious Liability', *Yale Law Journal*, 93 (1984), 1231.

[44] B. Wardhaugh, *Cartels, Markets and Crime: A Normative Justification for Criminalisation of Economic Collusion* (Cambridge University Press, 2014), p. 57.

'directing mind and will'.[45] It therefore means that individuals occupying the highest positions within the company (e.g. members of the board of directors, or very close) must themselves be personally responsible to establish culpability of the company itself. Such a narrow construct of corporate liability, too closely aligned to individual liability, seems particularly inadequate to collusive behaviour by large companies.[46] In effect, a company will be criminally liable only if the decision to enter into a cartel is made by the highest individuals of the hierarchy, and will be shielded from liability in all other circumstances. Such an approach will therefore not produce any incentive for shareholders to reduce the agency gap that may lead to collusive behaviour. In the UK, a possible reform of corporate criminal liability for economic crime followed criticisms of the impossibility of applying corporate liability in the existing framework.[47]

Another approach to liability is that of vicarious liability, understood here generally as the liability of companies, even if they do not initiate, encourage or know of the individual's act.[48] It is argued that vicarious liability is effective if the underpinning legal construct provides adequate incentives for companies to monitor their employees.[49] For the sake of conciseness, the remainder of the chapter will consider the impact of corporate sanctions, imposed vicariously, irrespective of their civil, administrative or criminal nature and different variations within it.[50] Vicarious liability echoes the existing approach to parental liability in corporate groups, as discussed in Chapter 4.

7.3.1.2 Insufficiency of Corporate Liability

In the absence of individual sanctions, corporate sanctions are seen to be effective when they induce companies to monitor individuals internally, provided that such controlling costs are not excessive and that they do not create perverse effects. Such incentive depends on the level of enforcement and probability of detection. When companies are not able to deter and detect illegal acts perpetrated by individuals, individual sanctions are required for greater deterrence of corporate sanctions.

7.3.1.2.1 UNDER-DETERRENCE OF CORPORATE SANCTIONS. A company has incentives to incur monitoring costs depending on its perception of the risk associated with cartel detection. If the probability of detection is very low, companies have little

---

[45] The leading case is *Tesco Supermarkets Ltd* v. *Nattrass* [1972] AC 153, accepted in Scots law in *Transco* v. *HM Advocate*, 2004 SCCR 553.

[46] Wardhaugh, *Cartels, Markets and Crime*, p. 67.

[47] Ministry of Justice, 'Corporate Liability for Economic Crime' Call for Evidence (2017).

[48] Sykes, 'The Economics of Vicarious Liability'.

[49] For discussion of vicarious corporate liability in the context of criminal sanctions, see Wardhaugh, *Cartels, Markets and Crime*.

[50] For a precise analysis of the different variations of criminal corporate liability and effects on deterrence, see ibid.

incentives, because corporate liability does not increment the agency problem between shareholders and managers anyway.[51]

Based on Becker's theory on crime, a sanction is a deterrent if the expected fine is greater than the expected gain from the infringement, the expected fine being equal to the nominal amount of the fine discounted by the probability that a cartel is detected and prosecuted.[52] Applying this to cartel sanctions on corporations, Wils finds that:

> Assuming a 10% price increase, and a resulting increase in profits of 5% of turnover, a 5-year duration and a 16% probability of detection and punishment, the floor below which fines will generally not deter price-fixing would be in the order of 150% of the annual turnover in the products concerned by the violation.[53]

Current levels of fines imposed at EU level and in other jurisdictions may be substantially lower than deterrence actually requires.[54] As a result, even after detection, the consequences of participation in a cartel do not substantially magnify the divergence of interests between shareholders and managers. Therefore, shareholders may have little incentive to incur agency costs to ensure compliance.

However, a broader range of parameters than just the level of fines required for deterrence can determine the impact that corporate fines may have on the agency relationship. Depending on the level of publicity, companies being fined may suffer from reputational costs, which may impact the business relations of the company. Shareholders suffer from reputational impacts to the extent that reputational costs are reflected in the stock price. A study on Dutch companies involved in cartel and dominance cases between 1998 and 2008 found that, on average, firms lose 2.3 per cent of their market value when an investigation is uncovered. The loss is explained in greater proportions by the adjustment effect and by reputational impact than by the actual fine.[55] Another study showed that the stock price of cartel companies fell by 10 per cent following a television show about the Dutch construction cartel, while information on this cartel was already publicly available. This drop suggests the possible significant reputational loss associated by publicity.[56]

If they have not left the company, managers within a firm may also suffer from the reputational damage associated with the prosecution of their company.[57] The business

---

[51]   P. Buccirossi and G. Spagnolo, 'Corporate Governance and Collusive Behavior' in W. D. Collins (ed.), *Issues in Competition Law and Policy* 1 (American Bar Association, 2008), p. 18.

[52]   Becker, 'Crime and Punishment: An Economic Approach', 169.

[53]   W. P. J. Wils, *The Optimal Enforcement of EC Antitrust Law* (Kluwer Law International, 2002) p. 200.

[54]   OFT1132, 'An Assessment of Discretionary Penalties Regimes', A Report Prepared for the Office of Fair Trading by London Economics (2009) 8.

[55]   S. van den Broek, R. G. M. Kemp, W. F. C. Verschoor and A. C. de Vries, 'Reputational Penalties to Firms in Antitrust Investigations', *Journal of Competition Law and Economics*, 8 (2012), 231.

[56]   J. J. Graafland, 'Collusion, Reputation Damage and Interest in Code of Conduct: The Case of a Dutch Construction Company', *Business Ethics: A European Review*, 2 (2004), 127.

[57]   Managers' personal reputation is affected more than shareholders' personal fame: it is more difficult to know the identity of shareholders, and dispersed shareholders are not supposed to have known about the cartel.

model and ethics of a company can be questioned even in the event that a company is cleared following an investigation.[58] Therefore, accounting for reputational impacts, monetary fines may have a deterrent effect even if their level is below the theoretical level of deterrence. As the deterrent effect determines the impact of a fine on the agency relationship, this means that broader elements associated with the actual corporate fines may magnify the agency problem between managers and shareholders.

A cartel that is not detected and prosecuted does not create a situation of moral hazard between managers and shareholders, because benefits and costs are aligned towards cartel detection.[59] Similarly, a very low fine imposed on shareholders is not likely to outweigh the accumulation of benefits from participation in the cartel. Thus, competition policy regimes should clearly aim to enhance the detection rate, since this critically impact incentives for internal control through its impact on the agency dynamics.

7.3.1.2.2 EFFECTIVENESS OF CORPORATE SANCTIONS. Taking the view that the level of fine imposed is sufficiently high, or that a company is sensitive to any type of risk associated with a prosecution, sanctions imposed on the principal may have the effect of magnifying the friction of the relationship between the shareholders and managers of a company.[60] The situation of moral hazard created by sanctions imposed on companies exclusively may translate into a regime that 'hurts the innocent (workers and shareholders) while leaving those responsible for the infringement (the managers) unscathed'.[61] When the *incentive* exists, corporate liability is deemed efficient if the company has the *ability* adequately to monitor the behaviour of individuals, to ensure that they act in the company's best interest. If a company's enforcement effort needs to be very costly because of a large interest gap in the agency relationship, such a cost may not outweigh the benefits of avoiding corporate prosecution. In addition, corporate sanctions may produce perverse effects that may deter companies from detecting misconduct internally.

'Ability' to Internalise

Although companies may have 'effective methods of preventing individuals from committing acts that impose huge liabilities on them',[62] this may not be the case in practice. Sanctions imposed exclusively on companies may target passive actors, the shareholders, who have no oversight of the cartel decision-making process in

---

[58] OFT1227, 'Drivers of Compliance and Non-compliance with Competition Law' (2010) 29.

[59] Benefits of cartel participation are likely to be common, but may be different in scope depending on several parameters: e.g. how increased sales profits translate into higher value of shares, and how increases sales profits impact on managers' remuneration.

[60] See Section 6.2.2.

[61] The word 'innocent' refers to the painting by Rubens, *The Massacre of the innocents*. See L. Ortiz Blanco, A. Givaja Sanz and A. Lamadrid de Pablo, 'Fine Arts in Brussels: Punishment and Settlement of Cartel Cases under EC Competition Law' in H. Hirita, E. Raffaelli and E. Adriano (eds.), *Antitrust Between EC Law and National Law* (Bruyland Emile Etablissements, 2009), p. 155.

[62] Unlike the position argued in R. A. Posner, *Antitrust Law: An Economic Perspective* (University of Chicago Press, 1976), p. 225; Wils, *The Optimal Enforcement of EC Antitrust Law*, p. 17.

practice. In large companies, especially those publicly listed, shareholders are widely dispersed and do not oversee the activities of the firm themselves. The function of control is delegated to the board of directors, who turn to officers to implement the day-to-day monitoring in managing the employees. Their option to sell or hold shares depends on whether earnings from the collusive profits can be expected. Targeting shareholders exclusively may not be efficient, especially in countries characterised by large publicly held companies, such as the UK and the United States. This is because the sanction does not harm those responsible for entering into and implementing the cartel.[63] In contrast, continental Europe's jurisdictions may be more responsive to strict corporate liability, as the corporate structure is characterised by more concentrated ownership.[64] Finally, even a credible threat of dismissal can be overcome by alternative employment opportunities; and a company's suit against employees is limited to the assets owned by the individual, which is likely to be lower than the harm caused by them.[65] Thus company's incentives to internalise cost may be undermined if they are greater than the expected benefits of avoiding liability.

The effectiveness of corporate liability also critically depends on how effectively mechanisms of corporate governance reduce the asymmetry of information and the interest gap between the company and its agents. Corporate governance mechanisms may fail to address this tension of interests, as exemplified by the corporate scandals in Enron or Parmalat. Corporate governance schemes that fail to reach the objectives for which they have been designed are not likely to be highly effective in preventing individuals from committing illegal acts, either. In addition, corporate governance guidance and rules logically focus on auditing and financial reporting requirements, while compliance with competition law (and other areas of law) is ancillary to the fiduciary duty of directors.[66]

'Perverse' Effects of Corporate Liability

The implementation of preventing and policing measures may increase the probability of the detection of illegal conduct by the authorities. A company that detects the wrongdoing of an agent is likely honestly to report the wrongdoing to relevant authorities. This is because companies may face higher penalties for not reporting the illegal act of an agent.

[63] K. J. Cseres, M. P. Schinkel and F. O. W. Vogelaar (eds.), *Remedies and Sanctions in Competition Policy: Economic and Legal Implications of the Tendency to Criminalize Antitrust Enforcement in the EU Member States* (Edward Elgar Publishing, 2006), p. 8.

[64] P. Massey, 'Criminalization and Leniency: Will the Combination Favourably Affect Cartel Stability?' in ibid, p. 180.

[65] A. M. Polinsky and S. Shavell, 'Should Employees Be Subject to Fines and Imprisonment Given the Existence of Corporate Liability?', *International Review of Law and Economics*, 13 (1993), 239.

[66] Although guidelines provided by the Organisation for Economic Cooperation and Development (OECD) and the Cadbury Report include the need to comply with the law and behave ethically as part of corporate governance responsibility; corporate governance rules that impose strict corporate governance requirements typically relate to subjects such as the independence of auditing, the certification and disclosure of financial information and criminal account manipulation etc. For the United States, see the Sarbanes–Oxley Act 2002, Pub. L. No 107-204, 116 Stat. 745 (2002).

In addition, the wrongdoing of the agent may eventually be discovered or reported to the authority. In weighing the costs and benefits of implementing internal enforcement measures, a company may decide not to incur any costs if it expects that the costs of detection are higher than the expected benefit of detecting the crime internally. Thereby, corporate liability may produce undesired or 'perverse' effects. The perverse effect of corporate liability exists even if companies do not systematically report all illegal practices. The mere fact that they expect an increased probability of detection may deter companies from implementing internal measures.[67]

In sum, corporate sanctions are effective when they induce companies to monitor individuals internally, providing that such controlling costs do not create perverse effects. Therefore, 'if the firm has different interests from its agents and cannot control them without cost – then simple vicarious liability may no longer be the preferred corporate incentive regime.'[68] Individual sanctions may enable the by-passing of corporate governance mechanisms that are not strictly focused on compliance with external legal obligations.[69]

7.3.2 *Individual Sanctions: Targeting the Agent in the Agency Relationship*

Antitrust sanctions that target individuals may take the form of monetary fines, imprisonment penalties and disqualification from the position of director. Individual sanctions can be of an administrative, civil or criminal nature. From a policy perspective, individual penalties may present a number of advantages over corporate sanctions in the way in which they affect the actors' incentives.[70] Individuals may be particularly responsive to prison sentences, while they may be less responsive to monetary fines due to their probable limited ability to pay a fine that corresponds to the total economic harm to society. Such an aspect of the discussion around the effectiveness is left aside in this section, as is the question around the enforcement cost of prison sentences over pecuniary penalties.[71]

This section will show that targeting the agent via individual penalties, in addition to sanctions on the principal, addresses some of the limitations of corporate liability. Individual sanctions have the overall effect of reducing the interest gap between responsible managers and shareholders when they have no oversight of the cartel decision-making process. Deterrence is particularly achieved with individual sanctions if these create agency problems towards participation in a cartel between various individuals within the firm.

---

[67]   J. Arlen, 'The Potentially Perverse Effects of Corporate Criminal Liability', *Journal of Legal Studies*, 23 (1994), 833.

[68]   Arlen and Kraakman, 'Controlling Corporate Misconduct', 690.

[69]   Cseres, Schinkel and Vogelaar (eds.), *Remedies and Sanctions*, pp. 12–13.

[70]   For example, W. P. J. Wils, 'Is Criminalization of EU Competition Law the Answer?' in ibid., pp. 78–85; Leslie, 'Cartels, Agency Costs, and Finding Virtue in Faithless Agents', 1644.

[71]   For an example of a study on the enforcement cost of prison sentences compared with that of financial penalties for individuals, see: T. L. Cherry, 'Financial Penalties as an Alternative Criminal Sanction: Evidence from Panel Data', *Atlantic Economic Journal*, 29 (2001), 450.

7.3.2.1 An Overview of Individual Sanctions

In the United States, the original version of the Sherman Act imposed criminal sanctions on individuals, from fines to imprisonment penalties.[72] Since 2004, it has been possible for an individual involved in a cartel to be given up to ten years in prison.[73] Prison terms have been regularly imposed, and the average sentence has gone up from eight months in the 1990s to twenty months over the last two decades.[74] At the EU level, sanctions are levied only against companies. However, individual sanctions, including prison sentences, can be imposed in a number of EU member states. In some member states, criminal sanctions (including fines of a criminal nature) can be specifically imposed for competition law infringements. Other regimes entail criminal sanctions, but for bid-rigging offences only. Finally, administrative fines can also target individuals.

In the UK, individual price-fixers may face disqualification, imprisonment and fines.[75] In Ireland, individuals are liable through the liability of the undertaking, and can face imprisonment penalties of up to ten years.[76] In France, individuals can have imposed a prison sentence of up to four years and a financial penalty of up to €75,000.[77] In Cyprus and the Slovak Republic there is a possibility of prison sentences for individuals.[78] The Estonian Competition Act entails the possibility of sanctioning individuals through fines or detention for up to three years.[79] In the Czech Republic, prison sentences of up to three years were introduced for individual price-fixers.[80] The Danish Competition Act entails the possibility of imprisonment for up to six years and criminal fines for individuals involved in a cartel.[81] Infringement of competition can be sanctioned, in Latvia, by up to two years' imprisonment and, in Romania, by between four months' and six years' imprisonment.[82] In Slovenia, individuals who breach competition law while performing a business activity can be prescribed a prison sentence ranging from six months to five years.[83] In Greece, competition policy provides for criminal

---

[72] Wils, 'Is Criminalization of EU Competition Law the Answer?', p. 71.

[73] Sherman Act, 15 USC§1.

[74] Department of Justice, Antitrust Division, Criminal Enforcement Trend Charts (2017), available at: www.justice.gov/atr/criminal-enforcement-fine-and-jail-charts

[75] Enterprise Act 2002, ss. 188 and 204.

[76] Irish Competition Act 2002, s. 8.

[77] Code de Commerce, Art. L420-6.

[78] Cyprus: The Protection of Competition Law, 2008, Part VIII; Slovak Republic.

[79] Competition Act 2006, para. 148.

[80] Czech Criminal Code, s. 248(2).

[81] Danish Competition Act, §23 (Consolidation Act No 23 of 17 January 2013); F. A. Bork, O. Koktvedgaard and S. Zinck, 'Cartel Regulation: Denmark (2017) Getting the Deal Through'.

[82] Latvia: Criminal Law, ss. 211 and 212; Romania: The Parliament of Romania Competition Law of 1996, Art. 63.

[83] Article 225(1) of the Criminal Code in A. Mitić and M. Rogl, 'The European Antitrust Review 2014: Slovenia', *Global Competition Review* (2014).

sanctions, including imprisonment.[84] In Malta, liability of directors for failure to pay a fine or to supply requested information can be joint with that of the firm, and they can be sanctioned to criminal fines as a consequence.[85] Imprisonment is a possible sentence in Italy, Austria, Germany and Hungary, Belgium and Croatia, but only for bid-rigging.[86] In Germany, besides criminal sanctions in bid-rigging cases, non-criminal financial fines of up to €1 million may be levied against individuals.[87] In the Netherlands, administrative fines of up to €450,000 can be imposed on natural persons.[88] In Belgium, administrative fines ranging from €100 to €10,000 can be imposed on individuals.[89] In Spain, an individual who directly took part in a collusion decision can be given a fine of up to €60,000.[90] The Portuguese Competition Act provides for the non-criminal individual liability of directors and individuals responsible for the management or supervision of areas of activity in which there has been a violation.[91] In 2015, Poland introduced administrative fines of up to €500,000 on managers responsible for participating in anticompetitive agreements.[92] Other member states, including Sweden and Finland, have expressly rejected cartel criminalisation.[93]

Notwithstanding the fact that a fair proportion of EU member states have sanctions against individuals, such provisions may not actually be actively enforced.[94] Although the UK had expected to be very active in criminal cartel enforcement since the introduction of the cartel offence in 2002, only four cases have reached court.[95]

---

[84] Article 44 of Law 3959/2011.
[85] Competition Act (Chapter 379 of the Laws of Malta) Arts 21 and 21a.
[86] Article 353 of the Italian Criminal Code; §168b of the Austrian Criminal Code (*Strafgesetzbuch*); s. 14 of Act XCI of 2005 amending the Hungarian Criminal Code, Act IV of 1978 and other Acts; §298 of the German Criminal Code; Art. 314 of the Belgian Criminal Code; Art. 254 of the Croatian Criminal Code.
[87] §81(4) of the German Act against Restraints on Competition (ARC).
[88] Dutch Competition Act, 2007, s. 57. M. Slotboom, 'Individual Liability for Cartel Infringements in the EU: An Increasingly Dangerous Minefield', Kluwer Competition Law Blog (2013).
[89] Article IV70. §2 Code de droit économique.
[90] Competition Act 2007, Art. 63.
[91] Portuguese Competition Act, Law 19/2012, Art. 73.
[92] Norton Rose Fulbright, 'Important Changes in Polish Competition Law' (2015).
[93] F. Wagner-von Papp, A. Stephan, W. Kovacic, D. Zimmer and D. Viros, 'Individual Sanctions for Competition Law Infringements: Pros, Cons and Challenges', *Concurrences*, 2 (2016), 14, 16.
[94] On criminalisation in Europe generally, see P. M. Whelan, *The Criminalization of European Antitrust Enforcement: Theoretical, Legal, and Practical Challenges* (Oxford University Press, 2014); M. Furse, *The Criminal Law of Competition in the UK and US: Failure and Success* (Edward Elgar Publishing, 2012).
[95] Marine hose case: *R v. Whittle, Allison, Brammer* [2008] EWCA Crim 2560; airline fuel surcharges case: *R v. George, Crawley, Burns and Burnett* [2010] EWCA Crim 1148 (trial collapsed upon discovery of 70,000 emails in evidence that had failed to be considered). *R v. Nigel Snee*, sentencing hearing, 14 September 2015; CMA (2017), 'Supply of precast concrete drainage products: criminal investigation' available at: www.gov.uk/cma-cases/criminal-investigation-into-the-supply-of-products-to-the -construction-industry

Only the *marine hose*, *galvanised steel tanks* and *construction product* cases resulted in sanctions – prison sentences and disqualification orders – against the responsible individuals. Lack of public support and legitimacy behind cartel criminalisation made it difficult to prove that individuals acted 'dishonestly', which was initially required for establishing a cartel offence.[96] Such a requirement was subsequently removed.[97] Another challenge in the UK relates to the high cost of bringing a criminal case to trial for the competition authority, compared with that of the civil procedure, in which the authority acts as investigator, and prosecutor.[98] In Ireland, only four cases have led to prison or financial sanctions against individuals.[99]

In other regimes, such as France, Greece and Romania, cartels are criminalised in a tenuous manner such that the offence relates more to fraud alone than a cartel offence and hence is much narrower than a true notion of criminal antitrust. This may also illustrate the reluctance of authorities to bring criminal charges against individuals.[100] In France, for example, criminal charges against individuals are, in practice, limited to cases in which there exist other types of infringements, such as the corruption or misuse of social assets.[101] The interplay of criminal proceedings for which courts are competent and administrative sanctions by the competition author-ity explains the extremely rare use of criminal antitrust sanctions in France.[102] Decentralised criminal enforcement means that cases are confined to local criminal courts that may lack experience or competition-law specific knowledge. In addition, criminal cases lack the media-coverage that cases dealt with by a national competi-tion authority may receive.[103] This explains a rather discreet type of criminal enforcement in Germany, where there are more criminal antitrust cases than are actually perceived by the public.[104] Prison sentences have regularly been imposed

[96] A. Stephan, 'How Dishonesty Killed the Cartel Offence', *Criminal Law Review*, 6 (2011), 446–55. For discussion of the UK cartel offence, see also J. Galloway, 'Securing the Legitimacy of Individual Sanctions in UK Competition Law', *World Competition*, 40(1) (2016), 121–57.

[97] Enterprise and Regulatory Reform Act 2013.

[98] Furse, *The Criminal Law of Competition*, p. 218. Stephan also points to problems associated with leniency raised by cartel criminalisation: A Stephan, 'Four Key Challenges to the Successful Criminalization of Cartel Laws', *Journal of Antitrust Enforcement*, 2 (2014), 333–62.

[99] *DPP* v. *Denis Manning*, Central Criminal Court (2007); *DPP* v. *Patrick Duffy and Duffy Motors (Newbridge) Ltd* [2009] IEHC 208. *DPP* v. *Pat Hegarty*, Circuit Criminal Court, Galway (2012); *DPP* v. *Aston Carpets & Flooring and Brendan Smith*, Central Criminal Court (2017). See details of criminal court cases at: www.ccpc.ie/business/enforcement/criminal-enforcement/criminal-court -cases/

[100] Jones and Harrison, 'Criminal Sanctions', 3.

[101] Example of cases: *Affaire des enrobés bitumineux*, Chambre criminelle de la Cour de cassation, 16 mai 2001, n 99-83467 et 97-80888; *Affaire de l'entretien et la rénovation partielle de l'éclairage public de la ville du Havre*, Chambre correctionnelle de la Cour d'appel de Rouen, 25 février 2002.

[102] Ministère de l'économie, de l'industrie et de l'emploi, Rapport sur l'appréciation de la sanction en matière de pratiques anticoncurrentielles (2010) 5.

[103] Wagner-von Papp et al., 'Individual Sanctions for Competition Law Infringements', 19.

[104] F. Wagner-Von Papp, 'What if all Bid Riggers Went to Prison and Nobody Noticed? Criminal Antitrust Law Enforcement in Germany' in C. Beaton-Wells and A. Ezrachi (eds.), *Criminalising Cartels, Critical Studies of an International Regulatory Movement* (Hart Publishing, 2011), p. 157.

on individuals since the introduction in 1997 of criminal sanctions against bid-rigging.[105] Administrative fines against individuals are also commonly imposed: between 1993 and 2010, the German Competition Authority fined, on average, one individual for each undertaking that it fined.[106]

Therefore, the level of enforcement of sanctions against individuals depends on the nature of the sanction – criminal or administrative – and varies from one jurisdiction to another. Individuals are likely to be sensitive to the level of enforcement they perceive. In case of low enforcement levels, the existence of individual sanctions may not impact the agency relationship significantly.[107]

7.3.2.2 The Case for Individual Liability: the Theory

Where directors and executives are personally liable for engaging in competition law infringements, they can no longer operate behind the shield of corporate liability.[108] In terms of incentives, individual sanctions align the cost of detection for the individual with that of the company. In the absence of personal punishment, the responsible individual may not bear the full cost of their behaviour, unless the company is able to punish the individual internally, or somehow recover the fine from the individual by way of a damages action or a derivative suit. Introducing individual sanctions may reduce the moral hazard situation characterising price-fixing conduct in a strict corporate liability regime.[109] Based on the optimal sanction theory, an individual has to discount the cost of a potential individual sanction from the benefit of cartel profits. An agent is expected to be reluctant to implement a cartel agreement if the cost of the expected personal sanction is greater than the benefits of implementing the collusive agreement.

As previously described, the implementation of a collusive agreement involves various agency relationships between different actors of the firm – that is, between the decision-makers, and those in charge of implementing the agreement. The introduction of individual sanctions has the potential to impact incentives of

---

[105] Between 1998 and 2013, 42 suspended prison sentences were imposed: Wagner-von Papp et al., 'Individual Sanctions for Competition Law Infringements', 18.

[106] BVerfG, 19 December 2012, 1 BvL 18/11, WuW/E DE-R 3766, paras. 52, 60–Verzinsungspflicht, available at: www.bverfg.de/entscheidungen/ls20121219_1bvl001811.html. Interestingly, Germany is one of the few jurisdictions in which individuals are primarily liable for breaching competition law (§9 OWiG). The undertaking may be liable for an administrative offence if the individual who infringed competition law has some degree of responsibility within the company (§30 OWiG). The owner of the company will be liable if there was a lack of supervision. Such a particular liability regime may explain why, in Germany, administrative fines are often imposed (§130 OWiG).

[107] However, the mere existence of criminalisation, even unenforced, is relevant in the context of extradition procedures: Wagner-von Papp et al., Individual Sanctions for Competition Law Infringements, 16.

[108] Cseres, Schinkel, and Vogelaar (eds.), *Remedies and Sanctions*, p. 8.

[109] This is based on the assumption that a collusive practice benefits both the principal and the agent in the agency relationship, and the cost of such behaviour depends on the liability regime attached to such infringements.

all such agency relationships within the company, even if not all the individuals are personally liable. Responding to a perceived risk of individual liability, an employee or manager may be reluctant to implement an illegal agreement and be 'faithless' to his direct manager. Fearing going to prison, Wayne Brasser, an employee of ADM, refused to cooperate in the lysine price-fixing conspiracy in which his company was involved.[110] The availability of personal sanctions surely affected the incentive of this employee. In this case, while being 'faithless' to the higher level of the hierarchy, the employee of ADM, Wayne Brasser, was indirectly 'loyal' to the shareholders of the company by refusing to cooperate, based on the assumption that they suffered from the legal consequence of the cartel. This is because he perceived that he could face a personal sanction in parallel to that imposed on the company.

The theoretical case for individual sanctions is straightforward: they reduce the interest gap in the agency relationship as now both the shareholders and individuals face sanctions. Individuals have a better incentive to act in the shareholders' best interests by avoiding entering into a price-fixing agreement for which both the shareholders and the individuals are liable.[111]

7.3.2.3 Effectiveness of Individual Sanctions

The responsiveness of individuals to sanctions depends on a number of external and internal factors, many of which are beyond the frame of (bounded) rationality.[112] Internal factors such as personal aversion to risk, the fear of being dismissed or the position occupied within the organisation affect the impact of sanctions and their effectiveness. As in the case of corporate sanctions, the perceived severity of enforcement, related to the probability of detection and how 'active' an authority might be, will be decisive. The nature of the sanction is obviously an important factor; an individual is likely to be more responsive to the risk of serving prison terms than to the threat of paying criminal fines.

Organisational factors may also mitigate the impact of sanctions beyond a corporate culture or remuneration schemes inducing breaches of competition law.[113] Individuals may also be provided with direct incentives that mitigate the liability risk. When it comes to monetary sanction, a company may commit to reimbursing any fine imposed on an individual, or may choose to inflate the level

---

[110] The employee was subsequently fired for not cooperating: J. M. Connor, *Global Price Fixing (Studies in Industrial Organization)*, 2nd edn (Springer, 2008), p. 357.

[111] See also Wardhaugh, *Cartels, Markets and Crime*, pp. 89–103.

[112] For criminology studies on the impact of criminal sanctions, see, e.g.: S. S. Simpson, *Corporate Crime, Law, and Social Control* (Cambridge University Press, 2002). More specifically, for an account of criminology studies on cartel conduct, see C. Hardin, 'The Anti-Cartel Enforcement Industry: Criminological Perspectives on Cartel Criminalisation' in C Beaton-Wells and A. Ezrachi (eds.), *Criminalising Cartels: A Critical Interdisciplinary Study of an International Regulatory Movement* (Hart Publishing, 2011).

[113] These factors were discussed in Chapter 6.

of compensation to anticipate any individual penalty. In addition, directors and officers may be externally insured against legal risks incurred, as part of Director and Officer ('D&O') liability insurances, for example.[114] Indemnification or insurance policies can foresee covering defence costs and potential damages arising out of the director or officer's function. Those costs would otherwise be funded by personal resources.[115]

Indemnifying or insuring individuals enables the risk of competition law breach to be shifted from the agent to the principal. If the company is fully capable of indemnifying its employees, individual sanctions may produce no effect on the agency relationship, in theory. This means that the principal bears the entire cost of the sanction, equivalent to situations of vicarious corporate liability. While monetary sanctions are easily covered by an indemnity equal to the amount of the fine, imprisonment sanctions may not be as easily indemnified, because an individual may suffer from losses that have greater implications than just a financial one.[116] However, in the heavy electrical equipment cartel, prosecuted in the United States in 1961, employees who served prison terms may have constituted 'scapegoats' to deflect criminal responsibility away from top executives.[117] Direct financial or promotion rewards may therefore be provided to designated individuals for taking liability risks (including prison terms) in the event of a cartel detection.

However, D&O insurances or companies cannot indemnify employees for all types of individual sanctions that they may face in their capacity as manager or director of the company. The UK Companies Act 2006, for example, prohibits companies from indemnifying against criminal fines or fines imposed by a regulatory authority to a director.[118] In particular, claims in relation to antitrust cases quite often seem to be explicitly excluded from the scope of D&O policies.[119] Therefore, it is unlikely that a director who personally took the initiative of entering in a cartel can hide behind the shield of a corporate indemnification or D&O policy.

---

[114]   Director and Officer liability insurance was introduced in the 1930s by Lloyd's of London and expanded in the United States in the 1960s, when it appeared that directors and officers, not just corporations, could face significant liability themselves in the context of security laws: R. Romano, 'Directors' and Officers' Liability Insurance: What Went Wrong?', *Proceedings of the Academy of Political Science*, 37 (1988), 76. The use of D&O liability insurance extended to the UK, Canada, South Africa, Australia, Ireland, Israel, France, Belgium, the Netherlands, Spain and Switzerland in the 1980s: Allianz Global Corporate & Specialty, 'Introduction to D&O Insurance, Risk Briefing', (2010), available at: www.agcs.allianz.com/assets/PDFs/risk%20insights/AGCS-DO-infopaper.pdf

[115]   StrategicRISK, Guide to Directors'& Officers' Liability Insurance (2012).

[116]   Wils 'Is Criminalization of EU Competition Law the Answer?', 86.

[117]   B. Fisse and J. Braithwaite, *Corporations, Crime and Accountability* (Cambridge University Press, 2010), p. 57; G. Geis, *White-Collar Criminal: The Offender in Business and the Professions* (Alberton Press, 2006).

[118]   Companies Act 2006, s. 234.

[119]   K. LaCroix, 'Professional Liability Insurance: The Antitrust Exclusion Isn't Just About Antitrust Claims' The D&O diary, 2012, is available at: www.dandodiary.com/2012/11/articles/d-o-insurance /professional-liability-insurance-the-antitrust-exclusion-isnt-just-about-antitrust-claims/

From a policy perspective, banning the indemnification of employees prevents the internalisation of liability cost and magnifies possible interest gap in a manner than enhances deterrence.[120] Mullin and Snyder, however, argue that companies should not be prohibited from indemnifying their employees as this triggers the risk of wrongly prosecuting companies that have not breached the law, and posits that deterrence can be achieved by targeting the company exclusively.[121]

7.3.2.4 Competition Disqualification Orders (CDOs) in the UK

In the UK, competition disqualification orders (CDOs) provide an illustration of the intersection of sanctions of competition law and corporate governance, the main concern of which is the reduction of the agency problem between shareholders and managers. The Company Directors Disqualification Act 1986 (CDDA), part of UK company law, entails the possibility of directors being disqualified for acting for a company in cases of certain misconducts. Initially, disqualification orders concerned wrongdoings in insolvency and broader corporate governance contexts.[122] Since an amendment of the CDDA by the Enterprise Act 2002,[123] such sanctions of corporate law can be used in the context of competition law infringements: directors can be disqualified if their company breaches competition law.[124]

In addition to the effect of the alignment of incentives generic to individual sanctions, CDOs may induce companies to enhance their general corporate governance systems. Directors need to be aware of compliance with competition law, in the same way that they are conscious of other corporate governance requirements. This implies that a director who fails to prevent or detect a breach of competition law is also unfit to ensure the corporate governance function. In practice, directors may be induced to put in place compliance programmes, internal reporting systems and so on, and have to pay greater attention to any suspicious information, including abnormal profits made in a particular department of the company.[125] Criteria to assess the unfitness of a director whose company has breached competition law consider not just the actual but also the constructive knowledge of the violation. The CMA guidelines confirm that directors who do not know about the conduct but who ought to have known are not less likely to be disqualified than those who actually knew.[126] This puts significant onus on a director to investigate internally

---

[120] C. Stone, 'The Place of Enterprise Liability in the Control of Corporate Conduct', *Yale Law Journal*, 90 (1980), 1; Kraakman, 'Corporate Liability Strategies and the Costs of Legal Controls', 857; F. Privileggi, C. Marchese and A. Cassone, 'Agent's Liability Versus Principal's Liability When Attitudes Toward Risk Differ', *International Review of Law and Economics*, 21 (2001), 181.

[121] W. P. Mullin and C. M. Snyder, 'Should Firms Be Allowed to Indemnify Their Employees for Sanctions?', *Journal of Law, Economics, and Organization*, 26 (2010), 30.

[122] E.g. conviction of an indictable offence, persistent breach of company legislation and fraud.

[123] Enterprise Act 2002, s. 204, modifying the Company Directors Disqualification Act 1986.

[124] Company Directors Disqualification Act 1986, ss. 9A–9E.

[125] Ibid.

[126] OFT1340, 'Company Directors and Competition Law' (2011), para. 2.4.

potential violation of competition law.[127] As with other types of individual sanction, the effectiveness of CDOs on the agency relationship depends on the ability to compensate a director. If a director is close to retirement, an early retirement package or generous severance package may be sufficient to mitigate the potential effect of CDOs on the agency relationship.[128] To date, disqualification under the CDDA has been successfully secured twice; in relation to an agreement not to undercut competitors' prices on Amazon, as well as in agreements between estate agents on minimum commission fees.[129]

To conclude, the disqualification of company directors enables aligning the incentives of directors and undertakings, for greater competition law compliance.[130] According to a study commissioned by the Office of Fair Trading (OFT), the CDO is perceived as one of the most powerful deterrent instruments, together with reputation cost and fines.[131] Individuals targeted by CDOs are characterised by a high level of education and experience, which may explain why there are a number of stories of individuals being promoted or employed shortly after being convicted.[132] Therefore, the threat of being banned from the profession may compensate for the inefficiency of the social stigma for certain high-profile executives.[133] In addition, CDOs are likely to receive greater public support than the cartel offence, which facilitates the prospect of bringing successful cases.[134] A fuller use of sanctions of corporate governance in the context of competition law would enable an even greater place for competition compliance among a director's other duties.[135]

---

[127]   N. Karr, 'The OFT's Revised Director Disqualification Guidance: Deterring Directors or Competition Law Breaches?' (2010) Linklaters.

[128]   A. Stephan, 'Disqualification Orders for Directors Involved in Cartels', *Journal of European Competition Law & Practice*, 2 (2011), 529, 533.

[129]   CMA, 'CMA Secures Director Disqualification for Competition Law Breach' (2016), available at: www.gov.uk/government/news/cma-secures-director-disqualification-for-competition-law-breach; CMA, 'Estate Agent Cartel Directors Disqualified' (2018), available at: www.gov.uk/government/news /estate-agent-cartel-directors-disqualified

[130]   Stephan, 'Disqualification Orders for Directors Involved in Cartels', 535.

[131]   OFT962, 'The Deterrent Effect of Competition Enforcement by the OFT, A Report Prepared for the OFT by Deloitte' (2007) 5.56, although a more recent study does not necessarily confirm such a finding: OFT1391, 'The Impact of Competition Interventions on Compliance and Deterrence', Final Report, by London Economics (2011) 3.36-41.

[132]   See below Section 7.5.1.

[133]   J. Schmidt, 'Germany: Merger Control Analysis of Minority Shareholdings – A Model for the EU?' *Concurrences*, 16. N° 2-2013387.

[134]   75 per cent of the British public believes that senior management involved in cartels should be barred from such positions, in contrast to only 27 per cent who believe such individuals should face prison sentences: J. Galloway, 'Securing the Legitimacy of Individual Sanctions in UK Competition Law', *World Competition*, 40 (1) (2016), 121, 151; A. Stephan, 'An Empirical Evaluation of the Normative Justifications for Cartel Criminalisation', *Legal Studies*, 37 (4)(2017), 621, 641.

[135]   P. Hughes, 'Director's Personal Liability for Cartel Activity', *European Competition Law Review*, 29 (2008), 632.

7.3.3 *Effectiveness of Sanctions: Targeting both the Agent and the Principal*

Cartels are formed and run by managers. A sanction policy must affect their incentives. This can be accomplished indirectly by imposing sanctions on firms. Individual liability is necessary if either the optimal enforcement policy requires the imposition of non-pecuniary sanctions, **or the principal-agent relationship cannot be shaped so as to efficiently pursue the principal's goals.**[136] (Emphasis added)

Overall, a sanction policy will not be efficient if it creates a situation of moral hazard between the agent and the principal, which the firm cannot address internally. If individuals operate behind the shield of corporate liability, they may not act in the best interest of the company as they themselves do not face the risk of detection. If corporations cannot address this internally, increasing the level of the corporate fine may not be optimal in terms of deterrence. Conversely, the reason for which it would not be satisfactory to punish individuals exclusively is that companies would operate behind the shield of individual liability, and could have strong incentives to encourage collusive behaviour by their employees.[137]

As a result, the discussion on the optimality of sanctions is merely a matter of whom to target among the agent and the principal. Companies repeatedly involved in cartel practices are likely to be large undertakings, formed of many business departments and various subsidiaries, where shareholders have limited oversight of the managers' actions. In those types of companies, the agency problem between shareholders and managers cannot be easily overcome. Therefore, individual sanctions have the overall effect of reducing the interest gap between responsible managers and shareholders who have no oversight of the cartel decision-making process. This is based on the assumption that it is in the long-term interest of shareholders that the company complies with competition law. In addition, individual sanctions have the potential to undermine the manner in which employees implement cartel-related instructions emanating from their managers.[138] Therefore, individual penalties are particularly deterrent if they create agency problems in the relationship between the employees and their managers, which in turn consists of aligning incentives of the agency relationship between shareholders and managers. In the light of their overall effect on the agency relationship, this book takes the view that individual sanctions are desirable. Deterrence considerations support the introduction of individual sanctions (be they of a criminal or an administrative nature) at EU level; and greater enforcement of existing provisions in the member states. Corporate sanctions alone will always have a limited effect because of the inherent agency issues affecting deterrence. Individual sanctions, and their introduction at

---

[136] Buccirossi and Spagnolo, 'Corporate Governance and Collusive Behavior', 20.
[137] Wils, 'Antitrust Compliance Programmes and Optimal Antitrust Enforcement', 59.
[138] G. Spagnolo, 'Cartels: Criminalization and their Internal Organization' in Cseres, Schinkel and Vogelaar (eds.), *Remedies and Sanctions in Competition Policy*, p. 142.

EU level (particularly in the form of prison sentences) raise a range of legal and practical challenges, including the existence of such competence in the EU, questions of procedural safeguards and human rights, the interaction with leniency policy, as well questions of public support and legitimacy.[139] Such questions will not be subject to further discussion.

7.4 ENFORCEMENT INSTRUMENTS THAT AIM TO DETECT CARTELS

This section will focus on instruments that purport to *detect* existing anticompetitive practices. Leniency policy and 'bounty' programmes are examples of instruments that are designed to undermine the stability of cartels, and are deemed to constitute a powerful detection device for competition authorities. For greater detection of cartels, leniency needs to be supplemented with strict sanction regimes including individual sanctions. Individuals also need strong incentives to report independently from the company (in the form of individual leniency or 'bounty' rewards). Leniency policy will effectively disrupt cartels only if the company and the responsible individual have aligned interests in seeking leniency. In contrast, individual leniency and bounty programmes will destabilise cartels only if they induce sufficient divergence of interest within the agency relationship. Practical and ethical considerations around whistle-blower schemes may, however, nuance such conclusion.

7.4.1 *Overview of Leniency Policy*

Leniency policy is a core public enforcement instrument, adopted unanimously in the United States and in EU competition laws. Leniency policies contribute to the fight against cartels, an illegal activity which is typically carefully concealed by its participants and which competition authorities have difficulties in uncovering.

The competition policies of all of the EU member states have leniency programmes, apart from Malta.[140] For the purpose of this section, leniency is understood as a 'catch-all' term referring to all types of immunity and reduced fines available in the various competition regimes.[141]

In the jurisdiction of the European Union the term 'leniency' refers to immunity as well as a reduction of any fine which would otherwise have been imposed on

---

[139]　For a more complete discussion, see Whelan, *The Criminalization of European Antitrust Enforcement*; Furse, *The Criminal Law of Competition*; Wardhaugh, *Cartels, Markets and Crime*.

[140]　EU Commission, 'Authorities in EU Member States Which Operate a Leniency Programme' (2012), available at: http://ec.europa.eu/competition/ecn/leniency_programme_nca.pdf. In June 2013, Malta opened consultation on the introduction of leniency regulations but leniency has not been introduced since then: ICLG, 'Cartel & Leniency, Malta' (2018): https://iclg.com/practice-areas /cartels-and-leniency-laws-and-regulations/malta#chaptercontent4

[141]　R. Whish and D. Bailey, *Competition Law*, 8th edn. (Oxford University Press, 2015), p. 440.

a participant in a cartel, in exchange for the voluntary disclosure of information regarding the cartel which satisfies specific criteria prior to or during the investigative stage of the case.[142]

In the EU, total immunity from fines can be granted to the first undertaking that brings convincing evidence of its participation in a cartel. Companies that do not qualify for full immunity can still benefit from a reduction in fines, if they can provide evidence that adds 'significant value' to the investigation. The reduction in the fine for the first company meeting these requirements ranges from 30 per cent to 50 per cent of the total amount that would have been imposed. Subsequent applicants can claim a reduction of up to 30 per cent.[143] In contrast, the US leniency programme grants immunity to only the first undertaking that reports the cartel.[144] Both leniency programmes entail the possibility of immunity when the cartel is undetected or when an investigation has already started. In both cases, immunity is conditional on the prompt termination of the cartel activity as well as to the full cooperation of the firm. The scope of leniency varies from one jurisdiction to the other, to adjust for the sanctions that individuals may face. Some programmes grant immunity from fines to corporations while providing blanket immunity to all the employees who may face personal sanctions.[145] In the EU, consistent with the absence of individual sanctions, the leniency programme grants immunity exclusively to the undertakings. Another important parameter is the interaction between leniency and rights of private parties to be compensated from competitive harm. In the United States, successful leniency applicants have a reduced exposure to follow-on civil actions, provided they cooperate with the private plaintiff.[146] In the EU, the Damages Directive has also restricted the scope of liability for leniency recipients.[147] It also clarifies that leniency statement documents may not be disclosed to parties claiming damages.[148]

---

[142]   Commission Notice on immunity from fines and reduction of fines in cartel cases [2006] OJ C298/11.
[143]   Ibid.
[144]   Department of Justice, 'Corporate Leniency Policy' (1993).
[145]   This is, for example, the case in the UK and in the United States: OFT1495, 'Applications for Leniency and No-Action in Cartel Cases' (2013); Department of Justice, 'Leniency Policy for Individuals' (1994)
[146]   Damages reduced from treble to simple damages. See Antitrust Criminal Penalty Enhancement and Reform Act, Pub L No 108-237, §213, 118 Stat 661, 666–67.
[147]   Directive 2014/104/EU of the European Parliament and of the Council of 26 November 2014 on certain rules governing actions for damages under national law for infringements of the competition law provisions of the Member States and of the European Union [2014] OJ L349/1 ('Damages Directive'), art. 11 (4).
[148]   Ibid, art. 6(6). For a discussion of the interaction and possible trade-offs between private enforcement and leniency, see: B. Wardhaugh, 'Cartel Leniency and Effective Compensation in Europe: The Aftermath of Pfleiderer', *Web Journal of Current Legal Issues*, 19(3) (2013); D. A. Crane, 'Why Leniency Does Not Undermine Compensation' in C. Beaton-Wells and C. Tran (eds.), *Anti-Cartel Enforcement in a Contemporary Age: The Leniency Religion* (Hart Publishing, 2015), p. 263; Laura Guttuso, 'Leniency and the Two Faces of Janus: Where Public and Private Enforcement Merge and Converge' in Beaton-Wells and Tran (eds.), *Anti-Cartel Enforcement in a Contemporary Age*, p. 273;

For the purpose of this analysis, the most relevant aspect of leniency lies in its interaction with individual sanctions. In addition to corporate leniency programmes, some competition policies have a leniency scheme for individuals, which enables them to seek amnesty or reduction of personal sanctions independently from their company. The United States incorporated an individual programme of leniency in 1994. An individual who is the first to report the cartel can be amnestied from any criminal sanctions that he would have faced.[149] The UK established an individual leniency programme in 2008, from which an individual who self-reports can benefit separately from their company, provided that the cartel conduct was unknown to the CMA. However, this does not guarantee immunity for other individuals of the firm or for the company.[150] In the Netherlands, the introduction of individual fines in 2007 was coupled with the establishment of an individual leniency scheme. The rules for the scope of the amnesty or fine reduction disregard whether the applicant is a company or an individual. If the undertaking applies for leniency, individuals can be 'co-applicant' in cooperating with the application made by the company.[151] In Germany, since 2006, natural persons have been able to seek leniency that automatically applies to the company and other individuals, unless specified otherwise.[152] To date, there is no reported experience of an individual benefiting from immunity while his company is prosecuted.[153]

7.4.2 *Effectiveness of Leniency*

The primary goal of leniency policy is to undermine the stability of relationships between cartel members. Unstable by nature, cartel relationships may be sustainable if cartel participants are able to monitor each other, and if the cost of a retaliation strategy prevents a member from unilaterally deviating from the agreement. Therefore, leniency strategy intends to weaken such cartel relationships, by rewarding companies that self-report.[154] Well-designed leniency programmes are expected to trigger a race in applications to competition authorities, while bringing highly

---

C. Cauffman, 'The Interaction of Leniency Programmes and Actions for Damages', *Competition Law Review*, 7 (2011), 18.

[149]   Department of Justice, 'Leniency Policy for Individuals' (1994).

[150]   OFT1495, s. 7.

[151]   Commission Notice on immunity from fines and reduction of fines in cartel cases [2006] OJ C298/11 (2007).

[152]   (If the natural person is authorised to represent the company); see Leniency Notice No 9/2006 (2006), para. 17.

[153]   In the lysine cartel case, Mark Whitacre could have benefited from immunity while his company was prosecuted, if he had not been found guilty of other breaches.

[154]   E.g. M. Motta and M. Polo, 'Leniency Programs and Cartel Prosecution', *International Journal of Industrial Organization*, 21 (2003), 347; C. R. Leslie, 'Trust, Distrust, and Antitrust', *Texas Law Review*, 82 (2004), 515 and 'Antitrust Amnesty, Game Theory, and Cartel Stability', *Journal of Corporation Law*, 31 (2006), 453; G. Spagnolo, 'Divide et Impera: Optimal Leniency Programs' (2004) CEPR Working Paper No 4840.

valuable evidence to competition authorities during the cartel investigation. *Ex ante*, leniency policy may reduce the expected cost related to the detection of the cartel, as successful applications result in immunity or the reduction of fines.[155] It is therefore essential for leniency to accompany a severe sanction regime; a generous programme together with mild sanctions (or low enforcement) could encourage cartel formation. The impact on the *ex ante* decision to form a cartel will not be further considered here, as the focus is on the detection of ongoing cartels.[156]

The effectiveness of leniency critically depends on who is targeted and whether the incentives towards a credible threat of sanctions are aligned; or whether it targets individuals and effectively disrupts any relation that is essential to the operation of the cartel.

7.4.2.1 Corporate Leniency Policy: Targeting the Principal in the Agency Relationship

The effectiveness of leniency largely depends on the distribution of incentives between individuals and the company.[157] In competition regimes that strictly target companies, leniency programmes logically give immunity only to companies. As previously stated, in the absence of individual sanctions, individuals may be able to reap benefits from their cartel participation without bearing the direct cost of its detection. The availability of a corporate leniency programme may not affect the individual incentives as it does not affect the employees' pay-offs, while the termination of a cartel means that the individual can no longer benefit from the cartel profits.[158] Therefore, if leniency policy makes a cartel collapse, the individual will be worse-off. If such an individual is reluctant to terminate the cartel or to cooperate with the investigation process, a tension of interests between the company and its employees can arise. In addition, individuals engaging their firm in the cartel may have different levels of information and perception of the threat of detection and sanction; together with a time-horizon limited to their period of employment. Individuals may well have left their company by the time that a cartel is expected to be detected and sanctioned. Therefore, weighing the costs and benefits, individuals may have little incentive to seek a leniency application. Empirical evidence on end dates of forty-three EU cartel cases (2002–14) suggests that a majority of cartels (twenty-three) were terminated once the leniency application was made. Only two cartels ended after leniency was sought, and they are the only clear cases of actual

---

[155] Adverse effects of leniency: see Motta and Polo, 'Leniency Programs and Cartel Prosecution', 347.

[156] For a literature review on the evidence on deterrence of leniency, see: C. Marvao and G. Spagnolo, 'What Do We Know about the Effectiveness of Leniency Policies? A Survey of the Empirical and Experimental Evidence' in Beaton-Wells and Tran (eds.), *Anti-Cartel Enforcement in a Contemporary Age*, p. 57.

[157] N. Zingales, 'European and American Leniency Programmes: Two Models towards Convergence?', *Competition Law Review*, 5 (2008), 5, 12.

[158] As stated previously, the assumption is that individuals somehow benefit from the cartel profits.

disruption of a well-functioning cartel. The rest of cartels terminated at the same time of the leniency investigation; based on which no conclusion may be drawn.[159] This may reflect the lack of consequences of leniency for the responsible individuals. In addition, some companies seem to be making a strategic use of leniency, as some companies are known 'leniency recidivists': Akzo Nobel obtained immunity or fine reduction in seven out of nine cartel decisions; Aventis received a leniency gain in all of its five cartel convictions (three full immunity and two fine reduction); BASF obtained fine reductions in nine out of eleven cartel cases etc.[160] Although these findings may be circumstantial, this tends to suggest that leniency may even confer benefits to companies who can make a strategic use of it.

Now we will consider the case in which individual sanctions are available, or in which a company is able to punish the responsible individual internally when the cartel is detected. Any instrument that potentially increases the probability of detection and cartel termination may be detrimental to the individual. This is because leniency does not protect such an individual from the sanctions that they may face afterwards. Therefore, if the application for leniency is in the hands of such individuals, they may try to avoid it in the first place. As a result, individuals will never seek to report the cartel. The sanction suffered by the individual is irrespective of whether their company or another one blows the whistle, or whether the cartel is detected by the competition authorities. In such circumstances, corporate leniency that does not also protect individuals may not generate a race in applications, because responsible individuals do not benefit from it personally. Therefore, one should consider the extent to which individual incentives in self-reporting parallel those of the company to understand the effectiveness of leniency policy. An important policy implication is that the introduction of individual sanctions may hamper the effectiveness of leniency programmes, unless they protect the individuals adequately.[161] The issue is relevant in the EU, where individuals cannot be prosecuted at EU level but still face the threat of individual conviction in their member state.[162]

Therefore, the disruptive effect of corporate leniency critically depends on how individual incentives are impacted. Individuals need to have aligned incentives towards the benefits of a leniency application. This may not be the case either when they do bear any of the consequences of cartel detection (absence of individual sanctions), or when leniency does not extend to individuals.

[159] A. Stephan and A. Nikpay, 'Leniency Decision-Making from a Corporate Perspective: Complex Realities' in Beaton-Wells and Tran (eds.), *Anti-Cartel Enforcement in a Contemporary Age*, pp. 146–50.

[160] C. Harding, C. Beaton-Wells and J, Edwards, 'Leniency and Criminal Sanctions in Anti-Cartel Enforcement: Happily Married or Uneasy Bedfellows?' in Beaton-Wells and Tran (eds.), *Anti-Cartel Enforcement in a Contemporary Age*, p. 259.

[161] D. Schroeder and S. Heinz, 'Requests for Leniency in the EU: Experience and Legal Puzzle' in Cseres, Schinkel and Vogelaar (eds.), *Remedies and Sanctions*, p. 163.

[162] Wils, 'Is Criminalization of EU Competition Law the Answer?', 93.

7.4.2.2 Individual Leniency Policy: Targeting the Agent in the Agency Relationship

Leniency programmes that contain an individual scheme produce a completely different effect on the incentive that an individual has to self-report. Individual leniency provides amnesty for an individual in distinction from his company.

First, individual leniency can address the tension of interests that can arise between the company and the individuals if they are not protected by corporate programmes of leniency. If the individual can join their application to that of the company, their incentives to self-report and to cooperate with the competition authority parallel that of the company. In that context, individual leniency programmes address the discrepancy of interest previously described.

Secondly, individual leniency can be granted to the individual of the company, without protecting his company. The possibility of a company being prosecuted as a result of an individual initiative to self-report has the potential to induce huge tensions of interests within the company. An individual wishing to benefit from leniency has to provide very valuable evidence to the competition authority. Evidence secured typically includes information regarding other persons responsible for initiating and implementing the cartel. Similar to corporate leniency, which enables the competition authority to prosecute other companies, individual leniency may trigger the conviction of other persons in the company. This is added to the sanction that the company as a whole faces.

Individual leniency destabilises the agency relationships within the firm, between those who initiate the cartel and those responsible for implementing it. The cost of operating a cartel is increased, as individuals need to ensure that others do not unilaterally report the cartel activity to the authorities. An employee may need to be bribed in exchange for promising not to blow the whistle.[163] Game theory insights teach us that the expectation about each other's reasoning is supposed to trigger an internal race to individual leniency applications. Expecting that individuals are likely to apply for individual leniency and depending on the degree of awareness, top executives then have every incentive to apply for leniency at the corporate level. Hammond expressed that phenomenon, stating that: 'The real value and measure of the Individual Leniency Program is not in the number of individual applications we receive, but in the number of corporate applications it generates.'[164]

As such, individual leniency seeks to undermine the horizontal relationships between cartel members, through the effect it has on (vertical) relationships within

[163] M. A. Han, *Vertical Relations in Cartel Theory* (Amsterdam Center for Law & Economics, 2011), p. 43.
[164] S. D. Hammond, 'Cornerstones of an Effective Leniency Program' (speech delivered to ICN Workshop on Leniency Programs, Sydney, 2004), available at: www.justice.gov/atr/public /speeches/206611.pdf

the firm.[165] This is exemplified by the lysine cartel, which was uncovered by the FBI through an employee of a participating company, Mark Whitacre. The prospect of being amnestied from any criminal sanction induced him to report the cartel. As a result of his action other executives received prison sentences, and a $100 million fine was imposed on his company, ADM. After exposing the cartel and working for three years with the FBI on the investigation, Mark Whitacre was eventually convicted and given a ten-and-a-half-year prison sentence, for other criminal infringements.[166]

Leniency policy is a cornerstone of competition law infringement against cartels throughout jurisdictions. Competition authorities heavily rely on such tools for detecting and investigating cartels. The so-called 'leniency religion'[167] may be questioned by empirical evidence suggesting that a majority of cartels may already be terminated when an application to leniency is sought.[168] In addition, companies have been using leniency strategically, as is shown by the examples of leniency 'recidivists'.[169] The anticipated 'race to the authority' may not be occurring according to the prediction coming from game theory. The nuanced disrupting effect may be explained on the ground of agency relationship. The agent (here, the individual who would trigger a leniency application) may have comparatively less to gain from leniency and more cartel benefits to forgo than the principal (the company). For greater effectiveness, individual sanctions are required (and immunity from such sanctions); as well as strong incentives given to individuals given to report independently from the company.

7.4.3 Bounty Programmes

Bounty or whistle-blower programmes are another instrument aimed at destabilising the agency relationships in companies, which in turn ought to undermine cartel stability. Whistle-blower programmes typically grant protection to individuals coming forward with information on a cartel, while not necessarily being involved in the cartel themselves. Individuals reporting the wrongdoing of third-parties need to be protected from possible retaliation from other individuals, and probable dismissal by the company, which may be convicted following an individual's action. In addition to individual protection, bounty programmes incentivise individuals with financial rewards. Only a few competition regimes include whistle-blower programmes. In 2017, the European Commission introduced a 'whistle-blower' tool by means of

[165] Argument developed in F. Thépot, 'Leniency and Individual Liability: Opening the Black Box of the Cartel', *Competition Law Review*, 7 (2011), 221. See the economic model in Han, *Vertical Relations in Cartel Theory*.

[166] Leslie, 'Cartels, Agency Costs, and Finding Virtue in Faithless Agents', 1643.

[167] Expression used in Beaton-Wells and Tran (eds.), *Criminalising Cartels*.

[168] Stephan and Nikpay, 'Leniency Decision-Making from a Corporate Perspective'.

[169] Harding, Beaton-Wells and Edwards, 'Leniency and Criminal Sanctions in Anti-Cartel Enforcement', p. 259.

which any relevant information on cartels can be submitted anonymously.[170] In the UK, the CMA may grant a reward of up to £100,000 to an individual who brings valuable evidence of the existence of a cartel in which he or she does not take part.[171] In Korea, the Cartel Informant Reward Programme provides a financial incentive of up to £2 million to an individual coming forward with information on cartel existence.[172] In Hungary, an individual reporting private information about a cartel may be granted at least 1 per cent of the fine eventually imposed (but no more than 50 million forints – the equivalent of about £140,000).[173] In the Slovak Republic, individuals who provide significant evidence on cartel activity are entitled to up to €100,000 as a reward.[174] In Pakistan, the Competition Commission offers reward of up to 5 million rupees (£30,000) in exchange of information that is useful for anti-cartel enforcement.[175] Informants are also rewarded in Singapore, where they can receive up to S$120,000 (£65,000) in exchange for cartel information.[176] Although 'bounties' are available in the United States for denouncing fraudulent claims against the government, as well as securities and tax fraud; there is no such appetite for rewards in antitrust cases.[177] The introduction of a whistle-blower programme that protects an innocent third party that denounces a cartel is envisaged

[170] DG Competition, Anonymous Whistleblower Tool, available at: http://ec.europa.eu/competition/cartels/whistleblower/index.html; A. Stephan, 'European Commission Launches New Anonymous Whistleblower Tool, But Who Would Use It?' (2017) Competition Policy Blog, available at: https://competitionpolicy.wordpress.com/2017/03/21/european-commission-launches-new-anonymous-whistleblower-tool-but-who-would-use-it/; Denmark, Germany, Romania and Poland also provides whistle-blowing functionalities to protect informant's anonymity in the provision of cartel information: ICLG, 'Cartels and Leniency 2018 – Individuals as Whistle-blowers', available at: https://iclg.com/practice-areas/cartels-and-leniency-laws-and-regulations/individuals-as-whistleblowers#chaptercontent5

[171] Competition and Markets Authority, 'Rewards for Information about Cartels', available at: www.gov.uk/government/publications/cartels-informant-rewards-policy. Following conviction in commercial vehicle cartel, the CMA specifically called for information about cartels in the motor industry against financial reward – see: www.gov.uk/government/publications/letter-from-the-cma-to-the-motor-industry-about-cartel-enforcement. There is no reported case of such a financial reward being granted to date. See the recent CMA campaign for cartel information: https://stopcartels.campaign.gov.uk/?utm_source=referral&utm_medium=press-release&utm_campaign=Cartels_2018&utm_content=CMA-release

[172] Since 2002, a total reward of KRW 540.56 million (£1.7 million) has been awarded for 76 cartel informants. In 2016, rewards amounting to KRW 730.21 million (£500,000) were awarded for the reporting of 15 cartels: Korea Federal Trade Commission, Annual Report (2017), available at: https://bit.ly/2wm2MZQ

[173] G. Bennett and B. Domineck, 'Hungary', *European Antitrust Review*, 2013.

[174] ICLG, 'Cartels and Leniency 2018'.

[175] Competition Commission of Pakistan, 'Revised Guidelines on "Reward Payment to Informants Scheme"', cl. 3, available at: www.cc.gov.pk/images/Downloads/guidlines/reward_paymentannexure_ii.pdf

[176] Competition Commission of Singapore, 'Reward Scheme', available at: www.cccs.gov.sg/approach-cccs/making-complaints/reward-scheme

[177] Department of Justice, 'The False Claims Act: A Primer', available at: www.justice.gov/civil/docs/forms/C-FRAUDS_FCA_Primer.pdf

in the United States. In the current bill (approved by the Senate but pending at the House of Representatives) no financial reward will be provided for individuals.[178]

The impact of bounty programmes on the relevant agency relationships resembles that of individual leniency. Bounty programmes have the potential to undermine the stability of agency relationships that exist in the operation of the cartel. The prospect of a financial reward may provide an incentive to an individual to report that outweighs the incentive to comply with cartel instructions. Also, the availability of a bounty may trigger a race to the authority, just to avoid the benefit of the programme being captured by other employees. In addition, the particularity of bounty programmes with respect to leniency programmes is that individuals not directly liable for the cartel may use the threat of reporting. Companies may need to align incentives with a greater range of individuals beyond those directly involved in the cartel for ensuring cartel sustainability (taking the form of, for example, monetary compensation).[179] In addition, an employee may find in the possibility of reporting the cartel a source of bargaining power to obtain a pay rise. This may create or aggravate agency problems that are not specifically related to the cartel operation.[180] For the cartel members, bounty programmes trigger an additional 'race' to the authority: cartel participants may now be in competition with non-cartel individuals from their or other companies.[181] The necessity to collect evidence in exchange for a financial reward further undermines cartel agency relationships.[182] Bounty programmes may increase the situation of moral hazard in the cartel operation *ex post*, while *ex ante* aligning the incentive of the informant individual with the long-term interest of shareholders, based on the assumption that they may be harmed by the legal consequences of cartel participation.

The ability of a bounty programme to undermine the agency relationship within the firm strongly depends on its design. In addition to a sense of loyalty that exists between employees and their company, duties of confidentiality may reduce one's incentive to report illegal conduct. Furthermore, the act of whistle-blowing is associated with considerable personal risks, such as dismissal, or problems with re-employment, and also carries consequences for family, personal and social life.[183] The tragic consequences of whistle-blowing are exemplified by the story of Stanley Adams, who reported to the European Commission illegal price-fixing practices

[178] Bill, Criminal Antitrust Anti-Retaliation Act of 2013, available at: www.govtrack.us/congress/bills/113 /s42/text; SEC, '2013 Annual Report to Congress on the Dodd-Frank Whistleblower Program' (2013) 1, available at: www.sec.gov/about/offi ces/owb/annual-report-2013.pdf. M. Stucke, 'Leniency, Whistle-Blowing and the Individual: Should We Create Another Race to the Competition Agency?' in Beaton-Wells and Tran (eds.), *Criminalising Cartels*, p. 218.

[179] A. Stephan, 'Is the Korean Innovation of Individual Informant Rewards a Viable Cartel Detection Tool?' in T. Cheng, B. Ong and S. Marco Colino (eds.), *Cartels in Asia* (Wolters Kluwer Law & Business, 2014).

[180] C. Aubert, P. Rey and W. E. Kovacic, 'The Impact of Leniency and Whistleblowing Programs on Cartels', *International Journal of Industrial Organization*, 24 (2006), 1241, 1264.

[181] Stucke, 'Leniency, Whistle-Blowing and the Individual'.

[182] Leslie, 'Cartels, Agency Costs, and Finding Virtue in Faithless Agents', 1668.

[183] Stephan, 'Korean Innovation'.

undertaken by his company, Hoffmann-La-Roche, in 1973. Following his act, he was sued in Switzerland for having disclosed confidential business information, faced retaliation measures from his company, and became bankrupt; and his wife reportedly committed suicide in response to the conviction of her husband and his being given a long prison sentence.[184] To counterweight possible huge personal costs, the reward for whistle-blowers must equate to a lottery win, and legal protection must be adequate.[185] Therefore, bounty programmes may destabilise the agency relationship only if they provide positive and defensive incentives that are strong enough to trigger a very peculiar and risky action.

This section only advocates the use of bounty programmes for their disrupting impact on cartels via their strong impact on individual incentives. The normative case for such programmes needs to account for a wider range of factors, and possible negative impacts both for the company and for competition law enforcement. For example, corporate culture may be tainted with distrust; and ethical concerns can exist if such processes are abused by individuals motivated by the prospect of financial gain. Also, there are concerns about how paying individuals may affect the integrity or the credibility of their testimony.[186] Finally, experience of whistle-blowers has involved individuals with peculiar personalities, as exemplified by the stories of Mark Whitacre and Stanley Adams.[187] This suggests that, particularly for such programmes, the strict framework of (bounded) rationality may have serious limitations.

In sum, the effectiveness of instruments that seek to detect cartels depends on their impact on agency relationships within the firm. Corporate leniency programmes are deemed not to be effective if there is a discrepancy of interest in applying for leniency between the shareholders and the managers. Leniency should be supplemented by severe sanction regimes, including individual sanctions. Individuals should also have incentives to report separately from their company through individual leniency and bounty programmes. If adequately designed, the value of these individual schemes stands in the destabilisation of stable agency relationships in companies that are part of a cartel.

7.5 EX POST: THE REACTION OF SHAREHOLDERS

In principle, corporate governance provides tools for shareholders to address the mismatch of interest that the company and individuals may have towards cartel

---

[184] Eric Newbigging, 'Hoffmann-La Roche v Stanley Adams – Corporate and Individual Ethics', (1986) Cranfield University Working Paper.
[185] Stephan, 'Korean Innovation'.
[186] Stucke, 'Leniency, Whistle-Blowing and the Individual'.
[187] Other information on Stanley Adams indicates that he was also a quite high-profile and unusual character. For example, in 1994 he was jailed for plotting the murder of his wife in the hope of getting huge life pension benefits. See 'Tearing Down the Facade of "Vitamins Inc."', D. Barboza, *New York Times*, 10 October 1999, available at: www.nytimes.com/1999/10/10/business/tearing-down-the-facade -of-vitamins-inc.html

detection. This section illustrates how, *ex post*, shareholders may take action against competition law breaches.

It is expected that shareholders do not receive favourably infringement decisions imposing high levels of fines on their companies and opening the door to follow-on damages actions. Potential reputational damages and the impact on the value of the shares may increment the negative impact on shareholders.[188] Collectively, or by way of activism, shareholders may have various means of actions onto the corporate governance of the company. It includes influencing the board composition, exercising proxy votes, or relying on the market for corporate control, which can also sanction exposing the company to consequences of a competition law breach. In addition, companies can take legal action against their own directors when they act against the company's interest. Such means of actions greatly depend on the type of company, ownership structure and jurisdiction. Literature on shareholder activism explores possible channels of influence on the corporate strategy; particularly when ownership is dispersed in large and publicly held companies.[189] Greater reliance on such mechanisms, when available, would constitute effective ways of aligning interests between shareholders and managers towards cartel detection.

7.5.1 *The Reaction of Shareholders: Examples*

Shareholders may publicly express their discontentment regarding the illegal acts of individuals in their companies, and require the resignation of top management. Following the conviction of ThyssenKrupp for its participation in the rail cartel in Germany, shareholders publicly expressed their disapprobation to managers for the harm that the infringement created to the company.[190] During its annual general meeting, a number of the shareholders called for the resignation of the chairman of the supervisory board, for his implication in the price-fixing scandal, and for other failed investments. He subsequently decided to step down from his position.[191] In 1996, following its conviction in several price-fixing scandals, including the lysine

---

[188] See discussion at Section 6.2.2 and A. Riley and D. Sokol, 'Rethinking Compliance', *Journal of Antitrust Enforcement*, 3(1) (2015), 31, 45.

[189] T. M. Jones and A. A. C. Keevil, '"Agents without Principals" Revisited: Theorizing the Effects of Increased Shareholder Participation in Corporate Governance' in M. Goranova and L. V. Ryan (eds.), *Shareholder Empowerment* (Palgrave Macmillan, 2015).

[190] C. Klahold – Chief Compliance Officer, ThyssenKrupp AG, 'Importance and Challenges of Antitrust Compliance for Large Corporations – Deterring EU Competition Law Infringements: Are We Using the Right Sanctions?', Conference by TILEC and the Liege Competition & Innovation (2012); Deutsche Welle, 'ThyssenKrupp to Face Fiery Shareholders' Meeting', available at: www.dw.com/en/thyssenkrupp-to-face-fiery-shareholders-meeting/a-16528518; 'Remarks By Dr. Heinrich Hiesinger Chairman of the Executive Board of ThyssenKrupp AG at the 14th Annual General Meeting on January 18, 2013 at RuhrCongress Bochum', available at https://goo.gl/UjokdG 14

[191] *Wall Street Journal*, 'ThyssenKrupp Chairman Gerhard Cromme to Step Down March 31', available at: www.wsj.com/articles/SB100014241278873233628804578348153890494668

cartel, shareholders' reactions brought about significant changes in the corporate governance structure of ADM. The number of external or independent directors on the board was increased, and directors' compensation levels were drastically reduced. The changes in corporate governance coincided with the end of a series of price-fixing scandals for ADM.[192]

However, it is not always the case that companies take disciplinary steps towards top executives being involved in anticompetitive infringements. While, in 1999, Robert Koehler was given a personal fine of $10 million for his participation in the graphites electrode cartel, he remained in the position of CEO of the company SGL until his retirement in 2014.[193] In addition, British Airways promoted to the company's board one of the sale executives allegedly involved in the fuel surcharge cartel case, a few weeks before he was due to appear in court, potentially facing a prison sentence.[194] A recent empirical study by González et al. on a sample of 248 publicly listed US companies convicted for cartel infringement also shows that managers of firms involved in cartels rarely face any legal consequences, and instead usually enjoy greater job security, higher bonuses and stock-based compensation.[195] Clearer and unambiguous commitment to compliance could be expressed by shareholders taking a much stricter stance on individuals responsible for engaging the company in a cartel.

7.5.2 *Derivative Actions*

In some cases, shareholders make use of a derivative action against top executives to recover from an antitrust fine imposed on the company. A derivative action or suit is a device of corporate governance through which shareholders – usually minority shareholders – are able to enforce the company's rights when directors have breached their duties.[196] The purpose of it, along with other corporate governance mechanisms, is to hold corporate executives accountable and ensure that they act in the company's best interest. Under certain conditions, shareholders may bring

---

[192] Changes were made sometimes fitfully, as, by late 1996, there were still more insiders than outsiders on the board of directors, following resignations: Connor, *Global Price Fixing*, p. 464.

[193] J. Harrington, *Optimal Deterrence of Competition Law Infringement* in 'Deterring EU Competition Law Infringements: Are We Using the Right Sanctions?', Conference by TILEC and the Liege Competition & Innovation (2012).

[194] *Financial Times*, 'BA Sales Chief on Price-Fixing Charge to Join Board' (28 Nov 2008). The sales executive was finally acquitted at trial.

[195] T. A. González, M. Schmid and D. Yermack, 'Does Price Fixing Benefit Corporate Managers?', NYU Working Paper No FIN-13-002 (2017).

[196] A. Reisberg, *Derivative Actions and Corporate Governance. Theory and Operation* (Oxford University Press, 2007), p. 1. See also, for instance: S. Thompson and R. S. Thomas, 'The Public and Private Faces of Derivative Lawsuits', *Vanderbilt Law Review*, 57 (2004), 1747; J. C. Coffee, 'New Myths and Old Realities: The American Law Institute Faces the Derivative Action', *Business Lawyer*, 48 (1993), 1407; R. Romano, 'The Shareholder Suit: Litigation without Foundation?', *Journal of Law, Economics, and Organization*, 7 (1991), 55.

a suit to seek compensation for damage suffered in relation to the breach of a director's duty.[197] Derivative actions or suits are available in almost all EU member states, in different variations.[198] Experience with derivative actions is particularly developed in the United States and the UK, while remaining quite rare in continental Europe jurisdictions.[199]

The US state of Delaware admitted the possibility of shareholders bringing a law suit against directors for failure of oversight in a violation of antitrust law. In *Graham v. Allis-Chalmers Manufacturing Co*, shareholders brought a suit against directors subsequent to the conviction of Allis-Chalmers for a price-fixing violation. Shareholders claimed that, having not implemented an internal monitoring scheme, directors should be liable for the antitrust violation as it resulted in failure to oversee the employees' price-fixing act.[200] The Supreme Court of Delaware absolved the directors, finding that they were entitled to rely on the honesty and integrity of their subordinates unless 'something occurs to put them on suspicion'.[201] Refusing to impose a duty for directors to 'install and operate a corporate system of espionage to ferret out wrongdoing', the Supreme Court's judgment opens the possibility that a director's duty includes a duty to monitor.[202] In *Re Caremark International Inc. Derivative Litigation*, the Delaware Court of Chancery specified that the necessary condition of directors' liability is to establish their lack of good faith, which consists in 'only a sustained or systematic failure of the board to exercise oversight-such as an utter failure to attempt to assure a reasonable information and reporting system exists'.[203] Endorsing the *Re Caremark* standard, *Stone v. Ritter* narrowed the condition to directors' liability, requiring to showing that directors either 'utterly failed to implement any reporting or information system or controls' or whether they 'consciously failed to monitor or oversee its operations thus disabling themselves from being informed of risks or problems requiring their attention'.[204] In *American International Group, Inc. v. Greenberg* the court inferred the lack of good faith from knowledge of the director's high-level in the managerial hierarchy, finding that it was unlikely that illegal bid-rigging in the insurance market would

---

[197] Corporate laws establish requirements for shareholders to have a standing for action, which may include some minimum proportion of shares ownership etc.: K. Grechenic and M. Sekyra, 'No Derivative Shareholder Suits in Europe – A Model of Percentage Limits and Collusion', *International Review of Law and Economics*, 31 (2011), 16.

[198] S. Kalss, 'Shareholder Suits: Common Problems, Different Solutions and First Steps towards a Possible Harmonization by Means of a European Model Code', *European Company and Financial Law Review*, 2 (2009), 324, 339.

[199] M. Gertner, 'Why do Shareholder Derivative Suits Remain Rare in Continental Europe?', *Brooklyn Journal of International Law*, 37 (2013), 843.

[200] *Graham v. Allis-Chalmers Mfg Co*, 188 A 2d (Del 1963).

[201] Ibid., para. 130.

[202] Ibid.

[203] *In re Caremark Int'l Inc Deriv Litig*, 698 A 2d at 959, 971 (1996).

[204] *Stone v. Ritter* 911 A 2d 362 (Del. 2006).

have occurred without their knowledge.[205] In *Robert F. Booth Trust v. Crowley* the Seventh Circuit Court of Appeal affirmed that a derivative action could also be brought in relation to the violation of section 8 of the Clayton Act provision on interlocking directorates.[206] Derivative suits have been made in several antitrust cases, to recover antitrust fines as well as for instituting internal mechanisms of compliance, as was the case in the derivative action in the Intel case.[207]

The recent case *Safeway v. Twigger* raised the question of the availability of a derivative action in the context of an antitrust infringement in the UK. Following the imposition by the OFT (ex-CMA) of an £11 million fine for illegal price-fixing behaviour in the dairy products market, Safeway brought a derivative action before the High Court against former employees who were supposedly responsible for the cartel practice.[208] Former directors were accused of taking part in and facilitating the price-fixing initiative, as well as not reporting the practice to the board of directors. Safeway alleged that the directors, in causing the company to breach competition law, had acted in breach of their fiduciary duties. Safeway sought to recover the fine imposed on the company, as well as the cost of the company's cooperation during the investigation. Relying on the principle of *ex turpi causa non oritur actio*, the former directors and employees applied for the claim to be struck out by the High Court. According to this principle, a legal action cannot be brought in relation to the claimant's own illegal act.[209] The High Court dismissed the defendants' application to strike out the claim. The Court considered that the illegal price-fixing conduct was the act of the directors and/or employees acting as agents for the companies. As such, the illegality came from the defendant's acts, rather than from the companies' personal actions. As a result, the Court considered that the claimants had a chance to defeat the defence's argument based on the *ex turpi causa* principle at the trial.[210] The High Court judgment opened up the possibility that companies, in spite of being the subject of the Competition Act provisions and liable for their infringement, could, in some cases, be 'innocent victims' of the hidden action of individuals in the context of the breach. In other words, this judgment would enable companies to use a device of corporate governance as a way to address issues of the agency relationship.

---

[205] *American International Group* v. *Greenberg* 965 A 2d 763, 795–99 (Del Ch 2009).
[206] *Robert F Booth Trust* v. *Crowley* 687 F 3d 314 (2012).
[207] J. S. Venit and A. L. Foster, 'Competition Compliance: Fines and Complementary Incentives' in P. Lowe and M. Marquis (eds.), *European Competition Law Annual 2011: Integrating Public and Private Enforcement of Competition Law – Implications for Courts and Agencies* (Hart Publishing, 2014) 80. *In re Intel Corp* Derivative Litigation, 'Stipulation of Settlement' Case 1:09-cv-00867-JJF (D Del. 25 May 2010) 13–16.
[208] Safeway admitted the breach of chapter 1 of the Competition Act 1998, following which it entered into an 'early resolution agreement': OFT Press Release, 'OFT Fines Certain Supermarkets and Processors Almost £50 Million in Dairy Decision' (10 August 2011).
[209] *Holman* v. *Johnson* (1775) 1 Cowp 341.
[210] *Safeway Stores Ltd and others* v. *Twigger and others* [2010] EWHC 11 (Comm), paras. 45 and 54.

The High Court interim judgment was subsequently appealed by the defendants to the Court of Appeal. In its judgment, the Court of Appeal struck out Safeway's claim against its former directors. The Court of Appeal reaffirmed that, based on section 36 of the Competition Act 1998, a company is liable for the violation of competition law prohibitions by its employees or directors. Therefore, the illegal action could not be attributed to individuals of the company because '[t]he whole hypothesis of the undertaking's liability is that it is personally at fault'.[211] This contrasts with the High Court's approach that Safeway could not be 'personally' at fault unless it could be shown that the former directors were the 'directing mind or will' of the company. The High Court rejected Safeway's subsequent application to appeal the Court of Appeal's judgment.

While the High Court's interim decision seemed to open the possibility of a company bringing a derivative suit in the context of a breach of competition law, the Court of Appeal reaffirmed that UK competition law applies to an undertaking strictly, disregarding the issues of corporate governance. The alternative conclusion would have implied that competition law is newly concerned with the relationship between a company and its executives.

The availability of a derivative action in the context of the breach of competition law would have been the recognition that competition law violations need to be addressed along the line of other corporate governance issues. The circumstances of *Safeway* v. *Twigger* were quite unusual, because Safeway was seeking to recover the penalty not from the directors themselves, but from its D&O insurers.[212] In addition, the action was brought after the company had been acquired by a rival supermarket, which makes the legal action slightly outside the scope of intra-company relations. For all these reasons, together with the capital market uncertainty that such legal action may trigger, it seems quite unlikely that the possibility of a derivative action will arise again in the UK. In addition, some have argued that such a possibility could have had adverse effects on other competition law instruments, such as leniency or settlement policies. Executives may be deterred from cooperating in the context of leniency or a settlement procedure because such cooperation may increase the potential for a derivative action against them.[213]

---

[211] *Safeway Stores Ltd and others v Twigger and others* [2010] EWCA Civ 1472, para 22. 'There is a liability it cannot be imposed on any person other than the undertaking, and the undertaking is personally liable for the infringement. If a penalty is imposed it will only be because the undertaking itself has intentionally or negligently committed the infringement. In those circumstances it is the undertaking which is personally at fault (there can be no one else who is), and once the maxim is engaged the undertaking cannot say that it was not personally at fault in order to defeat the application of the maxim. The whole hypothesis of the undertaking's liability is that it is personally at fault.'

[212] A. Morfey and C. Patton, 'Safeway Stores Ltd v Twigger: the Buck Stops Here', *Competition Law* (2011) 57, 63.

[213] P. Scott, 'Competition Law Briefing: Safeway v Twigger – Safeway's Claim Against Former Directors Reaches End of Shelf Life' (Norton Rose Case Brief, 2011).

7.6 CONCLUSION

The effectiveness of enforcement instruments critically depends on their effects on internal dynamics, analysed through the lens of agency relationships. This chapter has provided normative justifications for addressing effectively incentives of individuals. Prison or pecuniary sanctions imposed on individuals would greatly enhance the deterrence effect of corporate sanctions. This chapter has also clarified the key ingredients for effective leniency. Leniency policy may effectively disrupt cartels if, supplemented with a credible threat of severe sanctions, it aligns the incentives of the individuals and the company towards leniency application. Individuals should also have incentives to report separately from their company, through individual leniency and bounty programmes. Finally, a fuller use of corporate governance tools by shareholders could supplement and enhance the effectiveness of cartel enforcement instruments, towards better alignment of shareholders and managers' interests towards cartel detection. This would be particularly effective to remedy the current mitigated impact of sanctions on individuals in Europe.

8

Cartel Enforcement: Corporate Compliance Programmes

8.1 INTRODUCTION

Previous chapters showed that the effectiveness of enforcement instruments, in terms of deterrence and detection, critically depends on their impact on the agency relationship. This chapter discusses the significance of corporate compliance programmes, operating at the heart of corporate governance, as an enforcement tool against cartels. Compliance programmes refer broadly to the organisational and practical dimensions of companies' efforts to comply with competition law, with the aim of impacting durably the corporate culture and moral commitment to comply at all levels.[1] Compliance programmes typically encompass schemes designed to educate employees about illegal activities, monitor their behaviour, and discipline them in cases of illegal conduct.[2]

The main theoretical claim is that current enforcement challenges against cartels raise the need to move away from a strictly sanctions-based type of enforcement, to include self- or 'management-based' regulation.[3] Despite the increasing level of

---

[1] Wils defines compliance programmes as 'A set of measures adopted within a company or corporate group to inform, educate and instruct its personnel about the antitrust prohibitions [...] and the company's or group's policy regarding respect for these prohibitions, and to control or monitor respect for these prohibitions or this policy. Antitrust compliance programmes are thus a type of organizational control system aimed at standardizing staff behaviour, specifically within the domain of antitrust compliance' (W. P. J. Wils, 'Antitrust Compliance Programmes & Optimal Antitrust Enforcement', *Journal of Antitrust Enforcement*, 1 (2013), 52).

[2] C. Angelucci and M. A. Han, 'Monitoring Managers Through Corporate Compliance Programs', Amsterdam Center for Law & Economics Working Paper No 2010–14, 2. 'Compliance programmes' broadly refers to all the management tools used to prevent and detect misconduct: J Murphy in OECD, Policy Roundtable, 'Promoting Compliance with Competition Law' (2011) 14–15. Report available at: www.oecd.org/daf/competition/Promotingcompliancewithcompetitionlaw2011.pdf

[3] At one extreme of the enforcement spectrum lies the 'deterrence' or 'sanctioning' enforcement approach. At the other end, 'compliance'-based enforcement embraces a range of informal techniques including education, advice, persuasion and negotiation: R. Baldwin, M. Cave and M. Lodge, *Understanding Regulation: Theory, Strategy, and Practice*, 2nd edn (Oxford University Press, 2012), p. 239. Europe Economics, 'Etat des lieux et perspectives des programmes de conformité, Une étude

fines imposed on convicted companies, collusive behaviour remains a problem.[4] The hidden nature of cartel practices, and the related difficulty of detecting them, undermine the optimality of sanctions. Developments in algorithms and artificial intelligence are likely further to complicate detection of collusive behaviour.[5] Assuming a low probability of detection, the level of fines is currently suboptimal.[6] Individual sanctions constitute a possible solution to the impossibility of fining companies optimally, but alternative methods are advocated to complement a strict sanctions-based regime. Those methods entail addressing business perceptions of the morality of regulated behaviour.[7] Psychological studies suggest that a moral commitment to the norm is an important element that explains compliance with the law.[8] In addition, it is widely admitted that corporate culture is an important factor in explaining the engagement of companies in competition law infringements.[9] A decision to behave anticompetitively may emanate from the top of the hierarchy, and some companies have been known to perpetuate a tradition of antitrust infringements.[10] Establishing that cartel behaviour is morally 'bad', independently of its illegality, is as important as sanctions schemes.[11] In the context of this

réalisée pour le Conseil de la concurrence' (2008), para. 10.11, available at: www .autoritedelaconcurrence.fr/doc/etudecompliance_octo8.pdf. On Management-based regulation, see, for example: C. Coglianese and D. Lazer, 'Management-Based Regulation: Prescribing Private Management to Achieve Public Goals', *Law & Society Review*, 37 (2003), 691: 'A management-based approach requires firms to engage in their own planning and internal rule making efforts Management-based regulation directs regulated organisations to engage in a planning process that aims toward the achievement of public goals, offering firms flexibility in how they achieve public goals.'

[4] D. D. Sokol, 'Cartels, Corporate Compliance, and What Practitioners Really Think About Enforcement', *Antitrust Law Journal*, 78 (2012), 201, 202; A. Riley and D. Sokol, 'Rethinking Compliance', *Journal of Antitrust Enforcement*, 3(1) (2015), 31, 33.

[5] Challenges of the new economy for the study of collusive practices are discussed in, e.g., A. Ezrachi and M. Stucke, *Virtual Competition* (Harvard University Press, 2016); OECD, Algorithms and Collusion: Competition Policy in the Digital Age (2017).

[6] Empirical studies estimated a probability of detection between 13 per cent and 17 per cent of cartels that have been eventually detected. See: P. G. Bryant and E. W. Eckard, 'Price Fixing: The Probability of Getting Caught', *Review of Economics and Statistics*, 73 (1991), 531; E. Combe, C. Monnier and R. Legal, 'Cartels: The Probability of Getting Caught in the European Union', Bruges European Economic Research papers (2008), 2. Wils also concludes that, based on such a probability of getting caught, the deterrent level of fine would be about 150 per cent of the annual turnover in the products concerned by the infringement. W. P. J. Wils, *The Optimal Enforcement of EC Antitrust Law* (Kluwer Law International, 2002), p. 200.

[7] A. Riley and M. Bloom, 'Antitrust Compliance Programmes – Can Companies and Antitrust Agencies do More?', *Competition Law Journal* [2011] 21, 22.

[8] W. P. J. Wils, 'Is Criminalization of EU Competition Law the Answer?', *World Competition: Law and Economics Review*, 28 (2005), 117.

[9] Factors that are external to the companies also play a key role in explaining the rate of infringements in certain industries. See Section 6.3.2.

[10] J. Sonnenfeld and P. R. Lawrence, 'Why Do Companies Succumb to Price Fixing?', *Harvard Business Review* (1978),145.

[11] For a legal theory discussion on the relationship between law and morality, see: J. Garner, 'Ethics and Law' in J Skorupski (ed.), *The Routledge Companion to Ethics* (Routledge, 2010).

discussion, the question is whether a culture of compliance, via the adoption of compliance programmes, is an effective 'moral' avenue to controlling conduct with regard to compliance (in combination with the 'legal' means that are sanctions).[12]

Despite acknowledging the value of corporate compliance programmes, competition authorities across jurisdictions are reluctant to provide concrete incentives (either positive or negative) for their implementation. The European Commission has affirmed that compliance programmes cannot constitute a mitigating factor in the context of a conviction.[13] The United States Department of Justice has, until recently, refused to consider compliance programmes in antitrust infringements.[14] The UK and Italian competition authorities, however, may respectively grant a 10 per cent or 15 per cent reduction of a fine for having effective compliance measures.[15] In the field of anti-corruption, in contrast, companies in some jurisdictions can avoid completely liability for having implemented 'adequate procedures'.[16]

After providing an overview of the existing regulatory approaches to compliance programmes (with a focus on the United States, the European Union (EU) and EU member states), this chapter will analyse the contribution of corporate compliance to the enforcement objectives of prevention and detection of anticompetitive collusive practices. Among the different incentives that may be used by authorities, this chapter focuses on the possibility of giving credit to compliance programmes, in the form of a fine reduction in the context of an alleged infringement of the cartel prohibition.

This chapter argues that competition authorities should steer companies' incentives towards implementing effective compliance programmes. Rewarding effective compliance programmes in the context of an investigation can improve the effectiveness of corporate sanctions in providing *ex ante* incentives to companies to deter and detect illegal behaviour internally. Outlining the key foundations of an effective compliance programme, this chapter also helps understanding how and when competition authorities should reward the compliance efforts of companies. As such, it addresses the fundamental concerns of rewarding compliance programmes in the context of competition law infringements.[17]

[12] S. Shavell, 'Law versus Morality as Regulators of Conduct', *American Law and Economics Review*, 4 (2002), 227.
[13] J. Almunia, Vice President of the Commission responsible for Competition Policy: 'The main reward for a successful compliance programme is not getting involved in unlawful behaviour. Instead, a company involved in a cartel should not expect a reward from us for setting up a compliance programme, because that would be a failed programme by definition' (SPEECH/ 11/268, 14 April 2011).
[14] See further developments at Section 8.2.2.2.
[15] CMA73, 'CMA Guidance As to the Appropriate Amount of a Penalty' (2018), para. 2.19; Linee Guida sulla modalità di applicazione dei criteri di quantificazione delle sanzioni amministrative pecuniarie irrogate dall'Autorità in applicazione dell'articolo 15, comma 1, della legge n. 287/90, 31 October 2014, para. 23.
[16] See, e.g., the UK: Bribery Act 2010, s. 7(2).
[17] Wils, 'Antitrust Compliance Programmes'.

In the literature, compliance programmes refer to a great variety of processes, from a simple 'check-list' to very sophisticated schemes.[18] No distinction in the degree of seriousness and sophistication of compliance programmes is made in the definition here. The terms 'corporate compliance' and 'compliance programmes' will be used interchangeably, to refer broadly to the organisational and practical dimensions of companies' efforts to comply with the competition law, with the aim of impacting durably the corporate culture and moral commitment to comply at all levels. In addition, 'compliance efforts' will sometimes be referred to as a synonym for compliance programmes or corporate compliance.

8.2 OVERVIEW OF REGULATORY APPROACHES TO COMPLIANCE

The implementation of compliance programmes is very much valued by competition authorities as a necessary avenue for the creation of a culture of compliance. A number of guidelines describe the steps that companies should take to avoid the risk of competition law infringement in the first place, while acknowledging that a 'one-size-fits-all' approach is not adequate in the context of compliance programmes.[19] In spite of acknowledging the value of corporate compliance programmes, most competition authorities, including the European Commission, refuse to consider the compliance efforts of a company. This characterises the 'black box' approach: what matters is the outcome of corporate compliance. The assumption is that a company that has infringed competition law has necessarily failed in its organisational effort to comply, precluding it from receiving any credit for its compliance programme. In other jurisdictions, such as the UK and the United States (since a recent change in approach) robust and credible compliance programmes may be rewarded, despite a non-compliance outcome. In this kind of approach, the manner in which compliance is organised matters for the competition authorities. At present, none of the legal systems examined has relieved a company of its liability on grounds relating to compliance programmes.[20] The maximum

[18] D. Geradin, 'Antitrust Compliance Programmes & Optimal Antitrust Enforcement: A Reply to Wouter Wils', *Journal of Antitrust Enforcement*, 1 (2013), 325, 327. Studies on the drivers of compliance have identified corporate compliance as being a very complex product of structure, culture and agency. See, e.g., C. Parker and S. Gilad, 'Internal Corporate Compliance Management Systems: Structure, Culture and Agency' in C. Parker and V. Lehmann Nielsen (eds.), *Explaining Compliance: Business Responses to Regulation* (Edward Elgar Publishing, 2011).

[19] The UK: Guidance provided by the CMA: 'Businesses: Competition Law Guidance', available at: www.gov.uk/government/collections/competing-fairly-in-business-advice-for-small-businesses, including OFT1341, 'How Your Business Can Achieve Compliance with Competition Law' (2011); France: Autorité de la Concurrence, 'Antitrust Compliance and Compliance Programmes, Corporate Tools for Competing Safely in the Market Place' (2012); in the EU: Commission (DG COMP), 'Compliance Matters, What Companies Can Do Better to Respect EU Competition Rules' (2012).

[20] Although in the United States there are a few old cases in which judges allowed companies to present their compliance programmes to juries in their defence in antitrust criminal cases: 'If [. . .] you find that Koppers Company acted diligently in the promulgation, dissemination, and enforcement of an

incentive witnessed for antitrust programmes is a reduction in fine. In other areas of law, however, a complete defence seems possible, under certain circumstances. This is the case for anti-bribery law in the UK. In the United States, the authorities may elect not to prosecute a company in the event of an effective compliance programme. In addition to the US and EU approaches, a sample of regulatory approaches available in EU national jurisdictions will be presented. Approaches to compliance programmes are not set in stone. Both the United States and France have very recently shifted their policy of rewarding companies' compliance efforts.

8.2.1 *The EU Approach: Compliance Programmes as a 'Black Box'*

The European Commission made it clear that it will not consider compliance efforts undertaken by a convicted company. In a speech in 2011, Joaquin Almunia, former Vice President of the Commission responsible for Competition Policy, reaffirmed that compliance programmes implemented in companies that infringe competition law are 'failed' and therefore cannot constitute a mitigating factor in the assessment of the level of fine to be imposed.[21] In that conception, solely the outcome of such programmes matters in the context of competition law enforcement. Such an approach may reflect either the willingness of the EU not to interfere with companies' freedom to organise compliance, or a regulatory approach that 'commands' but does not 'control or monitor' the achievement of compliance by itself. Although compliance efforts should not be used to aggravate the level of the fine, compliance programmes have been considered in liability attribution cases within corporate groups. In *Schindler* the Court found that 'the implementation of [a] code of conduct suggests [. . .] that the parent company did in fact supervise the commercial policy of its subsidiaries', thereby suggesting the exercise of decisive evidence, required for attributing liability for the parent company.[22] In *du Pont de Nemours*, the existence of a common compliance programme was an indication of the decisive influence of parent companies over their jointly owned subsidiary.[23] The question of compliance programmes in liability attribution cases has been discussed in Chapter 4, in which I argued that programmes should be positively considered as part of a parent's defence, for greater effectiveness of fines. A parent company showing that it has taken all the organisational steps to ensure compliance within a corporate group should be able to be relieved of parental liability.[24]

---

antitrust compliance program in an active good faith effort to ensure that the employees would abide by the law, you may take this fact into account in determining whether or not to impute an agent or employee's intent to the Koppers Company' (jury instruction in *US* v. *Koppers Co* Crim. No 79-85 (D Conn 1980)).

[21]   Almunia SPEECH/11/268.
[22]   Case C-501/11P *Schindler Holding and Others* v. *Commission* [2013] ECR I-0, para. 114.
[23]   Case T-76/08 *EI DuPont de Nemours & Co* v. *Commission* [2012] EU:T:2012:46, para. 73.
[24]   See Section 4.2.2.

Interestingly, past decisional practice shows that the Commission used to consider compliance programmes in competition law cases. In *National Panasonic*, a case of export prohibition infringing ex-Article 101(1), the Commission considered the quality of the antitrust compliance programme as a mitigating factor in its assessment of the level of fine:

> Th[e] constructive attitude [of conducting an audit and issuing a code of conduct] adopted by the management of MET [. . .] has also been taken into account in assessing the amount of the fine. The undertakings concerned have adopted a comprehensive practical detailed and carefully considered antitrust compliance programme, with appropriate legal advice.[25]

Over the following years, the Commission similarly took account of compliance programmes in other export ban cases, in *Fisher-Price/Quaker-Oats Ltd – Toyco*,[26] *Viho/Toshiba*[27] and *Viho/Parker Pen*.[28] In the abuse of dominant position cases, *Eurofix-Bauxo/Hilti* and *Napier Brown – British Sugar*, the Commission took into account the undertaking offered by companies to implement compliance programmes in its assessment of the amount of fines.[29] In spite of commitments to implement an effective compliance programme, British Sugar was later prosecuted for being part of a cartel. On this occasion, the Commission, for the first time, considered the existence of a compliance programme to be an *aggravating* factor.[30] Therefore, for a certain period, the Commission, via its decisional practice, provided defensive incentives to companies for the implementation of compliance programmes, although never in cases of hard-core cartels.[31] In its recent practice, the Commission has not considered compliance programmes as a factor when setting fines.[32] Some have argued that this change in its approach coincided with the

---

[25] *National Panasonic* (Case COMP IV/30.070) Commission Decision 82/853/EEC [1982] OJ L354/28, para. 68.

[26] *Fisher-Price /Quaker-Oats Ltd – Toyco* (Case COMP IV/31.017) Commission Decision 88/86/ EEC [1988] OJ L04/19, para. 27.

[27] *Viho/Toshiba* (Case COMP IV/32.879) Commission Decision 91/532/EEC [1991] OJ L287/39, paras. 28–30.

[28] *Viho/Parker Pen* (Case COMP IV/32.725) Commission Decision 92/426/EEC [1992] OJ L233, para. 24.

[29] *Eurofix-Bauxo / Hilti* (Case COMP IV/30.787 and 31.488) Commission Decision 88/138/EEC [1987] OJ L65/19, para. 10; *Napier Brown – British Sugar* (Case COMP IV/30.178) Commission Decision 88/518/EEC [1988] OJ L284/41, para. 86.

[30] *British Sugar plc* (Case COMP IV/F-3/33.708), *Tate & Lyle plc* (Case COMP IV/F-3/33.709), *Napier Brown & Company Ltd* (Case COMP IV/F-3/33.710), *James Budgett Sugars Ltd* (Case COMP IV/F-3/33.711) Commission Decision 1999/210/EC [1998] OJ L076/01, para. 208.

[31] 'Defensive incentives' refer to incentives available in the context of an infringement of competition (for example, consisting of a fine reduction in the event of prosecution).

[32] E.g. *Amino Acids*, para. 312: 'The Commission welcomes ADM's initiative to set up a compliance policy. However, as the present case indicates, this initiative came too late and cannot, as a prevention tool, dispense the Commission from its duty to sanction the infringement of the competition rules which ADM has committed in the past' (Case COMP/36.545/F3) Commission Decision 2001/418/EC

increasing importance given to leniency policy.[33] Another argument explaining a change in its position may come from the *British Sugar* case. The compliance programme that was rewarded did not impede the subsequent infringement. The Commission's confidence in assessing the credibility of a compliance programme may have been affected.[34]

8.2.2 *The US Approach: the Wind of Change*

The United States has long adopted a quasi-neutral approach towards compliance programmes in antitrust. US federal courts may in principle consider compliance programmes as a mitigating factor in the context of corporate crimes, but the conditions attached to it almost exclude this possibility for antitrust violations. In addition, most criminal cases against companies do not go to court but settle. This further limits the possibility of compliance efforts to be taken into consideration in antitrust cases. Finally, until recently the Department of Justice was expressly excluding the reward of compliance programmes in antitrust cases.

8.2.2.1 US Federal Courts

The US Sentencing Guidelines that set out federal courts' policy for individuals and companies convicted of felonies and serious misdemeanours, in general, foresees the possible reduction in the level of fine if a convicted corporation had in place at the time of the infringement an 'effective compliance and ethics programme'. This means that, in application of these guidelines, the United States considers the organisation of compliance in the context of a corporate crime conviction. There is, however, a rebuttable presumption that a compliance programme is not effective when the offence involves 'high-level' or 'substantial authority' personnel.[35] Antitrust infringement have usually involved individuals who are able to exercise substantial authority within the scope of their responsibility, such as setting prices, negotiating and approving commercial contracts etc.[36] Therefore, antitrust cases were typically falling within the categories of individuals that preclude a compliance defence for corporations. Under very narrow circumstances, however, the involvement of senior

[2000] OJ L152); see also *Elevators and Escalators* (Case COMP/E-1/38.823) Commission Decision 2008/C 75/10 [2007] OJ C075/19, paras. 631, 687 et seq., 753 et seq; *Calcium carbide and magnesium based reagents for the steel and gas industries* (Case COMP/39.396) Commission Decision 2009/C 301/14 [2009] OJ C301/18, para. 325.

33 Europe Economics, 'Etat des lieux'.

34 J. E. Murphy, 'Policies in Conflict: Undermining Corporate Self-Policing', *Rutgers University Law Review*, 69 (2017), 421, 463.

35 US Sentencing Guidelines Manual (2012) §8C2.5 Culpability Score, (f) Effective Compliance and Ethics Program.

36 Ibid., §8A1.2: 'The term [high-level personnel of an organisation] includes: a director; an executive officer; an individual in charge of a major business or functional unit of the organization, such as sales, administration, or finance; and an individual with a substantial ownership interest.'

executives does not rule out the possibility of receiving credit for an effective compliance programme. As part of the compliance programme, the compliance officer should have 'express authority to communicate personally' to the board or its audit committee 'promptly on any matter involving criminal conduct or potential criminal conduct'. In addition, this officer must report 'no less than annually' about the compliance programme.[37]

8.2.2.2 US Agencies

Until recently, the Department of Justice's Antitrust Division clearly excluded the consideration of compliance programmes in the context of antitrust:[38] '[T]he Antitrust Division has established a firm policy, understood in the business community, that credit should not be given at the charging stage for a compliance program.' The justification related to the supposed specificity of 'antitrust violations, [that] by definition, go to the heart of the corporation's business'.[39] The Federal Trade Commission had taken a more flexible approach towards compliance programmes, having listed specific corporate compliance elements in a settlement procedure.[40] In 2015, top officials from the Antitrust Division, including Brent Snyder, stated that the Division was actively considering ways in which it could credit companies that proactively implement or improve compliance programmes after coming under investigation.[41] This change in direction materialised in recent cases, in which compliance programmes implemented during the investigation were considered to be mitigating factors in the amount of fines imposed.[42] The Department of Justice clarified that only compliance programmes implemented or improved after the

---

The term [substantial authority personnel] includes high-level personnel of the organization, individuals who exercise substantial supervisory authority [...], and any other individuals who, although not a part of an organization's management, nevertheless exercise substantial discretion when acting within the scope of their authority (e.g. an individual with authority in an organization to negotiate or set price levels or an individual authorized to negotiate or approve significant contracts).'

[37]   Ibid., ch. 8, (f)(3)(C)(i) and §11.
[38]   J. E. Murphy, 'Making the Sentencing Guidelines Message Complete' (2013), available at: www .compliance-network.com/wp-content/uploads/2012/08/4-5-13-filing-.pdf
[39]   United States Attorney's Manual, 9-28.400, Special Policy Concerns (2008), available at: www.justice .gov/usao/eousa/foia_reading_room/usam/title9/28mcrm.htm
[40]   FTC: National Association of Music Merchants, Inc, Docket No C-4255 FTC File No 001 0203; 2009. See J. E. Murphy, 'The FTC and Antitrust Compliance Programs' Compliance & Ethics Professional (2012), available at: www.joemurphyccep.com/wp-content/uploads/2012/08/Finalpublishedarticle _Murphy_ARTICLEcopy.pdf
[41]   See, e.g., Deputy Assistant Attorney General Brent Snyder Delivers Remarks at the Sixth Annual Chicago Forum on International Antitrust (8 June 2015), available at: www.justice.gov/opa/speech /deputy-assistant-attorney-general-brent-snyder-delivers-remarks-sixth-annual-chicago
[42]   *US* v. *Barclays Plc*, No 3: 15-cr-00077-SRU, plea agreement, available at: www.justice.gov/file /440481/download; *US* v. *Kayaba Industry Co.*, Ltd, d/b/a KYB Corporation, plea agreement, available at: www.justice.gov/atr/case-document/file/791911/download

infringement may receive credit, and the Antitrust Division will retain full discretion so that companies cannot expect to receive credit for implementing 'cosmetic' or mere paper compliance programmes.[43]

The Sentencing Guidelines do not apply to private enforcement cases, because they are not concerned with the level of fine. Therefore, companies receiving a fine reduction are still exposed to damages actions by private parties, particularly so in the United States, where private enforcement is very developed.[44] However, in the non-antitrust case *Stender* v. *Lucky Stores, Inc* compliance material was used against the company to establish a basis for claiming punitive damages.[45]

8.2.3 EU Member States

In the EU, only the UK and Italy may provide defensive incentives for the implementation of compliance programmes. France also provided such incentives until 2017. Defensive incentives refer to credit given to companies for having effective compliance programmes, in the context of an investigation. This typically entails a reduction in the level of the fine for a convicted company. The Netherlands also has experience with considering compliance programmes as part of commitment decisions. Positive incentives could consist of advantages, acquired for having a compliance programme outside of an investigation, for example in the context of a tender procedure. Certification of compliance programmes, either from non-governmental bodies, or from the competition authorities, could constitute such positive avenues to compliance. No authority grants such incentives in the context of antitrust. Defensive incentives can either concern compliance programmes existing at the time of the infringement, so-called *ante-factum*, or those implemented following the discovery of the infringement, which are *post-factum*.

8.2.3.1 The UK – *Ante-Factum* and *Post-Factum*

In the UK, compliance programmes may be given recognition in the context of competition law infringement. Revised Competition and Markets Authority (CMA) guidance on the setting of fines confirms the inclusion of effective compliance programmes as a possible mitigating factor – a view confirmed by the Competition Appeal Tribunal.[46] The basic amount of the fine may be adjusted

---

[43]   See Brent Snyder remarks.
[44]   Murphy, 'Policies in Conflict', 435.
[45]   803 F Supp 259 (ND Cal 1992). For more discussion of this case, see ibid., 451.
[46]   *Kier Group and others* v. *OFT* (2011) '[S]ome discount should be given for a post-infringement compliance programme. The reasons for a discount are obvious: it serves as an inducement to infringers to take appropriate steps to avoid infringing in the future, and reflects the mitigating circumstance that the infringer intends not to do so. Further, although the OFT is correct in saying that a compliance programme is not a substitute for a general or specific deterrent, the decision-maker

where adequate steps have been taken with a view to ensuring compliance.[47] Such defensive incentives are available for steps taken either before the infringement, or soon after the company had knowledge of it.[48] Assessed on a case-by-case basis, effective compliance programmes, if appropriate to the size of the business and to its level of competition risk, may lead to a maximum of a 10 per cent reduction in the level of the fine. Companies need to demonstrate a clear compliance commitment that is disseminated throughout the organisation, as well as processes of risk identification, risk assessment and risk mitigation that are in place, and a plan for reviewing those processes.[49] Ordinarily, compliance programmes do not constitute an aggravating factor, except in particular cases in which, for example, they have been used by companies to dissimulate or facilitate a violation, or to mislead the competition authority during its investigation.[50] Compliance programmes may also be recognised following the discovery of the infringement.

As an example, in 2015, the CMA granted a 5 per cent fine reduction upon evidence that, after the infringement, senior executives had received compliance training and that the company had implemented a competition compliance manual.[51] In 2014, the Office of Fair Trading (OFT) considered that a 10 per cent fine reduction was appropriate on the basis that a compliance programme would be monitored and assessed by one of the board members, that comprehensive compliance training would be received by all relevant employees, and that contracts with trading partners and compliance policies would be reviewed.[52] Compliance programmes have also been considered a mitigating factor in the decisional practice prior to the adoption of this policy in the authority's documents. In a 2002 infringement decision, *Arriva plc and FirstGroup plc*, the OFT granted a 10 per cent fine reduction to Arriva plc for implementing a compliance programme, involving training of staff.[53] In the 2003 *Hasbro* case, the OFT considered compliance programmes in two different ways. A compliance programme was in place at the time of the infringement, in which senior management were involved. The OFT stated that the fact that senior management had blatantly ignored the compliance programme impeded the reduction in the level of fine.[54] However, the OFT gave

---

should in our view take such a programme into account in assessing any deterrent element in the penalty. For it may well have a bearing on specific deterrence.'
[47] CMA73, 'CMA's Guidance as to the Appropriate Amount of a Penalty', para. 2.19.
[48] OFT1341, 'How Your Business Can Achieve Compliance with Competition Law', para. 7.2.
[49] CMA73, para. 2.19 fn. 33.
[50] Ibid.
[51] Case CE/9827/13 Property Sales and Lettings Investigation, Decision dated 8 May 2015, para. 6.43.
[52] Case CE/9627/12 Investigation into the Supply of Healthcare Products, Decision dated 20 March 2014, para. 7.30
[53] Decision of the Director General of Fair Trading, No CA98/9/2002 Market sharing by Arriva plc and First Group plc, 30 January 2002 (Case CP/1163-00), para. 66.
[54] Decision of Director General of Fair Trading, No CA98/2/2003, Agreements between Hasbro UK Ltd, Argos Ltd and Littlewoods Ltd fixing the price of Hasbro toys and games, 19 February 2003 (Case CP/0480-01), para. 340.

10 per cent reduction as credit for the disciplinary steps taken towards responsible employees as well as for the organisation of new compliance schemes in subsidiaries and for sales employees and senior management, following Hasbro's discovery of the infringement.[55]

8.2.3.2 Italy – *Post-Factum*

Italy also gives credit for compliance programmes in the context of litigation. In the *Farmindustria/Codice di autoregolamentazione* case, the association of pharmaceutical companies in Italy, the competition authorities relieved the association of any fine, for cooperating during the investigation as well as for implementing a compliance programme.[56] A similar approach was taken in *Assirevi/Società di revisioni*. The case concerned the coordination of prices via Assirevi (the Italian Association of Auditors) that set out minimum hourly fees for audit services provided by seventeen companies, who were members of the association. Compliance programmes, as well as the cooperative behaviour of some firms during the investigation, were taken into account by the Authority in its assessment of the gravity of the infringement.[57] In 2014, Italy introduced fining guidelines confirming that a compliance programme may constitute a mitigating factor, with a possible reduction of up to 15 per cent of the amount of the fine.[58] By way of example, in 2017, the authority granted a 5 per cent reduction to companies involved in anticompetitive agreements in home ventilotherapy and oxygen therapy supply services, for having updated compliance programmes prior to receiving a statement of objection. The compliance programme included training sessions for all staff members, including senior executives.[59]

8.2.3.3 The Netherlands – *Post-Factum*

The competition authority of the Netherlands, the ACM ('NMa' before 1 April 2013) also has experience of providing incentives in the context of commitment decisions. Compliance programmes appear as a requirement for commitments in a few cases, although the ACM remains vague as to the role that such programmes play in the

---

[55] Ibid., para. 341.

[56] *Farmindustria/Codice di autoregolamentazione* I342, 1999/7807; L. Longo and A. Moretti, 'Chapter 10: Italy' in M. Holmes, and L. Davey (eds.), *A Practical Guide to National Competition Rules Across Europe* (Kluwer Law International, 2007), p. 213.

[57] *Assirevi/Società di revisioni* I266, 2000/7979.

[58] Linee Guida sulla modalità di applicazione dei criteri di quantificazione delle sanzioni amministrative pecuniarie irrogate dall'Autorità in applicazione dell'articolo 15, comma 1, della legge n. 287/90, 31 October 2014, para. 23.

[59] Emily Townsend, 'Compliance Programs – The Italian Competition Authority Highlights The Importance Of An Effective Implementation and Update', McDermott Will & Emery, available at: www.antitrustalert.com/2017/01/articles/italian-developments/compliance-programs-the-italian-competition-authority-highlights-the-importance-of-an-effective-implementation-and-update/

decisions.[60] In 2006 and 2007, following complaints about possible anticompetitive behaviour, the NMa started investigations in the pharmacy, real estate and advertising sectors. In the first two sectors, the NMa ended its investigation upon commitments offered by the members of the industry associations to implement compliance programmes. In the advertising sector, the NMa stopped its investigation due to a lack of evidence, and it welcomed an initiative by three large publishers to implement compliance programmes.[61] The recent fining guidelines published by the ACM do not clearly include or exclude the consideration of compliance programmes for the setting of fine, as either aggravating or mitigating circumstances.[62]

8.2.3.4 France – Until 2017: *Post-Factum* Approach

Until 2017, compliance programmes were rewarded in the context of settlement procedures.[63] The undertaking could be granted up to an extra 10 per cent reduction in the level of the fine if it offered a commitment to implement a new compliance programme or to enhance an existing one.[64] The compliance programme was subject to the following requirements: it should be clear, transparent, publicly adopted by executives, and with an individual who was sufficiently high in the hierarchy being responsible for it. Effective information flows and training of staff, as well as an effective control and reporting system, were also part of the requirements.[65] The French competition authority had applied this policy in several instances.[66] As an example, following a violation of competition law in the cat and dog food market, Nestlé and Mars were respectively granted 18 per cent and 20 per cent reductions in fines for waiving their right to challenge the charges and offering commitments related to their compliance programmes.[67] Apart from the settlement and commitment context, no recognition was given to compliance

---

[60] ACM Case 7191, *Landelijke Huisartsenvereniging* 2012; ACM Case 7138, *Thuiszorg Midden-Brabant* 2011; ACM Case 13.0612.53, *Mobiele Operators*, 2014 in E Lachnnit, 'Compliance Programmes in Competition Law: Improving the Approach of Competition Authorities', *Utrecht Law Review*, 10 (5), (2014), 36.

[61] ICC, 'Promoting Antitrust Compliance: The Various Approaches of National Antitrust' (2011), 3.

[62] ACM Fining Guidelines, arts. 3.13 and 3.15 in Lachnnit, 'Compliance Programmes in Competition Law'.

[63] Conditions set out in art. L. 464-2 III, Code de Commerce. Procedure of 'transaction' introduced by 'Loi Macron' of 6 August 2015 (replacing procedure of 'non-contestation des griefs').

[64] Autorité de la Concurrence, Document-cadre du 10 février 2012 sur les programmes de conformité aux règles de concurrence, para. 31.

[65] P. Hubert and K. Schallenberg, 'Moving in the Right Direction, France is Taking Antitrust Compliance Very Seriously', *Competition Law Insight* (2012) 18.

[66] A list of decisions in which compliance programmes were considered can be found on the Autorité de la Concurrence website, available at: www.autoritedelaconcurrence.fr/user/standard.php?id_rub=428

[67] Autorité de la Concurrence, Décision 12-D-10 du 20 mars 2012 relative à des pratiques mises en œuvre dans le secteur de l'alimentation pour chiens et chats, paras. 309 and 311.

programmes existing at the time of the infringement.[68] Nor was the internal discovery of a violation by a company, thanks to its compliance programme, considered in the assessment of the fine.[69] Therefore France provided defensive incentives in the context of cartel litigation, *ex post* the beginning of the investigation.

In 2017, the authority announced that compliance programmes would no longer be entitled to a fine reduction, and withdrew its policy document stating the conditions under which effective programmes could be considered. The authority explained that companies were now expected to adopt compliance programmes as part of their general management systems, for which additional incentives could not be given.[70] The authority may also be willing to align its approach with the requirements of the newly introduced anticorruption legislation ('loi Sapin 2') requiring large companies to implement compliance programmes.[71]

Other legal systems offer some incentives for the implementation of effective compliance programmes. In Brazil, an effective compliance programme can be considered a mitigating factor for the setting of the fine imposed as part of an infringement decision or a settlement procedure.[72] In Canada, compliance programmes can constitute a mitigating factor, and the implementation of compliance measures may be imposed as part of alternative forms of resolution.[73] Korea is known for reducing the severity of sanctions, not only with regard to rewarding an effective compliance programme but also for the use of the programme in its promotional materials.[74] Australia has developed a standard for compliance programmes, which consists of guidance principles that are provided to companies (not specific to competition law).[75] In parallel, the Australian competition authority may consider compliance measures as an acceptable formal administrative undertaking, in the context of a settlement procedure.[76]

---

[68]   However, if a company does not qualify for leniency, it may receive a fine reduction if it had effective corporate compliance at the time of the infringement, provided that it can prove that the infringement ceased earlier than the start of the investigation. This concerns non-horizontal agreements cases. (Autorité de la Concurrence, Document-cadre du 10 février 2012, para. 28).

[69]   Ibid., paras. 23 and 27.

[70]   Autorité de la Concurrence, 'Communiqué du 19 octobre 2017 relatif à la procédure de transaction et aux programmes de conformité' (2017), available at: www.autoritedelaconcurrence.fr/doc/communi que19oct17_transaction_conformite.pdf

[71]   M. Hindré et C. Diot, 'Intégrer les risques liés au droit de la concurrence dans les programmes de conformité et s'assurer de leur effectivité : entre nécessité et opportunité !' in A. Dumourier, *le Monde du Droit* (9 November 2017).

[72]   CADE, Guidelines Competition Compliance Programs (2016), para. 3.3.4.

[73]   Competition Bureau, Corporate Compliance Programs (2015).

[74]   ICC, 'Promoting Antitrust Compliance', 6.

[75]   See further developments below at Section 8.4.2.

[76]   Australian Trade Practices Act 1974, s. 87B.

8.2.4 *Anti-Corruption Regulations*

Anti-corruption policies across the jurisdictions offer an interesting point of comparison with competition policies, regarding the manner in which they consider compliance programmes.[77] The aim is to understand the extent to which approaches to compliance programmes are specific to competition law. Only a few competition policies give credit for compliance programmes in litigation, granting a maximum of a 15 per cent reduction in the fine. In contrast, some anti-corruption laws in the same jurisdictions offer the possibility that companies can be relieved from anti-corruption completely, on grounds related to compliance programmes. US antitrust policy has long been quasi-neutral to compliance programmes in the setting of fines. In comparison, the US anti-corruption policy foresees the possibility of not prosecuting the company at all, provided that it has an effective compliance programme:

> Nine factors are considered in conducting an investigation, determining whether to charge a corporation, and negotiating plea or other agreements: [. . .]

> - the existence and effectiveness of the corporation's pre-existing compliance program[78]

In the case of prosecution, companies can receive a reduction in their fine for having an effective compliance programme, according to the Sentencing Guidelines provisions.[79] The Morgan Stanley case, in which the company avoided charges despite corruption acts committed by a managing director, exemplifies such a contrasting approach.[80]

Anti-corruption legislation is defined at EU level by a framework decision of the Council.[81] Member states are free to implement measures to achieve the required goals set out in the decision, the performance of which is monitored by the European Commission.[82] Therefore, national governments define their regulatory approaches towards compliance programmes in that area.

National anti-corruption policies also display a contrasting approach to compliance programmes. In the UK, section 7 of the Bribery Act 2010 provides that companies can defend themselves from being liable for an employee's illegal

---

[77]   F. Thépot, 'Antitrust v. Anti-Corruption Policy Approaches to Compliance: Why Such a Gap?', CPI *Antitrust Chronicle*, 6 (2) (2015).

[78]   The Criminal Division of the Department of Justice and the Enforcement Division of the US Securities and Exchange Commission, 'A Resource Guide to the US Foreign Corrupt Practices Act' (2012), 53.

[79]   See Section 8.3.1.

[80]   Department of Justice Press Release, 'Former Morgan Stanley Managing Director Pleads Guilty for Role in Evading Internal Controls Required by FCPA' (24 April 2012).

[81]   Council Framework Decision 2003/568/JHA of 22 July 2003 on combating corruption in the private sector [2003] OJ L192/54, arts. 5-6.

[82]   European Commission, Migration and Home Affairs, Corruption, available at: https://ec.europa.eu /home-affairs/what-we-do/policies/organized-crime-and-human-trafficking/corruption_en

conduct if 'adequate procedures' are put in place by companies'.[83] In Italy, anti-corruption legislation also entails the consideration of compliance programmes as part of a company's defence, with a possible reduction in the level of the fine.[84] In France, anti-corruption law primarily target perpetrators, who are held personally and criminally liable for such violations.[85] Companies' criminal and administrative liability has been strengthened by recent legislative changes introduced by the 'loi Sapin 2'.[86] No defence is available based on the implementation of compliance programmes, since this is now a legal requirement. In the Netherlands, although not systematically, companies are criminally liable for the wrongdoing of their employees. A defence is available to them based on grounds related to 'meaningful' compliance efforts.[87] The contrast in regulatory positions towards compliance programmes is even perceptible in documentation of the Organisation for Economic Cooperation and Development (OECD). In anti-corruption, the provision of positive incentives for the adoption of effective compliance measures is clearly advocated.[88] The OECD report of the roundtable on Promoting Compliance with Competition Law in 2011 illustrates the much more mitigated attitudes of its participants towards the reward for compliance programmes.[89]

Comparison between the anti-corruption and the competition law regulatory approaches reveals an interesting contrast. Anti-corruption regulations seem much

---

[83]   UK Bribery Act, s. 7(2): Evidence brought by the company in its defence will be analysed on a case-by-case basis, in light of matters such as the level of control over the activities of the responsible employee and the level of corruption that requires prevention. See Ministry of Justice, 'Guidance about procedures which relevant commercial organizations can put into place to prevent persons associated with them from bribing' (2010), para. 43.

[84]   Decreto Legge no 231/2001: a company can demonstrate that, before the violation was committed, it adopted and effectively implemented a model of organisation, management and control.

[85]   Articles 435-1 *et seq.* of the French Criminal Code (French Statute of 13 November 2007, as amended by French Statute of 17 May 2011), Domestic corruption: arts. 432-11 *et seq.* and 433-1 *et seq.* of the French Criminal Code (persons holding a public function) and articles. 445-1 *et seq.* of the French Criminal Code (persons not holding a public function). In a pioneering decision in 2012, the French tribunal of commerce prosecuted the company Safran for corruption acts committed in Nigeria, while relaxing the responsible individuals from liability: Les Echos, 'Safran condamné pour corruption active' (2012), available at: www.lesechos.fr/05/09/2012/lesechos.fr/0202249707571_safran-con damne-pour-corruption-active.htm

[86]   Loi 'sapin 2' imposed new requirements upon large companies, including the legal obligation to implement internal compliance mechanisms. It also introduced administrative fines imposed on companies, with the creation of the 'Agence Française Anticorruption' Transparency International France, Guide pratique pour la mise en oeuvre des mesures anticorruption imposées par la loi aux entreprises' (2017).

[87]   OECD, 'Phase 3 Report on Implementing the OECD Anti-Bribery Convention in the Netherlands', para. 37; Aldo Verbruggen, 'The Anti-Bribery and Anti-Corruption Review – Edition 6, The Netherlands' (January 2018).

[88]   OECD, Working Group on Bribery in International Business Transactions, 'Recommendation of the Council for Further Combating Bribery of Foreign Public Officials in International Business Transactions' (2009), para. 9.

[89]   OECD, Policy Roundtable, 'Promoting Compliance with Competition Law' (2011), 14–15.

less reluctant to open the 'black box' of compliance than competition authorities, even within a given country. The practice of producing audit reports and issuing certificates seems better developed in the field of anti-corruption.[90] This may illustrate the fact that a company has more chance of avoiding liability in that field.

8.3 OPENING THE 'BLACK BOX' OF COMPLIANCE FOR GREATER EFFECTIVENESS OF ENFORCEMENT

The question of whether authorities should give credit to compliance programmes has been highly debated.[91] This chapter takes the stance that compliance programmes need to be given credit for greater effectiveness of enforcement. Based on a comparison with anti-corruption, this section explains that antitrust infringement has no specific characteristic that should systematically preclude the consideration of a compliance programme. Comparative insights particularly outline the significant interaction of compliance programmes with liability regimes. Thus, it is of utmost importance to consider the impact of compliance programmes on incentives, combined with that produced by other enforcement instruments. This section will discuss the extent to which corporate compliance undermines or strengthens the deterrence and detection impacts of sanctions and leniency.[92]

8.3.1 *The Nature of Antitrust Infringement: a Specific Regulatory Approach?*

This section discusses whether collusive behaviour is a specific type of crime that requires a specific regulatory approach, based on a comparison with corruption.[93] Corruption refers to the misuse of public power for private benefit.[94] It can take the form of bribing officials with money, extortion, embezzlement or fraud. For the purpose of this section, no distinction between the different types of corruption will be made. Corruption emanating from companies will be the focus. Both corruption and cartel practices can be regarded as unfair practices affecting the rules of competition and business between different players in a market. In companies, anti-corruption and antitrust compliance are often addressed together. However, a company can be relieved of liability on corporate measures grounds in the case

---

[90] See, for example: www.mazars.fr/Accueil/Expertise/Audit-financier/Certification-Anti-Corruption
[91] As an example of such debate, two articles published in the same issue of the *Journal of Antitrust Enforcement* show contrasting views. Wils suggests that competition authorities should solely regard the outcome of compliance programmes, while Geradin advocates giving credit for companies' efforts with respect to the implementation of effective compliance programmes: Wils, 'Antitrust Compliance Programmes', 52; Geradin, 'A Reply to Wouter Wils', 325.
[92] As is exposed in Chapter 7, the effectiveness of sanctions and leniency critically depends on their impact on the relevant incentives within the firm.
[93] As raised in both the articles by Wils and Geradin.
[94] S. Rose-Ackerman, *Corruption and Government: Causes, Consequences, and Reform* (Cambridge University Press, 1999), p. 91; OECD glossary of statistical terms: 'active or passive misuse of the powers of Public officials (appointed or elected) for private financial or other benefits'.

an act of corruption, but not in the case of a collusive behaviour committed by an employee. How different is antitrust infringement from corruption committed in a company? Does antitrust infringement resemble other types of white-collar crimes, such as bribery and embezzlement, which affect companies adversely? Understanding the nature of antitrust infringement requires a comparison of several dimensions of the infringement with that of corruption: first, one must explain whether the decision to engage in a cartel differs from the decision to engage in corruption practices. Do cartel practices emanate from the top of the hierarchy? In contrast, what kind of position is occupied by the individuals engaging in corruption? Secondly, attention must be devoted to the manner in which the infringement operates within the structure of the company: are cartel practices operated through the company's business processes? In contrast, do corruption practices stem from isolated act of 'rogue' employees? Finally, understanding how the benefits of cartel practices are divided between the company's actors provides further insight as to the potential nature of the violation. Abstracting from the morale dimension of both types of crimes, I will now focus on the dimensions of the wrongdoing that are specifically related to the company.

As was revealed in Chapter 6, it is not uncommon that cartel practices involve senior executives of companies.[95] This is one of the reasons for the Department of Justice Antitrust Division refusing to give credit for a compliance programme in antitrust.[96] It is, however, not evident that senior executives are systematically involved. Sales people – not necessarily at a high level within the hierarchy – may initiate collusive practices. Also, the complex corporate structure of some companies implies that a subsidiary's senior executives may take part in a cartel, without the senior executives of the whole undertaking being involved. In addition, such characteristics of antitrust infringement also seem to be shared with other types of corporate crimes. This is exemplified by the Siemens corruption scandal, in which senior managers, up to board level, were directly involved in the policy of making corrupt payments.[97] While Siemens was heavily fined both in Germany and in the United States, a defence based on compliance efforts remains a possibility: the involvement of an employee in a position of authority, in cases other than antitrust,

---

[95]   A. Stephan, 'See No Evil: Cartels and the Limits of Antitrust Compliance Programs', *The Company Lawyer*, 31 (2010), 231, 236. In some cases, the top level of management was personally involved, and in others the top management permitted the collusion while not being directly involved.

[96]   J. E. Murphy, 'Making the Sentencing Guidelines Message Complete', letter to the Department of Justice: Proposed Revision to the Sentencing Guide, available at: www.compliance-network.com /wp-content/uploads/2012/08/4-5-13-filing-.pdf; M. Volkov, 'Antitrust Compliance and Credit for an Effective Compliance Program', available at: http://corruptioncrimecompliance.com/2013/09/anti trust-compliance-and-credit-for-an-effective-compliance-program/

[97]   'Statement of Siemens Aktiengesellschaft: Investigation and Summary of Findings with respect to the Proceedings in Munich and the US' (2008), 11–12.

does not preclude the consideration of a company's compliance efforts.[98] Despite corruption acts being committed by one of Morgan Stanley's managing directors, the company avoided liability for violating anti-corruption regulations, on grounds related to the compliance procedures that were in place.[99] Although cartel practices may involve a higher level of employees than in corruption on average, this is not necessarily always the case. Therefore, no absolute rule can be established on such a basis.[100]

Another possible aspect of the uniqueness of antitrust infringement is that it goes to the 'heart of businesses'. The Department of Justice Antitrust Division had advanced this specificity of antitrust infringement to explain that compliance efforts could not be credited.[101] In some industries, cartels indeed appeared as being the operational mode in use.[102] However, price-fixing practices can also originate from the isolated actions of sales employees, or from a 'rogue employee' who departs from accepted business standards. Once more, the example of the Siemens corruption scandal shows that a violation as a business operation standard is not exclusive to antitrust infringement. In that case, the corruption seemed to have been organised as a 'standard operating procedure'.[103] Cash desks were located within the company so that employees could withdraw large sums of cash up to € 1 million euros at a time. In addition, Post-it notes were used to sign payment authorisations so that the

---

[98] The US Sentencing Guidelines establish conditions for companies to obtain credit for their compliance programmes even when senior people are involved: see Section 8.2.2.1. US Sentencing Guidelines manual (2012), ch. 8, (f)(3)(C)(i) and §11.

[99] 'Morgan Stanley maintained a system of internal controls meant to ensure accountability for its assets and to prevent employees from offering, promising or paying anything of value to foreign government officials. Morgan Stanley's internal policies, which were updated regularly to reflect regulatory developments and specific risks, prohibited bribery and addressed corruption risks associated with the giving of gifts, business entertainment, travel, lodging, meals, charitable contributions and employment. Morgan Stanley frequently trained its employees on its internal policies, the FCPA and other anti-corruption laws. [. . .]. Morgan Stanley's compliance personnel regularly monitored transactions, randomly audited particular employees, transactions and business units, and tested to identify illicit payments. Moreover, Morgan Stanley conducted extensive due diligence on all new business partners and imposed stringent controls on payments made to business partners.[. . .] After considering all the available facts and circumstances, including that Morgan Stanley constructed and maintained a system of internal controls, which provided reasonable assurances that its employees were not bribing government officials, the Department of Justice declined to bring any enforcement action against Morgan Stanley related to Peterson's conduct.' (Department of Justice, Press Release, Former Morgan Stanley Managing Director Pleads Guilty for Role in Evading Internal Controls Required by FCPA).

[100] Geradin, 'A Reply to Wouter Wils', 329; and Murphy, 'Making the Sentencing Guidelines Message Complete', 7.

[101] United States Attorney's Manual, 9-28.400, Special Policy Concerns (2008).

[102] Sonnenfeld and Lawrence, 'Why Do Companies Succumb to Price Fixing?' gives examples of industries in which price-fixing was widespread.

[103] 'Bribery was nothing less than standard operating procedure for Siemens' (Department of Justice, Press Release, 'Siemens AG and Three Subsidiaries Plead Guilty to Foreign Corrupt Practices Act Violations and Agree to Pay $450 Million in Combined Criminal Fines' (15 December 2008)).

identity of the subscriber could be concealed in cases of payment control.[104] Most corruption cases do not seem as organised as the Siemens case. However, the widespread use of corruption in some countries may suggest that companies take account of such reality in their standard business practices.[105] Thus, competition authorities disregard compliance efforts because of characteristics that cannot systematically be attributed to the nature of antitrust infringement.

Finally, understanding how the benefits of cartel practices are divided between the company's actors provides further insight into the potential nature of the violation. Competition authorities are reluctant to consider compliance programmes because the company seems largely to benefit from the colluded prices. The profitability of an undetected and sustained cartel is not questioned.[106] A breach of anti-corruption law can also bring considerable economic advantages. Bribing an official with money can serve the purpose of getting favoured treatment in contracts, concessions or licensing processes, or of obtaining some relevant information or influencing the terms of contracts. The economic benefits stem from the substantial competitive advantage over other companies, acquired outside the scope of the fair competitive process.[107] Therefore, a breach of either antitrust or anti-corruption law by an employee can bring considerable economic advantage to their company. Chapter 8 identified several layers of agency relationships in cartel decision-making and operation. The cost and benefit of a cartel engagement therefore differ from one actor to another. These different types of agency relationships, which are not specific to antitrust violation, suggest that considering a company as acting in unity of will and action may yield erroneous conclusions. The same considerations surely hold for corruption infringements.[108] Further developments on the complexity of internal relations in the context of a corporate crime will be provided in the next section.

No definite answer emerged from the comparison of antitrust infringement with corruption. Even though cartel offence, on average, may take place at a higher level than corruption acts, this, in my view, does not justify a systematic rejection of a company's compliance efforts. Therefore, the specific nature of antitrust infringement does not provide a satisfying justification for different regulatory approaches towards compliance programmes.

---

[104] K. Sidhu, 'Anti-Corruption Compliance Standards in the Aftermath of the Siemens Scandal', German Law Journal, 10 (2009), 1343, 1346.

[105] Ibid. However, this does not seem to be the case in the jurisdictions of interest in this chapter.

[106] See Section 6.2.

[107] R. Calderón Cuadrado and J. L. Alvarez Arce, 'The Complexity of Corruption: Nature and Ethical Suggestions': Working Paper 05/06 Facultad de Ciencias Económicas y Empresariales Universidad de Navarra, 26–27.

[108] Acknowledging the need to understand a more complex view of corporate crime does not imply that companies should not be responsible for their employees' acts.

8.3.2 *Antitrust Versus Anti-Corruption: Different Approaches to Liability*

It is not the nature of the 'crime' that explains a different stance towards compliance programmes. Instead, different liability regimes in the case of antitrust and anti-corruption laws infringement may provide a more satisfying explanation.[109] In the EU, cartel sanctions and provisions are of an administrative nature and addressed to companies, not individuals. In addition, notwithstanding the fact that a fair proportion of EU member states have sanctions against individuals (of a criminal, civil or administrative nature), there is currently a low enforcement level of such provisions. In anti-corruption legislation, sanctions are typically of a criminal nature, targeting responsible individuals in the first place.[110] In addition, criminal liability of individuals does not necessarily extend to corporations in some jurisdictions. This is the case, for example, in Bulgaria, in which companies are not held liable for corruption committed by their employees.[111] Some other European countries have only recently introduced corporate liability, as is the case in Ukraine.[112]

In most of the jurisdictions under examination, companies may not be automatically charged if corruption acts are committed by an employee. In Hungary, for example, corporate liability depends on whether the corruption act benefited the company, and was committed intentionally by certain individuals within the company.[113] In Italy, companies are liable if the crime is committed to the benefit of the company.[114] In contrast, 'undertakings' are the designated subjects of competition law infringement decisions. Anti-corruption and competition laws have different 'default' liability rules. In anti-corruption, the extension of liability to companies has not always been, and is still not, automatic in many jurisdictions. This may explain that the company's role in fostering, detecting or preventing the occurrence of such action currently receives more attention for the purpose of the attribution of liability in anti-corruption. In spite of targeting corporate crimes, both competition law and corruption laws have evolved in different directions due to a different approach to liability in the first place.

8.3.3 *Compliance Programmes and 'Traditional' Enforcement Instruments*

As exemplified by the previous comparison with anti-corruption, discussing the necessity for competition authorities to consider compliance programmes requires analysing its potential articulation with sanctions. Chapter 7 established that

---

[109]   The following developments are based on Thépot, 'Antitrust v. Anti-Corruption Policy Approaches to Compliance'.

[110]   All the 26 countries covered by the *CMS Guide to Anti-Bribery and Corruption Laws* impose criminal sanctions on individuals for corruption: *CMS Guide to Anti-Bribery and Corruption Laws* (2016).

[111]   Criminal Code, Administrative Offences and Sanctions Act.

[112]   *CMS Guide to Anti-Bribery and Corruption Laws* (2016).

[113]   Section 2 of the Corporate Sanctions Act.

[114]   Legislative Decree No 231/2001.

sanctions that target individuals in addition to companies are desirable whenever the
corporate structure is such that it is difficult for shareholders to have tight control
over the actions of executives. Based on the similar analytical framework, this
chapter will discuss the combined impact of sanctions and corporate compliance
on internal incentives. Insights into anti-corruption liability regimes will shed some
light on a different approach to compliance programmes. This chapter argues that
compliance programmes may enhance the effectiveness of corporate and individual
sanctions, and can remedy some of their limitations. This section will consider
antitrust infringements in the longer run – that is, when the cartel is detected and
sanctioned. The effectiveness of compliance programmes will be assumed here.
The more practical dimension of the value and effectiveness of compliance programmes will be addressed in the second section of this chapter.

8.3.3.1 Compliance Programmes and Corporate Liability

An important value of considering compliance programmes, in the presence of
corporate and individual liability, stems from the informational advantage held by
the company. This section assumes that detection of the collusive practice can be
expected.[115] Corporate liability, in the absence of liability of individuals, exacerbates
the agency problem between shareholders and managers. This is because it imposes
the sanction on shareholders and not on the responsible managers.[116] Therefore,
a company that is willing to reduce the agency problem needs to incur some costs.
To do so, a company can seek to mitigate the risk that individuals expose the
company to liability.[117] In response to the threat of corporate sanctions, companies
may have a natural incentive to implement a compliance programme. Corporate
liability is optimal only if it induces 'firms to implement optimal compliance
programmes, self-report, and cooperate with the authorities'.[118] However, corporate
liability does not automatically translate into corporate compliance.[119] First,
the incentive to adopt compliance programmes may be mitigated by the 'perverse'
effects of vicarious corporate liability. A company may fear that implementing
internal measures to prevent and detect the wrongdoing of its employees will
increase the probability of detection.[120] In weighing the costs and benefits of
implementing a compliance programme, a company may decide not to incur any

[115] If the probability of cartel detection is low, harsh penalties may not translate into organisational
compliance See Section 7.3.
[116] Assuming that managers do not hold a significant part of the stock, in which case the agency problem
is reduced.
[117] This depends on the level of the fine and the probability of detection.
[118] '[C]orporate criminal sanctions will not deter corporate crime effectively unless they induce corporate policing: specifically, monitoring, self-reporting, and cooperation' (J. Arlen, 'The Failure of the
Organizational Sentencing Guidelines', *University of Miami Law Review*, 66 (2012), 321, 336).
[119] Sokol, 'Cartels, Corporate Compliance'.
[120] J. Arlen, 'The Potentially Perverse Effects of Corporate Criminal Liability', *Journal of Legal Studies*,
23 (1994), 833–67.

of those expenses if it expects that the costs of detection are higher than the expected benefit of detecting the crime internally.

In addition, companies may not have 'effective methods of preventing individuals from committing acts that impose huge liabilities on them'.[121] As was discussed in Chapter 7, the mismatch of interest may be too severe, because companies may have neither the incentive nor the means to address it. The extent to which a company has the ability to monitor its employees adequately depends on the quality of corporate governance that is in place. Corporate governance schemes that fail to reach the objectives for which they have been designed are not likely to be highly effective in preventing individuals from committing illegal acts. Giving credit to compliance programmes can help to mitigate the discrepancy between managers and share-holders, in a manner that makes corporate liability more effective. Therefore, compliance programmes can complement corporate liability regimes by directly impacting the internal dimension of compliance, and particularly so when companies lack the incentive and ability to achieve compliance internally.

8.3.3.2 Compliance and Individual Sanctions

Introducing individual sanctions may reduce the moral hazard situation that characterises collusive conduct in a regime of vicarious corporate liability. In contrast with the previous situation, individuals can no longer operate behind the shield of their company's liability. What would be the value of giving credit to companies in that situation?

Individual sanctions typically concern specific categories of people within the company's hierarchy. In the case of individual liability, companies still face the risk of huge fines being imposed upon them. Even though the incentives of some individuals may be aligned with those of the company towards sanctions, there may still be some mismatch of interests between the individual and the company. In addition, Chapter 4 identified several layers of agency relationships in cartel decision-making and operation. This enabled us to understand that cartel participation involves various actors, who incur different costs and benefits with regard to their cartel participation. By acting on the social norms of the company, effective compliance programmes may reduce the possible discrepancies that remain between the different actors, which in turn enhance the effectiveness of sanctions.

In the presence of individual sanctions, compliance programmes potentially have a greater effect on company's employees than when they are not personally liable.[122] A senior executive may pay greater attention to compliance training if pecuniary or

[121] R. A. Posner, *Antitrust Law: An Economic Perspective* (University of Chicago Press, 1976), p. 225; Wils, *The Optimal Enforcement of EC Antitrust Law*, p. 200.
[122] Argument also developed in F. Wagner von-Papp, 'Compliance and Individual Sanctions for Competition Law Infringements' in J. Paha. (ed.), *Competition Law Compliance Programmes – An Interdisciplinary Approach* (Springer, 2016), pp. 135–88.

jail sanctions are part of the non-compliance risk. More effort may be put into internal prevention and detection in the presence of individual sanctions. Therefore, compliance programmes may yield much greater value to the company.

Authorities should leverage the potential of greater value that compliance programmes constitute for companies. Promoting compliance programmes puts the onus *ex ante* on prevention and internal detection rather than on prosecuting the infringement. Prosecuting an individual is indeed a costly and lengthy process that requires a huge amount of evidence, which makes it beneficial to 'recruit' companies in the fight against cartels.[123] Competition authorities should seek to reward compliance programmes that affect social norms and direct corporate culture towards increased compliance.[124] A stronger corporate culture, in turn, is deemed to reduce agency costs: if a culture of compliance emanates from the top and is spread throughout the company, fewer resources are necessary to monitor the lower layers of the hierarchy.[125] As a result, the reward for compliance programmes by competition authorities could have a 'spillover' effect of increasing compliance, through its potential effect on social norms, thereby offsetting the competition authorities' resources that are dedicated to this. On a more conceptual note, competition policies that include individual sanctions admit the value of considering subunits – or 'opening the black box' of companies. Therefore, a similar interest in the internal working of companies could logically be dedicated in the context of compliance programmes. An important normative question is whether a company could obtain full defence for implementing an effective programme. Would the incentives be reduced to prevent the infringement internally? This depends on the type of evidence required, and on whether competition authorities can verify the effectiveness of compliance programmes. If cosmetic compliance is made possible, the possibility of a full defence could, at the margin, amount to a situation of strict individual liability, in effect, shielding the company from detection consequences.

8.3.3.3 Compliance Programmes and Leniency

The heavy reliance on leniency in competition law enforcement may also explain why competition authorities are more reluctant to give credit to compliance efforts (as they are in anti-corruption). Leniency programmes are designed to undermine cartel stability by granting immunity to companies that self-report, under certain conditions. Some have argued that giving credit to compliance programmes may undermine the value of leniency policy because it modifies the cost of detection,

---

[123] J. E. Murphy and D. Boehme, 'Fear No Evil: A Compliance and Ethics Professionals' Response to Dr. Stephan' (2011).
[124] For a discussion of the concept of social norms, see A. Stephan, 'Cartel Laws Undermined: Corruption, Social Norms, and Collectivist Business Cultures', *Journal of Law and Society*, 37 (2010), 345, 354.
[125] Sokol, 'Cartels, Corporate Compliance', 216.

thereby changing the pay-offs of the cartel members with regard to cartel activity. As a result, the incentive to self-report would not be as strong if a company could otherwise benefit from a fine reduction for its compliance programme.[126]

This chapter takes the contrary view that leniency programmes can be enhanced if compliance programmes are encouraged. The discrepancy of incentives to apply for leniency between a company and the individuals that exist when individuals are either not liable personally, or not covered by the immunity scheme, can be addressed by encouraging effective compliance programmes. A company that is better able to prevent and detect an infringement internally is also equipped with better tools to constitute a leniency application. In addition, this can help the company to detect the infringement earlier than the other cartel members.[127] In 2004, Lufthansa implemented a compliance programme that enabled the company to detect internally the air cargo cartel of which it had been part since 1999. Such internal measures enabled the company to file a leniency application and to benefit from full immunity.[128]

Some have argued that compliance programmes could even be required from leniency recipients.[129] As was shown in the previous chapter, the deterrent effect of leniency is questioned by evidence of its repeated use by some companies. Imposing the implementation of effective compliance measures may therefore reduce the risk of recidivism. Although most authorities affirm the value of corporate compliance, almost none of them consider it as a strategic tool as part of leniency.[130]

8.3.4 Conclusion: Corporate Compliance in the Enforcement Toolbox

Should competition policy encourage compliance programmes? No definite answer emerged from the comparison of antitrust infringement and corruption. Even though, on average, cartel offences may take place at a higher level than corruption acts, this does not justify the systematic rejection of a company's compliance efforts. A more insightful approach has been to consider compliance programmes in the light of other enforcement instruments. Corporate compliance programmes should form part of the cartel enforcement toolbox. Compliance programmes can help to mitigate the mismatch of interests that alters the effectiveness of corporate sanctions. The consideration of compliance programmes by competition authorities, under

[126] Wils, 'Antitrust Compliance Programmes', 69.
[127] Geradin, 'A Reply to Wouter Wils', 342.
[128] H. Bergman, and D. D. Sokol, 'The Air Cargo Cartel: Lessons for Compliance' in C. Beaton-Wells and C. Tran (eds.), *Anti-Cartel Enforcement in a Contemporary Age: Leniency Religion* (Hart Publishing, 2015), p. 310.
[129] This is argued by B. Fisse, 'Reconditioning Corporate Leniency: The Possibility of Making Compliance Programmes a Condition of Immunity' and J. E. Murphy, 'Combining Leniency Policies and Compliance Programmes to Prevent Cartels' in Beaton-Wells and C. Tran (eds.), *Anti-Cartel Enforcement in a Contemporary Age: The Leniency Religion.*
[130] For an overview of competition authorities approach to compliance programmes as part of leniency requirement, see Fisse, 'Reconditioning Corporate Leniency'.

certain conditions, affects the pay-offs of the actors engaged in a cartel, in a manner that may enhance the effectiveness of sanctions. When individuals are personally liable, compliance programmes potentially have a greater impact on the agent in the agency relationship. Therefore, competition authorities should leverage this potential in considering a company's compliance effort. Competition authorities, facing the issue of cartel detection, would then benefit from the informational advantage that companies have with regard to their managers and employees. Leniency programmes are also deemed to have limited impact on cartel termination if there is a mismatch of interests between an individual and the company when seeking leniency. A compliance programme could then enhance the effectiveness of leniency if it enabled companies to monitor and collect information relevant to a leniency application better. For now, this chapter posits that competition policies should consider compliance programmes, but not to the point of fully relieving a company from liability.

Accordingly, an optimal enforcement regime is composed by a combination of corporate and individual liability, with the possibility of obtaining a substantial sanction reduction if a company proves that it has an effective compliance programme. Internal measures could also be required as part of well-designed leniency programmes. The benefits of leniency, as a key instrument of cartel deterrence and detection, could be leveraged to enhance internal detection and prevention of cartels via effective compliance programmes. The following section will suggest how, in practice, competition authorities may encourage compliance programmes for greater effectiveness of enforcement.

8.4 FOR A PRAGMATIC AND INCENTIVE-BASED APPROACH TO CORPORATE COMPLIANCE

This section provides a regulatory framework for considering compliance programmes in practice.[131] An adequate regulatory approach is one that incentivises

---

[131] This section is largely informed by a range of interviews conducted with eleven general counsel or compliance officers of multinational or large companies headquartered in the UK, Germany, France, the Netherlands and Switzerland, between August and October 2013. Large companies were targeted because only such companies have personnel specialising in competition law compliance; large companies characterised with complex corporate structures also fit well with the theoretical framework of this thesis. The companies on the panel are from different jurisdictions and types of industries, and have diverse infringement backgrounds. The first contact with them was made by email. The email presented the research and the context, and introduced the specific input sought from the interviews. The format of the interviews, conducted on the phone, was open ended, but similar types of questions were posed. The first questions concerned the specific organisation of the compliance function in the company (such as whether it was a distinct unit for the purposes of competition law). These were followed by questions on the various challenges faced by the organisation of compliance (e.g. resources, and how to organise compliance in a company that has subsidiaries in multiple jurisdictions). Then, individuals were consulted on the possible strategic use of compliance, either within the company or with third parties (Had any innovative process been

companies to endorse a culture of compliance that is materialised by concrete organisational steps. Competition authorities should adopt a two-fold pragmatic attitude towards compliance programmes. First, competition authorities should build a positive discourse around the organisation of compliance, showing the potential strategic dimension of the voluntary implementation of compliance programmes. Secondly, competition authorities should strengthen the potential strategic interest of companies, and leverage the benefit that can arise if companies adopt compliance programmes as part of their business strategy. Further options available to competition authorities to strengthen the potential strategic interest of companies will then be discussed.

8.4.1 *The Potential Strategic Use of Compliance Programmes*

Competition authorities should engage in building positive motivations for the voluntary implementation of compliance programmes. This section will outline the potential strategic dimension of the organisation of compliance that competition authorities should stress and promote. Working in an ethical environment and avoiding the reputational and monetary cost of a prosecution are among the strategic interests of a company to comply with competition law. Assuming the value of complying with the law, I will focus on how the organisation of compliance can be a source of competitive advantage if it is addressed strategically.

8.4.1.1 Compliance and Risk Management

Companies face various regulatory constraints, which, in addition to other sources of uncertainty, constitute the risk that needs to be taken into account. Risk management is used by companies strategically to minimise the cost of the occurrence of uncertainty. Competition law is regarded by companies as a serious source of risk.[132] Thus, compliance programmes can be seen as an 'investment in risk management'.[133] In dealing with such a risk, companies can optimise the way in which they identify the business units and practices that are particularly prone to such practices and the manner in which they tackle them.[134] The effectiveness of

developed? Was compliance used in communication with third parties? Did the company consider the compliance of business partners?). Individuals were also invited to describe and compare the organisation of competition compliance with that of anti-corruption compliance in their companies. The concluding part of the interview collected their views on the possibility of certifying compliance programmes and competition authorities' approaches to compliance programmes. Additional interviews were conducted with three (non-in-house) legal and compliance experts on similar issues.
[132]   Survey by Baker McKenzie (2008): 'Anti-trust/competition was most frequently identified as the number one legal risk (18.1% of respondents) and was the most likely to be identified in the top three legal risks (38.6% of respondents).'
[133]   Riley and Bloom, 'Antitrust Compliance Programmes', 21.
[134]   For example, there exists guidance on how to assess the legal antitrust risk: Baker McKenzie, 'Conducting an Effective Global Antitrust/Competition Risk Assessment' (2013).

resources and processes is partly determined by the assessment of risk in the first place. Prioritising high-risk areas and employees enables resources to be allocated in a strategic manner, which is paramount to the effectiveness of corporate compliance. In its Antitrust Compliance Toolkit, the International Chamber of Commerce (ICC) provides practical guidance on how the antitrust risk should be assessed. It is suggested that a company should link its approach to antitrust risk to that of the company's general risk management methodology.[135] The CMA rightly provides a risk-based framework for the organisation of compliance, so that compliance can be tailored to the specific risks of a company.[136] As such, the CMA also encourages companies to address competition risk as part of a wider risk management strategy, which enables antitrust compliance to be more integrated into business practice. In other words, there is a strategic choice to be made, prior to the implementation of a compliance programme.

8.4.1.2 The Organisation as a Source of Competitive Advantage

As long as there is no prescription from the public authorities, companies are free to implement compliance within their budget constraints, tailored to the needs of the company.[137] This does not mean that the organisation of compliance does not require resources. Yet, there is room for using resources in a manner that confers competitive advantage over companies that would spend resources with a view to avoiding risk. For example, Murphy proposes an organisation of compliance to small companies for 'a Dollar a Day' that meets the principles set out in the US Sentencing Guidelines and the OECD Good Practice Guidance.[138] The key is to use management tools to set up a culture of compliance, from the top, which is then materialised by concrete managerial steps to make the compliance happen. In other words, 'the same types of management tools that make a company run successfully also need to be used to make sure it runs legally and ethically'.[139] This also means that a company can incorporate antitrust compliance in other processes of internal control or existing programmes. As long as antitrust benefits from sufficient resources, a holistic approach to antitrust compliance presents a number of advantages. For example, if antitrust appears among other central corporate risks,

---

[135]   ICC, 'The ICC Antitrust Compliance Toolkit, Practical Antitrust Compliance Tools for SMEs and Larger Companies', 16.

[136]   OFT1341; CMA, 'Competition Law Risk: A Short Guide' (2017).

[137]   J. E. Murphy, 'A Compliance & Ethics Program on a Dollar a Day: How Small Companies Can Have Effective Programs' (2010), available at: www.hcca-info.org/Portals/0/PDFs/Resources /ResourceOverview/CEProgramDollarADay-Murphy.pdf

[138]   OECD, 'Good Practice Guidance on Internal Controls, Ethics, and Compliance' (2010). This guidance particularly addresses compliance with anti-bribery rules, but set principles that can be applied to other areas of compliance.

[139]   Murphy, A Compliance & Ethics Program on a Dollar a Day', 3–4.

appropriate procedures can be designed more easily and implemented consistently within the company.[140]

The management of compliance may even be regarded as an investment in improving the internal organisation of a company. Wagner and Dittmar explain how some companies have adopted a strategic approach to compliance with Sarbanes-Oxley regulations to improve the quality of their existing processes (such as internal control, audit management and documentation systems).[141] Similar improvements could be witnessed in the context of competition law. Following convictions for antitrust or anti-bribery infringements, some companies reported drastic changes in their organisation of compliance.[142] Changes aimed at strengthening compliance concerned the role of compliance and legal functions within the firm, as well as internal control processes. Surely these changes also serve wider purposes than just compliance with a specific area of the law. In addition, a company could also gain informational advantage if a compliance programme enhances the company's awareness and adaptability regarding changes in the law, which could affect business decisions.

Bagley also posits that legally astute management teams practise strategic compliance management in viewing the cost of compliance as an investment, and not an expense. Instead of just complying with the letter of the law, they adopt operational changes that enable them to develop innovations based on regulatory obligations.[143] Companies that face budgetary constraints employ creative methods for the organisation of compliance. The use of technology for compliance purposes, including the use of 'serious games', may constitute innovative approaches to compliance.[144] Screenings, which may be very valuable tools to detect collusion in some markets, may also be used internally by companies.[145] Companies that face the challenge of being very large corporations, spread across various countries, elaborate techniques to deliver training online in an interactive fashion. In such cases, the companies can either make use of innovative tools that are in place, or create such tools that can then be used for other purposes.

[140] ICC, 'ICC Antitrust Compliance Toolkit', 7.
[141] 'Two approaches to Sarbanes-Oxley predominate. Some executives dutifully meet SOX requirements, but at minimum cost and utilizing the fewest possible resources. Others leverage the resources expended on compliance to obtain a return on their investment' (S. Wagner and L. Dittmar, 'The Unexpected Benefits of Sarbanes-Oxley', *Harvard Business Review*, 84 (2006), 133).
[142] Heads of competition law and compliance and general counsel of companies that have received major fines for cartel and corruption infringements.
[143] C. E. Bagley, *Winning Legally: How to Use the Law to Create Value, Marshal Resources, and Manage Risk* (Harvard Business School Press, 2005) and 'Winning Legally: The Value of Legal Astuteness', *Academy of Management Review*, 33 (2008), 378, 386.
[144] See, e.g., Michelin using 'a serious game' to train its employees to antitrust compliance: N. Siharath 'Michelin forme ses 3,000 commerciaux avec un serious game' (2012), available at: www .exclusiverh.com/articles/serious-game/michelin-opte-pour-une-formation-ludique-avec-son-serious -game-antitrust.htm
[145] A. Deng, 'Cartel Detection and Monitoring: A Look Forward', *Journal of Antitrust Enforcement*, 5 (2017), 488, 500.

8.4.1.3 The External Dimension of the Strategic Use of Compliance

Antitrust compliance may also be used strategically in the context of relationships with third parties. The intuition is that customers, suppliers and investors have an interest in interacting with a company that complies with competition law. The interaction with such actors is crucial to the performance and development of a company. Therefore, companies may be willing to invest in compliance if they can signal to third parties that effective compliance steps have been undertaken. The question of compliance programmes' certification by competition authorities or non-governmental organisations (NGOs) will be discussed in the next section.

Investors may be reluctant to invest in companies that have a reputation for not complying with competition law. Gaining investors' confidence can confer a real strategic dimension to the organisation of compliance.[146] A company that fixes prices with its competitors is likely to offer inflated prices to its customers. A supplier may also be negatively affected by a downstream company that abuses its dominant position, or may not be able to sell its products at an interesting price if companies downstream collude or engage into bid-rigging. Codes of conduct, covering a wide range of compliance areas, to be signed off by business partners illustrate a strategic interest in dealing with compliant suppliers.[147]

With a view to protecting itself from purchasing from cartelised upstream indus-try, Deutsche Bahn introduced a system of 'cartel damages prevention'. The key idea is to increase compliance awareness among potential bidders. The system consists of identifying four categories of cartel risk among potential bidding companies. To each risk group are assigned various compliance requirements. The riskiest companies – for instance, those for which an infringement decision has been issued – are requested to comply with a higher standard of compliance in order to participate in the tendering procedure launched by Deutsche Bahn. This includes a contractual clause of 'liquidity damages' that need to be paid to Deutsche Bahn in the event of future cartel conviction. In addition, companies may even be excluded from a call for tenders. Categories of companies for which there exists clear suspicion of cartel risk – for example because of an ongoing investigation – need to provide evidence of high compliance standards that are applied consistently within the company. Companies operating in industries that present characteristics prone to cartelisation must also comply with the compliance standards of cartel prevention defined by Deutsche Bahn. Finally, low-risk companies can also receive compliance support and need to sign a general integrity clause.[148] This demonstrates a strong strategic

---

[146] Interviews with heads of competition law of multinational companies (headquartered in the UK, Germany, Switzerland and the Netherlands).

[147] See, for example, code of conducts by Deustche Bahn, available at: www.deutschebahn.com /en/group/compliance/geschaeftspartner/verhaltenskodex-1212586

[148] Deutsche Bahn, 'Comply with Antitrust Law and avoid serious violations', available at: www .deutschebahn.com/en/group/compliance/geschaeftspartner/kartellrecht-1212628; 'Der DB-Konzern

incentive for companies to signal to third parties that compliance measures have been implemented internally. In the case of Deutsche Bahn, the third party takes the initiative of imposing on its business partners a certain standard of compliance.[149] Other companies could be willing proactively to signal the quality of their compliance organisation. In that context, the development of standards could enable companies voluntarily to adopt compliance programmes instead of merely complying with requirements imposed by other companies. For example, a company reported that it would readily recognise a company's own programme if it were based on similar principles set out in its code of conduct.[150]

A collective strategic interest in the organisation of compliance is witnessed in particular in the area of corruption. Collective actions are designed to create a business environment of compliance, in industries or countries that are particularly prone to corruption. Because a single company has no incentive to comply if corruption is a commonly accepted practice, collective efforts of compliance are more attractive to the business community. In antitrust, even though challenges of compliance may be different, similar actions could be undertaken by companies that find a strategic interest in cooperating in compliance.[151] However, the benefits of collective actions would need to be balanced with competition risks associated with any types of cooperation between competing companies. Collective actions may then be undertaken specifically to tackle risks of collusion in trade association meetings, which are typically prone to the discussion of anticompetitive agreements.[152] The ICC suggests undertaking due diligence on the activities of trade associations. Ensuring that a definite agenda for the meeting is circulated beforehand, and seeking legal advice before reaching agreements on potentially sensitive competition issues, are examples of initiatives that help to create a business environment of compliance with competition law, via the trade association.[153] As suggested by the ICC, these steps can be undertaken by an individual company. One can imagine these measures being endorsed by the trade association, in order to set a clear compliance message for the collective benefit of company members. Once more, such a collective interest stems from the importance of having business partners and competitors playing by the same rules.

---

steht für nachhaltiges und verantwortliches Handeln', available at: www.deutschebahn.com/de
/konzern/compliance/geschaeftspartner/verhaltenskodex-1191674

[149] Importance of compliance by business partners also appeared in the interviews.

[150] Interview with Head of Competition Law and Compliance of a multinational company.

[151] World Bank Institute, Fighting Corruption Through Collective Action, Presentation, available at: www.unglobalcompact.org/docs/news_events/8.1/fighting_corruption_through_collective_action.pdf

[152] Department of Justice: J. M. Griffin, 'An Inside Look at a Cartel at Work: Common Characteristics of International Cartels', ABA Section of Antitrust Law 48th Annual Spring Meeting (2000): 'Another characteristic of international cartels is that they frequently use trade associations as a means of providing "cover" for their cartel activities.'

[153] ICC, 'ICC Antitrust Compliance Toolkit', 53.

The antitrust risk presented by a company can also impact its relationships with various other actors. Customers may be reluctant to trust and cooperate with a company that has been convicted for an infringement of competition law. In addition, joint venture or merger projects may be undermined if the target company does not have adequate compliance procedures in place.[154] The acquisition price can be affected if a company presents an antitrust risk that is not adequately mitigated by internal compliance procedures. In addition, it is very important for an acquiring company to ensure that a culture of compliance can be easily implemented post-merger. The ICC advocates and provides guidance on the conduct of antitrust due-diligence prior to entering into joint ventures or merger and acquisition deals. Due diligence consists of identifying the antitrust risk of the target and assessing how it could affect the acquiring company post-transaction. In that respect, due diligence involves checking the history of antitrust convictions and verifying that a compliance programme is in place and that compliance is part of the corporate culture.[155]

The exposition of all of the potential strategic benefits may suggest that companies have a natural incentive to implement effective compliance programmes. One could conclude that competition authorities do not need to provide further incentives. However, this strategic dimension of compliance programmes is only a part of the bigger picture. Various types of challenges exist in the short run.[156] For example, companies, especially small ones, may have very limited resources to dedicate to competition compliance, compared with other areas of compliance. Another challenge for large companies stems from the complex corporate structure of multinational companies. Delivering consistent but tailored compliance training is difficult for large companies. Added to the substantial benefit of not complying and the difficulty that competition authorities have with regard to detecting cartels, challenges for organising compliance should be taken into account. In other words, competition authorities should convince companies that there is potential for a strategic organisation of compliance, and should steer such a strategic interest. As a result, positive discourse needs to be endorsed so that companies see compliance programmes not just as a burden to avoid risk but also as a potential source of value. In that respect, the French Competition Authority rightly employs a positive narrative in the guidance provided to companies: the guidance refers to the implementation programmes with terms such as 'useful risk management' or 'winning investment'. The guidance outlines the 'positive impacts in terms of [. . .] commercial development' that can, among other things 'increase the confidence of customers'.[157] Therefore, the French Competition Authority encourages companies

---

[154]   Interview with the head of competition law and compliance of a multinational company.
[155]   ICC, 'ICC Antitrust Compliance Toolkit', 54.
[156]   As reported by companies interviewed.
[157]   Autorité de la Concurrence, 'Antitrust Compliance and Compliance Programmes'.

to 'adopt proactive strategy' but, in 2017, stopped steering the company's incentives through fine reductions.

Without considering the effect of this specific guidance, I take the view that competition authorities should aim to convince companies proactively to implement an effective compliance programme, but they should also acknowledge that they can leverage this effect by 'steering' voluntary implementation. Competition authorities are right not to interfere with companies' internal matters, as this may affect the freedom of enterprise, and impose an unnecessary burden on businesses. However, authorities should build on the positive motivations behind the organisation of compliance, and exploit the potential strategic interest of companies in the organisation of compliance. Authorities themselves have a strategic interest in promoting the implementation of compliance programmes: that of placing further emphasis on *ex ante* enforcement, and hence theoretically balancing the need for (and cost of) *ex post* enforcement. Competition authorities should direct their efforts not only to detecting and punishing violations, but also to inducing the business community to direct social norms towards more compliance. An enforcement regime requiring a compliance programme as part of well-designed leniency could achieve detection of current practices, together with lowering future risks of collusion.

8.4.2 *For an Incentive-Based Regulatory Approach to Compliance Programmes*

This section provides practical suggestions regarding how competition authorities may provide concrete incentives to companies for implementing effective compliance measures. Two options will be examined: first, the possibility of companies being rewarded (in the case of an antitrust conviction, settlement procedure, or outside the scope of an infringement); and, secondly, the possibility of certifying the adoption of corporate compliance.

8.4.2.1 Rewarding Companies for the Implementation of Compliance Programmes

Providing incentives to companies to implement compliance programmes in the form of reward poses a number of issues. Prior to discussing the manner in which competition authorities should reward companies, it is required to discuss the concept of 'effective compliance programmes'. What steps undertaken by a company reflect the real endorsement of a compliance culture? While no 'one-size-fits-all' detailed standard for corporate compliance can be established, the key foundations of an effective compliance programme will be outlined. In addition, verifying and testing the effectiveness of compliance programmes is a core challenge in rewarding of compliance efforts. What constitutes 'adequate procedures'? How can competition authorities make sure that they are not rewarding 'cosmetic' compliance programmes? A related issue stems from the possible perverse incentives provided by a badly designed reward system.

8.4.2.1.1 THE KEY FOUNDATIONS OF AN EFFECTIVE COMPLIANCE PROGRAMME. One of the core issues around compliance programmes lies in the identification of what constitutes an effective compliance programme. The CMA and the Autorité de la Concurrence commissioned studies to understand the drivers of compliance and to identify the steps that companies need to undertake to achieve compliance.[158] Subsequently, guidelines were issued by the authorities, outlining the key features of effective compliance programmes. Business organisations also provide guidance to the authorities, and the ICC even issued a guidance document. This section will outline the key factors for a successful compliance programme.[159] Practical examples will be provided to illustrate what can constitute effective internal mechanisms. Examples draw from the literature, from interviews I conducted with persons responsible for in-house competition law compliance,[160] as well as from a survey of compliance practices conducted with over eighty-six large companies in Germany, Austria and Switzerland in 2013 and 2014 by Götz, Herold and Paha.[161] The Air Cargo cartel case study also provides insightful elements into the organisation of compliance.[162]

As pointed out above, a compliance programme encompasses all types of compliance efforts and processes taken by a company, designed to impact durably the corporate culture and translating into a strong moral commitment to comply at all levels. Corporate compliance is a matter of degree, and resources allocated to achieving compliance and cannot be equated to a mere code of conduct or training sessions.

Culture of Compliance Set from the Top

The first essential foundation of effective corporate compliance lies in the culture embedded from the top of the hierarchy. A strong culture of compliance at the top is particularly important because senior executives may be the most at-risk individuals. Personal commitment to compliance is essential, particularly in light of all the business matters that may otherwise take priority.[163] A clear and unambiguous commitment by senior management serves the purpose of setting the high compliance standard throughout the firm.[164] For such a core commitment to be

---

[158]   OFT 1227, 'Drivers of Compliance and Non-compliance with Competition Law (2010)'; Autorité de la concurrence: Europe Economics, 'État des lieux'.

[159]   Based on all of this literature, as well as on interviews conducted with those responsible for in-house competition law compliance.

[160]   See n. 131.

[161]   G. Götz, D. Herold and J. Paha, 'Germany, Austria and Switzerland on How to Prevent Violations of Competition Laws' in Paha (ed.), *Competition Law Compliance Programmes*, pp. 37–58.

[162]   Bergman, and Sokol, 'The Air Cargo Cartel'.

[163]   Murphy describes the busyness or arrogance of some top executives and how this may undermine corporate compliance: J. E. Murphy, 'Policies in Conflict: Undermining Corporate Self-Policing', *Rutgers University Law Review*, 69 (2017), 421, 470.

[164]   OFT1341, paras. 2.1–2.3.

communicated strongly within the company, it must be reflected in the actions of the top management. The board members need to be part of the compliance effort. Having one board member who is expressly responsible for questions of compliance enables compliance issues to be steered from the top.[165] In the case of the *air cargo* cartel, a change in corporate culture at Lufthansa was triggered by strong support of compliance initiatives by the senior management: in 2003, the general counsel Von Ruckteschell and chief financial officer Kley, a lawyer himself, directly approached the newly appointed CEO Mayrhuber to gain support for implementing a competition law compliance programme. The CEO clearly endorsed the introduction of the programme by adding a foreword to the document of the compliance policy.[166] As will be discussed below, however, a clear tone from the top needs to be evidenced by more than just a mere signature of a code of conduct by the CEO.

Clear Communication

Communication constitutes another key dimension of compliance programmes. Communicating a strong message of compliance throughout the organisation involves holding training sessions to teach employees about the compliance risks and procedures, especially those exposed to competitors. In addition, compliance programmes need to motivate the employees, to raise the compliance awareness within the company.[167] Therefore, compliance needs to work hand in hand with communication to 'impact emotionally' and avoid training fatigue. In practice, almost all companies (97 per cent) surveyed by Götz, Herold and Paha provide training within their company, raising awareness of the legal risks associated with non-compliance, but only 69 per cent communicate on the socially detrimental and ethical consequences of collusive behaviour.[168] Communication is also essential with respect to relationships with third parties. A written code of conduct supported by a strong compliance programme directed to business partners signals a clear commitment. Larger companies may also be able to impose compliance-related requirements on their partners. As exposed previously, corporate compliance stands to be more effective if the business environment is compliant.

A Compliance 'Ambassador'

Related to the communication dimension, the organisation of compliance must be supported by an 'ambassador' of competition law compliance, or a 'chief ethics and compliance officer.'[169] With a sufficient degree of responsibility, this person, as part of either the legal services or the compliance department, needs to have credible means to advocate competition law compliance. The issue of compliance cannot be diluted and given a lower level of priority compared with other areas of business, and

---

[165] Even though it depends on the function of the board (supervisory or executive).
[166] Bergman, and Sokol, 'The Air Cargo Cartel', 308.
[167] Interviews with heads of compliance and general counsel of multinational companies.
[168] Götz, Herold and Paha, 'Germany, Austria and Switzerland', 48.
[169] Murphy, *Policies in Conflict*, p. 473.

such a role needs to be given to a person of high authority within the firm. Although especially true for large companies, the need for a 'compliance ambassador' also stands for smaller companies that can hand the compliance responsibility to someone who is particularly sensitive to this issue. In the case of Lufthansa, the general counsel von Ruckteschell managed to convince the board of the necessity to introduce a compliance office within the legal department, and to appoint a dedicated lawyer. The counsel received the title of Chief Compliance Officer, by which he clearly endorsed the role of 'compliance ambassador' within the organisation.[170] This role was then instrumental to the internal discovery of cartel practices within Lufthansa.

Risk Mitigation Processes

Risk mitigation is a key component of compliance. Training is important but should not be the only dimension of risk mitigation; effective corporate compliance entails procedures of prevention, detection and response, reflecting a proactive approach to compliance. Training needs to be delivered to employees in a targeted fashion, with a view to preventing them from putting the company at risk, including senior executives. In addition, an effective compliance programme needs to ensure that codes of conduct and training sessions translate into actual compliance. To do this, procedures to monitor risky business activities and provide legal advice need to be clearly established. This may entail, for example, having clear rules on participation in trade association meetings. Companies can control who may participate, raise awareness of legal risks specific associated with such meetings, and require submission of relevant documentation to the legal department, including the meeting agenda, or minutes of the meeting.[171]

A compliance programme needs to impact incentives to comply in all its dimensions, and cannot solely rely on 'trust as a control'. Prevention, including training staff and communication compliance towards employees, should therefore be supplemented by solid internal mechanisms of detection and reporting. Risk mitigation thus entails proactively investigating the occurrence of misconduct. Sophisticated techniques such as screening can be used to detect the red flags of cartel behaviour.[172] In practice, screening or active investigation of collusive conduct within the firm may be integrated within broader auditing procedures, conducted either regularly or upon suspicion of wrongdoing. Auditing procedures may involve review of contracts with business partners, minutes of meetings, or interviews with employees. Such investigation could be undertaken via internal audit, or external services.[173] The definition of accounting benchmarks or targets may help companies to flag situations of increased collusive risk that should trigger an internal investigation. Corporate alert systems should also be provided to enable the internal

---

[170]   Bergman, and Sokol. 'The Air Cargo Cartel'.

[171]   Götz, Herold and Paha, 'Germany, Austria and Switzerland', 49.

[172]   R. M. Abrantes-Metz, P. Bajari and J. E. Murphy, 'Enhancing Compliance Programs Through Antitrust Screening', *The Antitrust Counselor*, 4.5 (2010), 4.

[173]   Götz, Herold and Paha, 'Germany, Austria and Switzerland', 52–54.

reporting of misconduct, with careful consideration of questions of confidentiality and protection against retaliation. A key challenge is that some other legal requirements may undermine such aspects of compliance. The exclusion of in-house lawyers from legal privilege protection in the EU may limit the ability of employees to raise concerns internally over competition law infringement. In Europe, helplines that can be used anonymously are therefore generally operated by third-party counsel.[174] Privacy and confidentiality concerns, particularly so with the recent legislative changes in the EU, may also undermine such mechanisms.[175]

Sanction schemes should be available and, most importantly, must constitute a credible threat. These should be clearly communicated within the organisation, and closely implemented in the occurrence of a breach. Disciplinary measures commonly used by the surveyed companies range from letters of warning, and training requirements, to dismissal. Although 88 per cent of the companies surveyed declared having these in place, only 44 per cent of companies previously involved in cartels did make use of such sanctions. This limits the credibility and deterrence effect of having such internal penalties.[176] Some 42 per cent of the companies reported having an internal 'leniency' approach to employees confessing wrong-doing to the compliance or legal department, and declared providing legal assistance including support with litigation cost to their employees. This illustrates the critical importance of effective implementation of internal policies.

Economic and Business Risk

Companies should respond proactively to any market indicators that may suggest an increased cartel risk. Demand shocks may be a factor of collusive risk. For example, the *Irish Beef* cartel was formed to remedy a decrease in demand due to the BSE crisis. Similarly, the cartel between Christie's and Sotheby's was created at a time of economic difficulties in the art market. The cartels of carbonless paper, professional videotapes, thread, or TV and monitor tubes producers may also have followed a persistent reduction in demand. Entry of a new competitor, or periods of intense competition, may be prone to cartel formation.[177] Companies should thus develop a precise understanding of how such market changes may impact the incentives to collude, through, for example, their impact via remuneration schemes. As was exposed in Chapter 6, managerial incentives based on short-term indicators may be conducive to collusion. Therefore, market indicators could be designed to alert the compliance officer to an increase in antitrust risk.

The survey of companies, however suggests that companies put relatively little emphasis on the economic and business dimension of the competitive risk. Only a minority of the companies consider reduction of profits, or entry of a new

---

[174] Riley and Bloom, 'Antitrust Compliance Programmes'.
[175] Murphy discusses how privacy regulations and legal privilege may undermine compliance programmes:, 'Policies in Conflict', 453–60.
[176] Götz, Herold and Paha, 'Germany, Austria and Switzerland', 51.
[177] Ibid., 44.

competitor, or intensified competition from imports as a risk factor.[178] Assessment of business and economic risk may be appealing to small businesses because it is relatively less costly than conducting legal auditing, for example. A greater understanding of risk factors can enable a targeted and tailored approach to risk mitigation.

In summary, companies need to adopt a strategic and proactive approach to compliance management, appropriate to their risk level, and in awareness of other legal requirements. Effective compliance goes well beyond training; it encompasses credible mechanisms of prevention, detection and sanction, reflected in clear commitment at the top. The provision of concrete incentives by competition authorities is therefore necessary to help companies overcome some of the compliance organisational hurdles.

8.4.2.1.2 THE VERIFIABILITY OF COMPLIANCE PROGRAMMES. Most of the debate about compliance programmes crystallises around the verifiability of the quality of the compliance programme. Some argue that the inherent difficulty in evaluating a compliance effort may create perverse incentives: companies will then adopt 'cosmetic' compliance programmes to ensure a reduction in the level of the fine.[179] As a result, infringing competition law would become less costly. This argument may be rejected on grounds similar to those advocating the use of leniency programmes. The fine eventually imposed no longer matches the gravity of the infringement, in order to stimulate the level of detection. Competition authorities operate a trade-off between reducing the potential deterrent effect of fines, at the benefit of an increased level of detection. In addition, companies are still subject to private actions, and other negative consequences of being investigated for breach of the law.

This chapter takes the stance that the effectiveness of compliance programmes can be verified. The difficulty of testing the quality may stem from the hesitation of competition authorities to penetrate the boundaries of the firm. As has been exposed at several instances, undertakings are the subjects of competition law. Competition authorities, especially in the EU, are reluctant to address the internal workings of companies, including in the field of sanctions. As a result, competition authorities have rarely had the opportunity to really analyse competition law issues from the perspective of the company. For example, the CMA and the French Competition Authority commissioned studies to enable them better to understand the internal dimension of compliance.[180] Incidentally, those competition authorities subsequently admitted the possibility of considering compliance programmes (until 2017 only, for France).

---

[178]   Ibid., 45.
[179]   Wils, 'Antitrust Compliance Programmes'.
[180]   OFT 1227, 'Drivers of Compliance and Non-compliance with Competition Law (2010)'; Autorité de la concurrence: Europe Economics, 'Etat des lieux'.

In contrast, in anti-corruption, authorities have not been reluctant to address and learn about compliance programmes. For example, in the United States, programmes are typically imposed on companies, with monitors assigned to ensure that the programmes are implemented.[181] The authorities examine the effectiveness of compliance programmes during their investigation, during which they undertake a detailed inquiry into company materials and interview company employees. This process can reveal whether a programme is credible. The burden of proof is on the undertaking, requiring the company to evidence each of the elements of an effective programme. Some agencies, such as the FBI in the United States, have even implemented their own internal compliance programme, showing a greater comfort with internal compliance mechanisms.[182] In addition, the anti-corruption legislation targets individuals as well as companies. Being more conversant with the internal dimension of the infringement, these authorities may possess better tools to assess the quality of compliance programmes. Competition authorities should learn from the experience of authorities that manage to assess the quality of a compliance effort. Competition authority staff should strengthen their practical understanding of compliance by undertaking in-house training, for example.[183]

Based on the foundations of effective compliance programmes, tangible elements can be required by competition authorities to demonstrate appropriate compliance efforts. To attest that there is a core commitment to competition compliance, competition authorities could require evidence that compliance is being discussed regularly at board meetings and that senior management has attended training. A compliance tone at the top cannot simply be evidenced by a CEO's signature of a compliance programme.[184] A code of conduct or compliance programme being regularly used by the CEO (e.g. on the desk), or evidence of any proactive compliance requirement by senior executives (e.g. from business partners) could signal clear endorsement of a compliance culture.[185] The mention of compliance in top executives' speeches or other internal communication, as well as the involvement of a communication department in compliance, can attest to an effective communication of compliance.

The authority may also verify that there is an empowered, independent senior officer responsible for compliance, and the frequency with which the compliance unit reports to the board. Evidence of the independence and empowerment may be

---

[181] Transparency International, USA, The Verification of Anti-Corruption Compliance Programs, *Compliance Monitors*, 4.3 (2014), available at: www.transparency.nl/wp-content/uploads/2016/12/TI -USA_2014_verificationreportfinal.pdf

[182] Department of Justice Review: 'FBI's Integrity and Compliance Program', available at: https://oig .justice.gov/reports/2011/e1201.pdf

[183] Interview with general counsel of a multinational Company: a Commission official asked how to know of the validity of a compliance programme. The general counsel responded in saying 'come on secondment'.

[184] Murphy, 'Policies in Conflict'.

[185] J. E. Murphy, '"Wow" Factors in Compliance & Ethics Programs' (2016), available at: radicalcom pliance.com

available in the employment contract. The communication dimension of an effective compliance programme lies in internal communication and training material, based on which its accuracy and its emotional impact may be assessed. The availability of a code of conduct adopted internally, and directed to business partners, is part of compliance communication, but only if it is actually implemented. Evidence of termination of a business relationship on the ground of non-compliance would substantiate the credibility of the measures in place. The actual implementation of compliance can be evidenced by training attendance records, and through the simple act of talking to company employees during an investigation. Competition authorities can request proof that senior executives, sales managers and other high-risk positions have attended training, and whether or not anyone was disciplined for not attending. Companies can also demonstrate that clear procedures are in place, in hiring employees (human resources can indicate that an employee has no history of antitrust infringement) and in monitoring risky business areas, such as trade association meetings. In addition, the availability of sanctioning procedures and the history of sanction cases are signs that compliance comprises a wider range of procedures than just training sessions. The availability of corporate compliance audit reports signals a willingness continually to adapt the compliance programme and to search for actual misconduct.[186] A clear understanding of economic risks may also be evidenced by the company, which can be required to explain the red flags in place within the organisation.

8.4.2.2 When Should Compliance Programmes Receive Credit?

Competition authorities should give credit to compliance programmes, but only in the context of an investigation. Upon cooperation and sufficient evidence of adequate compliance efforts, a company should benefit from a reduction – possibly substantial – in the level of the fine, assessed on a case-by-case basis. The amount of benefit given to a company for its programme should thus be along a continuum, reflecting the seriousness of the offence, any involvement of senior management on the one hand, and the degree of the programme diligence on the other hand. Because it holds an informational advantage over the competition authorities, the burden of proof should lie with the company. In terms of timing, rewarded compliance programmes may have proven effectiveness at the time of the infringement. A commitment from a company to introduce or improve an existing compliance programme may be rewarded.[187]

---

[186] Based on an interview with the head of competition law and compliance of a multinational company.

[187] One may wonder whether, and how, compliance efforts with respect to third parties may be rewarded. While, in principle, this would promote the adoption of a culture of compliance within business networks (suppliers, customers), granting the reward may raise further legal issues if several undertakings are potentially involved. (e.g. how to attribute the reward among the different undertakings, what types of evidence would be required, and burden of proof issues).

However, the reward should not just focus on post-infringement compliance programmes. The objective is to encourage the implementation of compliance efforts *ex ante*. *Ex post* consideration of compliance may undermine the impact that such a reward is designed to have on the prevention of cartels in the first place. *Ex ante* consideration of compliance efforts also supports the view that despite all of the efforts to mitigate antitrust risk, a residual risk exists. As with any other compliance area in which the concept of residual risk is admitted, a company that organises compliance in the most effective manner still faces the eventuality that an individual may put the company at risk. In addition, such an occurrence typically involves hidden behaviour, which complicates the risk mitigation. This view contrasts with that of the Commission, according to which a company's compliance efforts have necessarily failed in the event of a conviction.[188] Recidivism should seriously affect the prospect of getting a fine reduction. Fine reduction should be greater in case of smaller-scale or isolated misconduct, and the scope of the rewards should depend on the position of the responsible individuals within the hierarchy. Top executives blatantly disregarding a compliance programme that they were publicly supporting should preclude the company from getting a fine reduction.

8.4.2.3 The Question of Certification and Standards

The certification and standards for compliance programmes may further steer the voluntary implementation of compliance programmes by companies. As was suggested previously, a company may have a strategic incentive to signal that it has implemented an effective compliance programme. The use of certification based on a standard could help companies to implement compliance voluntarily, with broader objectives than solely to reduce antitrust risk. In the context of requirements imposed on suppliers or bidding companies, a widely accepted standard may encourage a company voluntarily to adopt a compliance programme on their own instead of adopting the principles imposed by the third-party company.

Initiatives to certify compliance programmes do exist. In 2014, the nongovernmental body ISO has developed the corporate compliance standard 19600, inspired from the Australian/New Zealand 3806–2006 standard for compliance programmes. Not specific to competition compliance, this standard provides principles and guidance for the design, implementation, maintenance and improvement of an effective compliance programme. The aim is to offer companies the possibility to demonstrate their commitment with compliance, based on a standard recognised internationally.[189] The ISO 19600 standard sets out twelve principles

---

[188] While in the field of corruption the Department of Justice understands that 'no compliance program can ever prevent all criminal activity by a corporation's employees' and it does not hold companies to a standard of perfection: United States Attorney's Manual, 9-28.400.

[189] International Organization for Standardization, ISO 19600:2014 Compliance Management Systems – Guidelines, available at: www.iso.org/standard/62342.html

grouped into four categories: commitment, implementation, monitoring and maintenance, and continual improvement. These aspirational principles set the basis for a voluntarily implementation by companies.

In 2011, the German Public Auditors' Institute put in place an audit standard called 'Principles of proper auditing of compliance management system'. The standard encompasses three layers of audit. The first type of audit consists of assessing the conceptual content and documentation of the compliance system. The actual design corresponding to the compliance principles set out by the company is the object of the second layer of the audit. The effectiveness of the processes in place is tested in the third type of audit.[190] Management and supervisory boards can then request a targeted type of auditing, according to the particularities of their company. ThyssenKrupp AG was the first company to have its compliance programme audited following this standard, and it advertised this certification widely.[191]

Certification and standards for compliance programmes seem to be a good concept, but they are difficult to establish, for various reasons. Businesses welcome these initiatives, while acknowledging the lack of experience and the potential cost of conducting an external audit. In addition, the current standard and certification systems rely on wide and vague concepts. A more effective approach to certification would be to elaborate a standard based on flexible but more concrete requirements. They could also suggest a desired number of compliance officers, and frequency of trainings, and indicate the types of procedures that need to be available for a certain range of size and the degree of risk.[192] Following a procedure of certification (or equivalent) by an external body, companies could be granted a label of 'antitrust compliance' that would send a positive signal to third parties.[193] Companies could also have their antitrust compliance system certified as part of other compliance areas. The voluntary dimension of the adoption of such a standard would reduce the risk of fraudulent compliance programmes.

Resources spent on voluntary compliance standards would constitute a strategic investment for a company, which would be decided along with other strategies, possibly sending a strong signal to third parties. Also, the certification of a compliance programme may facilitate cooperation with competition authorities in the event of an investigation. The compliance incentive would certainly be strengthened if the certification were coupled with the possibility of obtaining a fine reduction, under conditions described above. The investment in compliance certification should remain a business incentive rather than a systematic guarantee of benefiting from a fine reduction. Competition

---

[190] Institut der Wirtschaftsprüfer, Standard IDW PS 980, available at: www.idw.de/idw/verlautbarun gen/idw-ps-980/43124
[191] ThyssenKrupp, audit reports available at: www.thyssenkrupp.com/en/company/compliance/audit-reports/
[192] Interview with the head of competition law and compliance of a multinational company.
[193] Although one must bear in mind the potential risk of setting up too detailed standards: the minimum standards becoming the maximum.

authorities should take the opportunity to engage in such an exercise, as it constitutes a potential source of preventive measures against competition law infringements.

8.5 CONCLUSION

This chapter has provided theoretical and practical arguments supporting the desirability of opening the 'black box' of compliance programmes. Competition authorities rarely give credit to companies' compliance efforts. In contrast, other areas of compliance, namely anti-corruption regulations seem to consider compliance programmes differently. No systematic difference in the nature of antitrust and corruption infringements can explain these divergent regulatory approaches. Rather, regulators in both fields seem to display different mind sets. Competition rules that target the undertaking rather than the individual seem more hesitant to address the internal dimension of companies than anti-corruption regulators.

Rewarding effective compliance programmes should form part of the cartel enforcement toolbox. Compliance programmes help to address the mismatch of interest between shareholders and managers, in a manner that addresses the potential shortcomings of sanctions and leniency. Despite the increasing levels of fines and the introduction of individual sanctions, competition authorities face the difficulty of preventing and detecting cartels. The consideration of compliance programmes could then leverage the potential deterrent effect of harsh sanctions. In addition, compliance programmes could be required from leniency recipients, whereby detection of existing cartels could be achieved together with prevention of future infringements.

Companies can find a strategic interest in the organisation of compliance, with respect to internal processes and in relationships with business partners and potential investors. Competition authorities should steer this strategic interest and provide incentives for the voluntary implementation of effective compliance programmes. Giving credit to effective compliance programmes seems possible and desirable in the context of an investigation. Competition authorities should also engage further with the development of certification and standards that would facilitate the strategic use of compliance programmes by companies. Although not systematically, certification coupled with a defensive incentive could further strengthen the compliance efforts of companies. Greater engagement with companies' compliance efforts would help to align the incentives of companies and competition authorities in the fight against cartels.

Conclusion of Part II

Part II has provided a distinctive understanding of the issue of collusive behaviour that remains one of the greatest challenges of competition law enforcement. Cartels are first and foremost the products of individual behaviour, explained by a wide range of individual and organisational-specific factors. The agency relationship, featuring issues of imperfect information and opportunistic behaviour, approximates adequately the complexity of the internal drivers of collusive behaviour. Mechanisms of corporate governance that seek to impact incentives within the firm are significant components of the collusive narrative.

The main normative claim is that traditional enforcement tools, based on punishment and deterrence, should be complemented by tools that encourage self- or 'management-based' regulation.[1] Regarding traditional enforcement, corporate sanctions are necessary but insufficient. Their effectiveness may be mitigated by issues of imperfect information and by the inability systematically to prevent collusive behaviour internally. Individual sanctions should supplement the threat of harsh sanctions imposed on companies, in a manner that align incentives towards cartel detection. Leniency policy, a cornerstone of cartel enforcement throughout jurisdictions, will be an effective disruptive tool only if internal incentives are aligned in seeking detection. Finally, making greater use of sanctions of corporate

---

[1] On one extreme of the enforcement spectrum lies the 'deterrence' or 'sanctioning' enforcement approach. At the other end of the spectrum, 'compliance'-based enforcement embraces a range of informal techniques, including education, advice, persuasion and negotiation: R. Baldwin, M. Cave and M. Lodge *Understanding Regulation: Theory, Strategy, and Practice*, 2nd edn (Oxford University Press, 2012), p. 239. See also Europe Economics, 'Etat des lieux et perspectives des programmes de conformité, Une étude réalisée pour le Conseil de la concurrence' (2008), para. 10.11, available at: www .autoritedelaconcurrence.fr/doc/etudecompliance_oct08.pdf. On management-based regulation, see, for example: C. Coglianese and D. Lazer, 'Management-Based Regulation: Prescribing Private Management to Achieve Public Goals', *Law & Society Review*, 37 (2003), 691: 'A management-based approach requires firms to engage in their own planning and internal rule making efforts Management-based regulation directs regulated organizations to engage in a planning process that aims toward the achievement of public goals, offering firms flexibility in how they achieve public goals.'

governance is another means of effectively targeting those responsible for internal compliance within the company.

Promoting the voluntary implementation of compliance programmes may enhance the effectiveness of cartel enforcement. Compliance programmes help to address the shortcomings of sanction policies. In spite of the increasing levels of fines and the introduction of individual sanctions, competition authorities face the difficulty of preventing and detecting cartels. The consideration of compliance programmes could then leverage the potential deterrent effect of harsh sanctions. In addition, compliance programmes could be required from leniency recipients, whereby detection of existing cartels could be achieved together with prevention of future infringements.

9

Conclusion

9.1 INTRODUCTION

While summarising the main findings, this last chapter will highlight the theoretical contribution and policy implications of the conclusions reached in this book. This book has discussed the relevance of the boundaries of the firm set by competition law to establish its substantive reach vis-à-vis corporate governance. It has advocated a greater competition law inquiry into the conventional boundaries of the firm for cartel enforcement purposes.

9.2 THE FIRM AS A 'BLACK BOX' TO COMPETITION LAW

This book has explained that competition law, via the concept of undertaking or single entity, establishes a clear dichotomy between the firm and the market. Competition law considers the firm as a 'black box', which means that internal relations or mechanisms, including that of corporate governance, generally do not matter for competition law. The 'black box' perception of the firm exists regarding both the substantive reach of competition law and questions of enforcement. As explained in Chapter 3, the notion of undertaking in European Union (EU) law, based on the concept of economic activity, is indifferent to the legal form: two entities having distinct legal personalities can still be part of the same undertaking for the purpose of competition law provisions. Once such a relationship has been defined as pertaining to one single entity, the legality of any relationship within that undertaking will not be questioned by competition law. The single entity doctrine is thereby used critically to distinguish one undertaking from another, and to determine whether entities will be subject to competition law either separately or jointly. As Chapter 4 and Chapter 5 discuss, the application of the single entity to complex relations is critical because of its binary outcome: arrangements will either be immune or be submitted to provisions on agreements, with possibly drastic implications in the event of breach.

Regarding enforcement, the 'black box' conception of the firm exists in relation to liability attribution within undertakings composed by legally independent but economically affiliated entities. As was explained in Chapter 4, in the EU, competition law may be indifferent to the legal reality of what is defined as a single entity, when it attributes liability to a parent for the wrongdoing of its subsidiary, or to the principal in a commercial agency relationship. In doing so, it disregards the principles of legal separation and limited liability.

In addition, enforcement tools target the undertaking without much consideration of the internal subunits or individuals. As explained in Chapter 7, monetary sanctions imposed on the undertaking are the form of sanction most commonly used to punish an infringement. In EU competition law, no sanctions are directed to individuals. In other jurisdictions, sanctions target business participants within the firm, with relatively limited actual enforcement practice. In terms of deterrent impact, corporate sanctions target the incentive systems of companies as a whole, without further consideration of incentives within the organisation. The approach to compliance programmes, presented in Chapter 8, also illustrates the indifference of competition law enforcement to internal relations. While they provide guidance to companies, most competition authorities refuse to recognise a company's compliance efforts in the context of an infringement: in the EU, what matters is only the compliance outcome – the 'output' of the 'black box' – and, as such, no credit can be given to internal compliance processes. The United Kingdom (UK) is one of the few jurisdictions to consider compliance programmes as a possible mitigating factor. Therefore, what matters is only the compliance outcome that emanates from the 'black box'.

9.3 THE COMPETITION LAW CONCEPTION OF THE FIRM

This book has constructed the competition law conception of the firm, relevant for establishing its substantive reach and for matters of enforcement and liability. The main theoretical claim developed throughout this book is that these two distinct types of inquiries require a differentiated approach to the conception of the firm.[1] In the 'substantive reach' function, the boundaries of the firm are established to protect private agreements made among business participants. In its 'liability attribution' function, the firm is defined in terms of its rights and liabilities as an actor within a market or in society.[2] Understanding the distinct internal or external regulation purposes clarifies the need for distinct paradigms in setting the boundaries of the firm.

---

[1] This is a competition law adaptation of Orts's adaptation of H. L. A. Hart's approach to the legal boundaries of the firm. 'HLA Hart's admonition ... [is] the nature and boundaries of the firm depend on the nature of the question being asked': H. L. A. Hart, 'Definition and Theory in Jurisprudence' in *Essays in Jurisprudence and Philosophy* (Oxford University Press 1983); E. W. Orts, *Business Persons: A Legal Theory of the Firm* (Oxford University Press, 2013), p. 108.

[2] Orts, *Business Persons*, pp. 223–5.

9.3.1 *Substantive Reach and Moving Boundaries*

This book recognises the relevance for competition law of defining the boundaries of the firm: establishing the limits of the substantive reach of competition law provisions brings legal clarity to companies that need to comply with competition rules. Clearly endorsing an economic vision, competition law thus recognises the efficiency of alternatives to the market, and does not purport to interfere with such alternative forms of transactions. As such, agreements within what forms a single entity are outside its scope; and boundaries are drawn by competition law to protect the private ordering of firms. Likewise, public services functions that may fail to be provided in markets are protected from the reach of competition law. Essential in a world of scarce resources for competition authorities, confining the reach of competition law provisions also limits the negative effects on economies of too much enforcement.[3]

Moving boundaries between the firm and the market challenges the application of the competition law conception of the firm. In the modern economy, competition law faces a growing complexity of corporate structures; and the increasing disconnection between financial investment and operation of the economic activity complicates the assessment of control. In that respect, Chapter 4 shows that applying the single entity doctrine has been crucial in complex corporate groups composed of parent and subsidiaries, as well as in relationships between commercial agents and the companies that they represent. In addition, applying the single entity with care in horizontal relations is particularly important to identify instances in which competitors construct corporate arrangements to operate behind the shield of a single entity (Chapter 5). Too broad an application of the single entity defence could have important anticompetitive effects.

The theory of the firm provides relevant analytical features for the application of the single entity doctrine to complex relationships. The property rights theory, in particular, helps to distinguish what ought to be treated as a firm or a market transaction; in relationships such as joint ventures and parent and subsidiary, as well as in commercial agency agreements. In doing so it helps to minimise type I and type II errors. Efficient forms of economic transactions, including hybrid forms such as commercial agency relationships, are not deterred if treated as so by competition law. Arrangements that may produce anticompetitive effects, such as joint ventures, may also be captured adequately if they are correctly qualified in terms of property rights.

The competition law conception of the firm is, however, limited to catch anticompetitive effects of relationships that blur the market/firm boundaries. This is the case when competitors are connected via both a market and a corporate relationship, because of common ownership or board links. As was explained in Chapter 5, the

---

[3] Hence the preference for type II errors in competition law enforcement: F. H. Easterbrook, 'The Limits of Antitrust', *Texas Law Review*, 63 (1984), 1.

presumed enforcement gap in the EU around the issue of structural links stems from the inadequacy of the paradigm underlying the substantive reach. In contrast, US antitrust law has jurisdiction over competitive effects of structural links because US provisions around interlocking directorates and partial acquisitions are disconnected from the inter/intra entity paradigm. Regardless of whether an acquisition confers control over the target – indicating the end of a market-relationship – partial acquisitions capable of creating anticompetitive effects may be scrutinised. Capturing anticompetitive effects of such relationships may require adjustment of the substantive reach of EU competition law regarding the internal dimension of the firm.

9.3.2 Liability: the Firm as a Nexus of Agency Relationships

This book argues that an inquiry different from establishing the substantive reach demands a different conception of the firm. Instead of considering the firm a 'black box', the undertaking should be understood as a nexus of agency relationships for liability attribution purposes.[4] Relationships between a parent and a subsidiary, between a company and its commercial agent, or between shareholders and managers all involve the delegation of tasks from a principal to an agent. Issues of imperfect information and opportunistic behaviour characterise such economic relationships. The agency relationship approximates adequately the complexity of all these relations.

The single entity doctrine is, in the EU, critically used to attribute liability in case of undertakings composed by economically affiliated but legally independent companies. Part I demonstrated that the conception of the firm used in competition law is inadequate when used to attribute liability. Such an approach to liability is no longer relevant to the legal reality of complex corporate structures in the modern economy. The agency relationship provides an adequate framework for understanding the critical importance of incentives when financial ownership is remote from the operational control of the business activity. In addition, questions of liability are at the heart of discussions on cartels in Part II. It is shown that the 'black box' approach to liability for collusive behaviour in the EU is inadequate for the challenges of cartel enforcement. Cartels are, first and foremost, the products of individual behaviour, explained by a wide range of individual and organisational-specific factors. The agency relationship, featuring issues of imperfect information and opportunistic behaviour, reflects the complexity of the internal drivers of collusive behaviour.

The 'black box' approach to liability is inadequate because it is based on the premise that the *incentives* and the *ability* of actors coincide. Instead, liability should

---

[4] E. W. Orts, 'Shirking and Sharking: A Legal Theory of the Firm', *Yale Law & Policy Review*, 16(2) (1997), 265, 269.

be imposed, upon joint consideration of incentives and ability within relationships. Incentives may refer to the pay-offs – cost and benefits – that an actor may expect from an activity. The concept of ability, in turn, refers to the manner in which incentives may translate into behaviour. A parent company may have incentives aligned with that of a subsidiary in the cartel participation, but they may lack the actual ability to direct their conduct on the market. Similarly, a parent company that is remote from operational conduct may lack the ability to prevent the subsidiary from infringing competition law. Thereby, a critical question in liability attribution is whether those who bear the consequences of sanctions (incentives) have the ability to prevent and detect wrongdoing internally.

An effective liability regime is one that incentivises the principal to internalise the social cost of non-compliance, without their incurring excessive and wasteful expenses. The existence of imperfect information and opportunism that characterise relationships in large companies or within complex corporate groups may limit such ability. In addition, companies may decide not to proactively detect a breach internally if it increases the likelihood of its receiving fines.[5] Therefore, whenever the incentive gap is too wide, targeting the principal may significantly limit the deterrence effect of sanctions. Against this framework, this book has formulated important normative suggestions for greater effectiveness of enforcement. Better targeting of the agent together with providing incentives for the implementation of compliance mechanisms can help address some of the limitations of existing liability regimes.

9.4 MAIN POLICY IMPLICATIONS

This book has engaged with some of the most relevant issues of competition law in the modern economy: the everlasting cartel problem; the competition law treatment of corporate groups; and structural links that may produce novel or unchallenged types of anticompetitive effects. All three issues need to be addressed through a joint competition law and corporate governance perspective. This section summarises the conclusions reached in these three areas.

9.4.1 *Cartel Enforcement Through the Lens of Corporate Governance*

The main theoretical claim is that current enforcement challenges against cartels raise the need to move away from a strictly sanctions-based type of enforcement, to include self- or 'management-based' regulation.[6] Despite the increasing level of

---

[5] This is one of the perverse effects of corporate liability described by J. Arlen and R. Kraakman, 'Controlling Corporate Misconduct: An Analysis of Corporate Liability Regimes', *New York University Law Review*, 72 (1997), 687.

[6] At one extreme of the enforcement spectrum lies the 'deterrence' or 'sanctioning' enforcement approach. At the other end of the spectrum, 'compliance'-based enforcement embraces a range of informal techniques including education, advice, persuasion and negotiation: R. Baldwin, M. Cave

fines imposed on convicted companies, collusive behaviour remains a problem.[7] The hidden nature of cartel practices and the related difficulty of detecting them undermine the optimality of sanctions. Developments of algorithms and artificial intelligence are likely further to complicate enforcement against collusive behaviour.[8]

This book advocates the need for greater insight into the internal dimension of compliance by competition authorities and law makers. Understanding that cartels are, first and foremost, a product of individual and organisation factors is useful in every aspect of competition policy, from the design and assessment of provisions to their implementation and enforcement. From the decision to participate in a cartel through to its actual operation, cartel activity involves a wide range of actors, with different preferences, and agency relationships between them. The answer to the question 'Who benefits from the crime?' varies from one cartel case to another, and is therefore not straightforward. Looking at the costs and benefits of cartel participation for a few actors – shareholders, top executives and other employees – illustrates how incentives within the firm can differ. While the individual motivations behind cartel participation may be multiple, and the benefits are derived from different sources, competition law can directly affect the cost of cartel participation.[9] Identifying the interest gap of actors with regard to cartel participation has demonstrated the potential impact of enforcement instruments on internal incentives to collude.

Corporate sanctions are necessary but may be of limited effectiveness, particularly in large undertakings. This book advocates imposing more responsibility on business participants, top executives or managers, who have the incentive and ability to engage their company in collusive conduct. This would also clearly enhance the disruptive effect of leniency policy, provided that such individuals are adequately protected. Making greater use of sanctions of corporate governance, including disqualification of directors, is another means of effectively targeting those responsible for internal compliance within the company. The use of derivative actions, which is a possibility in the United States, could also mean that a failure of oversight over illegal price-fixing conduct may be considered a breach of a director's duties.

Encouraging the implementation of internal measures, within or added to existing mechanisms of control, is another important suggestion of this book. It has emphasised the significance of relying further on cooperative enforcement

---

and M. Lodge *Understanding Regulation: Theory, Strategy, and Practice*, 2nd edn (Oxford University Press, 2012), p. 239.

[7] D. D. Sokol, 'Cartels, Corporate Compliance, and What Practitioners Really Think About Enforcement', *Antitrust Law Journal*, 78 (2012), 201, 202; A. Riley and D. Sokol, 'Rethinking Compliance', *Journal of Antitrust Enforcement*, 3(1) (2015), 31, 33.

[8] Challenges of the new economy for the study of collusive practices is discussed in, e.g., A. Ezrachi and M. Stucke, *Virtual Competition* (Harvard University Press, 2016); OECD, Algorithms and Collusion: Competition Policy in the Digital Age (2017).

[9] This, of course, depends heavily on the perceived probability of detection.

encompassing some sort of self-regulation by companies. This can be achieved by providing strong incentives to implement effective compliance programmes, through substantial fine reduction in the case of an infringement. In 'recruiting' companies in the fight against cartels, competition authorities benefit from the informational advantage that companies have over them. The consideration of compliance programmes could then leverage the potential deterrent effect of harsh sanctions. In addition, compliance programmes could be required from leniency recipients, whereby detection of existing cartels could be achieved together with prevention of future infringements. Therefore, adopting enforcement strategies based on a combination of sanctions and cooperation, this book also emphasises the function of *prevention* held by competition law enforcement.[10]

9.4.2 *Competition Law and Corporate Groups*

This book has discussed some of the most critical issues regarding the competition law treatment of corporate groups. The relationship between financial ownership and corporate control is complicated by the increasing role of institutional investors. Has competition law adapted to the shifting boundaries of corporate relations, and to the growing complexity of corporate structures? The single entity doctrine was developed in relation to corporate groups. In *Copperweld* in the United States, and in *Viho* in the EU, the key question was whether a parent and a subsidiary could conspire, and whether they were subject to competition law jointly or separated. Since then, internal relations within corporate groups have been immune from provisions on agreements, whenever a parent and a subsidiary may be deemed to act on the market as a 'single economic unit'. The single entity here recognised the emergence of complex relational firms as alternative to more traditional forms of business firms.[11] As explained in this book, the property rights theory of the firm can help the application of the single entity to corporate groups. Both are based on 'looser' concepts than authority and hierarchy characterising the traditional form of business firms.

This book has also explained how, in the EU, the single entity doctrine has developed into a liability attribution tool, by which a parent is, in practice, almost always liable for the act of its wholly owned subsidiary. De facto attribution of liability to the parent of such subsidiaries is an exception to *entity liability* – the default approach around most of the legal relationships of business corporations across jurisdictions. *Entity liability* is founded on the principles of separate legal

---

[10]   In that respect, see developments regarding the prophylactic (preventive) function of enforcement in the context of remedies in I. Lianos, 'Competition law remedies in Europe: Which Limits for Remedial Discretion?' in I. Lianos and D. Geradin (eds.), *Handbook of EU Competition Law: Enforcement and Procedure* (Edward Elgar Publishing, 2013), pp. 362–455.

[11]   The term of 'complex relational firms' is used to describe the evolution of the corporate structure in Orts, *Business Persons*, ch. 5.

personality and limited liability. Within the *enterprise liability* approach, in contrast, a legal person may bear responsibility for the conduct of another legal person, in the same way that a company bears responsibility for the employees acting on its behalf. EU competition law seems to be aligned with the enterprise approach to parental liability. As Blumberg states, 'whether entity or enterprise law prevails depends on which doctrine best implements the underlying objectives and policies of the law in the particular area'. This book has therefore appraised the approach to liability in light of the identified policy objective: enhanced deterrence of corporate sanctions. It has demonstrated that the existing approach is suboptimal in terms of deterrence.

The current approach, illustrated by an analysis of the decisional practice, shows confusion between what characterises the *incentive* (organic elements associated with financial ownership) and *ability* (the actual ability to control the subsidiary's commercial conduct). As such, it ignores the agency nature of the relationship between a parent and its subsidiary, and the fundamental dynamics that impact deterrence. Against the liability framework developed throughout this book, I have argued that a parent company should be held liable only if it has the ability and incentive to direct the subsidiary's commercial conduct on the market. The presumption of incentive and ability that may reasonably exist in cases of full ownership should be rebuttable in practice, based on a clear distinction between organic and operational aspects of the parent–subsidiary relationship. In addition, a defence based on the legal standard of negligence should be available to parent companies, if they prove that they have implemented adequate internal measures for compliance.[12] This would align the approach to liability with the requirement of 'intentional or negligent' breach set by Regulation 1/2003 for imposing fines, reme-dying one of the concerns that a parent may be held liable irrespective of its behaviour. An approach to liability that integrates actors' behaviour is also one that incentivises greater control and oversight within the corporate group. In line with the overall framework for effective deterrence, this book thus advocates the need to consider internal mechanisms of compliance as part of the assessment of negligence.

Another important trend of evolution of the corporate landscape has been the proliferation of multinational firms in past decades.[13] This book has discussed the international dimension of corporate groups in the context of cross-border private actions. According to private European law provisions, a defendant can be sued in a member state in which a co-defendant is domiciled. This is very relevant in cross-border cases, since plaintiffs may choose to bring claims in the jurisdiction that offers the most favourable solution in terms of litigation costs and duration, and of

---

[12] N. I. Pauer, *The Single Economic Unit Doctrine and Corporate Group Responsibility in European Antitrust Law* (Kluwer Law International, 2014) and by B. Wardhaugh, 'Punishing Parents for the Sins of Their Child: Extending EU Competition Liability in Groups and to Subcontractors', *Journal of Antitrust Enforcement*, 5(1) (2017), 22.

[13] Orts, *Business Persons*, p. 190.

expected level of damages. Several cases have raised the question of whether a subsidiary domiciled in the UK could face private action for the conduct of its parent company, while it had no knowledge of it. In *Provimi*, the court noted that a wholly owned subsidiary could be held liable for the breach of its parent, thereby establishing the jurisdiction of a member state where a subsidiary (or 'anchor defendant') is domiciled.[14] In the United States, there is no such instance of suing a subsidiary company for reselling products of a cartel, where the subsidiary had no knowledge of the cartel.[15] Jurisdiction in cross-border cases depends, instead, on whether injury was caused by conduct that has an effect on US commerce.[16] Relying on the single entity doctrine to establish jurisdiction may have far-reaching implications. As in situations of parental liability, such cases go beyond the principles of legal separation and limited liability and even consist in 'reverse' corporate veil piercing. While holding a parent liable for the conduct of the subsidiary that it controls may be, under certain conditions, consistent with deterrence, holding liable the entity controlled by the infringer is not. Liability in such a case would be completely disconnected from any consideration of incentives and ability, as is advocated in this book.

9.4.3 *Structural Links*

This book is the first to discuss the issue of structural links from a systematic corporate governance and corporate law perspective. In the United States, recent empirical studies on possible anticompetitive effects of portfolio diversification strategies by institutional investors have provoked vivid scholarly debates.[17] In the EU, minority shareholdings not conferring control were at the heart of the project of merger control reform. Although the reform has not been pursued, the issue keeps its contemporary relevance.[18] This book also, quite uniquely, draws attention to the problems raised by widespread interlocking directorates in Europe. While such directorates among competitors are prohibited in the United States, there is no

---

[14] *Provimi Ltd v. Aventis Animal Nutrition SA* [2003] EWHC 96; *Cooper Tyre & Rubber Co & Others* [2009] EWHC 2609 (Comm) *KME Yorkshire Ltd and others and Toshiba Carrier UK Ltd and others* [2011] EWHC 2665 (Ch); *Nokia Corp and AU Optronics Corp* [2012] EWHC 731.

[15] B. Kennelly, 'Antitrust Forum-Shopping in England: Is Provimi Ltd v Aventis correct?', *CPI Antitrust Journal*, 2 (2010), 1, 5–6.

[16] The Foreign Trade Antitrust Improvements Act, 15 USCA §6a. For further discussion of international aspects of public and private enforcement of the application of the single entity doctrine to international corporate groups, see: E. Bouton, 'The Single Economic Unit Doctrine under EU Competition Law: Application and Consequences for the Scope and Enforcement of the Substantive Rules of Competition Law', unpublished LL.M. dissertation, University of Glasgow (2016).

[17] The most-cited study is J. Azar, M. Schmalz and I. Tecu, 'Anti-Competitive Effects of Common Ownership', *Journal of Finance*, 73(4) (2018).

[18] M. Vestager, 'Refining the EU Merger Control System' Speech, *Studienvereinigung Kartellrecht*, Brussels, 10 March 2016.

such prohibition in Europe, apart from in Italy where such links are prohibited in the banking and insurance industries.[19] Assessment of structural links involved two questions: What are the competitive effects of structural links, by which companies are tied both by a market and a corporate relationship? Is competition law equipped to address such possible anticompetitive effects? Competitive effects were assessed in terms of incentives and ability. This book has demonstrated that a closer look at corporate rights informs on the scope of anticompetitive effects, and whether there are rules that may mitigate those effects. As explained in Chapter 5, one central aspect of the debate in the United States is whether institutional investors have the ability to achieve a restriction of competition, and what the channels of influence may be.[20] In addition, one of the main issues featuring the emblematic *Ryanair* case was the presence of 'unwelcome shareholders'. The German example shows that legal constraints on information rights may, at least partially, address the risk of collusion between the acquirer and the target.[21] In the area of interlocking directorates, fiduciary duty may prevent a director from sharing sensitive information between companies on the boards of which he or she sits. However, a conflict of interest may arise for a director sitting on the boards of two competitors. In that respect, interlocking directorates could undermine both the rivalry between companies and the independence and loyalty of the director to their companies.

Legal constraints provided by corporate law do not bridge the regulatory gap that exists at the EU level. General principles of corporate governance, such as independence of decision-making, have a limited ability to address competitive concerns, even when they closely relate to common issues. Therefore, this book has explained that addressing the enforcement gap in the EU implies greater scrutiny of the internal dimension of companies. An EU-wide response to cover structural links may step in to bridge a gap that national corporate governance systems have so far failed to address. A comprehensive impact assessment of the extent of such issues in Europe should form part of any proposal for reform, and would supplement the identification of theoretical concerns provided in this book.[22]

---

[19] United States: s. 8 of the Clayton Act, 15 USC §19; Italy: Art. 36 of Decree Law No 201 of 6 December 2011, converted into Law No 214/2011: 'Protection of competition and personal cross-shareholdings in credit and financial markets.'

[20] See Section 5.3.1.1.2.

[21] J. P. Schmidt, 'Germany: merger control analysis of minority shareholdings – A model for the EU?', *Revue Concurrences*, 2-2013 (2013), 207. In the case of Germany, corporate rules did not entirely address anticompetitive concerns.

[22] Such a study is currently being carried out by the author in a collaborative empirical project. See preliminary results: I. Allemand, B. Brullebaut, E. Prinz and F. Thépot, 'Structure et évolution des réseaux d'administrateurs', Conférence internationale de gouvernance, 15–16 May 2017, Lausanne, Switzerland.

9.5 EPILOGUE

A conception of the firm, and of its boundaries, has been developed throughout this book, providing a framework for discussing some of the most important contemporary issues of competition law. This book validates the necessity for competition law to draw the boundaries of the firm, when it establishes its substantive reach; but the boundaries need adjustment to the reality of the modern economy. Reliance on economic relationships, rather than on legal concepts, should not be confined to the definition of an undertaking or a single entity. Economic relationships within the firm, or at the interface of the firm and the market, are also of paramount importance in competition law analysis. In that respect, the firm should not be a 'black box' to competition law. It should be understood as a nexus of agency relationships in which the allocation of ownership and control produces incentives with effects that matter both for competition law and for corporate governance.

This book has delivered a reflection on the goals of the firm, in examining whether competition law objectives could possibly be attached to that of maximising the firm's value. Objectives of firm performance and competitive markets may naturally conflict, from a theoretical perspective. However, considering firms as actors within a broader business and legal environment, this book has shown the existence of significant synergies between mechanisms and goals of competition law and corporate governance. This book has thus suggested that board members also need to take into account, in respect of their core duties, the long-term consequences of their decisions with regard to this broader environment, which encompasses the interests of the company's employees, suppliers and customers.[23] This may feed into an important body of literature in which constituents other than shareholders ought to shape business decision-making. As such, conclusions reached in this book may also enrich the argument developed in the corporate social responsibility scholarship.[24]

---

[23] This conclusion may be even more valid when taking a non-contractarian approach to corporate governance (which emphasises the need for the firm to pursue broader social objectives than just economic performance).

[24] See, e.g., C. Malecki, *Corporate Social Responsibility, Perspectives for Sustainable Corporate Governance* (Edward Elgar Publishing, 2018).

Bibliography

Abrantes-Metz, R. M., Bajari, P. and Murphy, J., 'Enhancing Compliance Programs Through Antitrust Screening', *The Antitrust Counselor*, 45 (2010), 4

AFEP-MEDEF, 'Code of Corporate Governance of Listed Corporations'

AFG, 'Recommandations sur le Gouvernement D'entreprise' (2018), 19, available at: www.afg .asso.fr/wp-content/uploads/2017/01/Recommandations_sur_le_gouvernement _d_entreprise_2018.pdf

Aghion, P. and Schankerman, M., 'On the Welfare Effects and Political Economy of Competition-Enhancing Policies', *The Economic Journal*,114 (2007), 800

Aguzzoni, L., Langus, G. and Motta, M., 'The Effect of EU Antitrust Investigations and Fines on a Firm's Valuation', *Journal of Industrial Economics*, 61 (2013), 290

Akaman, P., 'A Competitive Assessment of Platform Most-Favoured-Customer Clauses', *Journal of Competition Law & Economics*, 12(4) (2016), 781

Akman, P. and Kassim, H., 'Myths and Myth-Making in the European Union: The Institutionalization and Interpretation of EU Competition Policy', *Journal of Common Market Studies*, 48 (2010), 111

Akerlof, G., 'The Market for "Lemons": Quality Uncertainty and the Market Mechanism', *Quarterly Journal of Economics*, 84 (1970), 488

Alchian, A. A. and Demsetz, H., 'Production, Information Costs, and Economic Organization', *American Economic Review*, 62 (1972), 777

Alexander, C. R. and Cohen, M. A., 'Why Do Corporations Become Criminals? Ownership, Hidden Actions, and Crime as an Agency Cost', *Journal of Corporate Finance*, 5 (1999), 1

Allemand, I., Brullebaut, B., Prinz, E. and Thépot, F., 'Structure et évolution des réseaux d'administrateurs' Conférence internationale de gouvernance, 15–16 May 2017, Lausanne, Switzerland

Allen, F. and Gale, D., 'Corporate Governance and Competition' in X. Vives (ed.), *Corporate Governance, Theoretical and Empirical* (Cambridge University Press, 2000), p. 23

Allianz Global Corporate & Specialty, 'Introduction to D&O Insurance, Risk Briefing', 2010, available at: www.agcs.allianz.com/assets/PDFs/risk%20insights/AGCS-DO-infopa per.pdf

American Bar Association Section of Antitrust Law, *Antitrust Compliance: Perspectives and Resources for Corporate Counselors*, 2nd edn (ABA Publishing, 2005)

American Bar Association Section of Antitrust Law, *Interlocking Directorates: Handbook on Section 8 of the Clayton Act* (ABA Publishing, 2011)

Andreangeli, A., 'Between Economic Freedom and Effective Competition Enforcement: the Impact of the Antitrust Remedies Provided by the Modernisation Regulation on Investigated Parties' Freedom to Contract and to Enjoy Property', *Competition Law Review*, 6 (2010), 225

Angelucci, C. and Han, M. A., 'Monitoring Managers Through Corporate Compliance Programs', Amsterdam Center for Law & Economics, Working Paper No 2010–14 (2010)

Areeda, P. E. and Hovenkamp, H., *Antitrust Law, An Analysis of Antitrust Principles and Their Application*, 3rd edn (Aspen, 2006)

Arlen, J., 'The Failure of the Organizational Sentencing Guidelines', *University of Miami Law Review*, 66 (2012), 321

Arlen, J., 'The Potentially Perverse Effects of Corporate Criminal Liability', *Journal of Legal Studies*, 23 (1994), 833

Arlen, J. and Kraakman, R., 'Controlling Corporate Misconduct: An Analysis of Corporate Liability Regimes', *New York University Law Review*, 72 (1997), 687

Aubert, C., 'Managerial Effort Incentives and Market Collusion', Toulouse School of Economics, Working Paper No 09–127 (2009)

Aubert, C., Rey, P. and Kovacic, W. E., 'The Impact of Leniency and Whistleblowing Programs on Cartels', *International Journal of Industrial Organization*, 24 (2006), 1241

Ayres, I. and Braithwaite, J., *Responsive Regulation* (Oxford University Press, 1992)

Azar, J., Raina, S. and Schmalz, M., 'Ultimate Ownership and Bank Competition' (2016), available at: https://papers.ssrn.com/sol3/papers.cfm?abstract_id=2710252

Azar, J., Schmalz, M. and Tecu, I., 'Anti-Competitive Effects of Common Ownership', *Journal of Finance*, 73(4), (2018), 1513

Bagley, C. E., *Winning Legally: How to Use the Law to Create Value, Marshal Resources, and Manage Risk* (Harvard Business School Press, 2005)

Bagley, C. E., 'Winning Legally: The Value of Legal Astuteness', *Academy of Management Review*, 33 (2008), 378

Baily, M. and Gersbach, H., 'Efficiency in Manufacturing and the Need for Global Competition' in M. Baily (ed.), *Brookings Papers on Economic Activity: Microeconomics* (Brookings, 1995)

Baker, J., 'Overlapping Financial Investor Ownership, Market Power, and Antitrust Enforcement: My Qualified Agreement with Professor Elhauge', *Harvard Law Review Forum*, 129 (2016), 212

Baker, J. B., 'My Summer Vacation at the Commission', *The Antitrust Source* (2005)

Baker McKenzie, 'Conducting an Effective Global Antitrust/Competition Risk Assessment' (2013)

Baldwin, R., Cave, M. and Lodge, M., *Understanding Regulation: Theory, Strategy, and Practice*, 2nd edn (Oxford University Press, 2012)

Barboza, D., 'Tearing Down the Facade of "Vitamins Inc."', *New York Times* (1999)

Bardong, A., 'The "German Experience" in Merger Control and Minority Shareholdings: Time for a Change?', *Revue Concurrences*, 3 (2011), 14

Beal, K., 'The Sins of the Son or Daughter', *Competition Bulletin* (2013), available at: https://competitionbulletin.com/2013/05/19/the-sins-of-the-son-or-daughter/

Becker, G. S., 'Crime and Punishment: An Economic Approach', *Journal of Political Economy*, (1968), 76

Benham, A. and Benham, L., 'The Costs of Exchange' in P. G. Klein and M. E. Sykuta (eds.), *The Elgar Companion to Transaction Cost Economics* (Edward Elgar, 2010), 367

Bennett, G. and Domineck, B., 'Hungary', *The European Antitrust Review* (2013)

Bennett, M., 'Online Platforms: Retailers, Genuine Agents or None of the Above?' *Competition Policy International* (2013)

Bergman, H. and Sokol, D. D., 'The Air Cargo Cartel: Lessons for Compliance' in C. Beaton-Wells and C. Tran (eds.), *Anti-Cartel Enforcement in a Contemporary Age: The Leniency Religion* (Hart Publishing, 2015)

Berle A. A., 'The Theory of Enterprise Entity', *Columbia Law Review*, 47(3) (1947), 343

Berle, A. A. and Means, G. C., *The Modern Corporation and Private Property*, 2nd edn, (Harcourt, Brace and World, 1967)

E. Bernard, 'L'"activité économique", un critère d'applicabilité du droit de la concurrence rebelle à la conceptualisation', *Revue Internationale de Droit économique* [2009] 353.

Best in Procurement, *Das Magazin für Manager, im Einkauf und Logistik*, 'Kartell Prävention im Einkauf' (2013)

Bishop, J., 'Sitting Ducks and Decoy Ducks: New Trends in the Indemnification of Corporate Directors and Officers', *Yale Law Journal*, 77 (1968), 1

Blumberg, P. I., 'Limited Liability in Corporate Groups', *Journal of Corporation Law*, 11 (1985–86), 574

Blumberg, P. I., 'The Transformation of Modern Corporation Law: The Law of Corporate Groups', *Connecticut Law Review*, 37 (2005), 605

Bork, F. A., Koktvedgaard, O. and Zinck, S., *Cartel Regulation (Getting the Deal Through)* (online) (2017)

Bouton, E., 'The Single Economic Unit Doctrine Under EU Competition Law: Application and Consequences for the Scope and Enforcement of the Substantive Rules of Competition Law', unpublished LLM dissertation, University of Glasgow (2016)

Brandeis, L. D., *Other People's Money and How Bankers Use It* (Seven Treasures Publications, 1914)

Brander, J. A. and Lewis, T. R., 'Oligopoly and Financial Structure: The Limited Liability Effect', *American Economic Review*, 76 (1986), 956

Bronckers, M. and Vallery, A., 'No Longer Presumed Guilty? The Impact of Fundamental Rights on Certain Dogmas of EU Competition Law', *World Competition*, 34 (2011), 535

Bryant, P. G. and Eckard, E. W., 'Price Fixing: The Probability of Getting Caught', *Review of Economics and Statistics*, 73 (1991), 531

Buccirossi, P., and Spagnolo, G., 'Corporate Governance and Collusive Behavior', in W. D. Collins (eds.), Issues in Competition Law and Policy 1 (American Bar Association, 2008)

Buch-Hansen, H., 'Interlocking Directorates and Collusion: An Empirical Analysis', *International Sociology*, 29 (2014), 253

Buhart, J. and Lesur, L., 'Minority Shareholders and Competition: Is a European Reform Necessary?', *Revue Concurrences*, 4 (2013), 1

Burden, S. and Townsend, J., 'Whose Fault Is It Anyway? Undertakings and the Imputation of Liability', *Competition Law Journal*, 3 (2013), 294

Burnside, A. J., 'Minority Shareholdings Minority Shareholdings: An Overview of EU and National Case Law', e-Competitions N° 56676 (2013)

Burt, R. S., *Corporate Profits and Cooptation* (Academic, 1983)

Calderón Cuadrado, R. and Alvarez Arce, J. L., 'The Complexity of Corruption: Nature and Ethical Suggestions', Working Paper 05/06, Facultad de Ciencias Económicas y Empresariales Universidad de Navarra

Caronna, F., 'Article 81 as a Tool for Controlling Minority Cross Shareholdings Between Competitors', *European Law Review*, 29 (2004) 485

Cauffman, C., 'The Interaction of Leniency Programmes and Actions for Damages', *Competition Law Review*, 7 (2011), 181

Cheng, T. K., 'The Corporate Veil Doctrine Revisited: A Comparative Study of the English and the US Corporate Veil Doctrines', *Boston College International and Comparative Law Review*, 34 (2011), 329

Cherry, T. L., 'Financial Penalties as an Alternative Criminal Sanction: Evidence from Panel Data', *Atlantic Economic Journal*, 29 (2001), 450

Chu, C. Y. and Yingyi, Q., 'Vicarious Liability under a Negligence Rule', *International Review of Law and Economics*, 15 (1995), 305

Coase, R. H., 'The Nature of the Firm', *Economica*, 4 (1937), 386

Coase, R. H., 'The Problem of Social Cost', *Journal of Law and Economics*, 3 (1960), 1

Coffee, J. C., 'New Myths and Old Realities: The American Law Institute Faces the Derivative Action', *Business Lawyer*, 48 (1993), 1407

Coglianese, C. and Lazer, D., 'Management-Based Regulation: Prescribing Private Management to Achieve Public Goals', *Law & Society Review*, 37 (2003), 691

Combe, E., Monnier, C. and Legal, R., 'Cartels: The Probability of Getting Caught in the European Union', Bruges European Economic Research Papers (2008), 2

Comment, 'Combinations in Restraint of Trade: A New Approach to Section 1 of the Sherman Act', Utah Law Review (1966), 75

Competition and Markets Authority, Press Release, 'CMA Secures Director Disqualification for Competition Law Breach' (2016)

Competition and Markets Authority, Press Release, 'Director Sentenced to 6 months for Criminal Cartel' (14 September 2015)

Competition and Markets Authority, Press Release, 'Estate Agent Cartel Directors Disqualified' (2018)

Competition and Markets Authority, Press Release, 'Supply of Precast Concrete Drainage Products: Criminal Investigation' (15 September 2017)

Competition and Markets Authority, 'Rewards for Information About Cartels', available at: www.gov.uk/government/publications/cartels-informant-rewards-policy

Competition and Markets Authority, 'Stop Unfair Cartels', available at: https://stopcartels.cam paign.gov.uk/?utm_source=referral&utm_medium=press-release&utm_campaign =Cartels_2018&utm_content=CMA-release

Competition Commission of Pakistan, 'Revised Guidelines on "Reward Payment to Informants Scheme"', cl3, available at: www.cc.gov.pk/images/Downloads/guidlines/reward_paymentan nexure_ii.pdf

Connor, J. M., 'Cartel Detection and Duration Worldwide', *CPI Antitrust Chronicle*, 2 (2011), 2

Connor, J. M., *Global Price Fixing (Studies in Industrial Organization)*, 2nd edn (Springer, 2008)

Connor, J. M., 'Private International Cartels Full Data', 2012-4-13 2012-1 edn, Purdue University Research Repository (2012), available at: https://purr.purdue.edu/publications /2732/1

Connor, J. M., 'Recidivism Revealed: Private International Cartels 1990–2009', *Competition Policy International*, 6 (2012) 101

Connor, J. M. and Helmers, G., 'Statistics on Modern Private International Cartels', Working Paper 07–01: American Antitrust Institute (2007)

Conyon, M. J. and Mallin, C. A., 'Directors' Share Options, Performance Criteria and Disclosure: Compliance with the Greenbury Report', ICAEW research monograph (1997) in C. A. Mallin, *Corporate Governance*, 3rd edn (Oxford University Press, 2010)

Cooter, R. D. and Siegel, N. S., 'Collective Action Federalism: A General Theory of Article I, Section 8', *Stanford Law Review*, 63 (2010), 115

Corradi, M. C. and Tzanaki, A., 'Active and Passive Institutional Investors and New Antitrust Challenges: Is EU Competition Law Ready?', *CPI Antitrust Chronicle*, 3(1) (2017)

Cosset, J. C., Somé, H. Y. and Valéry, P., 'Does Competition Matter for Corporate Governance? The Role of Country Characteristics', *Journal of Financial and Quantitative Analysis*, 51 (2016), 1231

Crane, D. A., 'Why Leniency Does Not Undermine Compensation' in C. Beaton-Wells and C. Tran (eds.), *Anti-Cartel Enforcement in a Contemporary Age: The Leniency Religion* (Hart Publishing, 2015), p. 263

Crotty, J., *Capitalism, Macroeconomics and Reality: Understanding Globalization, Financialization, Competition and Crisis* (Edward Elgar, 2017)

Cseres, K. J., Schinkel, M. P. and Vogelaar, F. O. W. (eds.), *Remedies and Sanctions in Competition Policy: Economic and Legal Implications of the Tendency to Criminalize Antitrust Enforcement in the EU Member States* (Edward Elgar, 2006)

Dahlman, C. J., 'The Problem of Externality', *Journal of Law and Economics*, 22 (1979), 141

Davis, M. L., 'The Impact of Rules Allocating Legal Responsibilities Between Principals and Agents', *Managerial and Decision Economics*, (1996) 17, 413

De Geest, G., *Encyclopedia of Law and Economics* (Edward Elgar, 2000)

Demsetz, H., 'The Theory of the Firm Revisited', *Journal of Law, Economics & Organization*, 4 (1988), 141

Deutsche Bahn, 'Code of Conduct', available at: www.deutschebahn.com/en/group /compliance/geschaeftspartner/verhaltenskodex-1212586

Deutsche Welle, 'ThyssenKrupp to face fiery shareholders' meeting' (17 January 2013)

DG Competition, 'Anonymous Whistleblower Tool', available at: http://ec.europa.eu/compe tition/cartels/whistleblower/index.html

Department of Justice, Press Release 'Former Chairmen of Sotheby's and Christie's Auction Houses Indicted in International Price-Fixing Conspiracy' (2001)

Department of Justice, 'The False Claims Act: A Primer' (2011), available at: www.justice.gov /civil/docs_forms/C-FRAUDS_FCA_Primer.pdf

Department of Justice, 'Tullett Prebon and ICAP Restructure Transaction after Justice Department Expresses Concerns About Interlocking Directorates' (2016), available at: www.justice.gov/opa/pr/tullett-prebon-and-icap-restructure-transaction-after-justice-depart ment-expresses-concerns

Department of Justice Antitrust Division, 'Criminal Enforcement Trend Charts' (2017), available at: www.justice.gov/atr/criminal-enforcement-fine-and-jail-charts

Douma, S. and Schreuder, H., *Economic Approaches to Organizations*, 6th edn (Pearson Education, 2017)

Drago, C., Millo, F., Ricciuti, R. and Santella, P., 'Corporate Governance Reforms, Interlocking Directorship Networks and Company Value in Italy (1998–2007)', CESIfo Working Paper (2011)

Driguez, L., *Droit Social et Droit de la Concurrence* (Bruylant, 2006)

Dubrow, J. B., 'Challenging the Economic Incentives Analysis of Competitive Effects in Acquisitions of Passive Minority Equity Interests', *Antitrust Law Journal*, 69 (2001), 131

Easterbrook, F. H., 'The Limits of Antitrust', *Texas Law Review*, 63 (1984), 1

Easterbrook, F. H. and Fischel, D. R., 'Limited Liability and the Corporation', *University of Chicago Law Review*, 52 (1985), 89

Eichenwald, K., 'U.S. Wins a Round against Cartel', *New York Times* (30 January 1997)

Elhauge, E., 'Essay: Horizontal Shareholding', *Harvard Law Review*, 129 (2016), 1267

Enriques, L. and Volpin, P., 'Corporate Governance Reforms in Continental Europe', *Journal of Economic Perspectives*, 21 (2007), 117

EU Commission, 'Authorities in EU Member States Which Operate a Leniency Programme', available at: http://ec.europa.eu/competition/ecn/leniency_programme_nca.pdf

EU Commission, 'Cartel Statistics' (2017), available at: http://ec.europa.eu/competition/cartels/statistics/statistics.pdf

EU Commission, 'Statistics on Fines Imposed by the Commission Between 1990 and 2017' (2017), available at: http://ec.europa.eu/competition/cartels/statistics/statistics.pdf

Ezrachi, A. and Gilo, D., 'EC Competition Law and Regulation of Passive Investments Among Competitors', *Oxford Journal of Legal Studies*, 26 (2006), 327

Ezrachi, A. and Stucke, M., *Virtual Competition* (Harvard University Press, 2016)

Falce, V., 'Interlocking Directorates: An Italian Antitrust Dilemma', *Journal of Competition Law and Economics*, 9 (2013), 457

Fama, E., 'Agency Problems and the Theory of the Firm', *Journal of Political Economy*, 88 (1980), 288

Fama, E. and Jensen, M. C., 'Agency Problems and Residual Claims', *Journal of Law and Economics*, 26 (1983), 327

Faulkner, R. R., Cheney, E. R., Fisher, G. A. and Baker, W. E., 'Crime by Committee: Conspirators and Company Men in the Illegal Electrical Industry Cartel, 1954–1959', *Criminology*, 41 (2003), 511

Federal Trade Commission, 'Red Ventures Holds and Bankrate', N°1710196 (2018), available at: www.ftc.gov/enforcement/cases-proceedings/file-no-1710196/red-ventures-holdco-bankrate

Federal Trade Commission, 'Statement of FTC Chairman Jon Leibowitz Regarding the Announcement that Arthur D. Levinson Has Resigned from Google's Board' (2009), available at: www.ftc.gov/news-events/press-releases/2009/10/statement-ftc-chairman-jon-leibowitz-regarding-announcement

Federal Trade Commission, 'Third Point Funds Agree to Settle FTC Charges that They Violated U.S. Pre-merger Notification Requirements' (2015), available at https://perma.cc/F9HZ-S8YP

Ferraro, F., Schnyder, G., Heemskerk, E. M., Corrado, R. and Del Vecchio, N., 'Structural Breaks and Governance Networks in Western Europe' in B. Kogut (ed.), *The Small Worlds of Corporate Governance* (MIT Press, 2012), p. 151

Fich, E. M. and White, L. J., 'CEO Compensation and Turnover: The Effects of Mutually Interlocked Boards', *Wake Forest Law Review*, 38 (2003), 935

Fich, E. M. and White, L. J., 'Why Do CEOs Reciprocally Sit on Each Other's Boards?', *Journal of Corporate Finance*, 11 (2005) 175

Fichtner, J., Heemskerk, E. and Garcia-Bernardo, J., 'Hidden Power of the Big Three? Passive Index Funds, Re-concentration of Corporate Ownership, and New Financial Risk', *Business and Politics*, 19(2) (2017), 298

Financial Times, 'BA Sales Chief on Price-Fixing Charge to Join Board' (28 November 2008)

Fisse, B., 'Reconditioning Corporate Leniency: The Possibility of Making Compliance Programmes a Condition of Immunity' in C. Beaton-Wells and C. Tran (eds.), *Anti-Cartel Enforcement in a Contemporary Age: The Leniency Religion* (Hart Publishing, 2015), ch.10

Fisse, B. and Braithwaite, J., *Corporations, Crime and Accountability* (Cambridge University Press, 2010)

Flochel, L., 'The Competitive Effects of Acquiring Minority Shareholdings', *Revue Concurrences*, 1–2012 (2012)

Fox, E. M., 'Monopolization and Abuse of Dominance: Why Europe Is Different', *Antitrust Bulletin* 59 (2014), 129

Freedman, C. E., 'Cartels and the Law in France Before 1914', *French Historical Studies*, 15 (1988), 462

Furubotn, E. G. and Richter, R. (eds.), *Institutions & Economic Theory, The Contribution of New Institutional Economics*, 2nd edn (University of Michigan Press, 2005)

Galloway, J., 'Securing the Legitimacy of Individual Sanctions in UK Competition Law', *World Competition*, 40(1) (2016), 121

Garner, J., 'Ethics and Law' in J. Skorupski (ed.), *The Routledge Companion to Ethics* (Routledge, 2010)

Gavil, A. I., 'Copperweld 2000: The Vanishing Gap Between Sections 1 and 2 of the Sherman Act', *Antitrust Law Journal*, 68 (2000), 87

Gavil, A. I., Kovacic, W. E. and Baker, J. B., *Antitrust Law in Perspective: Cases, Concepts and Problems in Competition Policy*, 2nd edn (Thomson West, 2008)

Geis, G., *White-Collar Criminal: The Offender in Business and the Professions* (Alberton Press, 2006)

Geradin, D., 'Antitrust Compliance Programmes & Optimal Antitrust Enforcement: A Reply to Wouter Wils', *Journal of Antitrust Enforcement*, 1 (2013), 325

Gerber, B. M., 'Enabling Interlock Benefits While Preventing Anticompetitive Harm: Toward an Optimal Definition of Competitors Under Section 8 of the Clayton Act', *Yale Journal on Regulation*, 24 (2007), 107

Gertner, M., 'Why Do Shareholder Derivative Suits Remain Rare in Continental Europe?', *Brooklyn Journal of International Law*, 37 (2013), 843

Ghezzi, F., 'Interlocking Directorates in the Financial Sector: The Italian Job (Art. 36 Law 214/2011) – An Antitrust Perspective', Università Bocconi (2012)

Gilo, D., 'The Anticompetitive Effect of Passive Investment', *Michigan Law Review*, 99 (2000), 1

Gilo, D., Moshe, Y. and Spiegel, Y., 'Partial Cross Ownership and Tacit Collusion', *RAND Journal of Economics*, 37 (2006), 81

Ginsburg, D. H., 'Are Administrative Fines the Best Way to Deter Infringements?', Deterring EU Competition Law Infringements: Are We Using the Right Sanctions?, Conference by TILEC and the Liege Competition & Innovation, 3 December 2012, Brussels

Ginsburg, D. H. and Wright, J. D., 'Antitrust Sanctions', *Competition Policy International*, 6 (2010), 3

Goffinet, P. and Puel, F., 'Vertical Relationships: The Impact of the Internet on the Qualification of Agency Agreements', *Journal of European Competition Law & Practice*, 6(4) (2015), 242

González, T. A. and Schmid, M. 'Corporate Governance and Antitrust Behavior', Swiss Institute of Banking and Finance, University of St. Gallen Working Paper 5 (2012)

González, T. A., Schmid, M. and Yermack, D., 'Does Price Fixing Benefit Corporate Managers?', NYU Working Paper No FIN-13–002 (2017)

Götz, G. Herold, D. and Paha, J., 'Germany, Austria and Switzerland on How to Prevent Violations of Competition Laws' in J. Paha (ed.), *Competition Law Compliance Programmes – An Interdisciplinary Approach* (Springer, 2016), p. 37

Graafland, J. J., 'Collusion, Reputation Damage and Interest in Code of Conduct: The Case of a Dutch Construction Company', *Business Ethics: A European Review*, 2 (2004), 127

Grechenic, K. and Sekyra, M. 'No Derivative Shareholder Suits in Europe – A Model of Percentage Limits and Collusion', *International Review of Law and Economics*, 31 (2011), 16

Griffin, J. M., Department of Justice, 'An Inside Look at a Cartel at Work: Common Characteristics of International Cartels', ABA Section of Antitrust Law, 48th Annual Spring Meeting (2000)

Grossman, S. J. and Hart, O. D., 'The Costs and Benefits of Ownership: A Theory of Vertical and Lateral Integration', *Journal of Political Economy*, 98 (1986), 691

Grow, N., '*American Needle* and the Future of the Single Entity Defense Under Section One of the Sherman Act', *American Business Law Journal*, 48 (2011), 449

Guttuso, L., 'Leniency and the Two Faces of Janus: Where Public and Private Enforcement Merge and Converge' in C. Beaton-Wells and C. Tran (eds.), *Anti-Cartel Enforcement in a Contemporary Age: The Leniency Religion* (Hart Publishing, 2015), p. 273

Hammond, S. D., 'Cornerstones of an Effective Leniency Program', speech delivered to ICN Workshop on Leniency Programs, Sydney (22–23 November 2004)

Han, M. A., Vertical Relations in Cartel Theory (Amsterdam Center for Law & Economics, 2011)

Harding, C., 'The Anti-Cartel Enforcement Industry: Criminological Perspectives on Cartel Criminalisation' in C. Beaton-Wells and A. Ezrachi (eds.), *Criminalising Cartels: A Critical Interdisciplinary Study of an International Regulatory Movement* (Hart Publishing, 2011), ch. 16

Harding, C., Beaton Wells, C. and Edwards, J., 'Leniency and Criminal Sanctions in Anti-Cartel Enforcement: Happily Married or Uneasy Bedfellows?' in C. Beaton-Wells and C. Tran (eds.), *Anti-Cartel Enforcement in a Contemporary Age: The Leniency Religion* (Hart Publishing, 2015), ch. 12

Harringon, J. E., 'How Do Cartels Operate?', *Foundations and Trends in Microeconomics*, 2 (2006), 1

Harrington, J. E., 'Optimal Deterrence of Competition Law Infringement', Deterring EU Competition Law Infringements: Are We Using the Right Sanctions?, Conference by TILEC and the Liege Competition & Innovation, 3 December 2012, Brussels

Harrison, J. L., 'Dr Miles Orphans: Vertical Conspiracy and Consignment in the Wake of Leegin', *Wake Forest Law Review*, 45 (2010), 1125

Hart, O., 'An Economist's Perspective on the Theory of the Firm' in P. J. Buckley and J. Michie (eds.), *Firms, Organizations and Contracts: A Reader in Industrial Organization* (Oxford University Press, 1996), p. 199

Hart, O., *Firms, Contracts and Financial Structure* (Clarendon Press, 1995)

Hart, O., 'Incomplete Contracts and the Theory of the Firm', *Journal of Law, Economics, and Organization*, 4 (1988), 119

Hart, O., 'The Market Mechanism as an Incentive Scheme', *Bell Journal of Economics*, 2 (1983), 366

Hart, O. and Holmström, B., 'The Theory of Contracts' in T. Bewley (ed.), *Advances in Economic Theory: Fifth World Congress* (Cambridge University Press, 1987), p. 71

Hart, O. and Moore, J., 'Incomplete Contracts and Renegotiation', *Econometrica*, 56 (1988), 755

Hawk, B. E. and Huser, H. L., '"Controlling" the Shifting Sands: Minority Shareholdings Under EEC Competition Law', *Fordham International Law Journal*, 17 (1993), 321

Hayek, F., 'The Use of Knowledge in Society', *American Economic Review*, 35 (1945), 519

He, J. and Huang, J., 'Product Market Competition in a World of Cross-Ownership: Evidence from Institutional Blockholdings', *Review of Financial Studies*, 30(8) (2017), 2674

Heimler, A. and Mehta, K. 'Violations of Antitrust Provisions: The Optimal Level of Fines for Achieving Deterrence', *World Competition*, 35 (2012), 103

Hein, E., Detzer, D. and Dodig, N. (eds.), *Financialisation and the Financial and Economic Crises: Country Studies* (Edward Elgar, 2016)

Hernstein, R. J. and Wilson, J. Q., *Crime and Human Nature* (Simon and Schuster, 1985)

Herold, D., 'Compliance and Incentive Contracts' in J. Paha (ed.), *Competition Law Compliance Programmes – An Interdisciplinary Approach* (Springer, 2016)

Herold, D., 'The Impact of Incentive Pay on Corporate Crime', MAGKS Discussion Paper No 52–2017 (2017)

Holmström, B., 'Moral Hazard in Teams', *Bell Journal of Economics*, 13 (1982), 324

Holmström, B. and Tirole, J., 'The Theory of the Firm' in R. Schmalensee and R. D. Willig (eds.), *Handbook of Industrial Organization*, vol. 1 (North Holland, 1989), p. 61

Horn, H., Lang, H. and Lundgren, S., 'Competition, Long Run Contracts and Internal Inefficiencies in Firms', *European Economic Review*, 38 (1994), 213

Hovenkamp, H., 'American Needle: The Sherman Act, Conspiracy and Exclusion', *Competition Policy International Antitrust Journal* (2010), 1

Hovenkamp, H., *Enterprise and American Law, 1836–1937* (Harvard University Press, 1991)

Hovenkamp, H., *Federal Antitrust Policy: The Law of Competition and its Practice*, 5th edn (Thomson West, 2016)

Hovenkamp, H., 'Resale Price Maintenance: Consignment Agreements, Copyrighted or Patented Products and the First Sale Doctrine', University of Iowa Legal Studies Research Paper [2010]

Hovenkamp, H. and Leslie, C. R., 'The Firm as Cartel Manager', *Vanderbilt Law Review*, 64 (2011), 813

Hubert, P. and Schallenberg, K., 'Moving in the Right Direction, France is Taking Antitrust Compliance very Seriously', *Competition Law Insight* (2012), 18

Hughes, P., 'Competition Law Enforcement and Corporate Group Liability – Adjusting the Veil', *European Competition Law Review*, 35 (2014), 68

Hughes, P., 'Directors' Personal Liability for Cartel Activity under UK and EC Law – A Tangled Web', *European Competition Law Review*, 29 (2008), 632

Hughes, P. and Rodger, B., 'EU Competition Law and Private International Law: A Developing Relationship' in I. Lianos and D. Geradin (eds.), *Handbook on European Competition Law: Enforcement and Procedure* (Edward Elgar, 2013)

Ignjatovic, B. and Ridyard, D., 'Minority Shareholdings, Material Effects?', *Competition Policy International Antitrust Chronicle* (2012) 7

International Chamber of Commerce, 'Promoting Antitrust Compliance: The various approaches of national antitrust' (2011)

International Chamber of Commerce, 'The ICC Antitrust Compliance Toolkit, Practical Antitrust Compliance Tools for SMEs and Larger Companies' (2013)

International Comparative Legal Guides, 'Cartels and Leniency' (2018)

International Competition Network, *Anti-Cartel Enforcement Manual* (2011)

International Organization for Standardization, New Work Item Proposal – Compliance Programs (2012)

Januszewski, S., Koke, J. and Winter, J. K., 'Product Market Competition, Corporate Governance and Firm Performance: An Empirical Analysis for Germany', *Research in Economics*, 56 (2002), 299

Jensen, M. C., 'Agency Costs of Free Cash Flow, Corporate Finance, and Takeovers', *American Economic Review*, 76 (1986), 323

Jensen, M. C., 'Value Maximization, Stakeholder Theory, and the Corporate Objective Function', *Journal of Applied Corporate Finance*, 14 (2010), 8

Jensen, M. C. and Meckling, W. H., 'Theory of the Firm: Managerial Behavior, Agency Costs and Ownership Structure', *Journal of Financial Economics*, 3 (1976), 305

Jones, A., 'The Boundaries of an Undertaking in EU Competition Law', *European Competition Journal*, 8 (2012), 301

Jones, A. and Sufrin, B., *EU Competition Law: Text, Cases, and Materials*, 6th edn (Oxford University Press, 2016)

Jones, K. and Harrison, F., 'Criminal Sanctions: An Overview of EU and National Case Law', e-Competitions N° 64713 [2014]

Jones, T. M. and Keevil, A. A. C., '"Agents without Principals" Revisited: Theorizing the Effects of Increased Shareholder Participation in Corporate Governance' in M. Goranova and L. V. Ryan (eds.), *Shareholder Empowerment* (Palgrave Macmillan, 2015), 103

Joshua, J., Botteman, Y. and Atlee, L., '"You Can't Beat the Percentage" – The Parental Liability Presumption in EU Cartel Enforcement', *European Antitrust Review* (2012), 3

Kalbfleisch, P., 'Minority Shareholdings in Competing Companies', 'Merger Control and Minority Shareholdings: Time for a Change?', *Revue Concurrences*, 39–2011 (2011), 14

Kallifatides, M., Nachemson-Ekwall, S. and Sjoestrand, S. E., *Corporate Governance in Modern Financial Capitalism: Old Mutual's Hostile Takeover of Skandia* (Edward Elgar, 2010)

Kalss, S., 'Shareholder Suits: Common Problems, Different Solutions and First Steps Towards a Possible Harmonization by Means of a European Model Code', *European Company and Financial Law Review*, 2 (2009), 324

Karr, N., 'The OFT's Revised Director Disqualification Guidance: Deterring Directors or Competition Law Breaches?', Linklaters (2010)

Kass, C., 'Holding Parents Liable For Antitrust Violations – Differences in US And EU Corporate Governance', *The Metropolitan Corporate Counsel* (2010), 38

Katz, M. L., 'Vertical Contractual Relations' in R. Schmalensee and R. D. Willig (eds.), *Handbook of Industrial Organisation*, vol. 1 (North Holland, 1989), p. 655

Kennelly, B., 'Antitrust Forum-Shopping in England: Is Provimi Ltd v Aventis Correct?', *CPI Antitrust Journal*, 2 (2010) 1

Kershaw, D., *Company Law in Context: Text and Materials*, 2nd edn (Oxford University Press, 2012)

Kishoiyian, B. 'The Intra-Enterprise Conspiracy Doctrine in International Business: The Case for the Extraterritorial application of Antitrust Law', *Touro International Law Review*, 6 (1995) 191

Klahold, C., 'Importance and Challenges of Antitrust Compliance for Large Corporations', Deterring EU Competition Law Infringements: Are We Using the Right Sanctions?, Conference by TILEC and the Liege Competition & Innovation, 3 December 2012, Brussels

Klein, B., 'Single Entity Analysis of Joint Ventures After *American Needle*: An Economic Perspective', *Antitrust Law Journal*, 78 (2013), 669

Klein, B. and Lerner, A. V., 'The Firm in Economics and Antitrust Law' in W. D. Collins (ed.), *Issues in Competition Law and Policy*, vol. 1 (American Bar Association, 2008)

Klein, B., Crawford, R. G. and Alchian, A. A., 'Vertical Integration, Appropriable Rents, and the Competitive Contracting Process', *Journal of Law and Economics*, 21 (1978), 297

Klein, P. G., 'New Institutional Economics' in B. Bouckaert and G. De Geest (eds.), Encyclopedia of Law and Economics (Edward Elgar, 2000)

Koenig, C., 'An Economic Analysis of the Single Economic Entity Doctrine in the EU Competition Law', *Journal of Competition Law & Economics*, 13 (2017), 281

Kogut, B. and Walker, G., 'The Small World of Germany and the Durability of National Networks', *American Sociological Review*, 66 (2001), 317

Korea Federal Trade Commission, Annual Report (2017), available at: https://bit.ly /2wm2MZQ

Kornhauser, L., 'An Economic Analysis of the Choice Between Enterprise and Personal Liability for Accidents', *California Law Review*, 70 (1982), 1345

Kovacic, W. E., 'Competition Policy in the European Union and the United States: Convergence or Divergence in the Future Treatment of Dominant Firms?', *Competition Law International*, 4 (2008), 8

Kovacic, W. E., Mavroidis, P. C., and Neven, D. J., 'Merger Control Procedures and Institutions: A Comparison of the EU and US Practice', *Antitrust Bulletin*, 59 (2014), 55

Kraakman, R., 'Corporate Liability Strategies and the Costs of Legal Controls', *Yale Law Journal*, 93 (1984), 857

Krauss, J. G. and Cronheim, C. T., 'Partial Acquisitions After Dairy Farmers: Got Answers?', *Antitrust* magazine, ABA Section of Antitrust Law [2006], 49

Kühn, K. U., 'Fighting Collusion by Regulating Communication Between Firms', *Economic Policy*, 16 (2001), 167

Kühn, K. U. and Vives, X., *Information Exchanges Among Firms and their Impact on Competition* (Office for Official Publications of the European Communities, 1995)

La Porta, R., Lopez-de-Silanez, F., Shleifer, A. and Vishny, R. W. 'Law and Finance', *Journal of Political Economy*, 106 (1998), 1113

La Porta, R., Lopez-de-Silanez, F., Shleifer, A. and Vishny, R. W., 'Legal Determinants of External Finance', *Journal of Finance*, 52 (1997), 1131

LaCroix, K., 'Professional Liability Insurance: The Antitrust Exclusion Isn't Just About Antitrust Claims', The D&O Diary (2012)

Land, R. H. and Davis, J. P., 'Comparative Deterrence from Private Enforcement and Criminal Enforcement of the U.S. Antitrust Laws', *Brigham Young University Law Review* (2011), 315.

Leslie, C. R., 'Antitrust Amnesty, Game Theory, and Cartel Stability', *Journal of Corporation Law*, 31 (2006) 453

Leslie, C. R., 'Cartels, Agency Costs, and Finding Virtue in Faithless Agents', *William & Mary Law Review*, 49 (2008), 1621

Leslie, C. R., 'Trust, Distrust, and Antitrust', *Texas Law Review*, 82 (2004), 515

Letwin, W., 'Congress and the Sherman Antitrust Law: 1887–1890', *University of Chicago Law Review*, 23 (1956), 222

Leupold, B., 'Effective Enforcement of EU Competition Law Gone Too Far? Recent Case Law on the Presumption of Parental Liability', *European Competition Law Review*, 34 (2013), 570

Levenstein, M. C. and Suslow, V. Y., 'What Determines Cartel Success?', *Journal of Economic Literature*, 44 (2006), 43

Lianos, I., 'Commercial Agency Agreements, Vertical Restraints, and the Limits of Article 81 (1) EC: Between Hierarchies and Networks', *Journal of Competition Law & Economics*, 3 (2007), 625

Lianos, I., 'Competition Law Remedies in Europe' in I. Lianos and D. Geradin (eds.), *Handbook on European Competition Law: Enforcement and Procedure* (Edward Elgar, 2013), p. 362

Lianos I., 'Cross-border Damages Actions in the EU: Managing Inter-Jurisdictional Competition in the EU Mixed Enforcement System', CLES Research Paper series/2014 (2014)

Lianos, I., 'La Transformation du Droit de la Concurrence par le Recours à l'Analyse Economique' (Bruylant/Sakkoulas, 2007)

Lianos, I., Davis, P. and Nebbia, P., 'Cross-Border Damages Actions in the EU: Managing Inter-Jurisdictional Competition in the EU Mixed Enforcement System' in *Damages Claims for the Infringement of EU Competition Law* (Oxford University Press, 2015)

Longo, L. and Moretti, A., 'Chapter 10: Italy' in M. Holmes and L. Davey (eds.), *A Practical Guide to National Competition Rules Across Europe* (Kluwer Law International, 2007)

Macey, J. R., 'Agency Theory and the Criminal Liability of Organizations', *Boston University Law Review*, 71 (1991), 315

Macey, J. R. and Mitts, J., 'Finding Order in the Morass: The Three Real Justifications for Piercing the Corporate Veil', *Cornell Law Review*, 100 (2014), 99

Machlup, F., 'Theories of the Firm: Marginalist, Behavioral, Managerial', *American Economic Review*, 57 (1967), 1

Malecki, C., *Corporate Social Responsibility, Perspectives for Sustainable Corporate Governance* (Edward Elgar Publishing, 2018)

Mallin, C. A., Corporate Governance, 5th edn (Oxford University Press, 2014)

Malueg, D. A., 'Collusive Behavior and Partial Ownership of Rivals', *International Journal of Industrial Organization*, 10 (1992), 27

Manne, H. G., 'Mergers and the Market for Corporate Control', *Journal of Political Economy*, 73 (1965), 110

Marshall, R. C. and Marx, L. M., *The Economics of Collusion* (MIT Press, 2012)

Martin, S., 'Endogenous Firm Efficiency in a Cournot Principal-Agent Model', *Journal of Economic Theory*, 59 (1993), 445

Marvao, C. and Spagnolo, G., 'What Do We Know About the Effectiveness of Leniency Policies? A Survey of the Empirical and Experimental Evidence' in C. Beaton-Wells and C. Tran (eds.), *Anti-Cartel Enforcement in a Contemporary Age: The Leniency Religion* (Hart Publishing, 2015), p. 57

Mason, C., *The Art of the Steal* (GP Putnam & Sons, 2004)

Massey, P., 'Criminalization and Leniency: Will the Combination Favourably Affect Cartel Stability?' in K. J. Cseres, M. P. Schinkel and F. O. W. Vogelaar (eds.), *Remedies and Sanctions in Competition Policy: Economic and Legal Implications of the Tendency to Criminalize Antitrust Enforcement in the EU Member States* (Edward Elgar, 2006)

Matheson, J. H., 'The Modern Law of Corporate Groups: An Empirical Study of Piercing the Corporate Veil in the Parent-Subsidiary Context', *North Carolina Law Review*, 87 (2009), 1091

McCahery, J., Sautner, Z. and Starks, L., 'Behind the Scenes: The Corporate Governance Preferences of Institutional Investors', *Journal of Finance*, 71(6) (2016), 2905

Menard, C., 'The Economics of Hybrid Organizations', *Journal of Institutional and Theoretical Economics*, 160 (2004), 347

Menell, N. G., 'The Copperweld Question: Drawing the Line Between Corporate Family and Cartel', *Cornell Law Review*, 101 (2016), 467

Merlino, P., 'Edison: A Glimpse of Hope for Parent Companies Seeking to Rebut the Parental Liability Presumption?', *Journal of European Competition Law & Practice* (2014), 2

Meyers, R. P., 'Ownership of Subsidiaries, Unity of Purpose, and Antitrust Liability', *University of Chicago Law Review*, 68 (2001), 1401

Milgrom, P. and Roberts, J., *Economics, Organization and Management* (Prentice Hall, 1992)

Miller, S. R., Raven, M. E. and Went, D., 'Ownership Interest Acquisitions: New Developments in the European Union and United States', *Competition Policy International Antitrust Chronicle* [2012], 1

Mitić, A. and Rogl, M., 'The European Antitrust Review 2014: Slovenia', *Global Competition Review* (2014)

Mizruchi, M. S., 'What Do Interlocks Do? An Analysis, Critique, and Assessment of Research on Interlocking Directorates', *Annual Review of Sociology*, 22 (1996), 273

Moore, M. T., 'Private Ordering and Public Policy: The Paradoxical Foundations of Corporate Contractarianism', *Oxford Journal of Legal Studies*, 34(4) (2014), 693

Moore, M. T. and Walker-Arnott, E., 'A Fresh Look at Stock Market Short-Termism', *Journal of Law and Society*, 41 (2014), 416

Morfey, A. and Patton, C., 'Safeway Stores Ltd v Twigger: The Buck Stops Here', *Competition Law* (2011), 57

Motta, M., *Competition Policy, Theory and Practice* (Cambridge University Press, 2004)

Motta, M. and Langus, G., 'On the Effect of EU Cartel Investigations and Fines On the Infringing Firms' Market Value' in C. D. Ehlermann and I. Atanasiu (eds.), *European Competition Law Annual 2006: Enforcement of Prohibition of Cartels* (Hart Publishing, 2006)

Motta, M. and Polo, M., 'Leniency Programs and Cartel Prosecution', *International Journal of Industrial Organization*, 21 (2003), 347

Mullin, W. P. and Snyder, M., 'Should Firms be Allowed to Indemnify Their Employees for Sanctions?', *Journal of Law, Economics, and Organization*, 26 (2010), 30

Murphy, J. E., 'A Compliance & Ethics Program on a Dollar a Day: How Small Companies Can Have Effective Programs' (2010), available at: www.hcca-info.org/Portals/0/PDFs/Resources/ResourceOverview/CEProgramDollarADay-Murphy.pdf

Murphy, J. E., 'Making The Sentencing Guidelines Message Complete' Letter to the Department of Justice: Proposed Revision to the Sentencing Guidelines (2014), available at: http://antitrustconnect.com/2014/07/28/making-the-sentencing-guidelines-message-complete/

Murphy, J. E., 'The FTC and Antitrust Compliance Programs', *Compliance & Ethics Professional* (2012)

Murphy, J. E., 'Policies in Conflict: Undermining Corporate Self-Policing' Rutgers University Law Review, 69 (2017) 421

Murphy, J. E. and Boehme, D., 'Fear No Evil: A Compliance and Ethics Professionals' Response to Dr. Stephan' (2011), available at: http://papers.ssrn.com/sol3/papers.cfm?abstract_id=1965733

Nalebuff, B. J. and Stiglitz, J. E. 'Information, Competition, and Markets', *American Economic Review*, 73 (1983), 278

Nalebuff, B. J. and Stiglitz, J. E., 'Prices and Incentives: Towards a General Theory of Compensation and Competition', *Bell Journal of Economics*, 14 (1983), 21

Nelson, B., *Law and Ethics in Global Business: How to Integrate Law and Ethics into Corporate Governance Around the World* (Routledge, 2006)

Newbigging, E., 'Hoffmann-La Roche v Stanley Adams – *Corporate and Individual Ethics*', Cranfield University Working Paper (1986)

Newman, H. A. and Wright, D. W., 'Strict Liability in a Principal–Agent Model', *International Review of Law and Economics*, 10 (1990), 219

Nickell, S. J., 'Competition and Corporate Performance', *Journal of Political Economy*, (1996) 104–724

Nickell, S. J., Nickolitsas, D. and Dryden, N., 'What Makes Firms Perform Well?', *European Economic Review*, 41 (1997), 783

Nili, Y., 'The Corporate Governance of Sovereign Wealth Funds', available at: http://blogs .law.harvard.edu/corpgov/2014/08/07/the-corporate-governance-of-sovereign-wealth-funds/

Norton Rose Fulbright, 'Important Changes in Polish Competition Law' (2015)

O'Brien, D. and Waehrer, K., 'The Competitive Effects of Common Ownership: We Know Less than We Think', *Antitrust Law Journal*, 81(3) (2017) 729

Odudu, O., 'The Meaning of Undertaking Within 81 EC', *Cambridge Yearbook of European Legal Studies*, 7 (2005), 211

Okeoghene, O., 'Collective Dominance Clarified?', *Cambridge Law Journal*, 63(1) (2004), 44

Ono, H., 'Lifetime Employment in Japan: Concepts and Measurements', *Journal of the Japanese and International Economies*, 24 (2010), 1

Orbach, B. Y., 'The Antitrust Curse of Bigness', *Southern California Law Review*, 85 (2012), 605

Organisation for Economic Cooperation and Development, 'Algorithms and Collusion: Competition Policy in the Digital Age' (2017)

Organisation for Economic Cooperation and Development, 'Annual Report on Competition Policy Developments in Brazil', DAF/COMP (2010)

Organisation for Economic Cooperation and Development, 'Cartel Sanctions Against Individuals' (2003)

Organisation for Economic Cooperation and Development, 'Common Ownership by Institutional Investors and its Impact on Competition', DAF/COMP/WD (2017), 10

Organisation for Economic Cooperation and Development, 'Competition and Corporate Governance' (2010)

Organisation for Economic Cooperation and Development, Competition Committee, 'The Concept of Merger Transaction' (2013)

Organisation for Economic Cooperation and Development, Competition Committee, Working Party No. 3, Public Prosecutors Program (2005)

Organisation for Economic Cooperation and Development, 'Good Practice Guidance on Internal Controls, Ethics, and Compliance' (2010)

Organisation for Economic Cooperation and Development, Phase 3 Report on implementing the OECD Anti-bribery Convention in the Netherlands (2012)

Organisation for Economic Cooperation and Development, Policy Roundtable, Minority Shareholdings (2008)

Organisation for Economic Cooperation and Development, Policy Roundtable, Promoting Compliance with Competition Law (2011)

Organisation for Economic Cooperation and Development, 'Principles of Corporate Governance' (2004)

Organisation for Economic Cooperation and Development, Working Group on Bribery in International Business Transactions, Recommendation of the Council for Further Combating Bribery of Foreign Public Officials in International Business Transactions' (2009)

Ortiz Blanco, L., Givaja Sanz, A. and Lamadrid De Pablo, A., 'Fine Arts in Brussels: Punishment and Settlement of Cartel Cases under EC Competition Law' in H. Hirita, E. Raffaelli and E. Adriano (eds.), *Antitrust Between EC Law and National Law* (Bruyland Emile Etablissements, 2009)

Orts, E. W., *Business Persons: A Legal Theory of the Firm* (Oxford University Press, 2013)

Orts, E. W., 'Shirking and Sharking: A Legal Theory of the Firm', *Yale Law & Policy*, 16(2) (1997), 265

Pace, L. F. and Seidel, K., 'The Drafting and the Role of Regulation 17, a Hard-Fought Compromise' in K. K. Patel and H. Schweitzer (eds.), *The Historical Foundations of EU Competition Law* (Oxford University Press, 2013)

Paha, J., 'Antitrust Compliance: Managerial Incentives and Collusive Behavior', *Managerial and Decision Economics*, 38(7) (2017), 992

Parker, C., *The Open Corporation: Effective Self-Regulation and Democracy* (Cambridge University Press, 2002)

Patel, M. S., 'Common Ownership, Institutional Investors, and Antitrust', Antitrust Law Journal (2018)

Pauer, N. I., *The Single Economic Unit Doctrine and Corporate Group Responsibility in European Antitrust Law* (Kluwer Law International, 2014)

Pennings, J. M., *Interlocking Directorates: Origins and Consequences of Connections Among Organizations' Board of Directors* (Jossey-Bass Inc Pub, 1980)

Perrot, A., 'Minority Shareholdings: Is there a Need for Reform?', Law & Economics Workshop, Institute of Competition Law (15 October 2013)

Petersen, V., 'Interlocking Directorates in the European Union: An Argument for Their Restriction', *European Business Law Review*, 27(6) (2016), 821

Petersone, A., 'Managerial Compensation and Cartel Behavior' (2010), available at: http://dare .uva.nl/cgi/arno/show.cgi?fid=222247

Phillips, N. J., 'Taking Stock: Assessing Common Ownership' (1 June 2018), Remarks to the Global Antitrust Economics Conference

Pindyck, R. S. and Rubinfeld, D. L., *Microeconomics*, 9th edn (Pearson, 2017)

Pini, G. D., 'Passive–Aggressive Investments: Minority Shareholdings and Competition Law', *European Business Law Review*, 23 (2012), 575

Pinotti, V., Sforza, M. and di Castelnuovo, N., 'Italy Chapter – Cartels' in N. Parr and C. Hammon (eds.), *Cartels, Enforcement, Appeals & Damages Actions* (Global Legal Group, 2012)

Platis, I., 'Competition Law Implications of Minority Shareholdings: The EU and US Perspectives', *Hellenic Review of European Law* [2013], 181

Polinsky, A., Mitchell, A. and Shavell, S., 'Economic Analysis of Law', 2nd edn, *The New Palgrave Dictionary of Economics* (Harvard University, 2008)

Polinsky, A. M. and Shavell, S., 'Should Employees Be Subject to Fines and Imprisonment Given the Existence of Corporate Liability?', *International Review of Law and Economics*, 13 (1993), 239

Posner, E., Scott Morton, F. and Weyl, E. G., 'A Proposal to Limit the Anti-Competitive Power of Institutional Investors', *Antitrust Law Journal*, 81(3) (2017), 669

Posner, R. A., *Antitrust Law: An Economic Perspective* (University of Chicago Press, 1976)

Prinz, E., *Les effets des liens personnels interconseils sur la performance de l'entreprise: une analyse comparée entre France et Allemagne* (Peter Lang, 2011)

Privileggi, F., Marchese, C. and Cassone, A., 'Agent's Liability Versus Principal's Liability When Attitudes Toward Risk Differ', *International Review of Law and Economics*, 21 (2001), 181

Rahl, J. A., 'Conspiracy and the Antitrust Laws', *Illinois Law Review*, 44 (1950), 743

Raith, M., 'Competition, Risk and Managerial Incentives', *American Economic Review*, 93 (2003), 1425

Ramirez Pérez, S. M. and van de Scheur, S., 'The Evolution of the Law on Articles 85 and 86 EEC [Articles 101 and 102 TFEU], Ordoliberalism and its Keynesian Challenge' in K. K. Patel and H. Schweitzer (eds.), *The Historical Foundations of EU Competition Law* (Oxford University Press, 2013)

Reisberg, A., *Derivative Actions and Corporate Governance Theory and Operation* (Oxford University Press, 2007)

Rhee, R. J., 'Corporate Short-Termism and Intertemporal Choice', *Washington University Law Review*, 96 (2018), 2

Riley, A. and Bloom, M., 'Antitrust Compliance Programmes – Can Companies and Antitrust Agencies do More?', *Competition Law Journal* [2011], 21

Riley, A. and Sokol, D., 'Rethinking Compliance', *Journal of Antitrust Enforcement*, 3(1) (2015), 31

Roberts, J., *The Modern Firm, Organizational Design for Performance and Growth* (Oxford University Press, 2004)

Rock, E. B., 'Antitrust and the Market for Corporate Control', *California Law Review*, 77 (1989), 1365

Rock, E. B., 'Corporate Law Through an Antitrust Lens', *Columbia Law Review*, 92 (1992), 497

Rock, E. B. and Rubinfield, D., 'Antitrust for Institutional Investors', NYU Law and Economics Research Paper No 17–23

Romano, R., 'Directors' and Officers' Liability Insurance: What Went Wrong?', *Proceedings of the Academy of Political Science*, 37 (1988), 76

Romano, R., 'The Shareholder Suit: Litigation without Foundation?', *Journal of Law, Economics, and Organization*, 7 (1991), 55

Rosch, J. T., 'Terra Incognita: Vertical and Conglomerate Merger and Interlocking Directorate Law Enforcement in the United States', Remarks of Commissioner, Federal Trade Commission, before the University of Hong Kong (2009)

Rose-Ackerman, S., *Corruption and Government: Causes, Consequences, and Reform* (Cambridge University Press, 1999)

Ross, S. A., 'The Economic Theory of Agency: The Principal's Problem', *American Review*, 63 (1983), 134

Salop, S. C. and O' Brien, D. P., 'Competitive Effects of Partial Ownership: Financial Interest and Corporate Control', *Antitrust Law Journal*, 67 (2000), 268

Santella, P., Drago, C., Polo, A., and Gagliardi, E., 'A Comparison of the Director Networks of the Main Listed Companies in France, Germany, Italy, the United Kingdom, and the United States', Working Paper (2008)

Scharfstein, D. S., 'Product-Market Competition and Managerial Slack', *RAND Journal of Economics*, 19 (1988), 147

Schmidt, J., 'The Case for a European Competition Disqualification Order', *Zeitschrift für Wettbewerbsrecht*, 8 (2010), 391

Schmidt, J. P., 'Germany: Merger Control Analysis of Minority Shareholdings – A Model for the EU?', *Revue Concurrences*, 2–2013 (2013), 207

Schmidt, K. M., 'Managerial Incentives and Product Market Competition', *Review of Economic Studies*, 64 (1997), 191

Schmidt, V. A., 'Privatization in France: The Transformation of French Capitalism', *Environment and Planning C: Government and Policy*, (1999) 17, 445

Schroeder, D. and Heinz, S., 'Requests for Leniency in the EU: Experience and Legal Puzzle' in K. J. Cseres, M. P. Schinkel, F. O. W. Vogelaar (eds.), *Remedies and Sanctions in Competition Policy: Economic and Legal Implications of the Tendency to Criminalize Antitrust Enforcement in the EU Member States* (Edward Elgar, 2006)

Scott, P., 'Competition Law Briefing: *Safeway v Twigger* – Safeway's Claim Against Former Directors Reaches End of Shelf Life', Norton Rose Case Brief (2011)

Sergakis, K., 'EU Corporate Governance: The Ongoing Challenges of the "Institutional Investor Activism" Conundrum', *European Journal of Law Reform*, 4 (2014), 726

Shavell, S., 'Law Versus Morality as Regulators of Conduct', *American Law and Economics Review*, 4 (2002), 227

Shavell, S., 'The Judgment Proof Problem', *International Review of Law and Economics*, 6 (1986), 45

Shleifer, A. and Vishny, R. W., 'A Survey of Corporate Governance', *Journal of Finance*, 52 (1997), 737

Sidak, G. and Teece, D. J., 'Dynamic Competition in Antitrust Law', *Journal of Competition Law & Economics*, 5 (2009), 581

Sidhu, K., 'Anti-Corruption Compliance Standards in the Aftermath of the Siemens Scandal', *German Law Journal*, 10 (2009), 1343

Siemens, Statement of Siemens Aktiengesellschaft: Investigation and Summary of Findings with respect to the Proceedings in Munich and the US

Simon, H., 'A Formal Theory of the Employment Relationship', *Econometrica*, 19 (1951), 293

Simpson, S. S., Leeper Piquero, N. and Paternoster, R., 'Rationality and Corporate Offending Decisions' in A. Piquero and S. G. Tibbetts (eds.), *Rational Choice and Criminal Behavior: Recent Research and Future Challenges* (Routledge, 2002)

Simpson, S. S., *Corporate Crime, Law, and Social Control* (Cambridge University Press, 2002)

Simpson, S. S., 'Making Sense of White Collar Crime: Theory and Research', *Ohio State Journal of Criminal Law*, 8 (2011), 481

Simpson, S. S. and Koper, C. S., 'Deterring Corporate Crime', *Criminology*, 30(3) (1992), 347

Slotboom, M., 'Individual Liability for Cartel Infringements in the EU: An Increasingly Dangerous Minefield', Kluwer Competition Law Blog (2013)

Smith, A., *An Inquiry into the Nature and Causes of the Wealth of Nations* (University of Chicago Press, 1776)

Sokol, D. D., 'Cartels, Corporate Compliance, and What Practitioners Really Think About Enforcement', *Antitrust Law Journal*, 78 (2012), 201

Sokol, D. D., 'Policing the Firm', *Notre Dame Law Review*, 89 (2014), 785

Sonnenfeld, J. and Lawrence, P. R., 'Why Do Companies Succumb to Price Fixing?', *Harvard Business Review* (1978), 145

Spagnolo, G., 'Criminalization of Cartels and their Internal Organization' in K. J. Cseres, M. P. Schinkel, F. O. W. Vogelaar (eds.), *Remedies and Sanctions in Competition Policy: Economic and Legal Implications of the Tendency to Criminalize Antitrust Enforcement in the EU Member States* (Edward Elgar, 2006)

Spagnolo, G., 'Debt as a (Credible) Collusive Device, or: "Everybody Happy but the Consumer"', Working paper of the Stockholm School of Economics, No 349 (2000)

Spagnolo, G., 'Divide et Impera: Optimal Leniency Programs', CEPR Working Paper No 4840 (2004)

Spagnolo, G., 'Managerial Incentives and Collusive Behavior', *European Economic Review*, 49 (2005), 150

Spark Legal Network and Queen Mary University of London, 'Support Study for Impact Assessment Concerning the Review of Merger Regulation Regarding Minority Shareholdings' (2016)

Spector, D., 'Some Economics of Minority Shareholdings', *Revue Concurrences*, 3–2011 (2011), 14

Staahl Gabrielsen, T., Hjelmeng, E. and Sorgard, L., 'Rethinking minority Share Ownership and Interlocking Directorships – The Scope for Competition Law Intervention', *European Law Review*, 36 (2011), 839

Stanevicius, M., 'Portielje: Bar Remains High for Rebutting Parental Liability Presumption', *Journal of European Competition Law & Practice*, 5 (2014), 24

Stephan, A., 'An Empirical Assessment of the European Leniency Notice', *Journal of Competition Law and Economics*, 5 (2008), 537

Stephan, A., 'Cartel Laws Undermined: Corruption, Social Norms, and Collectivist Business Cultures', *Journal of Law and Society*, 37 (2010), 345

Stephan, A., 'Disqualification Orders for Directors Involved in Cartels', *Journal of European Competition Law & Practice*, 2 (2011), 529

Stephan, A., 'European Commission Launches New Anonymous Whistleblower Tool, but Who Would Use It?', Compettion Policy Blog (2017)

Stephan, A., 'Four Key Challenges to the Successful Criminalization of Cartel Laws', *Journal of Antitrust Enforcement*, 2 (2014), 333

Stephan, A., 'How Dishonesty Killed the Cartel Offence', *Criminal Law Review*, 6 (2011), 446

Stephan, A., 'Is the Korean Innovation of Individual Informant Rewards a Viable Cartel Detection Tool?' in T. Cheng, B. Ong and S. Marco Colino (eds.), Cartels in Asia (Wolters Kluwer Law & Business, 2014)

Stephan, A., 'See No Evil: Cartels and the Limits of Antitrust Compliance Programs', *The Company Lawyer*, 31 (2010), 231

Stephan, A., 'Should Individual Sanctions Be Part of Deterrence Efforts?' Deterring EU Competition Law Infringements: Are We Using the Right Sanctions? Conference by TILEC and the Liege Competition & Innovation, 3 December 2012, Brussels

Stephan, A. and Nikpay, A., 'Leniency Decision-Making from a Corporate Perspective: Complex Realities' in C. Beaton-Wells and C. Tran (eds.), *Anti-Cartel Enforcement in a Contemporary Age: The Leniency Religion* (Hart Publishing, 2015), ch. 8

Stigler, J., 'The Economies of Scale', *Journal of Law and Economics*, 1 (1958), 54

Stokman, F. N., Ziegler, R. and Scott, J. (eds.), *Networks of Corporate Power* (Polity Press, 1985)

Stone, C, 'The Place of Enterprise Liability in the Control of Corporate Conduct', *Yale Law Journal*, 90 (1980), 1

StrategicRISK, 'Guide to Directors' & Officers' Liability Insurance' (2012)

Stucke, M., 'Leniency, Whistle-Blowing and the Individual: Should We Create Another Race to the Competition Agency?' in C. Beaton-Wells and C. Tran (eds.), *Anti-Cartel Enforcement in a Contemporary Age: The Leniency Religion* (Hart Publishing, 2015), ch. 11

Sykes, A., 'The Economics of Vicarious Liability', *Yale Law Journal*, 93 (1984), 1231

Temple Lang, J., 'How Can the Problem of the Liability of a Parent Company for Price Fixing by a Wholly-Owned Subsidiary Be Resolved?', *Fordham International Law Journal*, 37(5) (2014), 1481

Thépot, F., 'Antitrust v. Anti-Corruption Policy Approaches to Compliance: Why Such a Gap?', *CPI Antitrust Chronicle*, 6(2) (2015)

Thépot, F., 'Leniency and Individual Liability: Opening the Black Box of the Cartel', *Competition Law Review*, 7 (2011), 221

Thépot, F., Hugon, F. and Luinaud, M., 'Cumul de Mandats D'Administrateur et Risques Anticoncurrentiels: Un Vide Juridique en Europe?', *Revue Concurrences*, 1–2016 (2016), 1

Thépot, F. and Thépot, J., 'Collusion, Managerial Incentives and Antitrust Fines', Working Papers of LaRGE Research Center, 2017–06 (2017)

Thomas, S., 'Guilty of a Fault that One Has Not Committed: The Limits of the Group-Based Sanction Policy Carried out by the Commission and the European Courts in EU-Antitrust Law', *Journal of European Competition Law & Practice*, 3 (2012), 11

Thompson, R. B., 'Unpacking Limited Liability: Direct and Vicarious Liability of Corporate Participants for Torts of the Enterprise', *Vanderbilt Law Review*, 47 (1994), 2

Thompson, S. and Thomas, R. S., 'The Public and Private Faces of Derivative Lawsuits', *Vanderbilt Law Review*, 57 (2004), 1747

ThyssenKrupp, Audit Report, available at: www.thyssenkrupp.com/en/company/compliance/audit-reports/

ThyssenKrupp, Remarks By Dr Heinrich Hiesinger Chairman of the Executive Board of ThyssenKrupp AG at the 14th Annual General Meeting on 18 January 2013

Travers, A. H., 'Interlocks in Corporate Management and the Antitrust Laws', *Texas Law Review*, 46 (1968), 819

Tricker, B., *Corporate Governance, Principles, Policies and Practices*, 2nd edn (Oxford University Press, 2012)

Tzanaki, A., 'The Legal Treatment of Minority Shareholdings Under EU Competition Law: Present and Future' in *Essays in Honour of Professor Panayiotis I. Kanellopoulos* (Sakkoulas, 2015)

Umit Kucuk, S. and Timmermans, H. J. P., 'Resale Price Maintenance (RPM): The US and EU perspectives', *Journal of Retailing and Consumer Services*, 19 (2012), 537

United Nations Conference on Trade and Development, Note by the UNCTAD secretariat, 'The Use of Leniency Programmes as a Tool for the Enforcement of Competition Law Against Hardcore Cartels in Developing Countries' (2010)

Van den Broek, S., Kemp, R. G. M., Verschoor, W. F. C. and de Vries, A. C., 'Reputational Penalties to Firms in Antitrust Investigations', *Journal of Competition Law and Economics*, 8 (2012), 231

Van Veen, K. and Kratzer, J., 'National and International Interlocking Directorates Within Europe: Corporate Networks Within and Among Fifteen European Countries', *Economy and Society*, 40 (2011), 1

Venit, J. S. and Foster, A. L., 'Competition Compliance: Fines and Complementary Incentives' in P. Lowe and M. Marquis (eds.), *European Competition Law Annual 2011: Integrating Public and Private Enforcement of Competition Law – Implications for Courts and Agencies* (Hart Publishing, 2014)

Vestager, M., 'Competition in Changing Times', FIW Symposium, Innsbruck (16 February 2018)

Vestager, M., 'Refining the EU merger Control System', speech, Studienvereinigung Kartellrecht, Brussels (10 March 2016)

Vives, X., *Oligopoly Pricing: Old Ideas and New Tools* (MIT Press, 1999)

Volkov, M., 'Antitrust Compliance and Credit for an Effective Compliance Program', available at: http://corruptioncrimecompliance.com/2013/09/antitrust-compliance-and-credit-for-an-effective-compliance-program/

Voss, K., 'Preventing the Cure: Corporate Compliance Programmes in EU Competition Law Enforcement', *Europarättslig Tidskrift*, 16 (2013), 28

Wagner, S. and Dittmar, L., 'The Unexpected Benefits of Sarbanes-Oxley', *Harvard Business Review*, 84 (2006), 133

Wagner von-Papp, F., 'Compliance and Individual Sanctions for Competition Law Infringements' in J. Paha (ed.), *Competition Law Compliance Programmes – An Interdisciplinary Approach* (Springer, 2016), p. 135

Wagner-Von Papp, F., 'What if all Bid Riggers Went to Prison and Nobody Noticed? Criminal Antitrust Law Enforcement in Germany' in C. Beaton-Wells and A. Ezrachi (eds.), *Criminalising Cartels, Critical Studies of an International Regulatory Movement* (Hart Publishing, 2011), p. 157

Wagner-von Papp, F., Stephan, A., Kovacic, W., Zimmer, D. and Viros, D. 'Individual Sanctions for Competition Law Infringements: Pros, Cons and Challenges', *Revue Concurrences*, 2–2016 (2016), 14

Waldron, J., *The Right to Private Property* (Oxford University Press, 1988)

Wall Street Journal, 'ThyssenKrupp Chairman Gerhard Cromme to Step Down March 31' (8 March 2013)

Wardhaugh, B., 'Cartel Leniency and Effective Compensation in Europe: The Aftermath of Pfleiderer', *Web Journal of Current Legal Issues*, 19(3) (2013)

Wardhaugh, B., *Cartels, Markets and Crime: A Normative Justification for Criminalisation of Economic Collusion* (Cambridge University Press, 2014)

Wardhaugh, B., 'Punishing Parents for the Sins of Their Child: Extending EU Competition Liability in Groups and to Subcontractors', *Journal of Antitrust Enforcement*, 5(1) (2017), 22

Warner, J. B., Watts, R. L. and Wruck, K. H., 'Stock Prices and Top Management Changes', *Journal of Financial Economics*, 20 (1988), 461

Weber Waller, S., 'Corporate Governance and Competition Policy', *George Mason Law Review*, 18 (2011), 833

Weisbach, M. S., 'Outside Directors and CEO Turnover', *Journal of Financial Economics* (1988) 431

Werden, G. J., Hammond, S. D. and Barnett, B. A., 'Deterrence and Detection of Cartels: Using all the Tools and Sanctions' (2012)

Werden, G. J., Hammond, S. D., and Barnett, B. A., 'Recidivism Eliminated: Cartel Enforcement in the United States Since 1999', *Competition Policy International Antitrust Chronicle* (2011), 10

Whelan, P. M., *The Criminalization of European Antitrust Enforcement: Theoretical, Legal, and Practical Challenges* (Oxford University Press, 2014)

Whish, R. and Bailey, D., *Competition Law*, 8th edn (Oxford University Press, 2015)

Williamson, D. V., 'Organization, Control, and the Single Entity Defense in Antitrust', *Journal of Competition Law and Economics*, 5 (2009), 723

Williamson, O., 'Comparative Economic Organization: The Analysis of Discrete Structural Alternatives', *Administrative Science Quarterly*, 36 (1991), 269

Williamson, O., *Market and Hierarchies: Analysis and Antitrust Implications* (Free Press, 1975)

Williamson, O., *The Economic Institutions of Capitalism* (Free Press, 1985)

Williamson, O., 'The Economics of Organization: The Transaction Cost Approach', *American Journal of Sociology*, 87 (1981), 548

Williamson, O., *The Mechanisms of Governance* (Oxford University Press, 1996)

Williamson, O., 'The Vertical Integration of Production: Market Failure Considerations', *American Economic Review*, 61 (1971), 112

Williamson, O., 'Transaction-Cost Economics: The Governance of Contractual Relations', *Journal of Law and Economics*, 22 (1979), 233

Williamson, O. and Winter, S. G. (eds.), *The Nature of the Firm, Origins, Evolution and Development* (Oxford University Press, 1993)

Willig, R. D., 'Corporate Governance and Market Structure' in A. Razin and E. Sadka (eds.), *Economic Policy in Theory and Practice* (Macmillan, 1987), p. 481

Wils, W. P. J., 'Antitrust Compliance Programmes & Optimal Antitrust Enforcement', *Journal of Antitrust Enforcement*, 1 (2013), 52

Wils, W. P. J., 'Is Criminalization of EU Competition Law the Answer?', *World Competition: Law and Economics Review*, 28 (2005), 117

Wils, W. P. J., 'Is Criminalization of EU Competition Law the Answer?' in K. J. Cseres, M. P. Schinkel, F. O. W. Vogelaar (eds.), *Remedies and Sanctions in Competition Policy: Economic and Legal Implications of the Tendency to Criminalize Antitrust Enforcement in the EU Member States* (Edward Elgar, 2006)

Wils, W. P. J., 'Private Enforcement of EU Antitrust Law and Its Relationship with Public Enforcement: Past, Present and Future', *World Competition*, 40(1) (2017), 3

Wils, W. P. J., *The Optimal Enforcement of EC Antitrust Law* (Kluwer Law International, 2002)

Wils, W. P. J., 'The Undertaking as Subject of EC Competition Law and the Imputation of Infringements to Natural or Legal Persons', *European Law Review*, (2000), 99

Windolf, P. and Beyer, J., 'Co-operative Capitalism: Corporate Networks in Germany and Britain', *British Journal of Sociology*, 47 (1996), 2

Winterstein, A., 'Nailing the Jellyfish: Social Security and Competition Law', *European Competition Law Review*, 20 (1999), 324

World Bank Institute, 'Fighting Corruption Through Collective Action', presentation, available at: www.unglobalcompact.org/docs/news_events/8.1/fighting_corruption_through _collective_action.pdf

Wright, S. K., 'All in the Family: When Will Internal Discussion Be Labeled Intra-Enterprise Conspiracy?', *Duquesne Law Review*, 14 (1975), 63

Yeo, H. J., Pochet, C. and Alcouffe, A., 'CEO Reciprocal Interlocks in French Corporations', *Journal of Management and Governance*, 7 (2003), 87

Zajac, E. J. and Westphal, J. D., 'Director Reputation, Power, and CEO-Board the Dynamics of Board Interlocks', *Administrative Science Quarterly*, 41 (1996), 507

Zhang, A., 'Toward an Economic Approach to Agency Agreements', *Journal of Competition Law & Economics*, 9 (2013), 553

Zingales, N., 'European and American Leniency Programmes: Two Models Towards Convergence?', *Competition Law Review*, 5 (2008) 5

Index

Index

Printed by Printforce, United Kingdom